Second edition

LISTEN

A GUIDE TO
THE PLEASURES OF MUSIC

ROLAND NADEAU

WILLIAM TESSON

Northeastern University

Arthur Komar,
Consulting editor

ALLYN AND BACON, INC. BOSTON LONDON SYDNEY

To Beverly · To Jennifer

Library of Congress Cataloguing in Publication Data

Nadeau, Roland,
  Listen: a guide to the pleasures of music.

  1. Music—Analysis, appreciation. I. Tesson,
William, joint author. II. Title.
MT6.N144L6 1975   780'.15   75–14236

ISBN 0–205–04816–1

CONTENTS

LIST OF COMMENTARIES
AND ANALYSES

PREFACE

We are happy to have had the opportunity to revise *Listen: A Guide to the Pleasures of Music*. We have rewritten and reorganized the entire text, adding several new features that will help the reader listen to music in a direct and meaningful way.

There are now thirty listening guides integrated throughout the text, each entitled "Commentary and Analysis." We have intentionally emphasized the twentieth century; fourteen of these guides examine a variety of important works by Sibelius, Dohnányi, Debussy, Stravinsky, Berg, Gershwin, Varèse, Messiaen, and Cage, as well as jazz pieces by Louis Armstrong, Art Tatum, and Miles Davis. At the same time, however, the listening guides offer a panorama of music starting with works by Josquin and Byrd.

Part III of the text contains a new feature entitled "Chronological Biographies of Composers." This section amplifies the material in Part II: "History" by providing important life facts on 169 composers. This information, if placed earlier in the text, would impede the flow of ideas about music in its socio-historical perspective. Separately placed, it serves as a handy reference. An alphabetical index at the beginning of Part III facilitates finding each composer according to year of birth. The usefulness of such a compact body of essential biographical data needs no further amplification.

In addition to the new analyses and biographies, much new writing has been added throughout the entire text, most especially in Chapter 9, "The Other Side: Folk, Jazz, and Pop."

There is an abundance of new illustrative material.

Our constant aim is for the reader to get to the music itself, bringing to it an ever-increasing awareness of its essence.

Roland Nadeau
William Tesson

ACKNOWLEDGMENTS

Thanks are due

—to Arthur Komar, our consulting editor, for valuable suggestions arising from close scrutiny of the entire text;

—to Pembroke Herbert, art consultant, for her able and sensitive response to the text;

—to George J. Guilbault for his contribution to the section on American musical theater;

—to Louis Cooperstein and Benedetto Fabrizi of the Modern Languages Department, Northeastern University, for help with translations;

—to Jeanne Ryder for extensive research in the chronological biographies;

—to Inza Lyon for general research and assistance throughout the text;

—to Robert Patterson, Senior Editor at Allyn and Bacon, for his strong encouragement and constant support during the preparing of this text;

—to Mary Johnson, who copy-edited the text with an acute eye for detail;

—to Jane Wentzell, who designed the book; and

—to Phil Carver and Bob Page, who autographed the musical examples.

R. N.
W. T.

ELEMENTS AND MEDIA

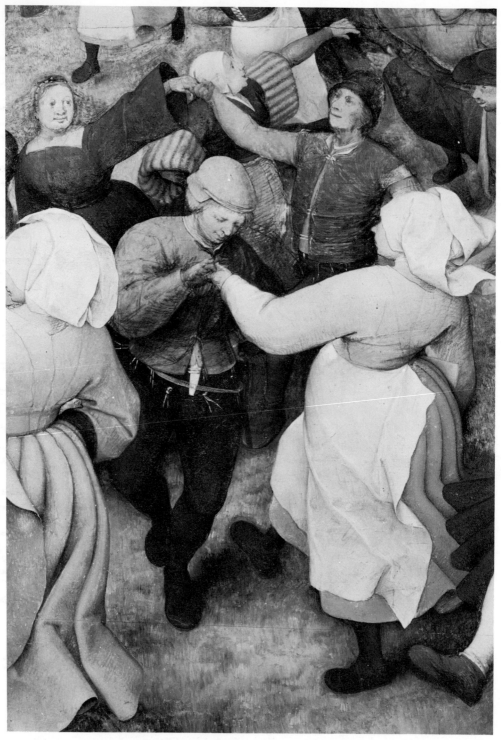

Figure 1. *The Wedding Dance* (detail) by Pieter Bruegel the Elder, Flemish c. 1525–1569. (From the collection of The Detroit Institute of Arts, Purchase, City Appropriation)

Chapter one

RHYTHM, MELODY, AND HARMONY

As natural creatures of the universe, we consider some experiences normal and others abnormal. Experiences that regularly recur are the ones we regard as normal. Deviations from the usual, such as a man eight feet or an August frost, we regard as abnormal. Those things that occur regularly we take for granted and accept as a normal part of our existence. The diastolic movement of our hearts is perhaps our closest connection with the movement of life. When we live at a normal pace, it beats regularly and at a certain speed. This is so taken for granted that the doctor uses its regularity and its speed as a check on our health. When we are excited or exert ourselves, it beats faster. When we sleep, it beats more slowly. From these facts of nature has arisen the theory that our heartbeats give to us the feeling of what is normal in the *pulse* or *beat* of music.

Thus, if a person's pulse beats eighty times per minute, a piece of music with eighty pulses or beats per minute will seem to be the norm or median with which all other pulses may be compared. Slower or faster pulses will seem less normal. Very fast pulses will feel exciting; very slow ones will feel numbing. Pulse in music, the regular recurrence of beats at various speeds, can then be considered as a basic ingredient underlying all musical movement. It is a strong sign of musical life and is the cause of the powerful, energizing force underlying all music —*rhythm*.

RHYTHM

In the broadest possible sense, musical rhythm can be said to include everything pertaining to the successive articulations of musical sound. More specifically, though, rhythm refers to time spans separating successive musical impacts. In effect, it is that element in music that sometimes causes us to tap feet, snap fingers, or set our whole body moving in sympathetic motion.

Note that the first statement uses the term *sound,* not pitch or tone. Though rhythm is usually inextricably bound up with melody and harmony, which in turn are themselves dependent on pitch and tone, it can exist without them. In the field of art music, especially that written in our day, pitchless or near-pitchless compositions exist. One example is the *Geographical Fugue* by Ernst Toch, written for speaking chorus. And many will have heard a jazz drummer "take a chorus" on his battery of percussion instruments, none of them pitched.

Despite the absence of pitch or tone, both of the above types of music can elicit emotional or aesthetic responses from an audience. If, as we said before, pulse is a strong sign of musical life, the very stuff of musical movement, then rhythm must be its breath and energizing power.

Rhythmic pattern

A rhythmic pattern (or figure) is a prominent succession of note values in a composition, often important enough to become a unifying structural element. The following rhythmic pattern has been isolated from its melody, which is shown in Example 1–2:

EXAMPLE 1–1

EXAMPLE 1–2   *Piano Concerto No. 3,* Opus 37, Mvt. I, Beethoven

Note that the symbols involved in the raw rhythmic pattern itself (Ex. 1–1) are those representing durational values only.

Certain melodies are dominated by one rhythmic pattern. One very celebrated theme by Paganini (Ex. 1–4)—used as the basis for extended compositions in variation form by Schumann, Brahms, Liszt, Rachmaninoff, and Blacher—is based entirely on this rhythmic pattern:

EXAMPLE 1-3

EXAMPLE 1-4   *Caprice No. 24*, Paganini

Longer compositions will usually contain several rhythmic patterns. These will contrast with one another and easily be identified as they return in the working out of the composition.

The examples given above are taken from melodies. But it should be remembered that rhythmic patterns also function as supportive elements, particularly in accompaniment patterns.

In this *aria*, the rhythmic pattern in the bass staff is repeated constantly and gives the music a dance character, in this case that of the habanera.

EXAMPLE 1-5   *Carmen*, "Habanera," Act I, Bizet

METER

Music is said to be metered when certain pulses are accented on a regular, predictable basis. These accented pulses are felt as primary *strong beats* to be distinguished from one or more intermediary *weak beats*. The primary characteristic of *meter* is alternation of strong and weak beats on a regular basis.

Let us examine the song "Clementine" to see how the feeling of meter arises from a simple melody. We assume that whoever first played or sang this melody felt accents on certain pitches. Anyone can feel the song's natural accents simply by singing the song strongly and rhythmically.

EXAMPLE 1–6   "Clementine"

Oh, my dar-ling, oh, my dar-ling, oh, my dar-ling, Cle-men-tine!

Thou art lost and gone for- ev - er, Dread-ful sor - ry, Cle-men-tine.

A glance at the rhythmic patterns underlying the melody provides further understanding of why these particular pitches feel as if they should be accented.

EXAMPLE 1–7

The circled notes are longer than the others and therefore receive a natural emphasis. The boxed notes are also accented because of their relation to the previous shorter note values. Underlying the whole, of course, is pulse.

If we again sing the song, now accenting sharply every third pulse starting on the first syllable of the word *darling*, we unmistakably feel meter and regular metrical accent. In this instance, because we have felt a regular accent every three pulses, the meter is called *triple*.

The example below shows "Clementine" with an arrow over each note of the

EXAMPLE 1–8

Pulse:

melody that receives a strong metrical accent. The equal-duration values below the melody represent the unit of pulse. These can be counted thus: one-two-three, one-two-three; or tapped.

Note that, between accents, the durational values of the melody itself will vary considerably; *they are not equal*. These differences in note duration are absolutely necessary for meaningful rhythmic patterns to occur. The counts or taps representing the beat or pulse, however, are steady and equal in duration.

Measures and bar lines

A convenient way for the composer to indicate precisely where the first strong metrical beat occurs throughout a piece of music is to place a vertical *bar line* on the staff immediately before it. The distance from one bar line to the next is called a *measure*. The first beat of each measure is called the *downbeat;* the last beat in the measure, the *upbeat*.

EXAMPLE 1–9

Bar lines are placed in the score to facilitate the task of reading the music. They indicate where strong metrical beats occur and can be numbered so that specific measures can easily be located.

Time signatures and meter

The performer, in addition to the visual aid he gets from the recurring bar lines, finds further help through the *time signature*. We have seen in the song "Clementine" that it has a natural metric accent occurring every three beats.

In addition to this, the notation of "Clementine" contains a double-number at the beginning of the music, telling the performer precisely what the meter will be. This time signature is in effect for the entire composition or until a new signature is introduced.

EXAMPLE 1-10

Time signature

For the purposes of understanding meter itself, only the top number of the signature need be considered. It tells the performer how many beats he will encounter in each measure.

$\frac{3}{4}$—three beats per measure

$\frac{2}{1}$—two beats per measure

$\frac{7}{8}$—seven beats per measure

$\frac{5}{16}$—five beats per measure

Simple and compound meters

Numbers most often found at the top of the signature are 2, 3, 4, 6, 9, and 12. The first three indicate *simple meter;* the last three, *compound meter.* In the case of simple meter, the upper number indicates precisely the number of beats per measure.

When the upper number in the time signature is 6, 9, or 12, however, the situation is more complicated. Taken at face value, a signature of $\frac{6}{8}$ would appear to indicate six beats to a measure. Thus, in the theme from Mozart's *Horn Concerto,* K. 447, one would normally expect to feel six beats—and we do indeed feel six beats. However, a metrical grouping of six beats tends also to be felt in two groups of three beats rather than the one group of six—especially in a quick tempo. To

EXAMPLE 1-11   *Horn Concerto, K. 447, Mvt. III, Mozart*

Counts: 6   1 2 3 4 5 6   1 2 3 4 5 6   1 2 3 4 5 6   1 2 3 4 5

experience this, one need only count six beats several times over, placing a slight emphasis on counts one and four. Therefore, the Mozart theme, which moves along at a lively pace, will not only be felt in six very fast beats, as in Example 1–11, but also in two slower beats, as shown on the next page.

EXAMPLE 1–12

Count ———→ 1   2   1   2   1   2   1   2

Thus, compound meter is aptly named. Beats can be felt and counted in two ways. Meters in 9 and 12 will also subdivide easily into three or four longer beats per measure. To see this, one simply divides the top number by three. Thus, a 6 meter can be felt in 2; a 12 in 4. The faster the pace of the music, the more easily this subdivision can be felt.

Asymmetrical meter

Meters other than those discussed above are termed *asymmetrical.* We have seen how compound meters can be subdivided into combinations of threes: a 6 meter into a combination of two threes; a 12 meter into a combination of four threes, etc. In all compound meters, the normal subdivided grouping is the same—in

EXAMPLE 1–13

threes. They therefore feel even. Asymmetrical meters such as 5, 7, etc., can also be subdivided into combinations. But as can be seen below, the groupings are not the same. The whole, therefore, feels uneven.

EXAMPLE 1–14

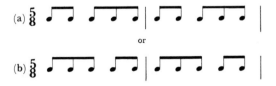

In the following example we see the time signature $\frac{5}{4}$ as used by Tchaikovsky

EXAMPLE 1–15   *Symphony No. 6*, Opus 74 ("Pathétique"), Mvt. II, Tchaikovsky

for the second movement of his *"Pathétique" Symphony.* While listening, we can count five beats fairly easily. But without considerable practice, it is possible to

EXAMPLE 1–16

Count ⟶ 1 2 3   4 5   1 2 3 4 5   1 2 3   4 5   1 2 3 4 5

lose the downbeat and miss the count. We actually feel more comfortable counting one-two; one-two-three; one-two; one-two-three, as is indicated in the example below. What we are feeling here, of course, is duple and triple meter alternating

EXAMPLE 1–17

Count ⟶ 1 2 1   2 3   1 2 1 2 3   1 2 1   2 3   1 2 1 2 3

on a regular basis. It is interesting to note that both compound and asymmetrical meters ordinarily subdivide into the two basic meters, duple and triple. In fact, all meter consists of either simple duple or triple, or their combinations.

> *Suggested Listening:* Ravel, "General Dance" from *Daphnis and Chloe, Suite No. 2*; Dave Brubeck Quintet, *Take Five.*

Mixed meter and polymeter

Mixed meter occurs when measures in different meter alternate. These are usually indicated by adjacent time signatures.

EXAMPLE 1–18   *Variations on a Hungarian Song*, Opus 21, No. 2, Brahms

Polymeter results when two or more meters occur simultaneously (Ex. 1–19). This term is used in the same sense as are the terms *polychord* and *polytonality*, which denote different chords or keys sounding simultaneously. Therefore, when discussing simultaneous meters, the term *polymeter* is much more exact than the usual but highly ambiguous *polyrhythm*.

EXAMPLE 1–19   *Don Giovanni*, Act I, Mozart

Changing meter

Changing meter occurs when time signatures change often enough so that regular downbeats do not come at the same place each time as expected.

EXAMPLE 1–20   Changing meter in Stravinsky's *The Rite of Spring*

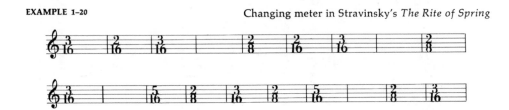

Syncopation

Syncopation refers to accents counter to the expected and regular flow of beats; simple syncopation occurs when weak beats are accented. The following example

EXAMPLE 1–21   *Symphony No. 44 ("Trauer"), Haydn*

shows a weak beat, in this case the second in a four-beat measure, strongly accented. This is common in music, especially so in the music of Beethoven.

EXAMPLE 1–22   *Variations on a Theme of Diabelli, Opus 120, Theme, Beethoven*

Jazz, perhaps more than other kinds of music, uses much syncopation—especially that produced by accented offbeats. That is, accents are placed consistently at various points between beats, with the last third of the beat favored. Underlying everything is an unflagging and steady pulse, much of the time organized in the meters $\frac{4}{4}$ or $\frac{2}{2}$. Regular but varied offbeat accents, constantly set against an orderly flow of metered beats, can produce a very exciting and lively effect.

TEMPO

Tempo deals with the pace of the beats. One sometimes hears the phrase "... in a fast rhythm." This is incorrect. What is meant is "... in a fast tempo," suggesting that the beats will follow one another quickly. Rhythm includes tempo as one important element, but the term *rhythm* should not be used when *tempo* is meant.

At the beginning of a piece or movement there is usually a tempo indication. For example, the German tempo indication *lebhaft* in a Schumann piano piece tells the pianist to play in a lively tempo. The French term *lent* in a Debussy prelude indicates a slow pace. These terms apply to the entire piece unless different tempo indications are subsequently introduced. For example, the tempo given at the beginning of Beethoven's *"Leonore" Overture No. 3* is *adagio*. This Italian term applies only until measure 37, when the term *allegro* replaces it. Later, at measure 514, Beethoven introduces the term *presto*. (Most tempo indications are given in Italian, even when the composer's native tongue is something other than Italian.)

It can readily be seen that terms for tempo are only general indications, helpful though never precise. There have been many attempts to find a system that would be accurate and constant in specifying the speed of a particular piece of music.

TABLE OF COMMON TEMPO INDICATIONS

ITALIAN	FRENCH	GERMAN
Presto—Extremely fast *Vivace*—Fast with vivacity *Allegro con brio*—Fast with brilliance *Allegro con spirito*—Fast with spirit *Allegro*—Moderately fast *Allegretto*—Not quite as fast as Allegro *Moderato*—Moderate *Andantino*—Not as slow as Andante *Andante*—Walking tempo *Lento*—Slow *Adagio*—Slow and calm *Largo*—Slow and broad *Grave*—Slow and solemn	*Animé*—Animated *Moderé*—Moderate *Lent*—Slow	*Lebhaft*—Lively *Mässig*—Moderate *Langsam*—Slow

Taken at face value, tempo indications would seem to suggest a very steady pulse. This is often true, especially in allegro movements of the baroque and classical periods. However, very little music is meant to be played in strict, inflexible tempo. Music in which the pace of the beats varies considerably is said to be in the *rubato* style, the term *rubato* taken as it applies to nineteenth-century romantic music. In earlier periods, it applied more to deviations from notated durational values than to fluctuations of pulse.

Beats gradually increasing in pace are indicated by the term *accelerando (accel.)*; *ritardando (rit.)* indicates the reverse.

DYNAMICS

One of the most important aspects of musical sound is volume. In much the same way that the level of volume in speech reflects emotion and meaning, so also does the level of volume in music. The frightened child's voice will not only sound at a high pitch, but at a high decibel level as well. Conversely, the mother will utilize low-pitched, soft inflections in her voice to calm and comfort the child. When music expresses majesty, dignity, or great heights of emotion, it will ordinarily be loud; the composer will place in his score indications for *forte* and *fortissimo*. On the other hand, when the music expresses peace, or deep, quiet sorrow, the music will be hushed; the markings will range from *pianissimo* to *mezzo-piano*.

Dynamics is the term used to cover levels of volume and changes from one level to another. The traditional language for indicating dynamics is Italian. Some of the most common dynamics markings appear in the table below:

Pianissimo (pp), very soft
Piano (p), soft
Mezzo-piano (mp), moderately soft
Mezzo-forte (mf), moderately loud
Forte (f), loud
Fortissimo (ff), very loud

The abbreviations in parentheses are the actual signs that are written in the score.

Two terms and signs are used to indicate gradual changes from soft to loud or from loud to soft:

Crescendo (<), meaning gradually getting louder, and *Decrescendo* or *Diminuendo* (>), meaning gradually getting softer.

The use of *crescendo* by the Mannheim (Germany) orchestra of the mid-eighteenth century produced such an exciting effect that it became known as the "Mannheim *crescendo*"; in certain dramatic sections of a piece the orchestra began very softly, and then by gradual degrees rose to a climactic *forte*. The application of *crescendo* through an entire section of a composition, or even an entire composition, can be most effective. A very well-known example, Ravel's *Bolero*, begins with a flute solo at a very low dynamic level, *pianissimo (pp)*, and ends 340 measures later with a thundering climax, *fortissimo (ff)*, for full orchestra.

The middle section of Debussy's orchestral *Nocturne No. 2*, entitled "Fêtes" (see analysis in Chapter 8), is another example of *crescendo* over a long span. Here the effect of growing volume has a special programatic aspect: The herald motive in the trumpets, *pp*, suggests the distant approach of a brass band. As the march continues, this motive is tossed from one instrumental choir to another as the volume increases. Finally the band marches by, its brazen sound confounded with the raucous noise of a holiday crowd. An interesting popular use of a similar effect is in the march "American Patrol" by F. W. Meacham.

The baroque period was noted for its terraced dynamics (see Chapter 5), in which *piano* and *forte* are achieved through a change in the number of players or number of organ stops or harpsichord couplings. Baroque composers rarely used explicit dynamics markings, however. Since the days of Mozart and Beethoven (Chapter 6), and particularly with rise of the piano, notated dynamics have become vital elements in musical composition. This includes *sforzando*, meaning a sudden loud accent, and abrupt changes from *piano* to *forte* or the reverse. A common marking in classical scores is a *crescendo* followed directly by *p*. *Sforzando-piano (sf/p)* is also common.

Composers of the nineteenth and twentieth centuries have continued the classicists' extensive application of dynamics markings, and some twentieth-century composers have even gone as far as to serialize these elements (see Chapter 10).

MELODY

What is melody?

There are many kinds of *melody*. From early times to the present day there have been as many different melodic styles on the part of the composer as there have been different tastes for melody on the part of the listener. But there are structural principles underlying these melodic styles that can be perceived in all periods of music. What, then, is melody? A simple definition would be: *the succession of single tones in time.*

Melodic process

A tone may be repeated.

EXAMPLE 1–23   "My Country 'Tis of Thee"

Or it may be superseded by another tone, a step higher;

EXAMPLE 1–24   *Academic Festival Overture*, Brahms

or change to a lower pitch by step;

EXAMPLE 1–25   *Academic Festival Overture*, Brahms

or leap up an interval of a 3rd,

EXAMPLE 1–26   *Symphony No. 3*, Opus 55, Mvt. I, Beethoven

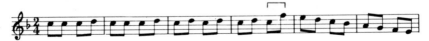

or more;

EXAMPLE 1–27   *Symphony No. 4*, Opus 36, Tchaikovsky

or leap down an interval of a 3rd,

EXAMPLE 1–28   "Swing Low, Sweet Chariot"

or more.

EXAMPLE 1–29   "None but the Lonely Heart," Tchaikovsky

Having looked at the several intervallic and directional possibilities of two-note combinations, it is clear that the prospects for variety in a melody lasting through many measures are manifold.

Melodic contour

As a melody spins itself out, it begins to assume an individuality of its own that could not be anticipated from the opening few notes. It now assumes what is variously called *shape, profile,* or *contour.* The shape of a melody may be seen by looking at the music as it is printed on the staff. In the well-known melody from Tchaikovsky's *Fifth Symphony*, notice the essentially rising character of the line

EXAMPLE 1–30   *Symphony No. 5*, Opus 64, Tchaikovsky

until the high point is arrived at in measure three. This type of melodic shape may be seen more clearly below.

EXAMPLE 1–31

Further abstracted, the shape of the melody looks like this:

EXAMPLE 1–32

Other melodic shapes often found are:

Gentle rise, gradual decline
Rise and fall of approximate equal length
Fall and rise of approximate equal length (Ex. 1–33)

EXAMPLE 1–33   *Concerto No. 1*, Opus 25, Piano and Orchestra, Mendelssohn

But no matter what the shape, the listener should observe the important high and low points of a melody. Further, these shapes may be combined and altered

in many ways, especially in melodies of greater length. The greater the length of the melody the more possibilities there will be for variety of contour and for subsidiary climaxes leading ultimately to the high point.

EXAMPLE 1–34   *Academic Festival Overture*, Brahms

Melodic range

In considering melodic style in relation to range it will be noted that melodies that are meant to be sung or are based upon vocal styles often stay within a relatively small range. *Gregorian chant*, for example, falls within a very small range. Note, in the following example, that the range lies within the interval of a 7th, from a high of A to a low of B.

EXAMPLE 1–35   *Dies Irae*

The theme that Beethoven used as the basis for the choral movement of his *Ninth Symphony* has a range of only an octave.

EXAMPLE 1–36   *Symphony No. 9*, Opus 125, Beethoven

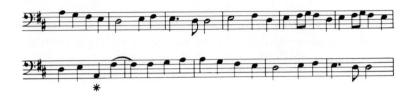

In the last movement of Brahms' *First Symphony* the main theme is not sung, but is based on a vocal "chorale" style and thus has a relatively small range.

EXAMPLE 1-37   *Symphony No. 1*, Opus 68, Brahms

Instruments have more range and flexibility than the voice, and composers have taken advantage of this in expanding the range of melody and in developing greater variety of contour.

EXAMPLE 1-38   *Symphony No. 2*, Opus 36, Beethoven

Conjunct and disjunct melodic motion

It will be noticed in the examples given above that vocal music uses step-wise or *conjunct motion* predominantly. On the other hand, instrumental melodies more often use leaps or *disjunct motion*.

HARMONY

Rhythm energizes music; melody and form give it definition; *harmony* provides it with depth and color.

Rhythm sets music in motion. It propels the musical fabric forward. Harmony, which provides forward motion through *chord progression,* can be defined as the simultaneous occurrence of three or more tones resulting in *chords,* and the relationships between these chords.

Though music does not actually exist in physical space, it is sometimes useful to think of it in terms of high, low, up, down, horizontal, vertical. When we discuss horizontal aspects, we refer to melodic elements that are represented in notation as going from left to right along the staff. This is also called the linear element of music. Tones occurring *simultaneously* in lower and higher parts of a staff represent vertical aspects.

Homophony refers to the homogeneity of texture that results from the rhythmic simultaneity of the voices. The Greek word *homo,* used as a prefix, means "the same." In homophony the notes of the various parts are articulated at the same time, and therefore sound like a harmonization of the melody and have no rhythmic independence of their own.

It may be shown that when chords are played in succession, the ear seeks to find the melody in the highest pitched tones, regarding any of the notes lower in pitch as only a reinforcement or thickening of the notes on top. A simple experiment at the keyboard will illustrate. Play several chords on the piano at random:

EXAMPLE 1–39

The ear hears these notes as the melody.

EXAMPLE 1–40

The harmonizations found in songbooks or hymnals are usually homophonic. "America the Beautiful" may serve as an example.

EXAMPLE 1–41   "America the Beautiful," Ward

This is almost pure homophony.

Chords are enormously powerful agents used by the composer to affect mood and atmosphere. Indeed, the plainest kind of tune can be metamorphasized by the subtle use of chords.

The well-known melody, "God Save the King," is harmonized very simply by Beethoven in his keyboard variations of 1804, though not quite as simply as it can

EXAMPLE 1–42   *Seven Variations on the National Song "God Save the King,"* Beethoven

be heard in its American version, "My Country 'Tis of Thee." In the coda to the

EXAMPLE 1–43   "My Country 'Tis of Thee"

variations, Beethoven not only changes the contour of the melody, but completely transforms the harmonic scheme from one of routine expectedness to one replete with poignant chords.

EXAMPLE 1–44   Coda, *Seven Variations on the National Song "God Save the King,"* Beethoven

Triadic harmony

Although it is true that *any* combination of three or more tones occurring simultaneously can be termed chords, it is also true that certain chords are more common than others. Indeed, one harmonic system—the triadic—has underscored Western music for centuries. A *triad* is a three-note chord built on intervals of thirds. These seem to many to be as eternal and normal as air and clouds, the color spectrum, or indeed anything experienced simply but surely in nature itself. The aural comfort and expectedness of triadic harmony has a basis in the laws of acoustics. The three tones of a major triad are derived from the first five tones

EXAMPLE 1–45

of the overtone series.

EXAMPLE 1–46

The overtone series is deeply imbedded in human aural experience. It follows that triads, tertian harmony, and the whole tonal system have been and perhaps for some time to come will be fundamental to musical experience.

Triads may be constructed on any note of the staff, including notes with accidentals.

EXAMPLE 1–47

We have said that triads are constructed in thirds. Visually, this can be ascertained by noting that all three notes of the triad are either on spaces or on lines. The distance between adjacent lines or adjacent spaces is always a third. The lowest note of the triad is termed its *root,* and the triad takes its letter name from it.

EXAMPLE 1–48

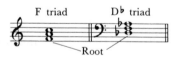

Chord connection

Heard singly, chords can be striking by themselves. But just as a single variety of flower seldom makes a garden, neither does a single type of chord make a piece of music.

The manner in which chords are connected is vital. Harmony textbooks refer to chord connection as *progression.* The jazz musician speaks of *changes.* But whatever it is called, logical chord connection is as important as syntax is to language. Just as certain ordered words make sense while others result in gibberish, chords go well together only in certain patterns. These patterns follow principles of chord progression that are consistent and logical.

To see this, one need only compare the melody in Example 1–49, harmonized

EXAMPLE 1–49   "Old Folks at Home," Foster

with a simple but appropriate set of chords, with the same melody harmonized with chords that do not follow well:

EXAMPLE 1–50

Although in any given musical situation a particular triad can connect with any other, certain triads combine much more smoothly than others. For example, a chord built on V (key of C major, Ex. 1–51)

EXAMPLE 1–51

will naturally lead to a chord built on I (Exs. 1–52 and 1–53).

EXAMPLE 1–52

EXAMPLE 1-53

V   I

Cadences

Chords, besides being supportive agents for melody, generators of musical movement through progression, and providers of color and depth, also can be powerful agents in dividing a composition into meaningful, cohesive, inner segments. Just as the eye would find it difficult to isolate phrases, sentences, and paragraphs if no punctuation were present, so would the ear find it difficult to identify intelligible musical statements without cadences. A *cadence* is a short progression of chords that either holds back or terminates completely the flow of music in a composition. Cadences are found at the joints of form: at the end of formal segments such as the phrase, period, part, section, or movement. They signal the ear that a musical statement has either just finished or has been interrupted before going on.

Modulation

The process of transition from one key to another is called *modulation*. Any key, major or minor, may be followed by another. The modulating passage may be short, long, simple, or complex, depending on the style, the historical period of the composer, and the work at hand. In general, the longer and more complex the composition, the more sophisticated will be the key scheme and the modulation techniques.

Chapter two

HOMOPHONIC AND POLYPHONIC STRUCTURES

HOMOPHONIC TEXTURES

Music is the most abstract of the arts.

Each tone glows, sometimes flames, then perishes to make room for those yet to come. Where has it gone? Time must elapse for music to be. The ear must not only assimilate several tones sounded together but also remember the ones that came before and anticipate those coming. Otherwise the music is not intelligible.

And beyond this, music, unlike painting or sculpture, must be re-created each time it is heard. Thus, the musical thoughts of the past masters are not directly available to an audience but must first be filtered through the personality of a conductor, a soloist, or an ensemble. These re-creations, or interpretations, necessarily will vary with each performance and with each individual performer or performers. In other words, a performer will not play a piece twice in the same way, nor will different performers play it the same. The listener, then, besides remembering and relating tones that flit by and then vanish, is faced with trying to assimilate and understand the whole composition, which is never heard the same way twice in live performance.

Despite this and without getting into a discussion of musical aesthetics, we will assume that it is patently evident to everyone that there is "meaning" in music; music does make sense. Its ephemeral and abstract nature notwithstanding, music can be the vehicle for vivid communication between composer and listener. This communication can never be completely understood or analyzed; nevertheless it is unquestionably felt to exist. The pervading force that makes this communication possible is musical form.

Musical form is the organization of tones, progressing in time, into patterns and shapes that the listener may organize and assimilate into a meaningful whole. The myriad formal structural patterns that exist and continue to be developed articulate the communication—emotional, aesthetic, intellectual—intended by the composer.

Unity with variety

Over a long period of time, and with much experimentation, forms such as sonata, rondo, theme and variations, etc., have evolved. These forms are not only treated differently by different composers, but are varied enormously by the individual composers themselves. Beethoven, for example, in his nine symphonies used sonata-allegro form for separate movements over and over again but never in precisely the same way. There is great freedom and transformation in his use of this formal structure from symphony to symphony.

However, underlying the great diversity in formal structures are certain principles that operate constantly. Of these, the most important are *unity* and *variety*. These principles are present in *all* music.

Unity

Unity is provided primarily by repetition. It occurs constantly and on many levels. *Themes, motives, rhythmic figures, chordal patterns and textures, sections of movements,* etc., all tend to be heard more than once.

Variety

Variety occurs through contrast. The ear needs to hear musical elements again, but it wants to hear them fresh. It also wants to experience the unexpected, the sharply different. A highly unified composition—for example, one built upon a single motive, a single rhythmic pattern, a single chordal texture—will be stale and uninteresting to the ear unless it is permeated with strong contrasts or variation.

Contrast comes in a great many ways. To name but a few of the most important, it may occur through change of chord, key, texture, articulation, melodic contour, range, rhythm, instrumentation, tempo, or form.

Contrast also comes with *variation*, the very essence of which lies in maintaining identity while introducing change. The substance of this section, in fact, deals with this primary musical technique. All the variation techniques described show the manifold ways that have been developed to satisfy the ear's need for identity with change. Variation techniques indeed point up the essential polarity of unity and contrast that exists in all good music.

A composition cannot be successful without both unity and variety operating in some kind of balance. We have said that music that emphasizes homogeneity at the expense of variety will be uninteresting. The reverse is true as well. A piece that emphasizes variety at the expense of unity will be unintelligible and meaningless. All effective music mixes unifying and contrasting elements.

Melodic elements

The motive

A *motive* is a short, seminal, melodic idea. It usually includes two or more tones.
Motives are normally striking and graphic, easily recognized and remembered:

EXAMPLE 2–1   *"Egmont" Overture*, Opus 84, Beethoven

Often they outline triadic shapes.

EXAMPLE 2–2   *Symphony No. 8*, Opus 88, Dvorak

Sometimes they are very brief,

EXAMPLE 2–3   *Tosca*, Scarpia's Motive, Puccini

other times rather extended:

EXAMPLE 2-4   *Madama Butterfly*, Love Motive, Puccini

But even though motives usually spearhead musical thought, they are only building blocks: vital musical components within a larger design.

It is sometimes possible to divide the motive into a smaller melodic structure
called a *figure*. The figure is also at the basis of many non-motivic passages, which
then are said to be figurative in character.

The theme

A *theme* is more extended than a motive. It can be a complete musical statement,
or it can be neatly tailored and clipped in a symmetrical sixteen-measure frame:

EXAMPLE 2-5   *Waltz*, Opus 34, No. 2, Chopin

The term *theme* itself is rather loosely used by composers. When the form is
labeled "theme and variations," the theme is often extensive enough to display
one of several simple forms to be discussed below, such as binary or ternary.

In general, a theme is a melodically striking component of a composition as
distinguished from the more figurative, less melodic elements. The motive, usually
shorter, will often itself be a component in the structure of the theme.

A *tune* is a simple melody easily played, sung, and remembered. Intervals in its
construction are largely diatonic, with limited range, and the whole will be more
complete in feeling than either a motive or a theme.

Units of form

Thus far we have dealt with materials—motive and theme—that in themselves do
not provide cohesion and definition for musical forms. They may be compared

to ideas that permeate accepted literary forms. For example, the idea suggested by the title of Emerson's essay "Self Reliance," does not by itself result in meaningful literary communication. Communication only occurs when ideas are developed and made articulate through the author's use of clear language and logic, conditioned by the structural principles of the literary form itself.

In the same way, motives and themes—the melodic "ideas" of a musical work—are made articulate in a total work only by the use of certain units of form. For purposes of analysis, these formal units may be measured according to the number of measures they span, and named according to function. From smallest to largest, these units are phrase, period, part, section, and movement.

The phrase

The *phrase* is the smallest formal unit in music. The phrase varies considerably in measure length according to the style of the music. Odd-numbered measure groupings such as 3, 5, 7, etc., are often encountered, especially in folk music and in contemporary works. But very often the phrase's structure will fall into the close-cropped framework of a four-measure unit, as in these examples.

EXAMPLE 2–6   "Auld Lang Syne"

EXAMPLE 2–7   "The Chase," Burgmüller

This kind of square, four-measure phrase often leads to another answering phrase, the whole then suggesting a larger formal unit called a *period*.

When the first questioning phrase ends as shown above, it is termed the *antecedent*. Its answer then becomes the *consequent*.

A pair of antecedent and consequent phrases usually start alike but end differently.

EXAMPLE 2-8   "The Chase," Burgmüller

Small complete structures: part-forms

When we consider small, *complete* forms, we encounter units more extensive than phrase and period. These are *parts*; and the forms themselves, *part-forms*.

What is a part?

A part consists of a few or several phrases often, but not always, organized into periods. These phrases will be alike in motive, texture, harmony, instrumentation, accompaniment pattern, key scheme, etc., so that they stamp the part as a single formal unit.

One-part form

The smallest possible *complete* form is termed *one-part form* and is simply labeled A:

EXAMPLE 2-9   *Prélude*, Opus 28, No. 7, Chopin

The one-part form, though minute, can be vivid and satisfying, especially in the hands of such masters as Bartók, Chopin, and Schoenberg.

Binary form

Encountered much more often are the *binary* and *ternary* part-forms. A *binary part-form*, AB, consists simply of two parts usually separated by a double bar.

EXAMPLE 2–10   *Violin Sonata No. 6*, Mvt. II, Haydn

Part A is frequently repeated, as is the following section, B. The pattern can be symbolized thus: A: ‖: B: ‖. The parts may be brief, as seen above, or rather extensive, as in the keyboard suites of J. S. Bach. In the more extensive AB forms, the second section will tend to be the larger of the two. Often it will contain at least a portion of the A section. When this happens, though the music may appear visually to be binary, it is at least partly ternary (ABA).

Ternary forms

The true *ternary form* consists of three parts, the third being a repetition, either exact or varied, of the first. The returning A section often spans approximately the same number of measures as the first A. Indeed, in *da capo* ternary forms, the returning A is not written out at all. The sign D.C. indicates to the player that he should simply repeat the opening section exactly as before. However, one of the pleasures in aurally tracing small ternary forms, other than da capo, lies in the recognition of the returning A section despite its being subtly transformed through variation techniques. We now can compare and distinguish between five complete small forms.

One-part form:	A
Binary form:	AB
Ternary da capo:	ABA
Ternary with varied return:	ABA¹
Hybrid binary-ternary:	AB + ½ A

Any of the parts within these forms may be repeated *before* the arrival of the following parts without changing the basic formal identity of the music. (Forms where successive *different* parts are generated beyond the B part are called *additive*: A, B, C or A, B, C, D, etc; see Rondo Form below.)

The complete part-forms discussed thus far are sometimes called *song* or *dance forms*. Although it is true that simple songs and dances easily fall into these patterns, music for other media and purposes also uses them. For example, simple binary or ternary forms underlie a great many of the *character pieces* for piano by Schumann, Schubert, Chopin, Brahms, and Mendelssohn.

Before going on to specifics about structure in the large forms, we will pause briefly to consider a striking facet of form in general. Small formal units are the basis for larger ones. Phrases group easily into periods that themselves are the basis for complete part-forms. Further, all these small units can be present and integral to larger units, soon to be discussed. Within the large pattern, smaller, often quite different, patterns operate. All are interdependent, and they reinforce and complement each other.

Larger single member forms

We are now prepared to discuss the larger *single member forms* of music, remembering that underlying all of them will be smaller, cohesive formal units. These larger forms can be complete in themselves, or they may represent one member of an aggregate work—e.g., a movement of a symphony.

The inner divisions of substantial forms such as sonata-allegro, rondo, and theme and variations are termed *sections*. In this text they will be named according to their role in the form, not labeled with letters as are parts. Therefore, part-forms will be labeled with capital letters, while sections will be described with words like *refrain* and *exposition*.

The section

Sections are distinguished from parts in several ways. Usually they are larger. Also, a section allows for greater inner diversity than the part. For example, a *development section* (see below) may be very extensive and include great musical contrasts. Within a section one or more part-forms may operate, while the part will itself only divide into phrases and periods. The minuet, when found in the symphony or other large forms, frequently shows each section divided into binary and/or ternary part-forms.

Three types of sections may appear in any larger single member form. They are the *introduction, coda,* and *transition.*

Introduction   The *introduction* often immediately precedes larger instrumental forms, which are in fast tempo. It is sometimes fragmentary, like the introduction to the first movement of the *Piano Sonata in B-flat Minor* by Chopin (four measures), or it may be lengthy, as in the finale of the *Symphony No. 1* by Brahms (61 measures). The tempo of the introduction is usually slow.

Coda   The *coda* occurs at the end of the larger forms. Like the introduction, its presence is optional and it can be of any length. It either continues in the tempo of the main movement or goes much faster, resulting in a brilliant finish.

It turns out, then, that the function of the introduction and coda are similar, in that each is optional and indeterminate in size and shape. The slow serious introduction sets the stage; the coda rounds out the form.

Transition

In contrast to the introduction and coda, the *transition* is almost always present, but its position in the form varies with the work. Its role is to link relatively stable melodic elements. Its effect is that of considerable musical motion, of "going somewhere." Modulation is characteristic, especially in the more extensive transitions. So is sequence. Often the music is highly figurative, featuring brilliant scales and arpeggios.

While introduction, coda, and transition occur in any of the larger forms, other divisions are integral to specific forms and will therefore be discussed below.

The movement

Sonata-allegro form: exposition, development, recapitulation

Sonata-allegro is a rather imprecise term used in formal analysis to describe a sophisticated movement prominently featuring development. The term was used initially to label opening allegros of multi-movement sonatas of the classical period. Because these opening allegros normally employed the formal plan of exposition, development, recapitulation, any form using this plan was called sonata-allegro. Thus, any movement using the above divisions, regardless of tempo or placement within the total work, is labeled *sonata-allegro* form (or simply *sonata-form*).

Sonata-allegro is a most felicitous form, combining the psychological satisfactions derived from ternary principles with the energy and excitement generated by development. The form is ternary because the recapitulation is a restatement of the exposition, albeit with important modifications. The development bridges the two sections.

Exposition   The role of the exposition is to present melodic and rhythmic materials in an orderly but vital manner. In standard works this is realized by contrasting themes appearing in succession, but often separated by transitions.

In the exposition of many works, two keys will prevail—the tonic for the opening theme, and either the dominant or mediant for later themes. Themes are numbered according to their order of entrance.

Development section   The development section is as free in shape as it is exciting in effect. As the term suggests, its role is to present in a new light the motivic materials already heard in the exposition. These materials are "treated" with an enormous array of compositional techniques, resulting in fascinating new musical shapes. Modulations occur very frequently, the total effect in more dramatic works being one of growing intensity and excitement until the arrival of the recapitulation section.

Recapitulation   The recapitulation closely follows the pattern of the exposition with but one major change. Whereas the exposition has two different keys, the recapitulation generally stays in one key, the tonic. A typical sonata-allegro form would then proceed according to the following plan:

Slow introduction	(optional).
Exposition	Presentation of themes with transitions and modulation to dominant or mediant key.
Development	Exploration of motives and themes and treatment by various compositional techniques. End of this section built on dominant chord, which leads to recapitulation.
Recapitulation	Return of exposition with all themes in tonic key and with other minor changes.
Coda (optional)	Usually in same tempo as exposition, development, recapitulation, but sometimes faster.

It should be remembered that the above outline of sonata-allegro form applies only to typical patterns. In the hands of the masters, details of structure can and do deviate from the norm. This is indeed true of all forms.

Suggested Listening: Beethoven, *"Leonore" Overture No. 3.*

Rondo form: refrain and episode

The *rondo* is often located as the finale in a multi-movement sonata. Its structural pattern is more variable than that of the sonata-allegro. There are two basic sections, the refrain and the episode, but these may be repeated often, and varied considerably. The one constant of the form is that the refrain returns no fewer than two times. Two very commonly seen arrangements of refrain and episode are *small rondo* and *large rondo*. Typical rondo patterns are:

Small, five-section rondo: Refrain, Episode I, Refrain, Episode II, Refrain.
Large, seven-section rondo: Refrain, Episode I, Refrain, Episode II, Refrain, Episode I, Refrain.

As we have seen, the distinguishing characteristic in sonata-allegro is the development section with its propulsive, eruptive power. But whereas sonata-allegro animates, the rondo charms. Its principal attraction lies in the refrain, which keeps coming back. Contrasting episodes separate these returns, and the ear delights during their latter portions in the anticipation of the refrain's return. In the simpler rondo, the refrain is likely to be repeated exactly as in its first entry. But in more extensive ones it often will appear in delightful mutations, including change of key and considerable variation. Sometimes Episode II itself takes on the character of development as it deals with thematic materials from the refrain. When this happens, the form becomes *sonata-rondo*, a hybrid. Codas regularly appear in rondos, but introductions only occasionally.

> *Suggested Listening:*   small rondo: Brahms, *Symphony No. 1,* Mvt. III; large rondo: Beethoven, *"Pathétique" Sonata,* Op. 13, Mvt. III; sonata-rondo: Haydn, *Symphony No. 88,* Mvt. IV.

Theme and variations

Theme and variations as a structural pattern can occur as a member of multi-movement works, but just as often it will be seen as a complete composition for any instrument or combination of instruments.

As in the rondo, the number of sections in the form is indeterminate. For example, Beethoven gives only three variations in the second movement of his *Piano Sonata,* Op. 14, No. 2, but thirty-three in the *Diabelli Variations,* Op. 120. In that sense it is an open-end form.

The theme itself, as we said earlier, often consists of a complete part-form. It may be borrowed from outside sources, from another composition by the composer, or may be specially written by the composer for the work at hand. Whatever its source, it tends to be of a simple and unadorned nature; thus will it lend itself more easily to expansion and change.

Variations are of two types: ornamental and characteristic. The *ornamental variation* is unpretentious. Interest lies in a graceful embellishment of the theme without major alteration of its basic length and shape.

EXAMPLE 2–11   "Clementine" in Ornamental Variation, Nadeau and Tesson

Indeed, it is sometimes possible to play or to sing the original theme simultaneously with any of the variations. The *characteristic variation* uses the theme as a touchstone. From within the theme itself, individual elements, such as motive, rhythmic pattern, and harmony, are isolated and used as the basis for variations of a "character" often wholly different from that of the theme. The connection

EXAMPLE 2–12   "Clementine" in Characteristic Variation, Nadeau and Tesson

between theme and ornamental variation is physiological; that between theme and characteristic variation is psychological.

Suggested Listening: ornamental variations: Mozart, *Variations on "Ah, Vous Dirai-je, Maman,"* K. 265, for keyboard; characteristic variations: Elgar, *Enigma Variations,* Op. 36, for orchestra.

Minuet (or Scherzo) with Trio

The standard terminology here is confusing, although the actual formal pattern used is very simple. The listener is presented with a form (frequently the third movement of a large structure) called *minuet.* However, its inner sections are labeled *minuet* and *trio.* The contradiction is obvious. How could the first section of the form be a minuet when the entire movement is a minuet?

The pattern used is ternary. The whole form, Minuet, takes its name from Section I, *minuet.* Section II is the Trio. The final section is the repetition of the first. Section I and Section II are frequently quite contrasted. Section II is often in a different mode or key, with its clearer texture differing vividly from that of Section I.

The minuet is also seen with two trios. The plan then becomes similar to that of a small rondo: Minuet-Trio I-Minuet-Trio II-Minuet.

The *scherzo* follows the same formal pattern as the minuet but differs in effect because of its considerably faster tempo.

Suggested Listening: minuet with trio: Mozart, *Symphony No. 41* ("Jupiter"), K. 551, Mvt. III; scherzo with trio: Beethoven, *Symphony No. 2,* Op. 36, Mvt. III.

Aggregate structures

Just as there needs to be pattern and logic within part-forms and within larger single member forms, so there needs to be some kind of organic unity and balance when two or more of these forms are joined in *aggregate structures.* Some of these are: symphony, concerto, quartet, solo sonata, suite, song cycle, oratorio, and opera.

In instrumental music aggregate forms unite their movements through certain techniques. The standard classical symphony, for example, will often show the same key for three of its four movements. The content in each movement will be such that there is follow-through as the work progresses. There will be a four-movement plan with a general tempo scheme of I fast, II slow, III moderate or fast, IV fast. The initial movement is almost always sonata-allegro, the third usually minuet or scherzo, and the last frequently rondo.

Beethoven's *Symphony No. 3*, Op. 55, *"Eroica"* (1805) is a large aggregate work based on the logical principles of the classical symphony. There are four movements:

Mvt. I: tempo—Allegro con brio
            form—sonata-allegro
Mvt. II: tempo—Adagio assai (Marcia funebre)
            form—ternary (ABA)
Mvt. III: tempo—Allegro vivace
            form—scherzo with trio
Mvt. IV: tempo—Allegro molto
            form—theme with variations

In this symphony Beethoven works in the traditional four-movement plan, with tempos and structures similar to those used by Haydn and Mozart in their symphonies. Each movement is internally cohesive but leads to the next movement with convincing musical logic. The instrumental forces used are modest. With the exception of the three French horns, the winds are in pairs; there are the usual string choir and two timpani.

Although this is an *absolute* symphony, manifesting the rigorous use of rational principles, it is filled with an expressive content that undoubtedly reflects the composer's spiritual travail at this point in his creative life. Conceived at the time of the Heiligenstadt Testament (see Chapter 6), the *"Eroica"* symbolizes Beethoven's spiritual catharsis. It is the musical parallel to Beethoven's new personal philosophy resulting from the physical crisis of his incipient deafness.

Cyclic form

Occasionally two or more movements will be linked physically by a *bridge passage*. Sometimes a kind of formal superstructure, termed *cyclic form*, will firmly relate the movements. This consists of one or more themes recurring in two or more movements, often in addition to the regular themes of the movement.

The romantic period is rich in symphonies whose formal superstructure is cyclic. Tchaikovsky's *Symphony No. 4*, Op. 36 is partially cyclic. The dramatic, herald-like theme from the introduction to the first movement interrupts the high spirits of the finale just before the coda. But the cyclic treatment is quite thorough in the same composer's *Symphony No. 5*, Op. 64. The theme from the introduction to Movement I is heard twice in the lyric second movement, once in the following waltz movement, and several times in the finale.

Both the *Symphonie fantastique*, Op. 14, and *Harold in Italy*, Op. 16, by Berlioz, make full use of cyclic themes. In the *Fantastique*, the cyclic theme—the *idée fixe* representing the beloved—occurs transformed in all five movements. A similar technique is used in the four movements of *Harold in Italy*. The Harold theme is played by the viola soloist and is present in every movement. Identity is achieved not only through a unifying cyclic theme, but by virtue of its being carried by the solo instrument throughout. Cyclic structure provides additional cohesion in an aggregate work. When a program is used, as seen below, oneness of concept is one of the prime considerations of the composer.

Berlioz, *Harold in Italy*, Op. 16

Program

Mvt. I: "Harold in the Mountains"—
            Scenes of melancholy, of happiness and joy
Mvt. II: "March of the Pilgrims"—
            Chanting their evening prayer
Mvt. III: "Serenade"—
            A mountaineer of the Abruzzi singing to his mistress
Mvt. IV: "Orgy of the Brigands"—
            Memories of past scenes

In aggregate vocal forms, such as opera, song cycle, masses, and oratorio, unity is largely provided by the text. In ballet, the plot itself cements the various scenes and dances.

Whether it be the briefest tune or a gargantuan two-hour symphony, unity, organization, logic, balance, and organic development are part of all intelligible music. And all this is tempered and leavened by the yeast of variety and contrast.

For further information and suggested listening on aggregate forms, both instrumental and vocal, see *Synoptic Listing of Musical Forms* (Appendix II).

POLYPHONIC PROCEDURE

The term *polyphony*, as derived from the Greek, means "many voices." Its usage, in musical terminology, denotes the combining and blending of two or more melodic lines. These lines may or may not be imitative. Voices or parts are distinguishable as separate melodies in direct proportion to the extent to which:

1. The "rhythmic diagrams" differ; this refers to both the lengths of notes and their moments of articulation.

2. The melodic contours differ.

Melody is linear and harmony is vertical. Therefore, polyphony—as a combination of melodies—is a multiple exposure of lines plus the concurrent tension and release inherent in simultaneous relationships. Polyphony is the most sophisticated of all compositional styles.

Even in homophony there is usually an attempt to keep each voice part some-what interesting by making its melodic contour different from that of the others. These differences in melodic contour may be seen in "America the Beautiful" (Ex. 1–40) by inspection of the parts. Note particularly the bass part, beginning with the upbeat to measure 9. Beginning here, and continuing through measures 9, 10, and 11, this part assumes a greater degree of individuality through its imitation of the soprano part in measures 1, 2, and 3. But whatever differences of melodic contour there may be among the four voices, they are of but minimal importance in any attempt to achieve a polyphonic style if the rhythmic articulations are simultaneous.

Applied polyphony

Counterpoint

Polyphony refers to music of any age in which the linear aspect is predominant. *Counterpoint* is a more specific term that refers to the planned setting of one melodic line against another.

The term *counterpoint* is derived from the Latin *punctus contra punctum,* "point against point," i.e., note against note. The common practice of counter-point in its early stages was to set another melody, at first note-to-note, against a melody already in existence, the *cantus firmus*, the "established tune." Later, more florid melodies were set against a cantus firmus. The florid melody set above was known as the *descant*. Composers throughout the centuries have been in-trigued with the idea of using a theme or melody from sacred or secular literature as a cantus firmus against which to write counterpoint.

Counterpoint, although de-emphasized during various periods of music history, has continued to the present day, achieving a new importance in the music of some twentieth-century composers. The styles of counterpoint have changed as the styles of music have changed. Contrapuntal style is dependent on many fac-tors, for example, the amount of dissonance and the way it is handled; the amount or kind of imitation between the parts; the melodic style, which may be vocal or instrumental, and the attendant amount of conjunct or disjunct motion and rhythmic emphasis. Thus, we may speak of sixteenth-century counterpoint and eighteenth-century counterpoint as related but different manifestations within the broad realm of polyphony.

Non-imitative Polyphony

Polyphony can be in two or more parts. Two-part music is the easiest to listen to, but in some ways the most difficult to write. In addition, two-part writing by its very nature cannot have one voice remain silent for any considerable length of time.

Two-part writing also excludes any extensive use of *parallel* and *similar motion*, as this would tend to reduce the separate individuality of the two parts. The two parts may vary in their comparative importance. In simple two-part writing, one part may consist of basically long notes against which there is a more florid second part.

In the example below we see, in measures 2–4, two-part writing that is mostly note against note. The two parts maintain their identities chiefly through their differing melodic contours.

EXAMPLE 2–13   *Piano Sonata, Op. 49, No. 2, Beethoven*

Quodlibet

Quodlibet, which means "as you please," is the name given to the process by which two or more melodies, often popular tunes that originally existed separately, are made to go together. This practice goes back to early music, and has been a part of popular culture until the present day. The first example of quodlibet combines two tunes of American origin. They are put together with some slight adjustments of the original melodies.

Because they are not only fun, but require some ingenuity, quodlibets are not only found in popular culture but have been explored by the master musicians as well. The more incongruous the borrowings in either tune or text, the more chal-

EXAMPLE 2–14   "Dixie," Emmett
"Old Folks at Home," Foster

lenging they are. Quodlibets were one of the favorite pastimes of the Bach family through several generations of family get-togethers. Sacred and secular songs were put together, or songs with texts in different languages. Sometimes they were written out; often they were improvised. Quodlibets have found their way into more serious areas as well. Johann Sebastian Bach included a quodlibet at the end of the *Goldberg Variations*. The bass line shown is the basis of Variation 30.

EXAMPLE 2-15

Superimposed on this is a popular song of Bach's time, "Ich bin so lang,"

EXAMPLE 2–16

Ich   bin   so   lang nicht bei dir   g'west
I've   been   so   long a - way from you

shown in the second measure in the upper part (Ex. 2-18), and this is joined by another popular melody, "Kraut und Rüben."

EXAMPLE 2–17

Kraut   und   Rü - ben   hab - en   mich ver - trie - ben
Kale   and   beets have   driv - en   me   a - way_____

These two melodies constantly reappear in different voices throughout the variation.

EXAMPLE 2–18   *Goldberg Variations,* Variation 30: Quodlibet, J. S. Bach

Canon

The strictest kind of polyphonic writing is the *canon.* The term *canon* (meaning "rule") originally was not a title specifying a certain style as does *waltz,* or a certain form as does *rondo,* but was rather an instruction by which one voice was to be imitated by another in some specific way. This was the canon for that particular piece of music. Therefore, it was necessary to write out one melody only; the other was to be supplied by the performer according to the instruction. It was later that *canon* became a generic term referring to any composition in which the basic principle is strict *imitation* throughout.

Two things must be known about how the second voice should combine with the first:

1. What note it should start on.

2. When it should start.

One of the simplest two-part canons has intrigued many composers. This is the "Alphabet Song," also known as "Twinkle, Twinkle, Little Star."

EXAMPLE 2–19   "The Alphabet Song"

If the melody only is given, with the instructions "at the unison," and "with a time-lapse of one measure" the realization will sound as shown below.

EXAMPLE 2–20   Canon: "The Alphabet Song"

The round

The simplest kind of canon is the *round,* in which each voice continually returns to the beginning immediately upon the completion of the tune. The round consists of one melody only, but beginning the melody again in other voices sets the melody against itself, creating counterpoint. A round may be in two, three, or four parts, or sometimes more. Most readers of this text have sung "Three Blind Mice" or "Row, Row, Row Your Boat." "Frère Jacques" is another of the best known rounds. As in all simple rounds, each voice entrance is on the same note—in this case, middle C—and the entrances are spoken of as being "at the unison." After the start of the tune, the other entrances come in successively two measures later until all four parts are active.

EXAMPLE 2–21   "Frère Jacques," French Round

The second entry of a round can also begin upon a different tone, such as a fifth above the original entry of the subject. This entry would then be spoken of as "at the fifth."

A round is an *infinite canon* (or *perpetual canon*) because it may go on and on, its close coming about only through the arbitrary decision to allow each voice to drop out in succession or to come to a stop at some predetermined point wherever the individual voices may be.

A *finite canon* does not return to the beginning but continues on until it is desired to close, in which case the imitation must be broken, the voices concluding in free counterpoint.

Of special interest is the *riddle canon*. The single melody is written out in full, but no instructions are given as to the pitch or time lapse of the other voices. These have to be figured out by the performers.

Fugue

The *fugue* cannot be considered as a form in the same way that we have defined the structures above. The Latin term *fuga*, meaning "flight," was in use in the sixteenth century in connection with canonic writing. The idea of one voice fleeing from the other is more aptly stated as one voice being the leader and the imitating voice being the follower.

The fugue when spoken of today refers to the development that reached its peak in the writings of Johann Sebastian Bach. The fugue differs from the canon in certain important aspects. It is not confined to strict imitation, but rather uses imitation as a "springboard" into areas in which there is a freer treatment of the melodic materials than strict imitation would allow.

The subject

The chief characteristic of the fugue is that it "grows" out of one theme called the *subject*, which is of short to moderate length. The subject may be somewhat shorter or longer than those in the following example, but there are two requirements:

1. It must be long enough to be a theme.
2. It must not be so long as to be diffuse.

This single theme becomes the material for the entire fugue.

EXAMPLE 2–22

(a) *The Well-Tempered Clavier*, Book I, Fugue 6, J. S. Bach
(b) *The Well-Tempered Clavier*, Book II, Fugue 18, J. S. Bach
(c) *Messiah*, No. 28, Handel
(d) *Requiem*, K. 626, "Kyrie," Mozart

The fugue retains one of the basic characteristics of contrapuntal writing, the "overlapping of melodies." A melodic cadence in a single voice does not result in a "cadential feeling," since the melody in another voice is already on its way. In a fugue there are three important areas of interest: fugue exposition, working-out area, and closure.

Fugue exposition   In the *fugue exposition*, the subject is presented at least once in all voices. There is tonic-dominant emphasis.

Working-out area   The second important area consists of the working out of melodic materials, using various contrapuntal techniques, and exploration of other keys. The *working-out area* may be of any length.

Closure   In the *closure*, one voice returns to the subject in the home key; others may follow. There may be homophonic emphasis near the close, and there are one or more cadences in the home key.

Stretto

Our English word *strait* has the same origin as the Italian term *stretto*, meaning "narrow" or "tight." Stretto refers to various entries of the subject in such a short space of time that one statement of the subject is not complete before the next entry is begun. The subject may appear intact or it may be shortened or changed. Stretto creates excitement and tension and thickens the texture. The composer may use stretto anywhere in a work, but because of its inherent dynamism it often occurs in the last half of the fugue.

Augmentation

A form of rhythmic variation, *augmentation* occurs when the durational value of each tone of the subject is lengthened, usually by a consistent durational value. Typically the duration of each tone is doubled.

EXAMPLE 2–23   *The Well-Tempered Clavier*, Book I, Fugue 8, J. S. Bach

(a) Subject

(b) Augmentation (transposed)

Diminution

Diminution is the inverse of augmentation; the durational values are shortened rather than lengthened.

Figure 2. *The Violinist* by Degas. (Courtesy, Museum of Fine Arts, Boston, William Francis Warden Fund)

Chapter three

VOICES, INSTRUMENTS, AND PERFORMANCE

Sounds have fascinated the child in us all throughout the ages. As babies we were beguiled by the sounds of voices, clocks, cars, toys, animals. An essential part of being human is the ability to respond to sound and especially to take pleasure in musical sounds. The composer draws upon this human responsiveness, using instruments and singing, creating in us a new awareness of things as they are or might be—awakening us to new experiences. Although the composer works mainly with specialized musical sounds, he often imitates the basically non-musical sounds that we have known since birth. A flute may imitate a bird, a tympani roll may suggest thunder. And of course, the human voice constantly utilizes one of the most fundamental types of sound—speech.

How do we designate the various instruments that have served for so long? How do we speak of the differences of tone quality between one singer and the next? How do we fathom the limitless blending of these instruments and voices? And what of the performance experience itself?

VOICES

Singing is a natural and pleasant experience to almost everybody. When music suddenly rises to the surface of our consciousness, nudged there perhaps by a beautiful spring day, we want to sing. Undoubtedly if we carried a flute at that moment and could play it, we would. But for most of us, singing is the most natural and accessible way of making music, and by association, understanding it.

As soon as we can, we repeat nursery songs. At school, one of our first musical experiences is with song. Later on we sing at school gatherings, at rallies, at church, or with a community chorus. We can enjoy singing—on an unsophisti-cated level, to be sure—without the slightest technical training.

Even at a very sophisticated level of instrumental performance, the concept of song is not far away. The critics speak of a pianist's "singing tone," or we hear of "the eloquent voice" of the cello. And for the very reason that words are usually present, vocal music is easily assimilated. Indeed, we often think of a song in terms of its text, or its textual meaning, rather than its melody or harmony. In short, we easily relate to vocal music because of the words with specific or symbolic meaning. Singing is a natural, familiar way for us to express ourselves. In it are combined the directness and universality of the spoken word and the sensuous appeal of tones produced by the human voice. Thus, the voice rightly has been chosen by the masters as the appropriate medium for some of their most important musical creations.

Voice types

Men's voices differ from those of women primarily in pitch register. The female's total register is one octave higher than that of the male. When a mixed group sings a melody together at a public gathering, the melody is not at the same pitch level, but at the distance of one octave.

Beyond this basic division, men's and women's voices are divided further into voice types corresponding to high, middle, and low *pitch* registers. Thus, for the basic female voices we have, from high to low: *soprano, mezzo soprano,* and *contralto (alto)*. For the basic male voices: *tenor, baritone,* and *bass.*

EXAMPLE 3–1

The above examples are for normal voices. It is understood that many individual singers exceed these ranges to varying extents. The tenor Caruso could sing strong low notes ranging down through the baritone register. An exceptionally low chorus alto will sometimes be found who is able to sing all the tenor pitches as well as the usual alto pitches.

In mixed *choral music*—most often scored in four parts, soprano, alto, tenor, and bass (SATB)—parts are not often written for middle-range voices—mezzo soprano and baritone. Thus, if a baritone possesses an exceptionally high range, he may join the tenor section as a second tenor or the bass section as a first bass. In exactly the same way, the mezzo soprano must match her voice either with the altos or sopranos, depending on her range.

In certain vocal forms revolving around several solo parts, middle-range voices are often fully represented with parts written especially for them. For example, Verdi, in his last opera, *Falstaff,* assigned the leading solo parts to voices corresponding to the six mentioned before. The parts are:

Sir John Falstaff, a rotund knight	baritone
Bardolph ⎱ retainers of	tenor
Pistol ⎰ Falstaff	bass
Ford, a wealthy burgher	baritone
Alice Ford, his wife	soprano
Ann Ford, their daughter	soprano
Fenton, Ann's suitor	tenor
Dr. Caius, another suitor	tenor
Mistress Page, a neighbor of the Ford's	mezzo soprano
Dame Quickly	contralto

The soprano voice

Coloratura soprano *Coloratura soprano* is the highest and most agile of the soprano voices. A fine coloratura will negotiate easily precarious leaps, dizzying high notes, and cascading scales.

Though the music for this voice can be dramatic as in the "Queen of the Night" arias from Mozart's opera *The Magic Flute,* it most often is light, as in this example from Gounod's opera *Romeo and Juliet:*

EXAMPLE 3–2   *Romeo and Juliet,* Act I, Gounod

It should be remembered that although music for coloratura soprano often emphasizes virtuosity and vocal gymnastics, it also can be very melodic and lyric.

Also, the term *coloratura* is applied to any voice type when it engages in highly figurative, cadenza-like music.

Suggested Listening: Lucy's "Hello Aria," from Menotti's comic opera, *The Telephone.*

Lyric soprano   The *lyric soprano*, as the name suggests, is assigned song-like sustained melodies. Most of the female leading parts in French and Italian romantic opera are sung by lyric sopranos: Marguerite in Gounod's *Faust*; Violetta in Verdi's *La Traviata*; Mimi in Puccini's *La Bohème*. Just as the coloratura soprano has its lyric moments, so the lyric soprano is called upon often to perform scintillating runs and trills, and to reach dazzling high notes.

Dramatic soprano   A *dramatic soprano* sings in approximately the same register as does the lyric soprano. Like the lyric, she must often sing in an intimate, sustained manner as can be heard in the love song from Act I of Puccini's opera, *Tosca.* But for the most part, and especially in German romantic opera, she must sing with great volume of tone and dramatic intensity for long periods of time. Operas using dramatic voices ordinarily feature very large orchestras, sometimes totaling over 100 players, and a dramatic soprano must project all the resonance at her command. Beyond the enormous vocal challenges occurring on almost every page of the score, a full rich orchestra swells with throbbing sound around the vocal part.

Suggested Listening: Richard Wagner's opera *Tristan und Isolde*, Isolde's Act I Narrative and Act III "Liebestod."

Boy soprano   Though the *boy soprano* can attain most of the pitches in the female lyric soprano register, the quality of this voice is quite different. It lacks the voluptuous quality often heard in the female soprano. When well trained, it is remarkable for its purity of sound and has little of the *vibrato* often heard in the lyric soprano. There is also the *boy alto.*

Suggested Listening: Menotti's Christmas opera, *Amahl and the Night Visitors*, the part of the boy.

The *castrato*, or male soprano voice, was very popular in seventeenth- and eighteenth-century opera. It was used in church choirs as well as on the operatic stage. Castrati were adult eunuchs who combined the register of the boy soprano voice with the power of the tenor. For obvious reasons, they are not used in our time.

Operatic roles originally sung by castrati, such as Idamante in Mozart's *Idomeneo* and Orpheus in the opera *Orpheus and Eurydice,* are now performed by a soprano or mezzo soprano. (The real question is, why were castrati *ever* used? Probably because appearing on stage was not regarded as suitable for women.)

The mezzo soprano   As mentioned before, parts for this middle-register voice are seldom found in music for chorus. But solo *mezzo soprano* parts in opera abound. As in the case with the baritone voice, however, *leading roles* do not often come its way. Well-known exceptions are the flaming roles of Carmen in Bizet's opera of that name and Delilah in Saint-Saëns' opera *Samson and Delilah.*

EXAMPLE 3–3   *Carmen,* Act I, Bizet

> *Suggested Listening:*   Richard Strauss' opera *Der Rosenkavalier,* the part of Octavian.

The tenor voice

Lyric tenor   The *lyric tenor,* like the lyric soprano, is assigned many of the love-liest melodies in opera and operetta, and often gets top billing. Operatic heroes and lovers are traditionally tenors, while baritones and basses are often cast as villians, fathers, and uncles.

> *Suggested Listening:*   Gounod's opera *Romeo and Juliet,* the part of Romeo.

Dramatic tenor or heldentenor   Both the terms *dramatic tenor* and *heldentenor* refer to tenor roles in opera precisely like those of the dramatic soprano.

> *Suggested Listening:*   Beethoven's opera *Fidelio,* the role of Florestan; Verdi's opera *Aida,* the role of Radames; Wagner's opera *Tristan und Isolde,* the role of Tristan.

Countertenor   The *countertenor,* or *male alto,* is the voice closest in technique to that of the female coloratura. By using a technique based on *falsetto,* a fine countertenor reaches a pitch range considerably higher than that of the lyric or dramatic tenor. His tone quality, while escalating through the notes of the scale usually sung by females, is transparent and considerably less virile than that of other male voices.

The baritone voice

Though in opera and elsewhere the leading male role does not often come his way, the well-trained *baritone* does have certain advantages. For one, his highest notes often have a brilliance and carrying power close to that of the tenor. On the other hand, his voice tends to have a rich, dark cast usually associated with basses.

When the baritone voice has a pronounced dark cast and approaches the register of the bass, it is then called *bass-baritone.*

> *Suggested Listening:*   Richard Strauss' opera *Salome,* the part of John the Baptist.

The bass voice

The *bass voice* in choral music anchors the total sound. Though it often sallies forth with a melody of its own, especially in contrapuntal music, much of the time it provides a tonal cushion upon which the upper voices depend.

The solo bass, however, is much used in vocal forms and is almost as diversified in tone quality and use as is its opposite member, the soprano. In addition to the quasi-bass, officially called *bass-baritone,* mentioned above, the *lyric bass* (*basso cantante*) and the *comic bass* (*basso buffo*) find ample representation in the operatic repertory. These last two voices differ not so much in tone color and in range but in style of performance. The *buffo* emphasizes acting and character portrayal, sometimes to the marked detriment of beauty of vocal sound, while the lyric bass cultivates a singing style where beauty of voice is as important as it is with the lyric soprano or lyric tenor. This example shows a bass melody to be sung in *buffo style*.

EXAMPLE 3–4   *The Barber of Seville*, Act I, Rossini

The *basso profundo* is a bass with an unusually low range. An occasional chorus exists where the true basso profundo will be heard underlying the already dark sound of the other basses. Russian choruses often boast many extremely low basses who are able to plumb the depths with ease, thus lending extraordinary solidity and majesty to the choral sound. This subterranean voice is called *contra-bass*.

> *Suggested Listening:*   basso cantante: in Boito's opera *Mefistofele*, the part of Mephistopheles; basso buffo: in Richard Strauss' opera *Der Rosenkavalier*, the part of Baron Ochs.

Vocal performance media

Before advancing to a description of the various physical combinations of voices with one another and with instruments, it is important to distinguish early and clearly between vocal performance media and vocal forms.

Vocal forms are the various structural patterns inherent in the music to be sung; they exemplify how the music is organized without regard to how many or what kind of voices are involved. (See Chapter 2.) Performance media are the various physical singing forces required to produce music that is written in these forms.

Thus, the *lied* as a form is a song sometimes cast in a strophic pattern but just as often through composed, using a German poem as text. The performance medium used is the solo voice, of any pitch register, sustained by a piano accompaniment. But while the performance medium may change, as when Richard Strauss writes solo *lieder* with orchestra instead of piano, the basic formal structure of the music itself remains.

Vocal forms refer to musical ideas and patterns; vocal performance media, to how many and what type voices are used. This distinction applies as well to the instrumental forms and performance media discussed below.

The chorus

The term *chorus* as understood in the broadest possible sense simply means a body of people singing together. These may be few or many—male, female, or both—divided into parts or singing in unison, accompanied by instruments or not, articulating a text or humming, and singing any kind of music in almost any setting.

In practice, however, choruses are classified and named according to their size, their social function, the kind of literature sung, and other characteristics. These important variations will be discussed after certain basic facts applying to them all are discussed.

Choral music is ordinarily divided into parts corresponding to voice types covering the highs, middles, and lows of music. The most common division is in four parts: soprano, alto, tenor, bass. A chorus thus constituted is called a *mixed chorus*, and the letter symbols used to describe it are SATB.

Various choral groups

A *choir* is a chorus that is attached to a church or chapel. Although its repertoire will be primarily sacred choral music for performance at religious services, it will occasionally include secular music at special concerts or on tour. Church choirs ordinarily are peopled by nonprofessionals, but the largest church choirs, ordinarily found in large urban areas, will sometimes consist, at least in part, of professional singers.

Secular choruses vary greatly in type and function. They will run the gamut from the polished, disciplined, professional groups heard constantly on radio, on television, and in concert to the informal groups in colleges devoted to the cultivation of student songs.

The *community chorus*, depending on its locale, resources, and the ambition of its members, will vary in quality and number. Some will thrive on slight musical fare, while others each season will mount several large-scale performances of the greatest masterworks with full symphony orchestra.

The term *glee club* usually applies to a collegiate chorus, female, male, or mixed. But such is the interest in choral music at many colleges and universities that several choral groups may flourish simultaneously. There may be a large chorus, a chamber chorus, a men's chorale, a chapel choir, madrigal singers, and other groups. Some of these become so refined and competent that they sing and record with the finest symphony orchestras, and tour periodically, sometimes on an international scale.

Most of the kinds of choral groups mentioned above are rehearsed and directed by a conductor. Whether this person is a professor of music who leads the college glee club after teaching hours, the chorus master permanently attached to an opera house, or simply the best musician of the group who dares to stand up and lead, his role is vital—especially if the chorus is to be a good one. He must rehearse adequately for performances, choose repertoire, draw good overall tone quality from the group, monitor enunciation and pronunciation of words—often in foreign languages—and generally spark the group to produce effective and imaginative performances. Occasionally he will also need to direct a symphony orchestra or other instrumental group along with his chorus.

Small vocal ensembles

Ensembles, with but one voice to a part, are named according to the number of voices involved. Thus, the Brahms *Liebeslieder Waltzes,* for four solo voices (SATB) with piano duet, are written for what is called an accompanied vocal quartet. The medium here is the chamber ensemble. But while the repertory for such chamber groups is fairly wide, vocal ensembles are more often encountered as a part of other massed vocal media.

Solo ensembles abound in opera, where the several principals join voices in every possible combination. Typical of this is the melodramatic trio (STB) heard in the last moments of Gounod's opera *Faust.*

Solo ensembles joining large choruses in the performance of oratorios, cantatas, and other vocal forms are usually grouped in mixed quartet (SATB) with the small ensemble sometimes set in dramatic opposition to the massed chorus and at other times blending in with the whole.

Suggested Listening: Beethoven's *Symphony No. 9,* the final movement for mixed quartet, chorus, and orchestra.

The solo voice

As a performance medium, the solo voice is universally used in combination with a great variety of instruments and in the realization of many musical forms. To name but a few, the solo voice is heard in opera and related forms, sacred and secular choral music, the symphony, with instrumental chamber music, and in the smaller song forms often accompanied by the piano, but also by other instruments and instrumental ensembles.

One of the most rewarding of these forms is the German art song, or lied, with piano. Contrary to the view of some, this is really a chamber ensemble and rightly can be considered a duet. As developed by the master German composers of lieder, Beethoven, Schubert, Mendelssohn, Schumann, Brahms, Wolf, Strauss, and Mahler, the lied as a medium often allots as much importance to the piano part as to the voice part. The poems used are generally of a high order. Art songs are ordinarily heard in solo vocal recitals.

INSTRUMENTS

The composer, in addition to utilizing the structural elements of music—melody, harmony, and rhythm—is acutely aware of the unique sound of each instrument. Each sound, alone or in combination with other instruments, can be used to enhance, emphasize, or accent line or texture, or to add spice and variety.

Tone color, or *timbre*, is the quality of sound of an instrument that distinguishes it from any other. Most readers are familiar with the fact that a tuba, which is large, sounds lower than a trumpet, which is small. "Large" and "small," however, are general terms and more specifically include reference to two dimensions: the length and width of the bore. The tuba sounds lower than the trumpet only because its tubing is longer. Its bore is wider, but this affects quality of sound, not pitch.

Tone color is also dependent upon the materials from which the instrument is made and upon the manner in which the sound is produced, whether by blowing, scraping, striking, or plucking.

Ranges

The *range* of an instrument refers to the total number of pitches capable of being produced on that instrument, from the lowest pitch to the highest.

Four basic groups of instruments

All musical instruments belong to one of four groups: *strings, woodwinds, brass,* or *percussion*. Although there have been more scientific descriptions of instruments, the professional musician—composer, conductor, orchestrator, or instrumentalist—uses this terminology.

The strings

In the string family are the violin, viola, cello, and double bass. The tone on each of these instruments is produced by a bow drawn across a taut string. The body of the instrument acts as a resonator and an amplifier. Stringed instruments on which the tone is produced in different manner—such as the piano, harpsichord, and harp—will be treated separately.

The violin   Because of its extensive range in the upper register, its facility, and its expressiveness, the violin may be found in the hands of a Gypsy violinist pouring forth a sentimental melody in a dimly lit cafe, at a country dance playing a spirited jig, in the concert hall as the leading member of a string quartet or symphony orchestra, and in the hands of a great violin soloist.

The violin is held under the chin with the left hand. The right hand holds the bow. The tone of the violin has been described as similar to the human voice. This is a poor comparison. The tone of the violin lacks the basic distinction of the human voice, which is that its sound is the result of a column of air that comes from the lungs of the performer and passes through the vocal cords, setting them in vibration. This method of producing tone is similar to the manner in which the wind player produces tone. The brass player's lips are the "vocal cords." The similarity of vocal tone to that of a wind instrument is well understood by the composer. Examples in the sections on brass and winds will demonstrate this.

It is better to describe the violin as the stringed instrument that it is. No stringed instrument by itself can have the power of the voice or a wind instrument. Instead of power, however, the violin has in its upper range a steely intensity and in its middle range an insinuating lyricism; in its low range it can be dark, vibrant, and sensuous.

Suggested Listening: Paganini, *Concerto No. 1 in D* for violin and orchestra.

The viola   The viola has all the appearances of the violin, and is also held under the chin, but it is a slightly larger instrument and it is pitched lower. It is the alto

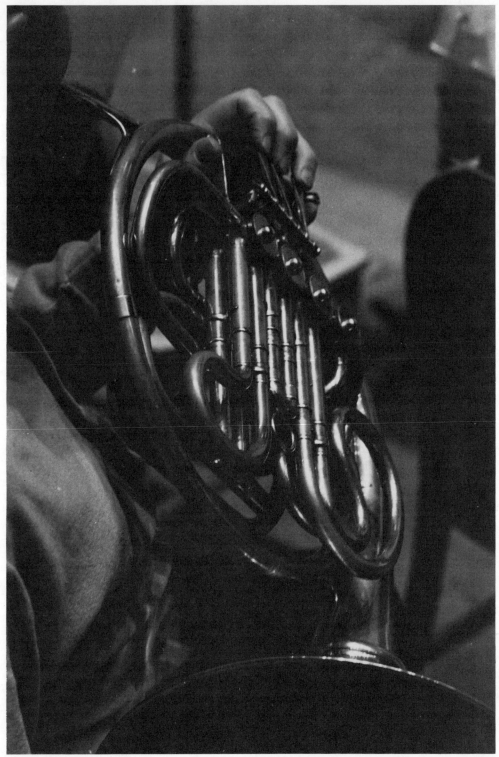

Figure 3. Courtesy, Boston Symphony Orchestra. (Creative Photographers)

to the violin's soprano, and, indeed, *alto* is the French name for the instrument. It has a darker and slightly more full-bodied sound than the violin, and just slightly less flexibility because the distances on the fingerboard from one tone to another are a fraction larger.

The composer not only uses the viola to fill out the middle register of the string section, but, aware of its expressivity and its uniquely introspective tone color, writes for it passages that portray a somber mood or a dark intensity. Sometimes the portrayal suggests a yearning, or possibly an introverted emotional turbulence.

Listen to the enchanting sound of the viola section in the opening measures of Tchaikovsky's *Sixth Symphony*. The violas enter in the fourth measure.

EXAMPLE 3–5   *Symphony No. 6*, Mvt. I, Tchaikovsky

The viola is a regular member of the string quartet and plays a prominent part in much other chamber music. Its solo repertoire is not extensive.

The cello   *Violoncello* is the full name of this instrument, but the shortened version, cello, is more often used. Because of its size it stands on the floor, using an extended end pin, and is held between the player's knees. This instrument has strings that are not only thicker than those of the viola, but twice as long. The cello is pitched an octave lower than the viola, and in its middle and upper range has a rich tenor sound that can be full and soaring. In its low range, it can be dark or warm as the composer requires. It can be quietly lyric, or it can give an effect of throbbing.

In addition to its use in the symphony orchestra, the cello is the lowest member of the string quartet. The solo repertoire for this instrument is considerable.

Suggested Listening: Dvorak, *Cello Concerto in B Minor.*

The contrabass   The contrabass is the largest instrument of the string family and the lowest-pitched. It is also called the *double bass* because it originally doubled with the cello on the bass line in the orchestras of the baroque and classical periods.

This instrument stands on the floor as does the cello, but, because of its size, the player either stands or sits on a high stool. With a deep, sometimes "gruff" sound because of the length and thickness of its strings, the contrabass is pitched nearly an octave below the cello.

The contrabass differs in certain aspects from the other instruments of the string section. On close inspection it will be noted that its shoulders are more sloping, and its back is flatter. These differing aspects are the result of its descent from the viol family. For this reason the contrabass is still called the *bass viol*. But there are some contrabasses that have incorporated the features of the violin family, not retaining the differences we have mentioned. The contrabass of the symphony orchestra today has an additional fifth string that extends the range of the instrument.

The contrabass is a standard member of the jazz orchestra, having replaced the tuba in the earlier part of the century and is frequently referred to as the *bass fiddle*, the *string bass*, or simply the *bass*. Its function in jazz is chiefly that of a rhythm instrument, and the manner of playing is usually that of pizzicato, although the bow is used to supply the foundation of the harmony in less rhythmic passages. In the jazz orchestra, the double bass has had a fifth string added to the usual four, but it is a string pitched higher than the other four, rather than lower.

The woodwinds

The term *woodwinds*, as a classifying name, was first used to differentiate wind instruments made of wood from those made of brass. This was not the only differentiating feature, but it did serve to classify, and it is still in use, in spite of the fact that some of the woodwinds are now made of metal.

Because of some basic differences in construction of woodwind instruments, the woodwind section of the orchestra has many more possibilities for variety of tone color than either the string section or the brass section. Note, for instance, that string instruments are basically the same in their proportions, materials, and manner of construction; they differ chiefly in size. The string section thus presents the most homogeneous sound of any section of the orchestra. The brass instruments, in spite of important differences in their bore measurements, are also reasonably similar in their proportions, materials, and manner of construction. The brass section sound is fairly homogeneous. By contrast, the instruments of the woodwind section are not "all of the same cloth," or even nearly so.

The flute   Originally of wood, the flute often is made of silver, and occasionally of platinum or gold. The instrument is held horizontally to the player's right; the tone is produced by blowing across an open tone-hole in somewhat the same manner as one blows across the open top of a bottle to produce a tone.

With the exception of the piccolo, the flute is the highest-pitched of the woodwinds and the most agile. The flutist can execute long lyrical passages, as well as ones of extreme technical complexity. The tone, acoustically, is the "purest" of the woodwinds because so few of the overtones are present in it. As it is the only instrument of the woodwind section that does not use a reed to set the air column in vibration, its tone has more of the quality of "wind" in it than the other woodwinds. Because it is not a reed instrument, its tone is the least insistent of all the woodwinds. In its middle register the flute's quality of tone may be suggestive of calmness or pensiveness. Through association with the shepherd's pipe, it sometimes suggests scenes of a pastoral nature. In its upper register the tone of the flute becames brighter, and in staccato passages, more bell-like. Aware of the flute's similarity to the human soprano voice in its middle and high registers, composers have often used the flute in duet style with the coloratura in florid operatic writing.

> *Suggested Listening:*   Donizetti, "Mad Scene," *Lucia di Lammermoor*, for soprano and flute.

In its low range the tone of the flute exhibits a quiet breathiness that can suggest an air of intimacy.

In addition to its use in the symphony orchestra, the flute is also a regular member of the concert band. In recent years it has become popular with jazz performers. This has been made possible with the aid of the microphone, whereas formerly the flute could not compete with the jazz instruments of greater volume.

The piccolo   "Piccolo" is short for *flauto piccolo*. The term *piccolo* by itself only means "little." This *petite flute,* as the French speak of it, is pitched an octave higher than the flute and adds not only range but brilliance to the upper register of the woodwind section. Its tone is much brighter than that of the flute and also much more penetrating. It is used in its middle and upper ranges to add sparkle to the orchestration. The tone of its middle range is somewhat comparable to a person's whistle, which is indeed in the same register. In the upper range the tone may be described as shrill or even piercing. Because of its great carrying power, the piccolo is used by composers rarely and with caution.

In the final pages of his opera *Salome*, Richard Strauss has made interesting use of the piccolo. As Salome carries the silver tray that holds the severed head of

John the Baptist, she is about to sing, "I have kissed your lips, Jokanaan." The following example shows the piccolo in octaves with the oboe in a figure that is played seven more times at varying time intervals, over trills and tremolos and generally shimmering orchestration. The effect is one of the most eerie in music.

EXAMPLE 3–6   *Salome*, Strauss

In the concert band the piccolo is used much more often than in the orchestra. In marches the piccolo often plays an *obbligato* high above the melody. Well known to many listeners is the piccolo obbligato in the trio section of Sousa's "Stars and Stripes Forever." In the interests of showmanship it is now traditional for the members of the flute section to stand as they play this piccolo obbligato.

The alto flute   The alto flute is pitched a fourth lower than the regular flute. It is a transposing instrument in G, somewhat longer than the flute, and with a larger bore. It is the alto to the flute's soprano, and has a larger, darker sound. It has lately attained wider use as a jazz instrument.

The recorder   The recorder is a woodwind instrument that was in common use from the sixteenth century to the eighteenth. It was eventually superseded by the flute for the same reason that certain other instruments lost favor; the flute had a more powerful tone. The recorder is end blown, and has a beaked wooden mouthpiece that fits between the lips in the manner of an ordinary wooden whistle. Its tone is unusually pure and is even more mellow and "hollow" than that of the flute.

To J. S. Bach "flute" meant recorder; when he wished to use the flute that we know today he wrote "flauto traverso" (transverse flute). There were several sizes of recorder making up a family, or consort; the most usual sizes were the descant, treble, tenor, and bass. The recorder has been revived in recent years for the proper performance of baroque music and also as a beginning instrument for children or adults.

The oboe   The double reed of the oboe imparts a tone quality to the instrument that is easily recognizable. Sometimes spoken of as nasal, its tone quality can perhaps be better described as reedy and quietly penetrating, as opposed to the clarinet tone, which is more bland. It often alternates with the clarinet in assuming the role of the soprano in the woodwind section, especially in a lyric, cantabile melody. There are many examples of its use as a solo instrument. This

EXAMPLE 3–7   *Swan Lake Ballet*, Scene I, Tchaikovsky

well-known example by Tchaikovsky shows the ability of the oboe to sustain an expressive legato line of quiet intensity in its middle range.

Suggested Listening: Brahms, *Symphony No. 1*, Mvt. II.

The oboe tone becomes thinner as it proceeds into the high range and its singing quality becomes less effective, but composers use the high range for special effects.

The oboe has no tuning slide as does a brass instrument, nor has it a mouthpiece that may be adjusted to lengthen the instrument as do the clarinet and flute. Thus the pitch is somewhat fixed, and the orchestra tunes to the oboe.

The English horn   The English horn is a double-reed instrument pitched a perfect fifth below the oboe. Larger and longer than the oboe, it is an alto instrument. In addition to its extra length, it may be distinguished from the oboe by the slight curve at its upper end and the globe-shaped bell at the lower. Its sound is darker and fuller than that of the oboe and has a husky plaintiveness that is unique. At times it may sound melancholy, and, on occasion, quietly raucous. Broad lyric lines become it. Rarely is it used in passages of a highly technical nature (as are the oboe and the bassoon), being favored by the composer for its interesting tone color.

Figure 4.   Seventeenth-century Dutch oboe. (Victoria and Albert Museum, London)

Suggested Listening: Berlioz, *Symphonie fantastique*, Mvt. III, "Scene in the Country."

The clarinet   Not only is the clarinet one of the most agile of instruments, but also, in its nearly four octaves, it has the greatest range of all the woodwinds. It also has the largest dynamic range of the woodwinds, varying from the lightest whisper to an impressive forte.

Brought into general use in the symphony orchestra by Mozart in his *"Paris"* *Symphony*, No. 31, the clarinet has remained there as a favored instrument of many composers, chiefly because of the wide variety of tone color of which it is capable. It can produce a wild shriek in its upper range. It can sound hollow or other-worldly in its lower, *chalumeau,* register. In its middle range, it can be lyrical and warm, or dry and light. And it can be bland as no other instrument can.

EXAMPLE 3–8   *Romeo and Juliet*, Tchaikovsky

Suggested Listening: Richard Strauss, *Till Eulenspiegel.*

The clarinet is most commonly pitched in B-flat, but there is also the clarinet in A, pitched a semitone lower. Both instruments are standard equipment for the clarinetist in a symphony orchestra.

The clarinet has had wide use in the playing of folk music and dance music in many countries. It has been used in orchestras in the United States ever since the Civil War, when it was borrowed from the marching bands of that day ultimately to become a standard instrument in the early jazz bands. Its use continues to the present day in dance orchestras and theater orchestras, where it is considered a "natural double" for the saxophonist. However, its use in the jazz orchestra has lately decreased.

The B-flat clarinet is a leading member of the concert band, the clarinet section equating in a general way with the violin section of the symphony orchestra.

The E-flat clarinet   A shorter and higher-pitched instrument than the B-flat clarinet, the E-flat clarinet extends the upward range of the clarinet section. This instrument has a tone that may be described as thinner and shriller than that of the B-flat clarinet. It is also somewhat more difficult to play in tune. At its worst it is strident; at its best, brilliant.

The alto clarinet (in E♭)   This instrument is longer than the B♭ clarinet and is pitched a fifth lower; its upper end is slightly curved because of the goodly length of the instrument. If it had a fuller sound, it would be an adjunct to the clarinet section in filling out the middle register. However, its tone being somewhat weak and shallow, it is not often used in the symphony orchestra. It is a regular member of the concert band, however, where it is not used as a solo instrument but stands in the same position in the clarinet section as the viola in the string section.

The bass clarinet   The bass clarinet is a fairly recent addition to the woodwinds, not coming into general usage until the second half of the nineteenth century. Sounding an octave below the B-flat clarinet, it is curved both at the upper end and at the lower end, with the lower curve turning upward into a bell shape. In its middle and lower range it has a tone color that may be described as "broad, but gentle."

Without the bite and the reediness of the bassoon, its volume is about the same. Therefore its tone can be easily covered by more sonorous instruments. The composer uses it often in exposing passages, in addition to having it supply the bass for quiet woodwind or string writing. In the upper part of the range, the tone of the bass clarinet "thins out." Its upper range is therefore used somewhat sparingly.

The bassoon   Music for the bassoon is written in the bass and tenor staves. In rare instances the treble staff is used.

It may be noted that its name in German, *Fagott*, or Italian, *fagotto*, is equivalent to the English word *fagot*, which means several sticks bound together. This was the "look" of the instrument in the earlier stages of its development when the workmanship was less refined. Now, although it retains its original shape, it is a sleek instrument made of maple, with a dark cherry finish brought to a high luster.

The English name, *bassoon,* refers to the fact that it is a bass instrument. With a range of three octaves or more and a surprising agility for a low-pitched instrument, the bassoon has many uses in the orchestra. In addition to providing the bass to the woodwind section, it is an excellent solo instrument with an expressive, individual sound. Its double reed gives its tone an edge, but it is a tone less penetrating than that of the oboe, its counterpart in the higher range.

In the orchestra of classical dimensions, the bassoon often doubles the cello or double-bass part, adding piquancy and verve to a fast-moving line. In its upper range it has a thinner, drier sound that has been used by Stravinsky with remarkable effect in the opening measures of *Le Sacre du printemps.*

The contrabassoon   Also known as the double bassoon, the contrabassoon is pitched one octave lower than the bassoon, and it is used by composers to achieve a depth not possible with any other instrument of the orchestra. Its lowest note is but a semitone above the lowest note on the piano, and when the instrument is played in its lowest range, the tone may almost be said to resemble a "rattle." Its use in the symphony orchestra is occasional, although it was used by Haydn in *The Creation* and by Beethoven in his Fifth and Ninth symphonies.

The saxophone   The saxophone is one of the few instruments that was invented as a complete family covering all the registers from soprano to bass. It is a hybrid instrument—made of brass, yet with a mouthpiece and single reed like those of the clarinet.

Invented by Adolphe Sax and patented by him in France in 1846, the saxophone did not gain acceptance into the symphony orchestra until the late 1800's, and since then its use has been somewhat sporadic. Richard Strauss introduced a quartet of saxophones into his *Domestic Symphony,* and Ravel wrote for three in his *Bolero.*

Suggested Listening: Debussy, *Rhapsodie* for saxophone and orchestra.

The chief use of the saxophone has been in American popular music and jazz. In the early 1900's it found its way into dance bands and jazz bands, and since then it has become the basic section of the large jazz orchestra, supplying the fundamental body of sound as do the strings in the symphonic orchestra. The alto saxophone, the tenor, and, to a lesser extent, the baritone, have been the instruments of some of the finest jazz soloists.

Suggested Listening: recordings by Coleman Hawkins, Charlie Parker, Gerry Mulligan, Stan Getz, and John Coltrane.

The soprano saxophone, pitched in B-flat, formerly made sporadic appearances as a jazz solo instrument, and has recently been in the spotlight again. The bass saxophone is rarely seen.

The brass

The instruments of the brass family include the trumpet, the French horn, the trombone, and the tuba. The modern symphony orchestra carries a minimum of three trumpets, four French horns, three trombones, and one tuba. This is the most sonorous section of the orchestra. Individually and as a section these instruments can produce more loud sustained sound than any other instruments. In sustained *tutti* passages, the brass dominate.

Listen to the opening measures of the overture to *Die Meistersinger*. Notice the predominance of the brass sound in spite of the fact that these instruments are, in number, only 11 out of the entire orchestra of more than 100 players.

The sound of all brass instruments is produced by a column of air set in motion. The air from the player's lungs causes the lips to vibrate. The lips control the pitch. The positioning of the player's lips on the mouthpiece is called *embouchure*. Special effects that can be obtained with different degrees of effectiveness on the various brass instruments include *double tonguing*, *triple tonguing*, and *flutter tonguing*.

Many mutes have been invented for the brass instruments, but there is only one that has become standard in the symphony orchestra. Made of metal or fibre, it is cone-shaped and is known as a *straight mute*. When the part specifies mute, it is understood that the reference is to the straight mute. The mute is fitted into the bell of the instrument, and not only softens the tone but changes its color completely so that it no longer has the basic sound of a brass instrument. The tone changes to one with an edge to it, more similar to the tone of a double-reed instrument. For example, the tone of the trumpet is changed in volume and tone color to such an extent that it is not too unlike the tone of the oboe. The straight mute is used principally in the trumpet and trombone sections, but on occasion even the tuba is called upon to use the mute. (This is a huge mute, since it has to fit the upright bell of the instrument, and the free-lance tuba player avoids carrying the mute with him if at all possible.) The cup mute, so called because of its shape, is rarely used in the symphony orchestra. It also softens the tone, but it gives the brass instrument a mellow sound more similar to the tone of a flute. The straight mute and the cup mute have long been standard equipment in the large jazz orchestras. The jazz musician has used many other devices to change the natural sound of the brass instruments. In addition to the straight mute and the cup mute, there is the harmon mute. This was originally used to produce a "wow-wow" effect (with the aid of the left hand), but now is more often used without this effect and used instead to produce an intense, yet soft sound. Some orchestras, such as that of Duke Ellington, have long used a "plunger"—this is actually the rubber end of a bathroom plunger—to produce a somewhat hollow sound, and in the hands of an expert trombonist it sounds oddly imitative of the human speaking voice.

Figure 5.   Town musicians playing trumpets, drums. (Museum W. Biecz, photograph by Kazimierz Slawski)

The trumpet   The trumpet is the soprano voice of the brass section. With tubing that is narrow-bored and mainly cylindrical, the trumpet has a brilliant, commanding tone that can "carry" above the entire symphonic orchestra playing at full volume.

Before the advent of valves in the early nineteenth century, the trumpet was employed to reinforce the fundamental harmonies and certain rhythmic figures of an orchestral work, often in conjunction with the timpani. Without valves the trumpet was limited to the notes of the overtone series based upon the fundamental tone of the instrument. In this respect it was similar to the bugle of today. This very limitation was the spur that drove trumpet players in the baroque period to develop the extreme high register since the overtones in the fourth octave of the harmonic series the notes are close enough together to enable the player to produce the notes of the major scale. To play in this octave is exceedingly demanding with regard to endurance and control, and is analogous to the performance of the coloratura soprano. A virtuoso school of trumpet playing developed—although these players were no less scarce than coloraturas—and composers of the time wrote for them. The trumpet part in the *Brandenburg Concerto No. 2* (Ex. 3–9) originally was written for a valveless trumpet, a larger and lower-pitched trumpet than the B♭ trumpet in use today. It was essentially an alto trumpet, pitched in F.

EXAMPLE 3–9   *Brandenburg Concerto No. 2,* J. S. Bach

With the addition of valves to the trumpet, virtuoso high-register playing died out, and today the baroque trumpet parts are usually played on a trumpet that is much smaller than the B♭ trumpet. This is the *piccolo trumpet* sometimes referred to as the *Bach trumpet,* pitched an octave higher than the B♭.

Most trumpet players in symphony orchestras have excellent control of the high register on the B♭ trumpet, producing a larger tone than is possible on the piccolo trumpet—more like the sound of the early baroque trumpet. Performances of the *Second Brandenburg* on the B♭ trumpet are few, however, because of the problem of endurance. In a way, it may be compared to playing the children's game, "King of the Mountain." It is not so much a matter of getting there as staying there.

The cornet   The cornet is occasionally called for in a symphonic score, but its chief use is in the concert band.

The tubing of the B-flat cornet and the B-flat trumpet is exactly the same length, in spite of the fact that the cornet looks shorter. The cornet appears to be shorter only because its tubing is coiled differently. In addition to their similar length, both instruments have the same valve system, so that anyone who can play the one instrument can play the other. The tone of the cornet is mellower than that of the trumpet because its bore is larger and more conical. The bore of the trumpet is basically cylindrical, which accounts for its more brilliant tone.

It has sometimes been said that the cornet is easier to play than the trumpet.

This is true in a very limited way; the more conical bore allows for a certain "easiness" in making the instrument speak and in the playing of a legato line. However, the chief reason that has always been advanced for its use as a leading member of the concert band is its mellowness of tone, the trumpet tone being regarded as too brilliant.

The fluegel horn in Bb   The fluegel horn in common use today is the one pitched in Bb, a soprano instrument with the same register and range as both the Bb trumpet and the Bb cornet. It is the descendant of a whole family of fluegel horns that came in many sizes and were pitched in all registers from the soprano fluegel horn in Eb (comparable to an Eb trumpet) to the contrabass (comparable to a BBb tuba).

This surviving instrument stands in relation to the cornet as the cornet does to the trumpet. That is to say: As the bore of the cornet is larger and more conical than that of the trumpet, and the sound is mellower, so the bore and the sound of the fluegel horn are even more so. Although its tubing is the same length as that of the Bb trumpet and the Bb cornet, the Bb fluegel horn appears shorter because of its coiling. The wider bore is apparent as well as the more conical tubing, which flares into a larger bell than that of the cornet. Its chief use has been in the concert band to add a mellow, darker sound in the soprano register. Separate parts have been written for it, but at times it has been used on the cornet parts, along with the cornets, to darken the cornet section sound. This is no longer common. The fluegel horn has lately found its way into the jazz field, where a few trumpet players have became intrigued with its broad, less incisive sound, using it chiefly in solo improvisation.

The French horn   The French horn, usually called simply the *horn*, is the alto instrument of the brass section. It has a natural tone that is somewhat mellower than that of the trombone. Its tone is further mellowed, or darkened, by a practice that is unique among the brass instruments—i.e., the normal method of playing the horn is with the player's right hand inserted into the bell, and the hand is "cupped" to somewhat muffle the tone.

The horn is also the only brass instrument in which the valves are played with the left hand. Before valves were invented, the horn was held with the left hand, the right hand being inserted into the bell in order to "manipulate" the tones by changing the air column enough to effect the pitch. This practice is known as "stopping," and continues today as a special effect. When the instrument was modernized, horn players—being accustomed already to using the right hand in the bell—developed the use of the left hand for the valves.

The mellow tone of the horn enables it to blend easily with the woodwinds as well as the other brass in the symphony orchestra. It is an excellent solo instrument, as the following example shows.

EXAMPLE 3–10   *Till Eulenspiegel*, Richard Strauss

The range of the horn is exceptionally large, as the Strauss example above shows. Note that the last three notes are on the bass staff. Since horn players sometimes specialize in "high horn" and "low horn," on occasion the last two notes of this solo are played by another member of the horn section.

The trombone   The trombone is a tenor instrument pitched an octave below the B-flat trumpet. Because its bore is narrow and mostly cylindrical, it has a tone brighter than that of the horn, and more akin to the trumpet. Its name, which is Italian, actually means "large trumpet."

The trombone historically is the oldest type of brass instrument widely used that still exists in its original form. Because of its slide, which can elongate the instrument through seven positions, thereby supplying seven different fundamental tones, it has always been able to play the entire chromatic scale. Playing a prominent part in early music, it did not come into use in symphonic writing until Beethoven introduced it in the last movement of his *Fifth Symphony*.

Although the trombone had not been accepted in symphonic circles in Mozart's time, Mozart made notable use of it in certain of his operas, often for the representation of the supernatural. In *Idomeneo* the trombones accompany the voice of the oracle speaking from the waterfall. This is their only use in this opera and the sounds come, not from the pit, but from backstage, accompanying the voice. In *Don Giovanni* Mozart again uses the trombone as part of a supernatural effect. He reserves their use throughout the entire opera until the appearance of the statue (or ghost) of the Commendatore whom Don Giovanni killed in a duel at the beginning of the opera. The trombones here also are backstage.

A unique piece of trombone writing is to be found in the "Tuba Mirum" in Mozart's *Requiem*. This is a part written for the trombone in duet with the bass (vocal) soloist. The first thirteen measures are considered to be by Mozart, with

EXAMPLE 3–11   *Requiem*, K. 626, "Tuba Mirum," Mozart

so - - - - - - num,

the following written by his amanuensis, Süssmayr. The solo is found in the second trombone part because in that day there existed the true alto tenor and bass
trombones, and Mozart wanted the tone color and range of a tenor trombone.

The trombone has had wide usage throughout all periods of jazz. In the early
days of jazz it was borrowed from the marching bands to play the bass line in
Dixieland, or "tailgate" from the back of a truck. It was one of the instruments of
the blues, and went from there into the large dance bands and jazz orchestras. Its
lyric voice was made prominent by Tommy Dorsey, and it continues today in big
bands, television studios, and in many jazz groups. The trombone has also been
a constant in the band, from the front line of the marching band to its position in
the concert band, which is basically similar to its position in the symphony
orchestra.

The tuba   The tuba most commonly used is the BB-flat (the double B-flat),
pitched an octave below the B-flat trombone, and with tubing twice as long. The
tuba has an extremely wide bore—wider in proportion to the length of its tubing
than that of any other brass instrument—and thus has a very broad, sonorous
sound.

The tuba, with the invention of valves, was the last of the brass instruments to
become a member of the symphony orchestra. It was invented in the 1820's. The
predecessors of the tuba were the *ophicleide,* which was the bass instrument of
the *keyed bugle* family, and the *serpent,* so named because of it shape.

Symphonic tuba players use a tuba in C, pitched one tone higher than the
BB-flat. This instrument provides a slight advantage in the upper range, and also
"manipulates" just a bit more easily. Its tone is slightly less obtrusive. More
rarely, smaller tubas pitched in E-flat and F are used in the symphony orchestra.

In the concert band, the BB-flat tuba is the standard instrument; but the tuba
in E-flat is also sometimes used. The chief reason for the E-flat tuba in the band
is its smaller size and lighter weight, which is more practicable for high school or
college students who may not have the "heft" necessary to handle the large instrument. This is especially true when the instrument must be carried while marching. A further aid to the tuba player in marching is the use of the model known
as the *sousaphone.* This is an instrument of the *helicon* type, in which the bell

faces forward; it was the innovation, although not the invention, of John Philip Sousa. The instrument encircles the player and "sits" on his shoulder.

The tuba has been in and out of orchestras in the popular and jazz fields since the late 1800's. At that time the most accessible and the least expensive instruments were those that had become "army surplus" after the Civil War. Thus it was only natural that the clarinet, trumpet, trombone, and "brass bass" (or tuba) should become prominent members of the early jazz bands. The tuba's position in the jazz band was gradually usurped by the bass fiddle, however, and by the mid 1930's it had become a rarity.

The percussion

The basic instruments of the percussion section have a history that anticipates that of the other families of instruments that have been discussed. The bass drum, the snare drum, and the timpani are but variants of the ancient drums of different sizes that were used in primitive cultures as an integral part of festivals or religious ceremonies, as signals in time of danger, or to set the rhythm for the dance. The ancient drums were made by stretching the dried and treated skin of an animal over one end of a hollowed-out tree trunk or gourd.

Timpani   The most refined of the membrane percussion instruments are the timpani. They are the only instruments of the membrane type that are tuned to specific pitches. There are hand screws on the upper rim that fine-control the tension of the head (membrane). The pitch of each of the timpani may be changed by a foot pedal that increases or decreases the tension of the head.

EXAMPLE 3–12   Timpani ranges

Diameter: 30-inch   28-inch   25-inch   23-inch

The classical orchestra usually employed two timpani (performed by one player), one tuned to the tonic of the key and the other tuned to the dominant. As noted in the section on the trumpet, the timpani and the trumpets were often used in conjunction with each other.

The timpanist is the principal player of the percussion section of the symphony orchestra. With the bass drum and the snare drum, the timpani are often employed in performing passages of a pronounced rhythmic nature, but in producing a definite pitch the timpani are also often the foundation of the harmony. Because of these two attributes of the timpani, it has been said, "If you don't have a good timpanist, you don't have an orchestra."

The snare drum   The snare drum differs from every other kind of drum in that it has a set of coiled wires stretched across the bottom head of the drum. These coiled wires are known as *snares*. When the top of the snare drum is struck, the snares add a crispness of sound that is useful in rhythmic passages requiring a dry, distinctive staccato effect.

A well-known use of the snare drum in the symphonic literature is found in Ravel's *Bolero,* where a single rhythmic figure is repeated throughout the entire work in a continuous crescendo to the end.

EXAMPLE 3–13   *Bolero,* Ravel

The snare drum is familiar as the instrument that plays the "street beat" in the marching band when other instruments are not playing. The snare drum is a basic part of the equipment of the jazz drummer.

The bass drum   The bass drum hardly needs to be explained or described, but it may be said that it consists of two heads of stretched membrane, each stretched over opposite ends of a barrel-type wooden (or metal) structure. Although bass drums vary in size, they are always the largest drums in either the band or the orchestra.

The bass drum has hand screws on both rims that control the tension of the heads. Although of indefinite pitch, the best *tone* for the purposes of the symphony orchestra or the concert band is that which is between the one extreme of a "boom"—which is too reverberating—and the other extreme of a "thud"—which has too little reverberation.

The importance of the bass drum cannot be overemphasized. In as much as correct tempo is the first requisite in performance, the rhythmic function of the bass drum is vital.

Cymbals   Piatti, which is the Italian term for "cymbals," literally means "plates." The term well describes the general shape of cymbals. Made of spun brass, they come in all sizes. The cymbals used in the symphonic orchestra and the concert band are eighteen inches or more in diameter, and are capable of a large dynamic range, from a whispering "z-z-z" to a resounding crash.

Figure 6. Angel musician with a tambourine, detail from one of the pilasters of the entrance to the Church of Saints Andrea and Bernardino in Perugia, by Duccio. (Alinari-Giraudon)

A pair of cymbals is played by one person. They are sounded by being struck against each other with a technique that might be described as "striking together obliquely."

There are also smaller cymbals, in various sizes, that may be played in different ways. The single cymbal may be struck with a felt-headed mallet, or a drumstick, or a roll may be played on a cymbal. In fact, the possibilities are many, and the twentieth-century composer often goes to great lengths to explain in the player's part just how he wants special effects produced. In the orchestra of the theater pit, the television studio, or the jazz orchestra, the suspended cymbal (or several of them in different sizes) is preferred to the larger "concert" cymbals.

The tam-tam   The tam-tam, or gong, is of Chinese origin. A giant disk, sometimes as large as four feet in diameter, it is struck with a round, soft-headed mallet to produce a reverberating tone that spans a range in volume from the softest whisper to a thunderous roar. The tam-tam has a lip at its outer edge, facing away from the player. Because of its immense size it is hung on a freestanding frame. The player on certain occasions starts the vibrations ahead of time by hitting it very lightly.

The xylophone   The modern xylophone is of comparatively recent origin, and because of its hard, dry staccato sound it is used in the symphony only in special passages. Its keyboard resembles a portion of the piano keyboard. The xylophone bars (keys) are made of wood.

Set horizontally on a stand, the xylophone is normally played with two mallets, but on occasion three or four mallets are used.

Suggested Listening: Saint-Saëns, *Carnival of the Animals*, "Fossils."

The marimba   The marimba, which is a larger version of the xylophone, has the added feature of resonance, which the xylophone does not have. Rare in its appearance in the symphony orchestra, it is used when the composer desires a deeper sound than the xylophone and a continuation of sound, which the xylophone cannot produce.

Also resembling the piano keyboard in its four-octave range, its bars are of wood that are played with from two to four soft rubber mallets. Under each bar there is a resonating tube that gives it its unique deep, hollow sound.

The marimba has occasionally been used in dance orchestras, but it is more commonly associated with the performance of the solo night club entertainer who performs on all of the "mallet" instruments.

Orchestra bells   The keyboard of the orchestra bells resembles that of the xylophone, but the instrument is smaller and its lowest C is pitched an octave higher. The bars are made of metal and, when struck with a hard-headed mallet, give off a sound similar to actual silver bells. Orchestra bells are also well-known by their German name, *glockenspiel.* They are standard equipment in today's symphonic orchestra, although their use is only occasional. The orchestra bells sound two octaves higher than the printed part indicates.

The use of the orchestra bells is far more common in the band for they are often given passages that accent a melody played in the brass or winds. They are also used as a solo instrument. Fast passages are impractical because of the carry-over of the sound: one tone will blur into the next for there is no dampening system on the instrument.

The orchestra bells, or glockenspiel, when used with a marching band, are referred to as the *bell-lyra,* as the bells are then in a vertical position, contained within a lyre-shaped frame.

Chimes   The chimes are long metal tubes, one and one-quarter or one and one-half inches in diameter, suspended vertically from a rack. They are struck at the top with a wooden hammer or a hammer covered with rawhide, and they give out a sound that resembles that of church bells. There is a foot pedal mechanism, which may dampen the tone or allow it to ring.

The triangle   The triangle is a round metal bar, about one-half inch in diameter, bent at two points to form the triangle shape, and open at the end. It is struck with a small metal bar and gives off a sound, indeterminate in pitch, that may best be described as a "ting."

The triangle was first used by Gluck. One of its more familiar uses is in Beethoven's "Turkish" variation of the choral theme in the *Ninth Symphony.* Here it is used simultaneously with the bass drum and cymbal to produce the "Turkish" effect.

The triangle is a standard part of the percussionist's equipment in symphony, the theater, and studio orchestra.

Suggested Listening: Beethoven, *Symphony No. 9,* Mvt. IV; Liszt, *Piano Concerto in E-flat.*

Other instruments

The piano

The piano is probably the most well-known of all musical instruments. With the exception of the organ, it has the largest range. Its eighty-eight keys arranged in semitones serve as a reference chart in designating the ranges of all other instruments.

The piano is actually a percussion instrument. Each tone is produced by the striking action of a felt hammer against the strings. And although the task of each pianist in playing a lyric or legato passage is to make the tone as sustained as possible, each tone begins to die away immediately after it is begun, in the same manner that the sound of a cymbal dies away after being struck.

The dynamic range of the piano is considerable, from crashing chords to a feathery wisp of sound. The piano has three foot pedals that add certain features to the expressivity of the instrument. When the damper pedal, on the right, is depressed it releases the dampers from the strings, allowing the strings to sustain the sound. The pedal on the left, the soft pedal, moves the hammers so that one less string produces the tone. The pedal in the middle (not practicable on some upright pianos) is the sostenuto pedal. This sustains the sound of selected tones during the playing of others that are not to be sustained.

Almost every major composer has written important works for the piano as a solo instrument, or in combination with other instruments.

The name *piano* is in reality an abbreviation of its original designation, *pianoforte*, signifying that it could play both softly and loudly from touch alone, in contradistinction to the harpsichord, which it superseded.

Invented in Italy in 1709 by Bartomoleo Cristofori, the piano was in general use by Mozart's time, but it had a much lighter sound and shorter keyboard than does our piano of today. It is interesting to note that Johann Christian Bach, an older contemporary of Mozart, wrote keyboard works in which he specified "harpsichord or forte-piano."

Suggested Listening: Schubert, *Piano Quintet in A,* "*Trout*," Op. 114; Beethoven, *Piano Sonata in F Minor,* "*Appassionata*," Op. 57.

The harpsichord

The harpsichord, usually in a shape similar to the grand piano, has a smaller range. The tone of the harpsichord, softer than that of the piano, is produced by a plucking action. When a key is depressed, a plectrum is moved upward, pluck-

Figure 7. *Young Woman Playing a Clavichord* by Jan van Hemessen, 1534. (Worcester Art Museum, Worcester, Massachusetts)

ing the string as it passes. A harpsichord often has two sets of manuals (keyboards), and these are often played in combination to achieve various nuances of sound. A system of foot pedals also permits coupling of the two keyboards in various ways, including octave doublings, which allows for a variety in expression that some find more interesting than that of the piano.

With the renewed interest in music of the baroque period in recent years, there has been a resurgence of interest in the harpsichord. It had been neglected for over 100 years but now makes its appearance frequently on the concert stage.

Suggested Listening: J. S. Bach, *The Well-Tempered Clavier.*

The virginal

The tone of the virginal is produced in the same manner as that of the harpsichord. Its shape is rectangular, and its much smaller size permits it to be carried from room to room and set on a table. Indeed, it might be thought of as a "portable harpsichord." However, it does not have the potential for expression of the harpsichord, being limited to one keyboard and having a smaller range. It was a favorite instrument for the home in sixteenth-century England, and much harpsichord music was performed on it. The best-known collection of music written specifically for the instrument is *The Fitzwilliam Virginal Book.*

The clavichord

The clavichord is the earliest of the keyboard instruments with strings. In the baroque period the clavichord was a sister instrument of the harpsichord. Of earlier origin, its tone was softer but nevertheless more expressive. The manner of producing the tone differed from that of the harpsichord. The tone is produced by a brass wedge (called a *tangent*), which touches the string. The force of the tangent may be varied by the pressure on the key that sets it in action. Thus, the control of volume is similar to that on the piano, although on a smaller scale. Also, since the tangent maintains its contact with the string while the tone is sounding, an expressive vibrato may be produced by the action of the player's fingers on the keyboard.

Music written for the clavier (keyboard) in the baroque period was performed on either the harpsichord or the clavichord, the choice being dependent upon the music's character and style.

The harp

The name *harp* derives from the Italian term for the instrument, *arpa*, which suggests the natural aptitude that the instrument has for playing arpeggios or broken chords. This natural aptitude is likewise its limitation. The strings are arranged, not in semitones, as in a piano or harpsichord, but in diatonic scale steps in the key of C-flat major. By a system of foot pedals the player can raise the pitch of each string by one semitone, or by one whole tone. There are seven foot pedals, each standing for one note of the scale in all octaves. There are three separate notches for each foot pedal. When all the pedals are in the highest notch the instrument is then in C-flat. Placing all the pedals in the middle notch shortens each string so that the instrument is then pitched in C. Placing each pedal in the lowest notch pitches the instrument still another semitone higher. Various combinations of the foot pedals allow for a limited amount of chromatic writing, but in anything but slow tempos, the harp is essentially a diatonic instrument.

The harp is one of the oldest instruments, but it did not make its way into the symphony orchestra until the nineteenth century. It is now a regular member of the symphony orchestra. In large orchestras there are two harps. The solo and chamber music literature for the harp is slight.

Suggested Listening: Ravel, *Alborada del Gracioso,* for orchestra (score includes two harps).

The organ

The organ is the most versatile of instruments; its capabilities are equivalent to those of an entire orchestra. A modern full-size organ offers virtually unlimited possibilities of *registration,* a term which refers to the various combinations of tone colors that may be produced by the operation of the organ *stops.* These stops, which may be adjusted by the player ahead of time or during the course of the music, change the quality of tone. The number of stops varies with each organ, and therefore the variety of tone differs with each instrument. Some of the stops are designated by terms such as *trumpet* or *oboe.* But to the organist these stops are not so much a means of imitation as (with the other stops) they are a means of differentiating the array of colors available on the organ.

The organ is one of the most ancient of instruments and was known as the *hydraulis* by the Greeks and Romans. Its golden age was the baroque period, but nineteenth-century French composers also showed much interest in the instrument.

In recent years there has been a renewal of interest in reproducing the smaller instrument that was used in the baroque period. This baroque organ may be a single instrument, or it may form a part of the design of a large organ. The return to the sound of the baroque organ parallels the return to the use of the harpsichord, both the result of a constantly burgeoning interest in the authentic performance of baroque music.

The solo literature for the organ is vast, and the organ occasionally makes its appearance with the symphony orchestra.

Most organs have at least two manuals and one pedal keyboard, allowing for possibilities of polyphony and contrast of color not available on any other keyboard instrument. The registration of the manuals may be kept distinct or they may be combined by the use of couplers.

The sound of the organ is produced by wind, which is forced through pipes that are of a whistle type (such as a recorder) or a reed type (such as a clarinet). The wind was at one time generated by hand pumping, a chore often performed by choirboys. The wind is now usually generated by an electric blower.

The celeste

The celeste (also called *celesta*) is a small keyboard instrument with a range of four octaves. The tones of the instrument resemble the sound of small silver bells. The sound is produced by a hammer action on small steel plates, similar to those of the orchestra bells, or glockenspiel, but enhanced by resonators.

Its first use in the symphony orchestra was by Tchaikovsky in the *Nutcracker Suite*.

EXAMPLE 3–14   *Nutcracker Suite,* "Dance of the Sugar Plum Fairy," Tchaikovsky

The celeste also figures prominently in the "Presentation of the Rose" scene from Richard Strauss' charming opera, *Der Rosenkavalier*.

The symphony orchestra

When the Pilgrims arrived in the New World in the year 1620, the piano had not yet been invented; the viol family of stringed instruments had not yet been superseded by the violin family; the brass instruments did not have valves; there was no such instrument as a tuba; and the beginnings of the symphony orchestra were over a hundred years away.

In the second half of the eighteenth century, the symphony orchestra, far smaller than now, was being shaped into an effective vehicle of expression that was to reach a peak in size by the beginning of the twentieth century. New instruments were added to expand the tonal palette of the orchestra. Tone color in all its variety became the goal of many composers.

The Mannheim orchestra, which impressed Mozart and influenced him to add clarinets to his later symphonic works, was considered at the time to be the finest orchestra in the world. According to one of Mozart's letters, the instrumentation of the orchestra consisted of the following: two flutes, two oboes, two clarinets, four bassoons, two trumpets, two timpani, ten or eleven first violins, ten or eleven second violins, four violas, four cellos, and four contrabasses. The score of Beethoven's *Fifth Symphony* calls for the following instrumentation: one piccolo, two flutes, two oboes, two clarinets, two bassoons, one contrabassoon, two horns, two trumpets, three trombones, two timpani, first violins, second violins, violas, cellos, and basses.

The size of the orchestra has been increased from 30 to 40 players to sometimes well over 100, although the usual symphony orchestra of today is now standardized at about 80 to 100 players (the chief differences being in the size of the string sections).

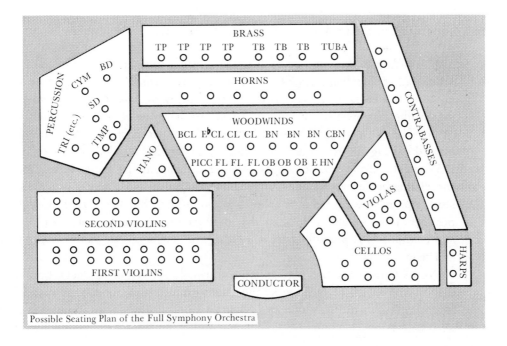

Possible Seating Plan of the Full Symphony Orchestra

Chamber orchestra

The term *chamber orchestra* most often means an orchestra small enough in size to play in a room for a more intimate gathering than would be found in a symphony hall. It is not possible to be precise about numbers. More to the point is the intent of the composer and the manner in which he handles the instruments. At the heart of the matter is the concept of treating the instruments more individually. Thus, there is often only one player on each type of instrument, for example, one clarinetist or one French horn player rather than a complete clarinet or French horn section. The strings are somewhat exceptional and may or may not be reduced to one player per instrument.

The term *chamber music* may specify music written for a chamber orchestra, but actually it is a more encompassing term and generally refers to music written for two or more players up to the limits of a chamber orchestra. The term also may refer to music with parts for voices as well as instruments. Some examples of chamber music are: Richard Strauss, *Serenade,* for two flutes, two oboes, two clarinets, four horns, two bassoons, and contrabassoon or bass tuba; Stravinsky, *L'Histoire du soldat,* for clarinet, bassoon, cornet, trombone, percussion, violin, and contrabass; Stravinsky, *Octet,* for flute, clarinet, two bassoons, two trumpets, and two trombones; Stravinsky, *Cantata,* for soprano, tenor, (small) female chorus, two flutes, two oboes (oboe II doubling on English horn), and violoncello.

Smaller chamber ensembles and solo performance

Also falling in the category of chamber music is music of a more soloistic character. Rather than being spoken of by the generic term, *chamber music,* however, music in this category is more often referred to by the specific traditional groupings of the instruments written for. These are the *woodwind quintet:* flute, oboe, clarinet, horn, bassoon; the *brass quintet:* usually two trumpets, horn, trombone, tuba; the *string quartet:* two violins, viola, cello; *string trio:* violin, viola, cello.

When the strings are joined by another instrument the group is specified by the distinguishing name of this instrument. Thus when a piano is added to a string quartet the ensemble is called a *piano quintet.* But the "Trout" Quintet of Schubert is an exception to this; the instruments are piano, violin, viola, cello, and contrabass. A *piano quartet* is a string trio plus a piano: piano, violin, viola, and cello.

Works written for two players are not usually spoken of as duets. Because of the soloistic nature of such works the two instruments are mentioned specifically, for example, *Sonata for Violin and Piano.* A work written for two pianos is called a *piano duo.*

There are many works for solo instruments, but the instruments with a super-abundance of such literature are the keyboard instruments: harpsichord, organ, and piano. Compositions for other solo instruments are much more unique, as well as often being a considerable challenge. On opposite sides of the spectrum are J. S. Bach's *Sonata in A Minor* for flute unaccompanied and Leonard Bernstein's *Elegy for Mippy II* for trombone and foot. (The foot keeps the beat by tapping on the floor.)

Suggested Listening: Francis Poulenc, *Trio for Oboe, Bassoon, and Piano.*

The concert band

Although the *concert band* is sometimes questioned as a performance vehicle for serious music, it actually has the potential for the presentation of the highest expression of any composer. The reason for the supercilious attitude toward the concert band is usually based not on its potential, which is great, but on the quality or type of music that has been performed by it in the past, and, in many cases, on the quality of the performance itself.

At the turn of the century and for many years after, the Sunday band concert in the park was a diversion for the average family. It was a light-hearted presentation of popular songs of the day, potpourri of well-known operatic selections, and usually some very "flashy" solo work by a cornet or trombone soloist, often in the form of variations on a theme. The soloists were outstanding technicians, and the well-known bands of Sousa and Pryor contained some of the best musicians of the day, but the musical fare was geared to the tastes of the average. In short, it was a commercial venture, rather than an artistic one. The concert band did not intend it to be otherwise, except perhaps in the presentations of transcriptions of symphonies. But this was only borrowed glory.

And here is the nub of the matter. In an attempt to play works of a more artistic nature, the Sunday afternoon band of necessity borrowed from works written for the symphonic orchestra or opera house. Although it might be said in some cases that the attempt was laudable, any attempt by a band to perform a work originally intended for orchestra can only be a miscarriage.

The popularity of outdoor band concerts began to decline with the advent of radio. With so many forms of entertainment now available at the turn of a dial, the band today exists mostly as a social outlet for students in high school or college. These are obviously not intended to be professional organizations. However, there are notable exceptions in colleges today, and a number of noncollegiate professional symphonic bands exist as well. Many symphonic bands perform original works for band exclusively, offering commissions to composers to write special works for them.

The concert band—or *symphonic wind ensemble*, as some prefer it—consists entirely of wind instruments, with the exception of the percussion section. The concert band evolved from the marching band, which of necessity used instruments that had the advantages of volume and portability. However, since the concert band has long since divorced itself from the marching band concept and moved into the concert hall, it has now made some exception to the concept of "wind instruments only" and has added string basses and timpani.

The basic sound of the symphony orchestra relies upon the strings; the basic sound of the concert band is winds. The concert band lacks strings, but in its woodwind section it has a far greater potential for variety of tone color than that of the symphony orchestra because of its greater number and variety of woodwind instruments.

In this century many outstanding composers have written for the concert band as an important vehicle for serious artistic expression.

> *Suggested Listening:*   Milhaud, *Suite Française*; Hindemith, *Symphony in B-Flat for Band*; Persichetti, *Divertimento for Band* and *Psalms for Band*; Holst, *Suites Nos. 1* and *2 for Band*; Vaughan Williams, *Folk Song Suite*.

PERFORMANCE

The composer as performer

In the past, composers who were merely competent as performers were rare. In fact, many were the supreme virtuosos of their time. J. S. Bach was perhaps better known for his technical facility and improvisations at the organ than for his compositions, while his contemporary in Italy, Domenico Scarlatti, electrified audiences with digital acrobatics at the keyboard. Mozart, Clementi, and Beethoven were legendary virtuosos of the keyboard. And, of course, Paganini, Mendelssohn, and Liszt were leading virtuosos of the romantic period. Berlioz and Wagner, though indifferent as players, yet managed to remain in intimate contact with performance and performers. They were leading conductors of the nineteenth century and performed their own as well as other composer's works. Wagner's *On Conducting* remains to this day an important handbook for aspiring students of the art.

The composer remained in direct contact with his audience, whether his listeners formed a church congregation, a circle of aristocrats in a gilded salon, a

Figure 8. Final scene of Haydn's opera *L'Incontro Improviso*, given under Haydn's direction at the Castle of Esterhaz, Hungary, 1755. (Theatre-Museum, Munich)

coterie of intellectuals gathered around a piano, or a massed audience in a large opera house. The composer/performer learned at first hand exactly how his listeners reacted to his music. The audience for its part saw and heard the composer present his own music in authentic performances. There was not the problem of the middle man/performer *interpreting* the composer's expression. The audience received the sense of the music directly.

During the nineteenth century, however, the unity that was composer/performer gradually disintegrated, and ultimately they were no longer one. As a specialist, the concert artist became a new force in the world of music. Pianists, such as Carl Tausig, Isidore Philipp, Ignacy Paderewski, Leopold Godowsky, retained certain credentials as composers but were of far greater significance in the musical world as concert virtuosos. At the beginning of this century the composer no longer felt the pressing need to mount the concert stage. For example, Debussy and others were less than matchless pianists. However, many twentieth-century composers took to the podium. The post-romantics, Mahler and Richard Strauss, were internationally known as conductors, and many more recent composers—including Stravinsky, Copland, Bernstein, and Boulez—have devoted much time to conducting as well.

Hindemith, perhaps lamenting the loss of the composer/performer as total musician, excelled as a violist and made it a point to play tolerably well most of the instruments for which he wrote. And the precedent of composer/virtuoso set by Paganini, Mendelssohn, and Liszt was not entirely lost. The Russian composers Rachmaninoff and Prokofiev and the Italian composer Busoni attained great virtuosity at the piano and established world reputations as concert artists.

Interpretation

Once the disengagement of composer from performer was a reality, a tremendously important concern arose: interpretation. If it is the role of the performing artists—pianist, violinist, conductor, singer—to transmit the composer's idea to the concert public, how is he to interpret the composer's wishes? When there is intimate communion between player and composer, as with the pianist Soulima Stravinsky and his father Igor Stravinsky, the task is less difficult. Piano rolls, or recordings made by composers of their own works, also help. But, essentially, the performing artist has to find for himself the musical voice of the composer. It goes without saying that he must attain great physical skills, and develop a powerful technique to enable him to conquer the most taxing compositions, but more important, he must steep himself in the life and work of the composer. He must analyze assiduously the composer's score, seizing upon its every detail to achieve as closely as possible the composer's intentions. He must consider matters of tone, dynamics, tempo, phrasing, and balance of melodic lines and harmonies. And he must know the tenor of the times in which the composer wrote. In other words, the concert artist faces an enormous challenge. He spends much of his life perfecting his interpretations of the masters.

Precisely because of this enormous technical and interpretive challenge many artists specialize in the music of one or two composers. For example, Wanda Landowska made a specialty of the harpsichord and clavichord music of J. S. Bach. Alfred Cortot, an extraordinary pianist of the early 1900's, was renowned for his Chopin playing. Arthur Schnabel made a reputation as a superb interpreter of Beethoven and Schubert. In recent years Rudolf Serkin has excelled at Beethoven and Brahms, Artur Rubinstein at Chopin, and Vladimir Horowitz at Liszt, Scriabin, and Prokofiev. In the world of opera, virtuoso singers have always been associated with certain roles—e.g., Joan Sutherland as Norma, Renata Tebaldi as Mimi (*La Boheme*), and Jon Vickers as Florestan (*Fidelio*).

Two important developments in the twentieth century have tended to shake the privileged position of the concert artist. One of these is the growth of jazz as an improvisatory art; the other is the recent surge of interest by composers in electronic media. The jazz artist again is a composer like the harpsichordist, organist, or violinist of earlier ages. Sometimes using a basic pattern such as the blues, or a well-known song or dance, but more and more using his own material, the jazz player improvises a statement that is uniquely his. With pure electronic music it is something else: the performer becomes obsolete. An object—tape recorder or synthesizer—totally replaces him. All that needs to be done is that the machine be switched on. A recreative artist, the middle man, is not needed; and traditional instruments, the tools of his trade, are likewise dispensed with. The composer is assured that his message will reach his audience exactly as he wrote it.

The conductor

What has been said of the performing artist's interpretive challenge applies as well to the conductor. He also searches for the meaning of the music as represented by the score. His pitch perception must be highly developed for he must always be aware of and be able to correct his players' intonation. He needs to be extremely sensitive to good balance between choirs, sections, and solo instruments.

What agile fingers, sensitive embouchure, controlled breath are to the soloist, baton technique is to the conductor. In its most basic aspect conducting technique refers to certain gestures traced by the right hand of the conductor which represent groups of beats. Following are three of the basic beat patterns:*

Patterns in two beats: Down, up

---

* Robert L. Garretson, *Conducting Choral Music*, 3rd Ed. (Boston, Mass.: Allyn and Bacon, Inc., 1970), pp. 6–8. © by Allyn and Bacon, Inc. Used by permission of the author.

Figure 9. Seiji Ozawa, conductor. (Courtesy, Boston Symphony Orchestra)

Patterns in three beats: Down, right, up

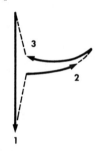

Patterns in four beats: Down, left, right, up.

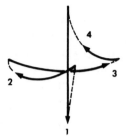

Other, more complicated rhythmic groupings resulting from compound or asymmetrical meter result in corresponding complexities in the conductor's gestures. This visual analogue of the beat is really not much more than a safeguard for the player, since he counts anyway to insure correctly timed entrances and exact ensemble. It is of much greater importance to the orchestra that the conductor also *controls the tempo*. Through his patterned rhythmic gestures he establishes a basic tempo, changing it when there are several different tempos within one composition. For example, a piece may begin in a *largo* tempo, switch to *allegro*, and end with a *presto*. Also, within a basic tempo, a pushing ahead (*accelerando*) or falling back (*ritardando*) of the beat is sometimes required by the composer. All this is indicated by the conductor's right hand. The left hand has its own, interdependent role. With it the conductor either cues for entrances or elicits dynamic effects and good balance. And, perhaps more important, the conductor must establish a rapport with his players, drawing out their best efforts while applying judicious discipline when necessary. The music director/conductor also plans programs and chooses guest artists over his entire season, and often tours and makes recordings.

The listener's part

The roles of composer and performer are very clear; the composer creates and the performer recreates. What then of the listener? What does he bring to the musical performance? Obviously he brings his attention and interest. This may be expressed by a quiet demeanor or by many sorts of active physical responses—depending on the kind of music heard. He may bring with him considerable listening experience sustained by extensive knowledge of the composer's cultural background and aesthetic outlook or, in the instance of folk music, he may understand its social or ethnic roots. But there is something much more important that the listener must bring to all serious musical expression, whether that expression is in the area of the "classics" or of jazz, folk, pop, or rock. The serious listener of music must have an attitude that is as conscientious as that of the composer and performer. In its deepest, most universal essence, music is the expression of the self. It voices the manifold aspects of human selfhood through the creativity of composer and performer. This self-expression is as unlimited as there are human modes of feeling and perception. Thus there are musical expressions reflecting states of nature, romance, philosophy, religion, humor, irony, sarcasm, optimism, pessimism, and intellectualism. Every listener, precisely because he is human, possesses a spark of creativity himself, no matter how latent or submerged it may seem to be. It was Freud who said that the poet or artist "forces us to become aware of our inner selves in which the same impulses are still extant even though they are suppressed." And Kant stated that the aesthetic experience "is represented as *universal*, i.e., valid for every man." The necessary conscientious attitude then is that of taking serious music seriously; of dredging from within oneself a creative responsiveness that will reverberate vividly to the sounds of genius. The listener must lend both his mind and heart to serious music. He must listen, not just hear.

The critic's role

The music critic is no more than a practiced and informed listener. As a professional he articulates his musical reactions that are then disseminated via the communications media. However, he often has become the arbiter and conditioner of mass taste, and the damnation or salvation of both creative and recreative musicians. Properly he should give the particulars, the what-where-when-who of the musical occurrence, and then follow with his opinion of the work, the performer, or both. Unfortunately, many critics either pass judgment as if in a court of law, or their opinion *is taken* as authoritative judgment. The absurdities indulged in by overly opinionated critics can readily be seen in the following excerpts from Slonimsky's *Lexicon of Musical Invective:* "Beethoven, this extra-ordinary genius, was completely deaf for nearly the last ten years of his life, during which his compositions have partaken of the most incomprehensible wild-ness. His imagination seems to have fed upon the ruins of his sensitive organs."*

One assumes that these comments applied to the last piano sonatas and string quartets, the *Missa Solemnis,* and the *Ninth Symphony,* now universally recog-nized as some of the most profound music ever written. And one can only marvel at the lack of musical perception by the great Russian novelist and dramatist, Maxim Gorky, as he reacted to a jazz concert:

> An idiotic little hammer knocks drily: one, two, three, ten, twenty knocks. Then, like a clod of mud thrown into crystal-clear water, there is wild screaming, hissing, rattling, wailing, moaning, cackling. Bestial cries are heard: neighing horses, the squeal of a brass pig, crying jackasses, amorous quacks of a monstrous toad . . . This excruciating medley of brutal sounds is subordinated to a barely perceptible rhythm. Listening to this screaming music for a minute or two, one conjures up an orchestra of madmen, sexual maniacs, led by a man-stallion beating time with an enormous phallus.†

Readers who follow critics closely should note Hume's astute epigram: "Al-though critics are able to reason more plausibly than cooks, they must still share the same fate." Critics are not infallible, not do they represent ultimate authority. The listener will do well to read the critics. Whether or not he has heard the per-formance himself, he should learn from and enjoy the critic's viewpoint, but only as another private, though informed, opinion. The listener's ultimate judgment should come only from hearing the music itself. Music means as many things as there are people to hear it.

---

* Nicolas Slonimsky, *Lexicon of Musical Invective,* 2nd Ed. (New York: Coleman-Ross Com-pany, Inc., 1965), p. 46 (W. Gardiner, *The Music of Nature,* London, 1837). © by Coleman-Ross Company, Inc.

† Ibid., p. 25.

Each age in history is, in fact, an age of transition. But in retrospect it seems that certain periods more than others were periods of stabilization. Tendencies, although sprung from different sources, lead toward the same focal point and finally merge. Though these merged tendencies seem clear enough now, it is often doubtful that during these periods the figures who now loom large to us as leaders would have thought of their times in terms of stability. To the philosopher, to the statesman, to the artist who is in the middle of the stream of thought or action, it is always a time of transition, a time of trying to reach some landing point that cannot yet be seen.

From our vantage point now, however, the smaller details blur and the large outlines remain, showing us the more important trends and their culmination points. Through hindsight we can check the truism that "every man is the product of his age." The age he lives in is the age he knows. "We sleep, but the loom of life never stops, and the pattern which was weaving when the sun went down is weaving when it comes up in the morning." And we are part of the texture. It is not more true of the artist than it is of the common man, but it is more important. It is more important because the artist leaves us an expression of his age.

In recognizing that each artist is a product of his age we should not attempt to equate the expression of one artist with that of another—to equate the output of the musician, for example, with the output of the architect. The inspiration of the painter and the musician, the author and the architect may all be triggered by the same environment, but their manners of expression will be individual. Similarities may be found in the ethos, but not necessarily in the expression of it. The uniqueness of the "comment" or expression of each artist will depend upon two things: the degree to which his expression is original, and the manner in which he handles his material.

Attempts to correlate the various expressions of artists have taken us to many a dead end. These attempts have resulted in describing baroque music as though it were baroque architecture; in characterizing impressionistic music in the terms of impressionistic painting; in equating the rhythms of jazz with the rhythms of certain twentieth-century paintings. Similarities and relationships are certainly apparent in these various pairings, and one in each pair may complement the other; but the essential differences among the arts must not be overlooked. Comparisons have gone even further, reaching the ultimate in vapidity in the phrase, "Architecture is frozen music." Neither music nor architecture can benefit from this association. This is not to say that comparisons of different types of works from the same period many not be illuminating; but the comparisons should not result merely in facile phrases.

No, each art form, each specific work must be considered as something unique. Instead of forcing superficial relationships upon the arts we should try to see how the same influences resulted in different expressions. Similarities will exist, but they will be of mood or style, not of design or form.

Each art will flower on its own branch. Thus we must look for the growth, the evolutionary progress, of music basically within its own historical perspective as an expression of the happenings of each age.

Chapter four

PRE-BAROQUE: BEFORE 1600

Sing joyously of God our strength;
Shout aloud of Jacob's God.
Raise the chant and beat the drum,
Both the pleasant harp and the lute.
Blow the trumpet at the new moon,
At the full moon on our festal day.
Psalm 81 *

These lines from the 81st Psalm are reminders that singing and the playing of instruments in religious ceremonies date back to early times. There are many other references in the Old Testament that testify to the Hebrew's long association with music. It was only natural that the early Christians were influenced by the music and the ritual of the synagogue.

During their first three centuries, the followers of Christianity were constantly persecuted by the powers in Rome, and many meetings had to be held in secret. In the fourth century certain things happened, affecting both the church and its music. In the year 312, Constantine, Emperor of Rome, embraced Christianity and gave it legal sanction. The Christians could now come above ground and conduct public services. Greek, the language of the New Testament and until this time the language of the church, was replaced by Latin. A vestige of Greek still exists in the language of the Mass. In the latter part of the century, Ambrose, bishop of Milan, gathered together a large number of hymns and antiphonal psalms for use in the church service. It is conjectural whether Ambrose contributed as a composer to this collection, but in any event this large body of work has come to be known as Ambrosian chant.

Inspired by the writings of Augustine, and with the foundations of the Roman Empire beginning to crack, more and more of the people turned to the church and away from the state. When the Empire disintegrated in the fifth century, the

---

* J. M. P. Smith, ed. & trans., *The Complete Bible: An American Translation* (Chicago, Ill.: University of Chicago). © 1939 by the University of Chicago. (The Apocrypha & the New Testament translation by Edgar J. Goodspeed.)

Figure 10. Illuminated Letter D; three monks singing. (The Metropolitan Museum of Art, Rogers Fund, 1912)

church became the dominant authority for many. The church grew and the body of its music grew, borrowing from various sources. These sources included Eastern as well as Western culture, pagan as well as religious, secular as well as sacred.

In the sixth century Gregory, who was Pope of Rome from 590 until his death in 604, felt it was time to draw together the loose ends of the heterogeneous—or, perhaps better, miscellaneous—collection of church music; to make choices out of the large abundance of materials that were in existence, to "purify" in some cases, and to establish an ideal of what the main body of sacred music should be.

That he was successful is only too well established. Gregorian chant, as this body of music came to be known, has served the church to the present.

THE MIDDLE AGES

Gregorian chant (plainsong)

Gregorian chant may be sung by a solo voice or a chorus singing in unison; this is known as *monophony*. It may be responsorial—alternating from solo to choral singing—or antiphonal—alternating from chorus to chorus. The range of chant is not large, very often being contained within an octave.

Gregorian chant, in the quiet undulating motion of its melody, conveys a feeling of purity and otherworldliness that lends itself well to the Catholic liturgy. The serene quality of this music is uniquely refreshing to ears accustomed to the more turbulent, emotional expression of later days.

The melodic style of the chant may be *syllabic*, one syllable to each tone; or *neumatic*, in which two, three, or four tones are sung to one syllable; or *melismatic*, in which an extended series of tones are sung to one syllable.

Guido

Guido d'Arezzo, a monk and a theorist of the eleventh century, must have had the sense of frustration that all trainers of choral groups often have in trying to teach singers how to remember pitch relationships. There was no table of reference for relative pitch names. It can only be imagined that when something went wrong in the learning of a new piece of music, Guido would often have to work from the beginning again. How long he searched for a system we do not know, but one way or another—and perhaps accidentally—he discovered that the beginning tone of each of the phrases of the *Hymn to St. John* was related to the other tones by step, and in an ascending pattern. As a memory device he decided that the Latin word or syllable sung to these tones could serve as the names of the tones and thereby be used to designate the relations of the pitches.

Hymn to St. John

	DERIVED SYLLABLES		DERIVED SYLLABLES
Ut queant laxis	Ut	Solve polluti	Sol
Resonare fibris	Re	Labii reatum	La
Mira gestorum	Mi	Sancte Iohannes	—
Famuli tuorum	Fa		

Ut has since been changed to *Do*, except in France. The syllable for the seventh scale step, *Si*, was added later (in the sixteenth century). One theory has it that *Si* was derived from the first letters of the last two words of the hymn.

Organum

The first deviation from the prevalent unison singing of Gregorian chant occurred sometime before the tenth century. There is only speculation as to how this started. It may have been in secular music, or in music of the church. At any rate, a second part was added, which was sung in fourths or fifths along with the basic chant. This parallel motion, called *organum,* in which the lower voice

EXAMPLE 4–1   Organum

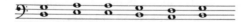

was a coupling with the upper, must indeed have sounded exciting after centuries of unison singing. The theory of organum was first described in *Musica Enchiriadis*, written in the ninth century.

In time the two voices of organum were doubled at the octave above. This is called *composite organum.* A further development, referred to as *free organum,* allowed more freedom of parts, especially at the beginning or end of the chant.

EXAMPLE 4–2   Free Organum

The next step shows the added part above rather than below the plain chant and the intervals varied so that the two parts show differing melodic contours.

Here are the seeds of polyphony. But one step more is needed to attain the true aspect of polyphony: to the differing contours of the separate melodies must be added rhythmic distinction. By the twelfth century this had been achieved. Against the plainsong the upper part is a weaving, florid line.

The setting of a florid part against the chant necessitates holding the tones of the chant longer. As the lower tones became stretched out, this lower part became known as the *tenor* (from the Latin, *tenere*, to hold).

Notre Dame

In Paris, in the twelfth and thirteenth centuries, the church of Notre Dame was the fountainhead of new developments in polyphony. Late in the twelfth century, Leonin, organist and composer, and his successor, Perotin, contributed many works. The thirteenth-century motet evolved out of their work, to become one of the most important forms of this period. To a melismatic portion of a plain chant, used as the tenor (and the basis) of the musical work, two upper parts (usually) would be added.

Unlike organum, which was mostly rhythmically free, the motet was organized into rhythmic patterns, but with the tenor part in longer note values. The melismatic portion taken from a plain chant as the basis for the motet would be changed into a fixed rhythmic pattern. This, in many cases, would be played by instruments. Above this would be added two or three parts with words of secular origin. The term *motet* arose out of the French *mot*, or word. In addition to the mixture of music derived from both sacred and secular sources, a poly-textual element was also introduced. One part above the tenor might be in French, another in Latin.

A further development toward rhythmic regularity can be seen in Latin songs, of this period. The *conductus*, for example, consisted of a tenor part not derived from the chant but composed; thus the complete work is now original. The parts are mostly homophonic.

Secular music

During the first ten centuries A.D. the systematic preservation of church music resulted in a body of music that is available to the musicologist. But there is no equivalent with respect to the secular music of these centuries. The church took great pains to preserve its music, but the preservation of music outside of the church was mostly ignored. Only in the last 100 years have scholars realized that the music of a people is an important part of their culture and therefore have made intensive studies in these directions. There is little secular music extant that

Figure 11.   *Le Jongleur.* (Bulloz)

precedes the tenth century. The largest body of secular music that has been preserved is from the eleventh and twelfth centuries.

In southern France in the twelfth century we find the *troubadour*, usually of noble birth, singing songs of love and of chivalry. The troubadour songs were in a style meant to communicate easily and directly. Travelling about from town to town the troubadour (and later in Northern France, the *trouvère*) would often have in his company a jongleur, a man of many talents but not of noble birth. The term *jongleur* originally meant jester or juggler, and to these talents the jongleur added singing and often dancing or playing an instrument.

In Germany the art of the troubadour was carried on by the *minnesinger* and the *meistersinger*. The meistersingers eventually formed guilds and awarded prizes for composition within specified "rules and regulations." This was actually a surrender of the original freedom of improvised song. An excellent illustration of the guild movement may be seen in Wagner's opera, *Die Meistersinger*.

"Sumer Is Icumen In"

The oldest example of a six-part polyphonic style that has been preserved now resides in the British Museum. Termed a *rota*, "Sumer Is Icumen In" is a canon (or round) for six men's voices. It is written so that four voices form the canon

EXAMPLE 4–3   "Sumer Is Icumen In"

From *Historical Anthology of Music*, Archibald T. Davison and Willi Apel, eds., Rev. Ed., Vol. 1 (Cambridge, Mass.: Harvard University Press, 1954), p. 44.

accompanied by two others that sing a bass line as a double ostinato. The canon is at the unison at a distance of four measures. "Summer Is Icumen In" is believed to be from about the middle of the thirteenth century.

A free rendering is given of the old English, so that the round is practicable for singing.

> Summer is a-coming in,
> Loudly sing cuckoo.
> Groweth seed and bloweth mead
> and springeth woodland new.
> Sing cuckoo.
>
> Ewe now bleateth after lamb,
> Low'th after calf, the cow,
>
> Bullock starteth, buck he grazeth,
> Merry sing cuckoo.
> Cuckoo, cuckoo.
> Well sing'st thou cuckoo,
> Nor cease thou never, now.

Pre-Renaissance

The flowering of an age is a fascinating display, and perhaps the most fascinating age of all is the Renaissance. Before the Renaissance, common man, when not worshipping God, had his eyes on the ground. On his shoulders were the burdens of tradition and superstition; feudalism dominated his way of life. His moral choices seemed to be for the most part between God and the devil; he was the victim of diseases of society as well as of the body; he was circumscribed by important limitations of the mind as well as those of his physical universe. He had yet to look beyond the horizon, not only of the Western ocean but of his limitations of knowledge. Perspective was yet to be found not only in painting, not only in the relation of the earth to other astral bodies, but in the relations of man to men.

There have been many attempts to pinpoint a single date as the beginning of the Renaissance, but no flower has a single root. The roots of the Renaissance are many and go back to the beginning of the fourteenth century. It was here that the sense of restlessness, the desire to become loose of the shackles, the itch to move out of the restrictions of manner and mode of thought and its expression were first most noticeably apparent.

The travels of the Crusaders had awakened many to the worlds that lay beyond their borders—worlds of other cultures and customs, of other moral and political beliefs. The desire for the expression of the individual led to the beginnings of a middle-class society, and serfdom began to fade.

Roger Bacon, who died about 1294, was an English monk in the Franciscan order. In his experiments in chemistry, optics, and astronomy we find the modern concept: the scientific method of inquiry as opposed to belief based on tradition. Dante, although in other respects a medieval man, made the greatest impress toward the use of a modern language (Italian) in his writings and is the first representative figure of the new language of the new age. Latin continued to be spoken and written in the universities in Italy. In 1305 Dante writes, and encourages others to write, in the best vernacular of the time. Not only Italy, but England and France as well, were at the beginnings of a national language and a national culture. In Chaucer's greatest work, *The Canterbury Tales*, the stories were medieval, but the language was new. And late in the fourteenth century, we have Wycliffe's translation of the Bible into the common tongue.

In the century that followed, the voyages of Columbus opened the way for further explorations and also established avenues for international trade and com-

Figure 12.   French court musicians. (Bulloz)

merce, which ultimately freed man not only from his physical insularity but from his insularity of thought, preparing him to acknowledge the existence of ideas and customs that could differ from his own.

More and more questions were raised about the individual's position in society. Dante had written, "We must now determine what is the purpose of human society as a whole. . . . There is . . . some distinct function for which humanity as a whole is ordained, a function which neither an individual nor a family, neither a village nor a city, nor a particular kingdom has power to perform. . . . The specific characteristic of man is not simple existence, . . . it is rather the possible intellect, or capacity for intellectual growth."

Ars Nova

A spirit of restlessness was apparent in the world of music as well. Early in the fourteenth century a treatise ascribed to composer, poet, diplomat, and bishop, Philippe de Vitry (1291–1361) was titled *Ars Nova* to describe the new styles in music as opposed to those of the earlier century. The music of the earlier century became then known as *Ars Antiqua*. The treatise was essentially a discussion of notation and rhythm, and advanced an argument for the use of duple as well as triple meter. The prior concept that triple meter was the "pure" meter stemmed from the traditional concept of three as the perfect number, the trinity being at the center of Christian theology. The title of the treatise was felt to express the spirit of the times, and it was taken up and adopted as a label to symbolize the new freedom of expression that was arising in France and, a little later, in Italy.

The "New Art" of the fourteenth century, as contrasted to the musical practices of the previous century, shows a greater use of thirds and sixths in part writing and a freer use of dissonance. The new interest in rhythm resulted in new means of expression. Regular rhythmic patterns had become, during Ars Antiqua, a part of the final development of organum and had been firmly established in Latin songs such as the *conductus*, which was mostly homophonic. Also, dance forms such as the *estampie* had carried this rhythmic regularity even further. The rhythms that had been in effect were now cast aside as being too restrictive. Now there was to be an interesting combination of a free polyphony that nevertheless carried within its framework repetitions of rhythmic patterns. The leading composer of this period was Guillaume de Machaut (c. 1300–1377), a Frenchman, who excelled in both sacred and secular works. In addition to setting the music to his own poetry in *Remède de fortune*, he established an important body of music in his ballades, rondeaux, and virelais as well as in his polyphonic chansons and motets.

Machaut was also the first composer to make a polyphonic setting of the Mass for voices and instruments. This work, the *Messe de Notre Dame* (1364), is one of the most remarkable compositions in the entire literature of Western music, and it may be regarded as the earliest masterwork that can be attributed to a known composer.

In Machaut's *Mass,* as well as in most of his motets, we see examples of the new rhythmic concept, *isorhythm.* This term refers to the repetition of similar rhythmic patterns within a polyphonic flow. Also, in the "Agnus Dei," from the same work, is seen the *hocket* ("hiccup"), which had appeared in the thirteenth century but was more extensively used in the fourteenth. The term refers to the interruption, by a short rest, of the syllable being sung. During the rest the singer would take a quick breath and then return to singing the interrupted syllable. Often during the rest another voice would insert itself, creating an "in-and-out" effect that added rhythmic variety and accent to the texture.

Another development of the fourteenth century was the use of chromatics, not written in the music, but introduced by the performer. Termed *musica ficta,* these would often occur at the end of a phrase in a melodic cadence, 7–8; or they might occur during the piece to make a smoother melodic line.

Burgundian school

In the early fifteenth century important developments in music sprang chiefly from a group of composers working for the court of Burgundy. We now see developments in polyphonic style taking place that will ultimately lead to the refined style of Lassus and Palestrina. The Burgundian school was influenced by the writings of John Dunstable in England whose use of imitation represented the beginnings of contrapuntal style. His interest in setting words in their "conversational" usage resulted in an expression the opposite of melismatic. And his use of vertical structures emphasizing thirds and sixths was to lead to a greater appreciation of the triad as a harmonic structure.

In the music of Guillaume Dufay, leading composer of the Burgundian school, we see the use of imitation. In the tenor part we may still have the cantus firmus, but the other parts are beginning to "loosen" into a flowing, expressive style.

Finally, the restriction of the lowest part to a cantus firmus was done away with, at first by putting another part below the tenor. This lowest part was ultimately called the *bass* part, and the part above the tenor became the *alto.* The voice above the alto, tenor, and bass (in the superior position) ultimately became the *soprano.* Thus, about the middle of the fifteenth century, the basic four voice parts were established and have remained as the norm for choral writing.

Figure 13.   Guillaume Dufay and Gilles Binchois. (Giraudon)

THE RENAISSANCE

Josquin

The roots of the Renaissance were in the fourteenth century. The Renaissance itself is most conveniently designated as the period from 1450 to 1600.

The first outstanding musical figure of this period is Josquin des Prez. He has been spoken of by some writers as the "first genius of modern music." His music is the first that registers with us as being of the musical language that we know. His melodic lines have continuity and coherence as we understand it, his harmonies are colorful and expressive, and his phrases and cadences have the rise and fall that are familiar to us.

Born about 1450 in the Netherlands, his name was Josse. The diminutive, Jossekin, became Josquin. He traveled widely, spending much time in Italy, at one time in the service of the ducal court at the Sistine Chapel in Rome and at other times serving as court composer in Milan and France.

From Ockeghem and others, he learned not only the highly complex devices common to the contrapuntal writing of the time, but also the art of musical expressiveness that goes beyond devices and makes of them a means rather than an end in themselves. Riddle canons had been the delight of composers of the time, but some of the composers had become lost in the presentation of the puzzle, losing sight of the musical end. The oft-quoted statement of Martin Luther bears repeating: "Josquin is a master of the notes; they have to do as he wills, other composers must do as the notes will." Naumann, in speaking of the Netherlands school in general, said "Henceforth counterpoint was but a means to an end, and art-music began to assume for the first time the characteristics of folk-music, i.e., the free, pure and natural outflow of heart and mind with invaluable addition, however, of intellectual manipulation." The way had opened for a musical expressiveness that was to find its culmination in the fugal style of Bach.*

COMMENTARY AND ANALYSIS

"Absalon, fili mi," Josquin

Absalon, fili mi	*Absalon, my son*
Qui det ut moriar prote	*Who wills that I would die for you!*
Absalon, fili mi	*Absalon, my son,*
Non vivam ultra	*I live no longer*
Sed descendam in inferum plorans	*But shall descend to hell, weeping.*

The motet, a composition with sacred Latin text for unaccompanied voices, was an important part of church music from the thirteenth century to the eighteenth.

Josquin des Prez, a contemporary of Leonardo Da Vinci, expressed in his music the essence of all Renaissance art: a flowering, a surging toward beauty that, al-

---

* Paine, Thomas, and Klauser, ed., *Famous Composers and Their Works*, Vol. I (Boston, Mass.: J. B. Millet Co., 1891), p. 16. © by J. B. Millet Co.

though based upon the traditions of the past, now sought a more personal expression.

Josquin's output of sacred masses and motets and secular chansons was copious. Of about 100 motets by Josquin, *Absalon, fili mi* is one of the most expressive in its wedding of words and music. The musical lines rise and fall as the text suggests.

The staggered entrances of the voices and the use of imitation are the forerunner of the fugues of Bach and his time.

Absalon, fili mi is in three parts based upon the text. The motet's opening subject begins in the soprano part in whole and half notes, establishing a broad, sedate style.

EXAMPLE 4–4

The alto, tenor, and bass voices make staggered entrances in imitation of the soprano in measures 3, 4, and 6.

The second part begins with the words "Qui det" (Ex. 4–5) and contrasts with the first part in several ways: a change of key, an intensification of materials through the use of shorter note values, and shorter breathing spaces in all parts.

EXAMPLE 4–5

A dramatic change occurs in part three, in the setting of the text beginning "Non vivam" (Ex. 4–6) where the sole use of homophony throughout this otherwise flowing polyphonic work is to be found. Notice also the dramatic change of key from the major mode to the minor.

EXAMPLE 4–6

The homophony lasts for just under two measures before the polyphonic style resumes. One of the most striking effects of the third section is the setting of the word *descendam* (Ex. 4–7), where the pitches actually descend, in literal imitation of the word being sung. This type of musical tone-painting was common to Jos-

EXAMPLE 4–7

quin's time. The words often suggested melodic contours to the composer. Thus, it is not remarkable that Josquin employed this imitational device, but rather that in using it he produced music of such rare beauty—music with a certain kind of vibrant pulsation occurring as the voices gradually descend in a commingling of emotional thrusts.

Figure 14. Martin Luther in his home. (Culver)

Luther was enchanted with polyphony. He speaks of how "other voices at the same time cavort about the principal voice in a most wonderful manner . . . They seem to present a kind of divine dance, so that even those of our day who have only a most limited amount of sentiment and emotion gain the impression that there exists nothing more wonderful and beautiful. Those who are not moved by this are indeed unmusical and deserve to hear some dunghill poet or the music of swine."*

Lassus and Palestrina

Longfellow's statement, "In character, in manners, in style, in all things, the supreme excellence is simplicity," is an overstatement, but as applied to the style of a work of art it does point up that certain great masterworks have a remarkable simplicity. Longfellow's thought is disarming because simplicity of this kind is the resolution of many complexities—complexities the artist has already dispensed with, whether through thought, or experiment, or previous works—and what is left is the pure simplicity. The "supreme excellence" that is simplicity may be found in Lincoln's Gettysburg Address, in the beauty of a gem, in a *haiku*, or in

---

* William Kimmel, "Martin Luther, Musician," *HiFi/Stereo Review* (December 1966), p. 50.

Da Vinci's *Mona Lisa*. It may be found also in the music of Lassus and Palestrina. Lassus and Palestrina, the one Flemish, the other Italian, both died in the year 1594, and it is this date that is usually taken as the close of the "golden era" of polyphony.

Lassus was born Roland de Lattre, in Mons, and was the last of the great masters of the Netherlands school. He is known either by the Italian form of his name, Orlando di Lasso, or the Latinized version, Orlandus Lassus. Like Josquin, he travelled widely, but his travels began under circumstances that are—to say the least—somewhat unusual. Because of the excellence of his voice as a boy, Lassus was kidnapped three times! The first two times he was recovered by his parents, but the third time marks the beginning of his journeys, which took him first to Milan and Naples and then to Rome, where he became a chapel master. At various times he visited France and England, and ultimately he married and settled in Munich. The profound *Penitential Psalms* are of this period. Writing music constantly, both sacred and secular, he became famous throughout Europe. Contrary to the experience of many composers, he received the rewards of an adoring society, was knighted, and received the Order of the Golden Spurs from the Pope. He was one of the most prolific composers of all time. For example, he left over 500 motets.

Giovanni Pierluigi was born in the town of Palestrina, not far from Rome. He has been called the greatest of the church composers, and his music is also considered to be the "purest expression" of the polyphonic school of the sixteenth century. Whereas Lassus travelled widely and wrote in all forms, both secular and sacred, Palestrina spent most of his life in the service of the church. As a result almost all of his large output is music for the church.

Palestrina at once represents the close of the Flemish school and the beginning of the Roman school in music for the church. He is considered to be the greatest composer of the Catholic church, and in him we find a purity of expression that seeks not to let earthly passion obtrude in the service of worship but rather to express the serenity and the other-worldiness of a hushed chapel. Versed in all the compositional techniques of the Netherlands school, Palestrina sought a "purer" expression. As the Lutheran chorale later would be the foundation for the music of Bach, so the Gregorian chant was the foundation upon which Palestrina built.

In the interest of purity, he reduced in his music the amount of chromaticism and dissonance that was common in the works of other composers. His musical lines are more conjunct than disjunct. When he did introduce leaps, they were often counteracted by a returning conjunct movement, which filled in the interval of the leap. Thus each voice was a gently undulating line, intended to propel the listener on gentle waves of sound.

The words of Palestrina show his earnestness in striving for the essence of purity in his music:

Music exerts a great influence upon the minds of mankind, and is intended not only to cheer these, but also to guide and to control them, a statement which has not only been made by the ancients, but which is found equally true today. . . . anxiously have I avoided giving forth anything which could lead anyone to become more wicked or godless. All the more should I . . . place my thoughts on lofty, earnest things such as are worthy of a Christian.*

The madrigal

One of the very special achievements of the late Renaissance was the development of the *madrigal* in Italy. It was a secular expression parallel to the sacred motet of the same period. It began to come into prominence early in the sixteenth century when musicians became more and more interested in the extremely expressive writings of the contemporary poets.

The madrigal grew out of the *frottola*, which was an Italian secular stanza song in chordal style, first in vogue near the beginning of the sixteenth century. In his musical settings of the poems each madrigal composer tried to express the emotional content of important words or phrases. This developed into a kind of word-painting that at times (in the hands of certain composers) was somewhat cloying, but at its best it evoked an extremely powerful kind of writing.

Where the frottola had been essentially homophonic, the madrigal grew more and more polyphonic until it was a felicitous combination of homophony and polyphony, the changing texture occurring as a result of the proper expression of the text.

The madrigal was freely composed, its length dependent upon the length of the poetic text. In the works of sixteenth century madrigal composers, such as Adrian Willaert (c. 1490–1562), Jacob Arcadelt (c. 1505–c. 1560), and Nicole Vincentino (c. 1511–1572), there is a charming use of word-painting as part of the new attitude toward expressive writing. If the text referred to sighing, the music would "sigh" with the text through a downward curve in the melodic line.

Much chromaticism was prominent by the time of Luca Marenzio (1553–1599), who set the final stamp on what may be called the mature Italian madrigal.

One other composer deserves mention here. Carlo Gesualdo (c. 1560–1613), considered to be outside the mainstream of composers of this time, carried the ideas of lyric expression and word-painting to the ultimate, in harmonies that foreshadowed both Wagner and Debussy 300 years later.

With the publication, in 1588, of a collection of Italian madrigals titled *Musica Transalpina*, the madrigal passed to England. The collections, mostly Italian madrigals with Italian and English words, contained many of the compositions of

---

* Paine, Thomas, and Klauser, ed., *Famous Composers and Their Works*, Vol. I (Boston, Mass: J. B. Millet Co., 1891), p. 31. © by J. B. Millet Co.

Marenzio, de Rore, Palestrina, and others, including, as well, William Byrd of England, who had previously seen the Italian madrigals in manuscript and had recognized their significance.

Figure 15.   Lute player. (The Metropolitan Museum of Art, Rogers Fund, 1929)

William Byrd (1543–1623) was the first of a long list of English composers, who, influenced by the madrigal of Italy, made the madrigal their own. The seed had landed in fertile ground, and a whole body of literature began to spring up.

Important composers of the madrigal in England, in addition to William Byrd, were: Thomas Morley (c. 1557–1603), Thomas Weelkes (c. 1575–1623), Orlando Gibbons (c. 1583–1625), John Dowland (c. 1562–1626), and John Wilbye (c. 1574–1638).

Along with the madrigal in England there was a development of the solo *ayre* with lute accompaniment. Most English madrigalists also wrote ayres or songs with lute accompaniment, but among the chief lutanist song composers of the late sixteenth century were: John Dowland, who was responsible for *The First Book of Songs or Ayres* (1597); Thomas Campion (1567–1620), doctor, musician, and poet; and Francis Pilkington (c. 1562–1638).

Many of the ayres or songs also lent themselves well to accompaniment on the virginal, which was the popular household keyboard instrument of seventeenth-century England. Here again we come upon the name of William Byrd, the chief composer for the virginal. One of the most important virginal books was *My Ladye Nevells Booke* (1551), which contains nearly 300 works.

COMMENTARY AND ANALYSIS

"The Carman's Whistle," Byrd

"The Carman's Whistle," chosen by Byrd as the basis for a set of keyboard variations, was a popular ballad in Elizabethan England. The ballad in the sixteenth century was a narrative song in which the music was repeated for each verse. It often dealt with events of the day or told a tale, amorous or witty, or both. "The Carman's Whistle" was known at least as early as 1592.

The text is from *The Ballad Literature and Popular Music of the Olden Time* by William Chappell (first published in 1859). There are twelve verses in the original, of which the first five are presented here.

EXAMPLE 4–8

As   I   a-broad was   walk-ing, By the break-ing   of — the day. In -

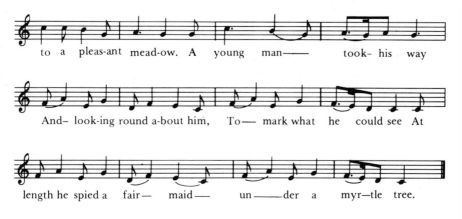

to a pleas-ant mead-ow. A young man—— took- his way

And- look-ing round a-bout him, To—— mark what he could see At

length he spied a fair— maid— un——der a myr—tle tree.

2. So comely was her countenance,
   And "winning was her air,"
   As though the goddess Venus
   Herself she had been there;
   And many a smirking smile she gave
   Amongst the leaves so green
   Although she was perceived,
   She thought she was not seen.

3. At length she chang'd her countenance
   And sung a mournful song,
   Lamenting her misfortune
   She staid a maid so long;
   Sure young men are hard-hearted,
   And know not what they do,
   Or else they want for compliments
   Fair maidens for to woo.

4. Why should young virgins pine away
   And lose their chiefest prime;
   And all for want of sweet-hearts
   To cheer us up in time?
   The young man heard her ditty,
   And could no longer stay,
   But straight unto the damosel
   With speed he did away.

5. When he had played unto her
   One merry note or two
   Then was she so rejoiced,
   She knew not what to do:
   O God-a-mercy, carman,
   Though art a lively lad;
   Thou hast as rare a whistle
   As ever carman had.

The carman (or carter), as opposed to the coachman, was considered in some quarters to be able to cheer his horses, when they got tired, with his whistling of a current ballad. The coachman, on the other hand, used oaths for his tired beasts.

Shakespeare, in *King Henry IV, Part 2,* had Falstaff say this of Justice Shallow: He "came ever in the rearward of the fashion, and sung those tunes to the over-scutched huswives that he heard the carmen whistle, and sware they were his fancies or good-nights."

The manuscript of William Byrd's set of variations on this tune is in a collection of virginal music preserved in the Fitzwilliam Museum, Cambridge, England. This collection, long known as *Queen Elizabeth's Virginal Book,* was printed for the first time in 1889 as *The Fitzwilliam Virginal Book.**

There are eight variations. In these there occurs a compositional practice that

---

* Reprinted by special permission from Roland Nadeau and William Tesson, *Scores and Sketches: An Anthology for the Listener* (Reading, Mass.: Addison-Wesley, 1971), pp. 19–20.

was to apply to variation form for more than 300 years. Sets of variations by Purcell, Rameau, Handel, J. S. Bach, Haydn, Mozart, Beethoven, and Brahms gain much of their interest from a progressive rhythmic animation from variation to variation. What happens is that shorter note values appear in each successive variation, while the tempo remains constant.

The tune's metrical unit is the dotted half-note ( ), which remains constant in tempo, but is divided into shorter note values in successive variations.

THEME

The actual tune does not start until measure 3. Measures 1 and 2 serve as a kind of short introduction where the tune's first few notes are played by the right hand, then imitated in the bass part played by the left hand. Listen for melodic embellishments that lend a decorative aspect to the simple, lilting folk ballad.

EXAMPLE 4–9

Beginning at measure 3 (see Ex. 4–9), the tune is supported by strong vertical chords suggesting the triadic tonality to be used by Mozart and Haydn two centuries later. However, close listening reveals that the harmony is actually based on the modal scales of antiquity. In Renaissance genres, such as the madrigal, the mass, the lute song, and the keyboard variations, harmony was transitional, retaining some of the old modal color, yet anticipating the major/minor key system of later times.

VARIATION I

Variation I begins exactly as did the tune in measure 3 (see Ex. 4–10). By the fifth measure quicker notes make their appearance. This eight-note motion enlivens the variation to its end.

EXAMPLE 4–10

VARIATION II

There is considerable rhythmic interest at the start of Variation II. The left hand, beginning in the first measure, plays syncopated half-notes against the tune above.

EXAMPLE 4-11

Eighth-note motion appears in the last half of the variation.

VARIATION III

Variation III has a generally descending melodic line in the bass, set against the tune in the soprano.

EXAMPLE 4-12

Melodic activity in the bass remains fresh and interesting throughout.

VARIATION IV

The bass part here is not only melodically fresh, but it manifests an entirely new motive.

EXAMPLE 4-13

Soon, however, steady eighth-note motion occurs, carrying the variation to a bright conclusion.

VARIATION V

For the first time the right hand does not begin with the exact notes of the tune. Instead it commences with a rest, following by an ornamented version of the tune's contour,

EXAMPLE 4–14

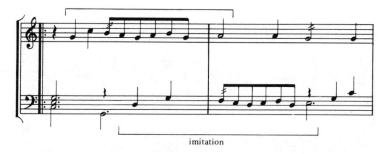

imitation

Quick-note motion begins in the first measure and persists with little change throughout. In the fifth measure listen for the melodic line played by the left hand.

EXAMPLE 4–15

It is an echo of the new motive established at the beginning of this variation (see Ex. 4–14).

VARIATION VI

Here the harmony is very colorful. Listen for the suggestion of the Aeolian mode* in the first two measures.

* Aeolian mode: the white note diatonic scale pattern starting on A.

EXAMPLE 4–16

Listen also for new modal color when an unexpected accidental, B flat, occurs in the upper line.

EXAMPLE 4–17

VARIATION VII

The feature of this variation is the brilliant figuration of constant running eighth-notes. The right hand begins with the tune against the eighth-notes of the left hand. Soon the right hand takes over the running figuration, and, towards the close, both hands play quick notes together. Variation VII functions as the rhythmic climax of "The Carman's Whistle."

VARIATION VIII

While Variation VII generates great excitement, it is Variation VIII that provides a majestic and fitting conclusion to the entire work. The most interesting aspect of this variation lies less in further melodic elaboration than in chordal color for its own sake. The variation begins with full chords in both hands.

EXAMPLE 4–18

That there are sometimes six notes in these dense chords suggests a true keyboard style in which massed chordal sounds are presented in their own right and not merely as support for the tune. The tune, which up to now has been no more than lightly decorated, is now virtually embedded within these dominating chords. We have here an early example of harmony taking the ascendant over melody.

Thus, as the sixteenth century turns into the seventeenth, we have seen vocal polyphony come to its full glory; we also notice the rise in the importance of instruments, and we approach the combination of instruments and voices in a new form—opera. Ultimately we will become aware of a surge that encompasses the development of instruments—and the writing for them—that will culminate, in central Europe, with the emergence of one of the most dramatic expressions of man: the symphony.

Chapter five

BAROQUE/ROCOCO

To the untrained listener, the music of the baroque period (approximately 1600–1750) is frequently perplexing. He searches hard but scarcely catches a tune. Sometimes so many tunes assail his ears at once that he cannot distinguish among them. The ones that he does isolate from the thick web of sound strike him as either jagged and spiky or rambling and diffuse. However, he does feel rhythm, indeed, sometimes a very insistent, steady beat. But he is likely to consider it to be monotonous, like the clacking of an old-fashioned treadle sewing machine. And what bothers him more than anything else is a kind of formidable façade of dignity and reserve that seems to keep his emotional responses at arm's length.

Thus, before musical enlightenment comes, he gives only part of himself to the fugues, concerti grossi, cantatas, and passions that he encounters from the period. This he does despite perhaps what we might call unconscious appreciation of the best-known pieces from the period. He glories in singing the carol by the great baroque master, Handel's "Joy to the World." He is touched by the same composer's *Messiah*, and he dearly loves the romantic composer Gounod's "Ave Maria" without realizing that it is based entirely on a prelude from J. S. Bach's *The Well-Tempered Clavier*.

The contrast that exists on the purely musical level between the baroque and the following periods is very pronounced. The prevailing texture in musical composition in the baroque period is polyphonic, while that in the classical and romantic periods is primarily homophonic. We who have been weaned on homophony in our immediate social activities with hymns, folksongs, and patriotic songs, take very readily to the clearly marked leading melodies, buttressed with the colorful harmonies of Haydn, Mozart, Beethoven, and Tchaikovsky. But we are puzzled at the thick tangle of melody lines and rich luxuriant detail of the Baroque. Thus, to enter into the beauties of much of the music of the Baroque we must undergo a certain amount of aural reconditioning. We must learn how to perceive and truly experience simultaneous melodic lines.

Similarly, the forms of the seventeenth and eighteenth centuries are not those with which we feel most comfortable. For example, the many elegant dance forms of the baroque and earlier periods are quite foreign to us as living dance vehicles. On the other hand, the waltz, which flowered in the nineteenth century, is still a popular dance today. The minuet, gavotte, and sarabande are emblems of a munificent, luxuriant society only encountered now in films. The instruments of the period—the harpsichord, clavichord, tracker organ, recorder, viola da gamba—have only recently become the object of renewed interest.

THE AGE OF REASON

The influence of science

Pascal said, "All the dignity of man consists of thought." The meaning of these words is germinal to most of the philosophical and scientific thought of the seventeenth and eighteenth centuries. Man had come into the security and certainties of rationalism. It was the Age of Reason.

Galileo and Kepler destroyed geocentric thinking and, as a fortuitous by-product, flattened the fossilized theories of the time. Chemistry replaced alchemy, and Harvey discovered that blood travels constantly throughout the entire body. Rational comprehensive explanations were found for phenomena that had puzzled men from the beginning of time.

Newton, the author of the monumental *Principia Mathematica*, hoped to explain all material occurrences with mathematically expressible rules. He said, "I wish I could derive all phenomena of nature by some kind of reasoning from mathematical principles. . . ." Thinking baroque man then believed that his world could be reasoned out, could be fully understood, and perhaps even fully controlled by the use of logic and the new methods as outlined by Newton and Descartes.

As in every musical period, it was inevitable that pervasive and compelling ideas such as these were reflected in the arts. Thus it is that the music of Vivaldi, Handel, Corelli, J. S. Bach strikes us as being so solid and rational. It seems to be suffused by iron bonds of logic. Once the musical thought in a Bach fugue—say the "Kyrie Eleison" of his *Mass in B Minor*—has taken root in our consciousness, the music's direction and plan seem self-evident, completely right and logical. The ideas follow naturally and surely.

On the technical musical level this sense of permeating, comprehensive order can be illustrated many times over. It will suffice to point out the prominence of *figured bass* (or *thorough-bass*) in the Baroque. Figured bass was simply a system of numbers placed on the score itself. These numbers indicated with considerable precision the vertical interval combinations to be realized by the keyboard player. The analogy between musical notation and the mathematical bias of baroque philosopher/scientists is obvious. Relationships of tonality, chord, interval, scale, and modulation had become so systematic and general, so logical, that they could now be represented by numerical figures.

The influence of the court

Besides this orderliness, there is also the feeling of luxuriance and richly decorative detail in many of the works. Again this reflects a very important aspect of baroque life.

There existed at that time an enormous social and ecomonic gap between the masses and the aristocracy. Despite the mid-seventeenth-century republican insurrection of Cromwell in England and that in the Netherlands earlier, it was a time of splendid yet despotic monarchies in Europe.

We can clearly perceive this social cleavage by looking at some of the facts surrounding the life and manners of Louis XIV, the Sun King, who reigned in France for nearly three-quarters of a century.

He thought that, "As he [the king] is of a rank superior to all other men, he sees things more perfectly than they do, . . . occupying, so to speak, the place of God, we seem to be sharers of His knowledge as well as of His authority." "L'état c'est moi." Indeed! His official residence, the chateau of Versailles, housed ten thousand inhabitants and consumed six out of every ten francs collected in taxes.

The pomp and splendor of the court extended even to the humblest functions. The noble chosen as the official bearer of the king's chamber pot was considered fortunate indeed.

H. G. Wells, in his *Outline of History*, mentions the ". . . sculpture in alabaster, faience, gilt wood-work, metal work, stamped leather, much music, magnificent painting, beautiful printing and binding, fine cookery, fine vintages. Amidst the mirrors and fine furniture went a strange race of gentlemen in vast powdered wigs, silks, and laces, poised upon high red heels, supported by amazing canes; and still more wonderful ladies, under towers of powdered hair and wearing vast expansions of silk and satin sustained on wire. Through it all postured the great Louis, the sun of his world, unaware of the meagre and sulky and bitter faces that watched him from those lower darknesses to which his sunshine did not penetrate."*

Most of the master composers of the period either were in the "employ" of this gilded aristocracy or were church musicians. Very few, like Handel, or John Gay,

* H. G. Wells, *The Outline of History*, Vol. II (New York: Garden City Books, 1949), pp. 825–826.

Figure 16.   French ball. (Giraudon)

became entrepreneurs, appealing directly to a ticket-paying, theater-going public.

It followed then that baroque secular music, written expressly for the aristoc-racy, should clearly reflect the sumptuous qualities of court life in general. In the music of the court—secular and sacred—there is much melodic ornamentation and exquisite detail of texture.

For many years Lully, founder of the French school of opera, was court com-poser for Louis XIV, writing masques and ballets in which both he and the king actively took part. Having glimpsed at the splendor of this court life it is small wonder that the Baroque should exemplify panoply, dignity, pomp, luxuriance.

The influence of the church

The third influence in baroque music was undoubtedly that of religion and the church. Many of the greatest works in the Baroque are religious in purpose: can-tatas, passions, oratorios, masses, te deums, and magnificats. Though outwardly ostentatious and elaborate, these religious works often represented the composer's innermost subjectivity. It was here that he could appropriately air his innermost sentiments.

There is a special quality in baroque music—its aliveness. Not so long ago it was fashionable to speak of baroque music as being dry, and arid—even academic. This was partly due to inept performers who considered the music of the early masters little better than finger exercises. Needless to say, their playing of J. S. Bach, Corelli, and Handel was deadly and antiseptic.

All this was partly due to the tremendous power and influence of Romanticism in the nineteenth century. Many musicians felt that music without the intense subjectivity and overt passion of Wagner, Chopin, and Schumann simply was dry. We now know differently. The music of the Baroque, particularly in its late phases, is extremely vital, especially in the area of rhythm. Sometimes it is as raucous and colorful as the satirical paintings of William Hogarth (1697–1764). John Gay's enormously successful *The Beggar's Opera* is the perfect counterpart to the work of Hogarth. And the high spirits in Henry Fielding's novel *Tom Jones* finds a perfect match in the finale of J. S. Bach's *Sixth Brandenburg Concerto*.

But from whatever impetus or for whatever purpose, individual movements, dances, choruses, arias, etc., in baroque music show great homogeneity of mood and expression. This oneness follows from the baroque doctrine of affects which dictated that all structural elements–rhythmic, harmonic, melodic—be representa-tive of a single affect or mood. Thus, within individual pieces or movements, there is strong continuity bordering on the uniform. For example, in the "Crucifixus" from Bach's *Mass in B Minor* (Ex. 5–13) all inner materials are continuously con-sistent with the mood to be established—in this case, intense pathos. A single subject (theme), one rhythmic pattern, a steady tempo, and a consistent texture underlie many of the single movements of composite baroque pieces.

GENERAL CHARACTERISTICS

Melody

Viewed from the standpoint of basic shape and type, baroque melody shows an interesting dichotomy. On the one hand, it is frequently highly expansive, personal, even romantic. At other times the "melody" is a mere fragment, a wisp of a tune that becomes important only through its elaboration and working out.

EXAMPLE 5–1   *The Well-Tempered Clavier*, Book I, Fugue 4, J. S. Bach

These few notes, followed by their blossoming into great music, remind us of the rationalistic philosopher Descartes' raising enormous edifices of wisdom on his simple yet potent idea: "I think, therefore I am."

Baroque melody frequently has an angular, rather jagged contour. Often it takes on life only through the poignant ornamentation dotting its surface.

Rhythm

There is a certain expectedness to baroque rhythms. Especially in many of the allegros we hear constantly repeated rhythmic patterns, propelled by an unflagging beat. And we do not hear a great variety of tempos, as we do in Beethoven, Chopin, or Tchaikovsky. All of this is apparent when we compare the dreamy, flexible chant from an earlier period with the straight-gaited beat of a late baroque choral work.

This rigidity, however, occurs only on the surface of baroque music. Underneath the rather plain rhythmic exterior exist perhaps the most subtle and sophisticated rhythmic structures of any period. Among the many rhythmic riches, perhaps the most exciting is that of syncopation. A great many baroque compositions make astonishing use of syncopation. If played with a steady, motoric underlying pulse, and if the melodic line is accented according to its natural beat, the music shown in this example is surprisingly close to jazz. Indeed, fine jazz artists of our day are increasingly admiring and playing baroque music.

EXAMPLE 5–2

Invention No. 6, J. S. Bach

Harmony

The Baroque is particularly interesting in the area of harmony. Of course, some impetus from the Golden Age of Polyphony remained; contrapuntal structures such as fugue, chaconne, and canon evolved and indeed tended to predominate. But, simultaneously, homophony came to the fore, with the musical center of gravity shifting to a single commanding melody. And although much of the music is either primarily polyphonic or homophonic, often there exists a masterful blend of the two. Thus, the Bach chorale not only is considered to be the fountainhead for all later tonal developments in vertical relationships, but also represents an ideal model for organizing four separate, but cooperating, melodic parts.

This development of massive polyphonic structures side by side with the homophonic, and the potent mixture of the two, could not have happened without the emergence of the two diatonic scales, the major and the minor. These were the foundation of a powerful homogeneous tonality. In the pre-Baroque the major scale (formerly Ionian mode) and the minor scale (formerly Aeolian mode) were only two of several possible scales underlying the structures of the Renaissance and earlier. But the hardy, homogeneous system of major-minor tonality was so satisfactory to many baroque composers that it must have seemed as eternal and fixed to them as the basic mathematical principles established by Newton and Descartes seemed to contemporary philosophers.

Figured bass can be seen as early as 1602. Later it became so universal that Rameau in his several treatises, including the *Treatise on Harmony*, incorporated figured bass into a comprehensive harmonic system. The principles of figured bass are not difficult to understand. Accompanying a bass line are certain numbers, either one or several, which indicate notes to be added above each bass note. These notes always were "figured" up from the bass, and were meant to be played by the keyboard performer. He would often use the resulting chords for extensive extemporaneous elaborations, accompanying the principal melody or melodies. In effect, this was a shorthand system that saved the composer much time and also allowed for interesting personal contributions from the player involved.

EXAMPLE 5–3   *St. Matthew Passion*, Recitative, J. S. Bach

Figured bass served a purpose similar to that of the chord system used in the popular music of our day. The player "realizes" a lead line accompanied by a

special system of chord letters and figures. Operating within the limits of major-minor tonality and figured bass were vertical sounds and progressions that are as trenchant and voluptuous as the vibrant colors in a Rubens painting.

Range and dynamics

Both range and dynamics in baroque music were limited in scope. Most of the music of the period fits comfortably within a range of four or five octaves.

Much of the music of the Baroque is polyphonic and therefore every voice—bass, tenor, alto, soprano—at times carries leading melodic parts. But the favored register is decidedly the high soprano. Instruments with the ability to climb very high, such as the trumpet (*clarino*) and soprano recorder, were much used. The baroque organ is distinguished by the many "mixture" stops that often highlight the brilliant upper soprano register. Many of the *trio sonatas* by Corelli are written for two violins, which frequently criss-cross, reaching high into the soprano. Beneath is the continuo part in the bass, played by cello and keyboard. The rather bare middle register area was left to be "filled in" by the keyboard player reading the figured bass.

Dynamics were most conservatively used. A modest forte or piano sufficed for most of the music. The phrase *terraced dynamics* refers to the abrupt juxtaposition of *piano* and *forte* without gradation. Significant crescendo and diminuendo were impossible on some keyboard instruments and sparingly used in general. It was not until the classical period, particularly with the orchestra at Mannheim, that colorful, graduated dynamics came into strong favor. Indeed, the mere fact that Rossini was called "Signor Crescendo" attests to the novelty of this effect.

Baroque masters were not unaware of the emotional impact derived from artfully utilized dynamics. But rather than rely on crescendo and diminuendo, or on extremes of dynamic levels, they preferred to use the sharp juxtaposition of forte and piano.

Performance and instruments

Performance standards were rather high in the Baroque. Daquin astonished all who heard him because of the brilliance of his passage work at the keyboard. Corelli, Torelli, Locatelli, and Vivaldi were all renowned violinists. Domenico Scarlatti astounded the courts of Italy, Spain, and Portugal with his digital gymnastics at the harpsichord. J. S. Bach was perhaps better known for his playing at the organ than for his compositions.

Of the 381 instruments owned by King Henry VIII in sixteenth-century Renaissance England, 272 were winds. Only 109 were strings, including keyboard instruments. Winds certainly predominated in the Renaissance; strings were emphasized in the Baroque. The seventeenth and early eighteenth centuries saw the flourishing of the master instrument builders at Cremona: Stradivari, Amati, Guarneri, and others. There is no question that the finest literature of the period is written for strings. The string family formed the backbone of many of the orchestras of the day.

Keyboard instruments—clavichord, harpsichord, organ—also were prominent. The piano, though existing in the late Baroque—J. S. Bach is known to have played on Frederick the Great's new Silbermann pianofortes—did not displace the harpsichord in the affections of musicians until the time of Mozart and Haydn.

Forms

Opera, cantata, passion, the liturgical mass, the chorale, and many other forms occupied a vital position in the musical thinking of baroque masters. In both vocal and instrumental music, polyphonic textures predominated. Bach felt so challenged by the fugue that in 1722 he wrote twenty-four preludes and fugues spanning all the major and minor keys in a volume known as *The Well-Tempered*

Figure 17. Harpsichord, Collegium Musicum, 1775. (Germanisches Nationalmuseum, Nuremberg)

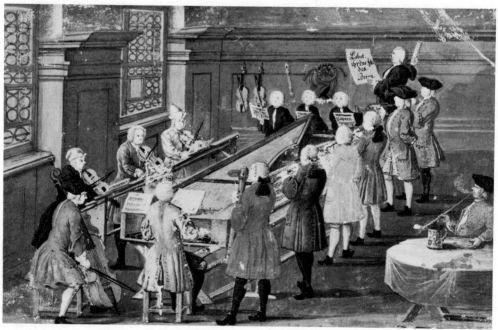

Clavier. Twenty-two years later he started over again and wrote a second volume of twenty-four more preludes and fugues. In this effort, however, he was anticipated by Johann Caspar Fischer who, in 1715, published twenty preludes and fugues covering nineteen different keys.

There is no question that the enormous technical challenges found in polyphonic composition appealed to the rationalist in the baroque composer. These ultra-sophisticated contrapuntal structures manage, in the hands of the masters, to achieve great emotional impact.

At the same time that traditional approaches to compositions were employed, many new forms appeared that were destined to achieve dominance in later periods. Thus, we see early forms of the concerto, symphony, and sonata. Each achieved ascendancy later in the classical and romantic periods. These early forms only anticipate in a general way the actual dramatic structures of the late eighteenth and nineteenth centuries. The baroque solo concerto is vastly different from the structures developed by Mozart and Beethoven. For example, the typically classical sonata-allegro structure was not used in the baroque concerto. The baroque concerto employed a considerable degree of polyphonic texture, while the later classical form is predominantly organized with tight homophonic textures. And, most important, the dramatic juxtaposition of soloist with orchestra only occurs in the later concerto.

The composers

It was a long time from the days of Monteverdi, at the turn of the seventeenth century, to the ripe musical days of J. S. Bach in the mid-eighteenth century. There is enormous contrast between the works of the early baroque masters and those of Bach and Handel, even more than between early Haydn and late Beethoven. It follows, then, that no single overriding aesthetic outlook permeates all the figures in this period. There was tremendous variety of style during these many decades. For example, a comparison of Antonio Vivaldi and J. S. Bach, contemporaries writing in similar idioms, uncovers tremendous differences. Among these are Bach's closely cropped textures and rhythmic complexity, as opposed to Vivaldi's near folk-song simplicity. Despite huge contrasts in their respective styles, Bach so admired Vivaldi that he transcribed (among other Vivaldi works) his *Concerto for Four Violins* into one for four claviers.

Early Italian composers

There are six major figures at the outset of the Baroque. Each had deep roots in the Renaissance and wrote many works clearly in the sixteenth-century style. Yet each was an innovator, breaching reactionary defenses and catapulting music into a new age. All were Italian: Giovanni Gabrieli (1551–1612), Don Carlo Gesualdo, Prince of Verona (1560–1613), Giulio Caccini (1546–1618), Jacopo Peri (1561–1633), Claudio Monteverdi (1567–1643), and Girolamo Frescobaldi (1583–1643).

Peri and Caccini collaborated on the first opera ever written, *Daphne*, but to Caccini alone goes the honor of writing the first opera published, *Euridice*. These men were in the artistic-intellectual group revolving around Count Giovanni Bardi, scholar and patron of music. This group, called the *Camerata*, wished to bring back the simplicity and directness of expression that they associated with ancient Greek culture. This resulted in the *monody* of Peri and Caccini, which might seem rather bland and anti-lyric now. In fact, much of it consists of little more than a recitative-like single line sustained by simple block chords. But to these men, accustomed to the thick, clustered web of ecclesiastical polyphony, this new, direct mode of musical expression seemed the perfect tool for the humanism that they advocated.

Gesualdo is an interesting figure, not only for his music, but in the details of his private affairs. The color and excitement generated by the extreme chromaticism of his madrigals is only surpassed by the romance of his life. He is the only major composer with the distinction of being a murderer. He is positively known to have arranged for the assassination of his wife's lover. If one is slightly disturbed at such a thought, one need only read Machiavelli's (1469–1527) *The Prince*. There he will find an eloquent apology for the murky backgrounds of brilliant men still to come, such as Gesualdo, the great sculptor Benevenuto Cellini (1500–1571), and others.

In such works as *Orfeo*, Monteverdi outstripped by far his predecessors in the field of opera. Although he did not write instrumental music as such, he greatly expanded the role of the orchestra in operatic music. He introduced novel effects, such as *pizzicato* and *tremolo* in the strings, which startled the musical world. With his unique harmony he anticipated much modern usage. Unprepared dissonances and unusual but trenchant juxtaposition of chords abound in his madrigals, operas, and songs. If Peri and Caccini were the founders of monody and opera, Monteverdi must be considered the founder of modern harmony.

Frecobaldi and Giovanni Gabrieli were both renowned organists. Both were vital in the development of instrumental forms. Frescobaldi in his *ricercari* anticipated one of the Baroque's most important structures, the *fugue*. Gabrieli created pieces for grouped instruments such as the *Sonata pian e forte,* where the winds are set opposite the strings in antiphonal style. He reveled in the color possibilities of antiphony, sometimes dividing his massed forces into four choirs singing back and forth.

Gabrieli is a particularly pertinent example of a great transitional figure. His uncle, Andrea Gabrieli (1520–1586), of whom he was a reverent disciple, was a grand figure in the Renaissance; his pupil, Heinrich Schütz, is considered to be of major importance in the development of the German Baroque.

Following closely on the heels of the composers discussed above was Giacomo Carissimi (1605–1674), who was important in the creation of the *oratorio*. That form at first was distinguished from early opera only by its sacred text. But with Carissimi's masterful balancing of choral and soloistic forces, and the addition of the narrator, the oratorio took on individuality and became a genre of tremendous meaning for the future.

Violinists-composers

Shortly after the blooming of the new vocal forms of opera, oratorio, etc., there developed an extensive and long-lived school of composers whose primary interest lay in music for the violin. It was Italy, the mother of *bel canto*, that produced this brilliant group of player-composers, and it was the Italian city of Cremona that produced the finest stringed instruments that the world has yet known. Inspired by the many magnificent instruments produced by Nicolo Amati (1596–1684), Antonio Stradivari (1644–1737), and Guiseppe Guarneri (1681–1742), Italian composers set about composing a multitude of violin sonatas, con-

Figure 18.   Antonius Stradivarius in his workshop. (The Bettmann Archive, Inc.)

ANTONIVS·STRADIVARIVS

certos, and single pieces of singular grace and lyric elegance. This long line of composers included Archangelo Corelli (1653–1713), Antonio Vivaldi (1692–1770), Francesco Geminiani (1687–1762), Guiseppe Tartini (1692–1770), and Francesco Veracini (c. 1690–1750). As can be seen, this line of composers spanned the better part of one hundred years and included several preclassical composers.

Corelli and Vivaldi

Perhaps the two outstanding figures in Italian baroque music were Corelli and Vivaldi.

Corelli, besides having systematized bowing on the violin, is said to have been the first to introduce *double stops*. But much more important than his fame as a player and innovator of violin technique are the nobility and profundity of his works. The solo violin pieces are still much esteemed by concert audiences, but it is with the *concerto grosso* and the *trio sonata* that Corelli's true greatness becomes apparent.

Vivaldi was an extremely colorful figure. His music now is beginning to rival that of J. S. Bach and Handel in popularity with concert audiences. Vivaldi was a clergyman whose pedagogical excellence matched his prowess with the violin and genius in composition. For thirty-six years Vivaldi directed a music school for indigent girls. According to Vivaldi's contemporary, De Brosses: "Indeed they sing like angels, play the violin, flute, organ, oboe, cello, bassoon—in short no instrument is large enough to frighten them. . . . I swear nothing is more charming than to see a young and pretty nun, dressed in white, a sprig of pomegranate blossom behind one ear, leading the orchestra and beating the time with all the grace and precision imaginable."*

Vivaldi's output was enormous; his 447 concertos for a wide range of instruments—including guitar, mandolin, and piccolo—represent a stupendous achievement. Particularly intriguing is the set of four violin concertos called *The Seasons*, each representing a different time of the year. They are studded with appealing moments of imagery, such as a summer storm and bird calls.

Not especially associated with the school of violinist-composers were two other masters, Alessandro Scarlatti (1660–1725) and Giuseppe Sammartini (c. 1693–1770). Both wrote instrumental music that anticipated the classical symphony. In addition, Scarlatti was a great master of late baroque opera and is credited with the perfection of the oratorio form.

---

* *Grove's Dictionary of Music and Musicians*, Vol. IX (New York: St. Martin's Press, Inc., 1960), p. 27.

COMMENTARY AND ANALYSIS

Concerto, "Winter," from The Seasons, Op. 8, No. 4, Vivaldi

The "Winter" concerto is made up of three movements, following the typical tempo plan of the late baroque concerto: fast-slow-fast. The orchestra is also typical for the time, especially for music composed in the Italian style. Except for the harpsichord, it consists entirely of strings: violins 1 and 2, viola, violoncello, and contrabass. The technical brilliance and characteristic touches in the solo violin part attest to the high development of the literature for the violin in the Italian baroque.

An Italian sonnet entitled "Winter" accompanies the concerto.

> *Shivering, frozen in the snow and ice,*
> *Battered by a terrible wind's harsh blow,*
> *Stamping your feet, to run while time seems slow;*
> *And from such cold your chattering teeth freeze;*
> *To spend, content by the fire, quiet days*
> *While the rain outside soaks things through and through.*
> *To walk over ice with pace so slow,*
> *Afraid to fall; to go, looking for ways*
> *To move on strongly; to slip to the earth;*
> *To start again on the ice; to run headlong*
> *Until the ice breaks up and opens a path;*
> *To feel, from the iron gates issuing,*
> *The southeast, north, all the winds' warring breath:*
> *This is winter, but joys it also brings.*

(translated by Martin Robbins)

Isolated phrases from this sonnet appear in the score identifying specific musical images.

MOVEMENT I. ALLEGRO NON MOLTO

Meas. 1 *Agghiacciato tremar tra nevi algenti:* to shiver, frozen in the snow and ice*

The concerto begins quietly with repeated single notes first in the cellos, and then accumulating harmonic mass as violas, second violins, and first violins progressively join in:

---

* The lines quoted by the composer do not match the precise wording of the original sonnet. Therefore, the English renderings here and below differ slightly from the complete translation given above.

EXAMPLE 5–4

As the chordal texture thickens, listen for the dissonant quality that results in a bleak and wintry atmosphere.

Meas. 12   *Al severo spirar d'orrido vento:*   battered by a terrible wind's harsh blow

The solo violin enters:

EXAMPLE 5–5

The virtuosic solo violin perfectly suggests the violence of the wind. You will hear this characteristic passage in the solo part three times, each time bridged by soft, repeated chords in the orchestra.

Next, a crescendo begins at measure 20, leading to charming tone painting for the words:

Meas. 22   *Correr battendo i piedi ogni momento:* to run, stamping your feet every moment

The orchestra and soloist play a sequential passage where a rush of notes suggests "stamping."

EXAMPLE 5–6

martellato (like hammer strokes)

After a long flowing passage for the violin solo followed by dramatic "tremolo" responses in the orchestra, the material from the opening of the movement returns (see Ex. 5–4).

Then comes a highly picturesque passage:

Meas. 47   *E pel soverchio gel battere i denti:*   and from such cold your teeth chatter

EXAMPLE 5–7

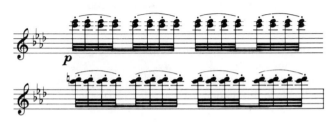

Listen for the repeated double stops in the violin solo giving a "chattering" effect made even more graphic through dissonances. This long passage is interrupted by a return of the stamping figuration of Example 5–6. The movement closes with a

majestic broadening of the tempo leading to a full cadence in the tonic key, F minor.

MOVEMENT II. LARGO

Meas. 64 *Passar dal foco i di quieti e contenti mentre la pioggia fuor bagna ben cento:* to spend quiet and contented days by the fire while the rain outside soaks things through and through

The second movement is simple in texture, warm in expression. The solo violin spins out a lovely cantilena melody over a quiet accompaniment in the lower strings.

EXAMPLE 5–8

At the same time, the first and second violins, playing pizzicato, supply more active accompanying material that suggests a gently falling rain.

MOVEMENT III. ALLEGRO

Meas. 82 *Caminar sopra il ghiaccio:* to walk over the ice

Movement III begins with a melody in the solo violin part made out of a "rolling" motive suggesting a careful tread.

EXAMPLE 5–9

Meas. 106 *E a passo lento per timor di cader, girsene intenti:* and with slow step for fear of falling, walk intently

At measure 106 the rolling sixteenth notes give way to more cautious eighth notes as the melodic contour changes:

EXAMPLE 5–10

Meas. 121   *Gir forte, sdrucciolar, . . . :*   to move on strongly, to slip and . . .

Meas. 129   *Cader a terra:*   fall to the ground

Meas. 132   *Di nuovo ir sopra il ghiaccio e correr forte:*   to start again over the ice and run hard

Meas. 170   *Sin ch'il ghiaccio si rompe, e si disserra:*   until the ice breaks and a path opens

Measure 170 becomes suddenly dramatic, ending with the inevitable crash through the ice.

EXAMPLE 5–11

Meas. 182   *Sentir uscir dalle ferrate porte Scirocco, Borea:*   to feel issuing from the iron gates the southeast wind (*Sirocco*), the north wind

Momentarily the mood quiets as the several winds gather fitfully:

EXAMPLE 5–12

Meas. 201   *E tutti i venti in guerra:*   and all the winds at war

   Then virtuosic scales for the soloist, answered by more "tremolo" from the orchestra, lead to a strong close in the tonic key.

Meas. 228   *Quest' è il verno, ma tal, che gioia apporte:*   This is winter, but it also brings joys*

Lully

Underlining the influence of Italian masters in the early Baroque is the fact that the first truly great French composer of the Baroque, the founder of French opera,

---

* Based in part on and reprinted by special permission from Roland Nadeau and William Tesson, *Scores and Sketches: An Anthology for the Listener* (Reading, Mass.: Addison-Wesley, 1971), pp. 32–33.

the creator of the disciplined court orchestra of Louis XIV, was a violinist from Florence by name of Jean Baptiste de Lully (1632–1687). He was a tremendous force in the music world of his time. Even the English acknowledged his luster. Roger North, a lawyer-turned-composer, in his *Memoires of Musick*, said, ". . . during the first year of Charles II all musick affected by the beau mond run in the French way; and the rather because at that time the master of the Court Musick in France, whose name was Baptista (an Italian frenchifyed), had influenced the French style by infusing a great portion of the Italian harmony into it, whereby the air was exceedingly improved."*

Lully's temper was said to match the power of his music. He died from an infection caused by striking his foot with his enormous baton while in a rage with his orchestra.

Other French masters

François Couperin (Le Grand) (1668–1733), the most illustrious of a family of musicians rivaling the Bach family for longevity, wrote much charming music for the clavecin (harpsichord). His colorful pieces, replete with delightful titles, are still popular with keyboard artists. Some of the finest of these are "Le Moucheron" (anticipating by two centuries the famous *Diary of a Fly* by Bartók), "Soeur Monique," and "L'Anguille," whose wiggling figurations charmingly suggest the slithering of the eel.

Jean Philippe Rameau (1683–1764), in addition to systematizing harmony, had a great influence on the theoretical thinking of composers after him. More important, however, is his music, especially the novel and majestic operas, such as *Castor et Pollux*. His pieces for clavecin rival those of Couperin for clarity, sophistication, and color.

Claude Daquin (1694–1772), the composer of the keyboard piece, "Le Coucou," was a rival of Rameau's and famed for the clean articulation of his organ playing.

Other important composers of French baroque music are Jean Baptiste Loeillet (1680–1730); Louis Marchand (1669–1732), Marc Antoine Charpentier (1634–1704) and Jean-Marie Leclair (1697–1764), a famous violin virtuoso.

The English

The English, after the luminosity of their many magnificent Renaissance composers such as Byrd, Dowland, and Morley, produced only a few baroque masters.

---

* David G. Weiss, *Samuel Pepys, Curioso* (Pittsburgh, Pa.: University of Pittsburgh Press, 1957), p. 49.

John Blow (1649–1708) was organist at Westminster Abbey before Purcell. John Christopher Pepusch (1667–1752), the collaborator with John Gay in the fabulously successful *Beggar's Opera*, was really a transplanted German. Dr. Thomas Arne (1710–1778) lived into the classical period.

Without question the leading composer of the English Baroque was Henry Purcell (c. 1659–1695). In his short thirty-six years, he managed to produce a great many profound works. In the geniality of his melody, the copiousness of his output in so short a lifetime, and the richness of his harmony, he is much like Schubert. Purcell's best-known works are the operas *Dido and Aeneas* and *The Fairy Queen,* adapted from Shakespeare's *Midsummer Night's Dream.*

German masters

Heinrich Schütz (1585–1672) is a major figure in the early Baroque, occupying a position of equal importance to that of Monteverdi in Italy. His opera. *Daphne,* now lost, was the first in the German language. The many sacred choral works such as the *Seven Last Words of Christ*, the Passions, and the *Christmas Oratorio* show a Bach-like power and intensity. There can be no doubt that the sacred choral works of this master were the cornerstone and inspiration of much of the works of J. S. Bach and Handel.

If the favorite instrument of the Italian Baroque was the violin, that of the German Baroque was the organ. The violin was an excellent instrument for the transmission of Italian *bel canto;* the organ, with its power and diversity of tonal color, was the ideal instrument for German polyphonic complexity. Just as the violin was perfected in the hands of the master craftsmen of Cremona, the baroque organ became highly developed in the northern countries of Holland and Germany.

These great organs, with their great clarity and substantial body of tone, were the ideal instruments for the fugues, toccatas, passacaglias, and chorale preludes that are so intrinsic to German baroque music. There are many who feel that the organs by Schnitger and others have never been surpassed.

An illustrious line of organist-composers arose beginning early in the seventeenth century. One of these was Johann Jakob Froberger (1616–1667), a student of Frescobaldi. Among many others were Johann Pachelbel (1653–1706) and Dietrich Buxtehude (1637–1707). Buxtehude's playing and compositions were of such high repute that J. S. Bach walked over 200 miles to hear him. Indeed, Bach overstayed his leave from his church position by three months in order to hear and study the master's music.

Georg Philipp Telemann (1681–1767), whose fame eclipsed that of J. S. Bach in his day, wrote many facile and entertaining suites, concertos, trio sonatas, and vocal pieces. His technique as a composer was such that he was said to be able to dash off an eight-part motet as easily as another would write a letter. Schumann quoted him as saying, ". . . a proper composer should be able to set a placard to music."

Handel and Bach

The German Baroque culminated with two majestic names in music: Georg Friedrich Handel (1685–1759) and J. S. Bach (1685–1750).

In some ways the lives of these two men parallel those of two later German masters who summed up the romantic period, Johannes Brahms and Richard Wagner. Brahms was a gentle, rather parochial conservative who worked mostly with the classical instrumental forms, while Wagner espoused opera and assailed the whole world with his "music of the future."

J. S. Bach, much like Brahms, stayed in Germany, and developed to a high level of perfection the sacred vocal and organ forms that he inherited from his predecessors. Although opera inundated the stages of the civilized world, it did not become part of his output. Handel, like Wagner, was much more of an entrepreneur, and much of his most important work was in the field of opera.

Johann Sebastian Bach was a member of a distinguished family of composers and players that thrived in Germany for over 200 years. Strong roots in the craft of his fathers and his own inclinations toward sober hard work may have kept him, perhaps, from wandering much in the world or from urgently seeking recognition. However, he did challenge the great French organist Marchand to a musical duel at the keyboard and was happy enough late in his life to visit and play for Frederick the Great at Potsdam. He held posts as Kapellmeister at important churches, and as court composer.

Bach's musical style exhibits an interesting dichotomy. On the one hand it is super-sophisticated at almost every level. The polyphony is of great intricacy, demonstrating the power of musical logic. The rhythms are more complex by far than anything in Mozart or Haydn. His unique handling of dissonance anticipates the music of our times. In short, Bach's music is highly intellectual, showing the highest flights of which the musical mind is capable. On the other hand, his music is rarely dry. No matter how cerebral it may be, it is always suffused by a warmth, a uniquely human quality. For example, the "Crucifixus" from the *Mass in B Minor* represents the highest kind of technical mastery in music. It is a chaconne, with utterly refined use of polyphonic variation over the repeated chromatic bass figure. Yet, despite the formal intricacies, the effect is sublime. The sounds emanating from the voices are as rich and satisfying as anything from Beethoven or the Romantics.

EXAMPLE 5–13   *Mass in B Minor, "Crucifixus,"* J. S. Bach

Where the intellectual is matched by the emotional, Bach is again very much like Brahms. Bach's best-known works are the *B Minor Mass*, the *St. Matthew Passion, The Well-Tempered Clavier,* the *Brandenburg Concertos,* the concertos for single or multiple instruments, the chorale preludes for organ, and the cantatas.

COMMENTARY AND ANALYSIS

Chorale Prelude, "Wachet auf, ruft uns die Stimme," Bach

This piece is particularly rewarding for analysis and study. It illustrates the highest kind of music by the master who is conceded to represent the very essence and culmination of the baroque style, Johann Sebastian Bach. It is rewarding from the historical point of view in that the form used, the chorale prelude, is of

major significance, with a long line of ancestry in German music. It is based on the
Lutheran chorale, itself a form of major significance in the German Baroque.

The chorale prelude *Wachet auf* is found in two versions: as an organ piece
(from the *Schubler Chorale Preludes*) and as the fourth number from *Cantata 140*
—for tenors, strings, and continuo. Thus, the music not only illustrates Bach's
habit of setting the same music for different performance media, but offers an
excellent opportunity to contrast the effect of the same music presented in different timbres. The chorale will already be familiar to many for it is included in
many modern Protestant hymn books.

EXAMPLE 5–14

Free translation:

> *"Wake up!" the voice calls us;*
> *The Watchman calls from high up in the tower,*
> *"Wake up, city of Jerusalem!"*

This chorale illustrates another important facet of Bach's genius. The tune is
actually by an earlier composer, Philipp Nicolai (1556–1608), but Bach adds to it
immeasurably by virtue of his beautiful harmonization.

The form of the chorale prelude as used here by Bach is one of several possible
chorale prelude forms. Bach creates an original melody and a bass line of exquisite
sensitivity. At certain points in the flow of these lines successive phrases of the
chorale are superimposed. Thus, the whole consists of three-part counterpoint,
each melodic part contrasting rhythmically with the others—the upper part quite
active, the lower part more stately, and the chorale most simple of all. In somewhat
more technical terms, the upper part consists mainly of eighth-and sixteenth-notes,
the lower part of quarter- and eighth-notes, and the chorale mostly of half-notes.

The chorale prelude begins with the typical jagged intervals found in so much
of Bach's music.

EXAMPLE 5–15

The rugged contour of the melody represents not one, but two melodic lines.

EXAMPLE 5–16

In measure 5, another complementary idea begins,

EXAMPLE 5–17

which leads to an interesting syncopated figure.

EXAMPLE 5–18

At measure 13, on the third beat, the chorale enters. The miracle of this moment is that the entrance is so natural.

EXAMPLE 5–19

The first 12 measures of two-part counterpoint are so absolutely satisfying in themselves that one marvels now at the arrival of a third melodic part that suddenly seems indispensable. We wonder if Bach might very well have been able to add a fourth and a fifth part with the same perfect ease and natural effect.

The first phrase of the chorale is heard with its accompanying counterpoint. Then the music thins to a two-part texture again, where we hear a firm modulation to the dominant key, B-flat major:

EXAMPLE 5-20

After a repetition of this material a new phase begins and the music shifts to another tonal area, the key of C minor:

EXAMPLE 5-21

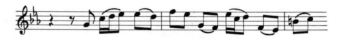

The two-part counterpoint touches briefly on G minor and soon after sinks back into E-flat major, the home key. At this point the last phrase of the chorale is heard. After it is completed, the last part of the prelude is taken up by the final spinning out of the florid melody of the beginning, the whole gradually coming to a majestic repose with a cadence in E-flat major on a simple tonic.

EXAMPLE 5-22

COMMENTARY AND ANALYSIS

Partita No. 1 in B♭ Major, Bach

J. S. Bach's keyboard dance suites go far beyond the functional. The dances within become idealized: dances for the imagination, not for the feet.

The dances from these suites are highly sophisticated; their contrapuntal texture alone is enough to make them into more than mere accompaniments to the dance. Each is an example of absolute music, contributing its individuality to the entire work, but reminding us always of the universal and elemental urge to dance.

> Whither by and by the dancing master came, whom standing by, seeing him instructing my wife, when he had done with her, he would needs have me try the steps of a coranto (courante), and what with his desire and my wife's importunity, I did begin, and then was obliged to give him entry-money 10s., and am become his scholler.
>
> Samuel Pepys
> *Diary*, May 4, 1663

The *B♭ Major Partita* has six sections:

No. 1 — Prelude	No. 4 — Sarabande
No. 2 — Allemande	No. 5 — Minuets 1, 2
No. 3 — Courante	No. 6 — Gigue

Each is in the tonic key, B♭ major.

NO. 1. PRELUDE

Form: free contrapuntal structure in three voices.
Meter: common time, four beats to the measure.

This prelude is written in the style of Bach's *Three-Part Inventions*. The subject is heard alternately in all three voices.

EXAMPLE 5–23

Follow the subject through the entire prelude; note that the thickening contrapuntal fabric provides a solid chordal texture near the end.

NO. 2. ALLEMANDE

Form: binary
Meter: common time
   There is a continuous flow of graceful melodic figures in this dance.

EXAMPLE 5–24

   The basic melodic idea (Ex. 5–24) is heard twice, once at the start of Part A (meas. 1) and once at the start of Part B (meas. 19). If you listen for both appearances of this melodic idea, you will have no difficulty tracing the allemande's binary structure. Remember, however, that each part is played twice (in a row); do not confuse the repetition of the first part with the first statement of the second part.

NO. 3. COURANTE

Form: binary
Meter: triple
   As in the preceding allemande, there is continuous motion. This time the constant unit is the triplet, rather than the sixteenth-note.

EXAMPLE 5–25

NO. 4. SARABANDE

Form: binary
Meter: triple

The sarabande is the most lyric of the dances in the suite and occupies a position similar to that of the slow movement in a sonata. In the keyboard suites, the sarabande is far removed from its original use and is normally played with great rhythmic freedom. It features a highly decorative melodic line that is both expansive and expressive.

Follow the intricate shape of the melody, mostly in the right-hand part, paying particular attention to the many ornaments added by the player.

EXAMPLE 5–26

NO. 5. MINUETS 1, 2

Form: binary
Meter: triple

The baroque suite often contains two dances of a single type in succession. When the first dance returns after the second, the structure is identical to the *minuet with trio* which was often used later in the classical period.

Thus, we have:

The baroque minuet.   Minuet 1–Minuet 2–Minuet 1 which becomes
The classical minuet.   Minuet–Trio–Minuet

The minuets of the Bach partita presented here typify the baroque minuet form; Minuet 1 reappears after Minuet 2. Note the contrast in melodic motion between the two minuets. The first uses steady eighth-note motion, while the second uses a variety of short and long note values.

EXAMPLE 5–27

Minuet 1

EXAMPLE 5–28

NO. 6. GIGUE.

Form: binary
Meter: common time

This gigue is a favorite of players and audiences alike. Perhaps one reason for this is the sight of the artist's left hand constantly crossing over the right. The melody, entirely in the left hand, consists of two-note phraselets in dialogue, high to low. The right hand plays supportive chordal arpeggiations throughout.

EXAMPLE 5–29

This gigue is difficult to play on the piano because the left hand tends to get tangled with the right hand. This difficulty disappears when the piece is performed on the concert harpsichord where there are two keyboards, rather than one.

The Bb *Major Partita* exemplifies the typical baroque suite for the harpsichord. It consists of five varied dances cast in binary form, preceded by a contrapuntal prelude. Unity is achieved by the use of a single form for the dances (binary) and a single key throughout (in this case, Bb major). Each dance goes beyond the practical function of accompaniment and represents absolute musical expression.

Handel was much more volatile and enterprising than Bach. He once fought a duel with the organist-composer Johann Mattheson and survived to enter the lists later in England with his bitter rival for operatic supremacy, Bononcini (1670–

1747). Early in life he traveled to Italy, met both Scarlattis, and quickly ascertained that his fortune lay with the stage. In his later years in London, where he achieved great fame, he wrote a great many operas in the Italian style, and oratorios, including the *Messiah*. The effect of Handel's music is much more immediate than that of Bach's. The texture is more open with much less dissonance. Though counterpoint is the cornerstone of his style, it is much less compact than Bach's. The harmony, though occasionally astonishing in its chromaticism, is usually rather bland. The rhythms are seldom as intricate as those in Bach, but his melodic lines are more fluid and lyric.

Handel is supreme in massed effects. Pieces such as the *Te Deum* are monumental in scope. In this respect Handel's music sounds well when sung by large choruses of 150 or more voices (though much of it was written for smaller groups), while that of Bach becomes almost unintelligible when done by anything larger than a chamber chorus.

Beethoven esteemed Handel above all others in the field of vocal music and asked for a complete edition near the end of his life.

Handel, like Bach, was almost blind for his last few years; however, he managed to play the organ in his own oratorios until his death in 1759.

COMMENTARY AND ANALYSIS

The Musick for the Royal Fireworks, Handel

The *Royal Fireworks Music* more than any other of Handel's pieces shows the cosmopolitan aspects of his career and musical style. Performed in a festive atmosphere it consisted of simple yet regal music suitable for massed outdoor listening. Handel supplied the score for the ceremonies in London's Green Park (1749) celebrating the peace of Aix-la-Chapelle, ending the War of the Austrian Succession.

Written in England by a renowned German immigrant composer, the *Royal Fireworks Music* was cast in the French style. Since France and England had been opposing factions in the War of the Austrian Succession, Handel's use of French dances and program titles was particularly proper for this event of state.

Twelve thousand people attending the rehearsal caused a mammoth traffic jam at London Bridge. A fire broke out in the pavilion during the fireworks display, and the designer of the display, the architect Le Chevalier Servandoni, angrily drew his sword on Charles Frederick, "Comptroller of His Majesty's Fireworks." Despite the unexpected excitement, the event was a brilliant success.

Compared to the exquisitely balanced later orchestras called for by Mozart, Mendelssohn, and Debussy, the preponderance of winds in the *Fireworks* score seems gauche. There are three first horns; three second horns; three third horns; three first trumpets; three second trumpets; three third trumpets; three pairs of timpani; twelve first oboes; eight second oboes; four third oboes; eight first bassoons, four second bassoons; and strings. What is certain is that the music could be heard by all.*

MOVEMENT I. OVERTURE

The Overture is inordinately long compared to the other pieces in the suite; the score shows forty-two pages covering this movement, while fourteen pages suffice for the remaining 5 movements. This disproportion suggests certain necessary time spans connected with the exhibition of fireworks to be "filled" with music. That this accommodation was an actual factor in the composition of the work can be surmised from Handel's original manuscript in which the composer indicates exactly how long certain dances were to be played. The final Menuet, for example, was to be played three times, presumably each time with inner repeats. Music can hardly be more functional.

The Overture is divided into three main sections:

Section A (Lentement)   Section B (Allegro)   Section C (Lentement)

Section A Section A, slow and regal, is marked by the dotted rhythmic figure characteristic of the French overture. The opening melody is notated like this:

EXAMPLE 5–30

VL, OB, HN, TB

However, the conventional French style required that the players lengthen some of the dotted notes while shortening some of the short notes. Although notation cannot capture precisely this conventional liberty in performance, the following transcription of the example above approximates what was probably heard:

EXAMPLE 5–31

---

* Based in part on and reprinted by special permission from Roland Nadeau and William Tesson, *Scores and Sketches: An Anthology for the Listener* (Reading, Mass.: Addison-Wesley, 1971), p. 28.

The harmony in Section A is particularly simple, as it is throughout most of the suite: during its deliberate 46 measures only a single chromatic tone (g sharp) sounds in an otherwise exclusive use of diatonic tones from the tonic key, D major. Because of technical limitations in brass instruments of the Baroque, they were necessarily assigned straightforward, non-chromatic parts. Handel knew what he was about in providing plain diatonic lines for the brass; with nine trumpets and nine French horns in his orchestra, some perhaps of unknown quality, tricky chromatic notes were written to be played by strings and woodwinds only.

Section B   Section B follows without a break. The tempo changes to a brisk allegro in triple meter. The trumpets with drums, answered by the strings and oboes, clearly establish the antiphonal style:

EXAMPLE 5–32

Section C   The French ceremonial style returns with typical dotted notes in very slow tempo. For the first time several chromatic tones are heard, while the key changes four times: D major leads to B minor, E minor, B minor, and a final cadence in F sharp minor. Significantly, brass and drums do not play in this section.

MOVEMENT II. BOURRÉE

The bourreé was a French seventeenth-century dance in quick duple time with a single note on the first upbeat. Typical of baroque dance forms, the bourrée's structural pattern was binary with each part repeated. It can be symbolized as: AA/BB, or A:‖ B:‖. All the dances following the Overture are binary. For his Bourrée, Handel has reduced his orchestra to near-chamber size. The brass and drums do not play.

EXAMPLE 5–33

MOVEMENT III. "LA PAIX," LARGO ALLA SICILIANO

MOVEMENT IV. "LA RÉJOUISSANCE," ALLEGRO

Both titles, "La Paix" (Peace) and "La Réjouissance" (Rejoicing), obviously relate to the treaty signed by the great powers at Aix-la-Chapelle. Both pieces are mildly programmatic in that they suggest the mood of peace, harmony, and happiness.

In "La Paix" Handel retains the reduced orchestra of the preceding Bourrée, although he brings back the French horns. Both its slow tempo and the rhythmic pattern in its melody (Ex. 5–34) are characteristic of the Siciliana, a dance that had become identified with a peaceful, pastoral mood.

EXAMPLE 5–34

Listen for the addition of soft, fluid running notes shortly after the above example and then for gentle trills in the violins and oboes.

For "La Réjouissance" the composer adds trumpets and drums, thus allowing for a full, bright sound needed for the celebration. The tempo is lively, while the tune is energetic and happy.

EXAMPLE 5–35

MOVEMENT V. MENUET

For this Menuet Handel again reduces his orchestra to that used in the Bourrée (no trumpets, horns, or timpani). As in the Bourrée this Menuet is cast in D minor (tonic minor). The shadowed minor key provides contrast in a suite that was purposely set in plain harmonic colors.

The following example shows the melodic line for the entire Menuet:

EXAMPLE 5–36

MOVEMENT VI. MENUET

It was proper that Handel conclude the suite with a Menuet; it was of French origin, its aristocratic background making it the perfect vehicle for the pomp and circumstance required. This final Menuet is in the tonic major (D major), an effective contrast to the minor in the preceding dance.

EXAMPLE 5-37

VL, OB, TP, HN

Since all instruments here play all the time, the music is entirely diatonic: There is not a single chromatic alteration. We can assume that the Menuet's plain harmony and simple melodic contour played in tune by the full orchestra—all this in conjunction with the fireworks—achieved a stunning climax.

IN TRANSITION: THE GALLANT STYLE OF THE ROCOCO

The next major period to be encountered after the Baroque will be the Classical, encompassing the lives of three giants: Mozart, Haydn, and Beethoven. The stylistic gulf that separates the densely intellectual, massively ornate Baroque from the directly expressive Classical is huge.

The music that fills this gap is called *Rococo*. The word is derived from the French, *rocaille*, meaning "rockwork," and refers particularly to the ornate arrangements of rocks in the gardens at Versailles. As it applies to music it means an emphasis on the elegantly embroidered, graceful, and charming. Its purpose is simply to please. It is intentionally shallow, reflecting the hedonism so apparent in the court of Louis XV.

Rococo music frequently is saturated with melodic ornaments, called *agréments* by the French. Homophony predominates, with the harmonies simple and affecting. Frequently, as we saw earlier with Couperin, catchy titles were used.

The exquisite hedonism of the Rococo is seen in the polished paintings of Watteau, where grace, sheen, and elegance reign supreme. The many scrolled mirrors at Versailles also reflect this accent on decoration, and the heightening of the pleasures of life. The new simplicity of the French Rococo was paralleled by developments elsewhere throughout Europe. We have already mentioned Gay's extremely popular *Beggar's Opera* (1728), which eventually routed the conservative *opera seria* (serious opera) from the boards of the English stage. In the Paris

Figure 19. *The Scale of Love,* by Watteau. (National Gallery, London)

of 1752 an intermezzo, *La Serva Padrona*, by Giovanni Pergolesi (1710–1736) ran for one hundred performances. This frothy piece in the new Italian *opera buffa* (comic opera) style precipitated the "War of the Buffoons." Through a series of polemical pamphlets, many of the finest minds in Paris debated the merits of the new popular *buffo* style versus the traditional *opera seria*. As could be expected, the philosopher Rousseau, as the champion of "natural man," favored the fresh expressive tide stimulated by Pergolesi's masterpiece. In 1752, the same year that marked the sensational debut of *La Serva Padrona* in Paris, Rousseau wrote his own opera buffa, *Le Devin du village*. And the preclassicism of the orchestral symphony, newly emerging at several European cultural centers, clearly pointed away from the severity of the late Baroque. The general term *gallant* indicates a sensual, direct, and immediately appealing kind of music; much of the music of the mid-eighteenth century is spoken of as being in the *style galant*.

Of the French composers discussed above those associated with the *style galant* are Couperin "Le Grand," Rameau, Daquin, and Leclair. In Italy, Domenico Scarlatti concerned himself much with music for the cembalo (harpsichord), on which he was renowned a virtuoso as was Liszt on the piano in the nineteenth century. His sonatas, numbering over 500, are frothy, piquant, and elegant, often displaying qualities similar to those of the French Rococo. However, one of Scarlatti's works, the *Cat's Fugue*, shows how very much rococo masters were rooted in the true Baroque. This piece, built on a subject supposedly originating from notes played by the household cat jumping on to the cembalo keyboard, is cast as a perfectly correct, baroque fugue.

In Germany the counterpart to the French rococo gallant style was the *empfindsamer Stil*. This musical expression can be heard in the slow movements of the keyboard sonatas of C. P. E. Bach (son of J. S. Bach and court musician to Frederick the Great). There is subtle nuance, varied expression, and a touching sensitivity throughout. C. P. E. Bach's own directions for realizing this style at the keyboard point up the emphasis placed on the effective representation of emotion in the *empfindsamer Stil*: "In languishing, sad passages, the performer must languish and grow sad. Thus will the expression of the piece be more clearly perceived by the audience."

Chapter six

CLASSICISM

Montaigne undoubtedly exaggerated when he said of man's progress in history, "We do not go; we rather run up and down and whirl this way and that; we turn back the way we came." Certainly it is true that history repeats itself, at least in part. Nothing is all new. There simply does not exist a totally new style of painting or musical composition. This is particularly apparent in successive musical eras. A new period or style may well have evolved in an atmosphere of violent reaction to the "artistic establishment" immediately preceding it. The development of spare and simple monodic forms by the Italian Camerata near 1600 as a strong protest to the elaborate polyphony of renaissance music exemplifies this principle. Yet that which is new—and worthwhile—is always powerfully rooted in the past and especially in the near past. Classicism is no exception to this.

Classicism sits squarely on the foundation built by baroque masters. In the field of harmony, Rameau and others had codified chord structure, chord progression, and major-minor tonality to such an extent that it sufficed basically unchanged for Haydn, Mozart, and Beethoven, and lasted into the twentieth century. Lyric homophony, which is the prevailing texture throughout the classical era, actually was fully developed in the Baroque, but was not given as much attention by composers as polyphony. The masters of Classicism took full advantage of the enormous growth of instrumental music, as well as the refinement of the instruments themselves in the Baroque.

The music of the classical masters often shows strong traces of the past. The slow introduction of Beethoven's last *Piano Sonata*, Opus 111, shows an unmistakable resemblance to the typically somber French overture of the Baroque (p. 170).

Beethoven's predilection for the fugue in his later years is well known. Mozart, besides writing many sterling fugues himself, arranged five fugues from J. S. Bach's *The Well-Tempered Clavier*. His additional accompaniments to four choral works of Handel—including the *Messiah*—shows an involvement in the Baroque beyond simple homage to the past.

EXAMPLE 6–1   *Piano Sonata*, Op. 111, Beethoven

Yet, aside from these obvious and necessary connections with the Baroque, classical music is strikingly original in sound. We have seen in Chapter 5 the distinguishing characteristics of baroque style: a splendid display of energy, drive, and passion tempered by utter dignity, and a luxuriance of detail made convincing by a complete logic of structure. Briefly, baroque music can be said to display an intense but thoroughly ordered musical expression.

In contrast to this, classical music typically emphasizes symmetry, reserve, a profound simplicity. Emotion is present—indeed sometimes it seethes to the surface as in the *Symphony No. 40* by Mozart—but it seldom is as obvious as in the Baroque. The classical goal was balance: a blending of form with content. Hellenistic simplicity, purity, symmetry, and universality were the ideals in all the arts of that time.

Jacques Louis David produced paintings such as "The Death of Socrates" and "Brutus" whose content and form were directly influenced by Greek and Roman aesthetic attitudes. Palladian architecture, with its emphasis on early classical symmetry and just proportion, permeated England and, of course, the North American colonies. The University of Virginia, designed by Thomas Jefferson, is a particularly fine example of early American use of Palladian architecture.

In the music of the Classicists, symmetry, purity, and simplicity reign. One beautifully chiseled phrase will be answered and balanced by another very much like it. There is much expectedness. Nothing is done to excess. Textures are open, simple, and pellucid.

Though polyphonic forms continued to be used—especially in sacred music—cleanly chiseled, diaphanous single melodies, supported by logically structured chords in various guises, predominated in the classical period. Lyric homophony was easier to understand, representing perhaps plainer, more direct expression; therefore it was ideal for the classical style.

Summing up, the transition from the Baroque to Classicism was one from complexity to simplicity, from a luxuriant vivacity to a serene, generally buoyant simplicity. Rhythms became simpler, melodic contours smoother, textures more open, forms easier to perceive. Homophony largely replaced polyphony. All of this was initiated during the transitional rococo period.

Figure 20.   Greek vase, youths and flute player going to a banquet. (The Metropolitan Museum of Art, Rogers Fund, 1941)

What, then, were some of the forces at work in society that conditioned musical thinking of the last half of the eighteenth century?

In the baroque period, Europe was politically divided by the Great Powers: France, England, Spain, Germany. A gilded, pampered aristocracy yoked and abused the great mass of suffering humanity. Imperialism, mercantilism, and absolutism reigned. Many courts had become corrupt. The longer their princes and kings reigned, the sillier and more unrealistic they became. Samuel Pepys in his diary noted, "On the night when our ships were burnt by the Dutch, the King did sup with my Lady Castelmaine, and there they were all mad, hunting a poor moth."

But counterbalancing this state of affairs were many free, independent souls, products of the Enlightenment, disgusted at the excesses of the courts, and at the pitiable state of the poor masses. John Locke, with works like *An Essay Concerning Toleration*, deeply influenced the American libertarian revolutionaries. In France, Rousseau, Diderot and the Encyclopedists, and Voltaire raised loud cries

of protest. And then, within a span of twenty years, two events occurred on different continents that were destined to shake the very foundations of the existing
social structure: the American Revolution of 1776 and the French Revolution of 1789. The height of the classical period in music coincided with these
two social upheavals.

To some it may seem strange to link together the graceful, somewhat detached
music of this period to the terror in France during the Revolution. The picture of
hundreds of patrician heads rolling into baskets, or gracing elevated pikes
throughout bloodthirsty, raging Paris, does not harmonize well with minuets,
romances, and serenades.

The French and American revolutions signaled a fundamental change in world
history and attitudes. Throughout history, there had been talk and theory of the
fellowship of man and of democracy and equality for all men. The Greeks and
Romans had eloquently spoken for it, but in practice it turned out to be a limited
democracy, only for those who happened not to be born slaves. The Cromwellian
Republic in England lasted but a few years, despite the magnificent proclamation
of the Rump Parliament "that the people are, under God, the original of all just
power."

In America, after the Revolution, four million people consciously set out to see
if democracy could work. In France, despite many regressions, a similar experiment had begun. This political adventure had enormous repercussions throughout
the world. Whether democracy succeeded or not in Europe and America was not
as important as the attempt. For the essence of the constant social revolution, beginning in the late 1700's and intensifying into the twentieth century, is the importance of man—of Everyman. Music somehow had to reflect emerging truths
about the nobility of common man, of the essential dignity of his reason and
emotions.

In the Renaissance, music was apt to reflect the serenity and repose of an ideal
world—a remote world accessible only through a churchly, pious life. Baroque
music mirrored an expanding, vital, growing world on all levels. It is enormously
energetic music, the lavish sonorities of its secular music reflecting the high gloss
or aristocratic life. Its sacred music mirrored both the depth and passion of the
Protestant Reformation and the sincerity and brilliance of the Counter-Reforma-
tion. Rococo music, emphasizing expression, sensibility, and ultra-refinement of
the sensual, reflected the jaded ennui of a fast decaying aristocratic society. In
this process it strove for directness and began the approach to what was to come
in Classicism. Jean-Jacques Rousseau, who with his opera *Le Devin du village*
(1752), wrote in an extremely direct, homophonic style, said of polyphonic devices that they "reflect disgrace on those who have the patience to construct
them." The very fact that Rousseau, the champion of "natural man" and of total
democracy, propagandized and publicized the new gallant style is highly signifi-

Figure 21. *Le Devin du village (The Village Soothsayer)*, opera by Jean-Jacques Rousseau, 1752. (Bulloz)

cant. It shows that the new, non-contrapuntal, melodic style dovetailed exactly with the revolutionary ideas about sentiment and the value of the individual.

The effect of this new, simply harmonic style on the sophisticated listening public must have been like that of Benjamin Franklin as envoy to France during the American Revolution. His public appearances, in plain clothes and without ceremonial wig, did much to win French hearts to the Republican cause.

In sum, the atmosphere of the time was conducive to an establishment of a direct, more personal style of musical expression. Through its emphasis on simplicity, reason, and directness of sentiment, Classicism paved the way for a truly *personal music*. This subjective, intimate factor began to appear in late Mozart and Haydn and finally flowered with Beethoven. It was then—at the turn into the nineteenth century—that music became the magnificent medium for the expression of the essence and uniqueness of all men. Thus, Classicism is a most significant era in the history of music.

GENERAL CHARACTERISTICS

We have already touched on some of the basic characteristics of classical music, its perfect lucidity and ideal proportion. Content—melodic and harmonic ideas—is perfectly matched to structure. Though there are serious moments replete with tender pathos in the secular music, the tendency is toward good humor, sparkle, and zest. The classicists aimed to please. They had to, if they wished to retain their princely patrons.

Sometimes the humor achieved rather robust proportions, as in *A Musical Joke* by Mozart. Here the composer flashes one tonal jest after another. For example, after a perfectly innocuous beginning in the Menuetto, the horns and strings are required to play an incredibly raucous passage:

EXAMPLE 6–2   *A Musical Joke*, K. 522, Mvt. II, Mozart

The third movement ends with a tongue-in-cheek whole tone scale, gracing a terribly obvious cadenza for the first violin.

The finale ends with a cadence in five different keys at once.

Melody

Mozart had declared, "I compare a good melodist to a fine racer, and counterpointists to hack post horses."

With the acceptance of homophony as the basis for much classical music, attention turned strongly toward melody, especially in its lyric aspect. Now that a single, predominating line received much of the compositional thrust, it had to be constructed so that it would instantly fix and hold the listener's attention. It therefore became simpler than either rococo or baroque melody. The classical emphasis on symmetrical phrase and period structure resulted in melodies neatly trimmed and tailored. They seemed more blocked out, and segmented, conforming to the inner divisions and dimensions of balanced classical forms.

Another striking contrast between baroque and classical melody is in the area of melodic rhythm. In the earlier period, melodic syncopation was commonly used. Sometimes melodic rhythms were so diffuse and irregular as to seem entirely independent of the given meter. Classical melody, on the other hand, is rhythmically simple. Underlying rhythmic patterns are often built upon a single rhythmic idea, and they usually fit easily into the ongoing metrical framework.

Harmony

A powerful yet flexible system of major-minor tonality underlies the tunefulness, clarity, and elegance of classical music. Mozart and Haydn inherited a system of chord structures, consonance-dissonance, and chord progression that had been systematized by Rameau and refined by J. S. Bach. The Bach chorale became the paragon of harmonic usage in the classical period. The prevailing key and scale was major. Of the symphonies attributed to Mozart, only two are in the minor mode: No. 25 and No. 40, both in G minor. Only two of the piano sonatas and two of the piano concertos are in the minor. The minor was used for music in the *patetico* style, and with Haydn and Mozart it was subjective and personal. Although the usual overall key scheme tended to be major, episodes or secondary themes in minor could be striking in effect.

The Andante cantabile from *Piano Sonata in C Major* by Mozart is a good example of this harmonic duality. The first section is dominated by a theme in F major.

EXAMPLE 6-3   *Sonata in C*, K. 330, Mvt. II, Mozart

The second section, in F minor, begins as shown below.

EXAMPLE 6-4

The sudden poignancy achieved through the change of mode is wonderful—especially after the serenity of the beginning.

One curious facet of classical harmony is that dissonance is encountered significantly less often than in the Baroque. At first thought, this would seem a regression, especially if increased dissonance is equated with heightened expression. It is a fact that the sinewy counterpoint and colorful chromaticism of J. S. Bach produced many more dissonant intervals and chords than did the diatonic harmony of the classical composers. This certainly points to a greater emphasis on emotion and expression in baroque music. However, equanimity being more important than pathos to the classicists, it is appropriate that they chose a lower level of dissonance.

Register

In one area, that of register and tessitura, Classicism was similar to the Baroque—both favored the soprano. If one considers the string choir in Mozart symphonies, it becomes apparent that the violins consistently have the better of it melodically. The cello and contrabass are largely supportive.

The same can be said about the other forces of the classical symphony. The most important winds were flutes, oboes, and trumpets. Bassoons were the only winds to anchor the total sound in the bass. The trombone, tuba, bass clarinet, or contrabassoon did not come into steady use until the nineteenth century.

Of course, there are many striking pieces emphasizing bass instruments or voices. One thinks immediately of the Mozart *Bassoon Concerto*, or the buffo parts in classical opera such as that of Leporello in Mozart's *Don Giovanni*. But high registers were primary in the classical period, suggesting a penchant for lucidity and brilliance.

Dynamics and tempo

We have already noted (see Chapter 5) the tremendous stir caused by the systematic use of crescendo and diminuendo by the composers of the Mannheim School in the preclassical period. Unquestionably, these surging dynamic effects excited the emotions of audiences of the day. Indeed, even today a well-managed crescendo or diminuendo is a powerful tool for creating excitement and mood. In the time of Mozart and Haydn the resulting expressivity was precisely in line with the developing need for a more personal music. With Beethoven it became a major tool for achieving searing dramatic effects.

Along with the traditional use of *forte* and *piano*, the *fp* and the *sf* attained much prominence. This last effect was especially useful in music for the pianoforte, which in contrast to the harpsichord, could effectively manage sudden louds followed by immediate softs within the body of a phrase or period.

However, a medium-loud forte and a gentle piano were the usual. It was not until Beethoven that *fortissimo* and its opposite, *pianissimo*, came consistently into use.

In a similar way, tempos were moderate. The Mozart presto was probably no faster than a Tchaikovsky allegro. Undoubtedly the wealth of detail and marvelous juxtaposition and combination of ideas can best be perceived if tempos are not excessive.

Performance and instruments

With the development of many resident orchestras, at Mannheim, in Paris, at Esterhazy, and elsewhere, players took pride in their profession. Virtuosity became common. Mozart had his Leutgeb, sometime cheese monger and brilliant player of the French horn, and wrote four concertos for him.

And there was the brilliant Anton Stadler, who did much to spur Mozart's interest in the clarinet. His playing was the inspiration for the *Clarinet Concerto,* the *Clarinet Quintet,* and many other works.

The travels of the boy Mozart and his sister, Nannerl, throughout the continent as prodigies of the keyboard are well known. In maturity, Mozart was an incredible virtuoso at the keyboard, particularly in performances of his own concertos. In like manner, young Beethoven was celebrated as a fiery, brilliant pianist, much more so than as a composer. His passionate improvisations affected audiences to such a degree that many in his audience wept.

Virtuosity on any of various instruments was much in vogue throughout the last half of the eighteenth century. Attesting to the public's hunger for any sort of instrumental virtuosity were the scintillating careers of two ladies, the English Marianne Davies and the German Marianne Kitchgessmer. Both were famed for their performances on the glass harmonica, an instrument perfected by Benjamin Franklin.

Forms

The shift of emphasis from the polyphony of the Renaissance and the Baroque to the homophony of Classicism resulted in enormous changes in melody, harmony, and rhythm. But most important of all was the new outlook on form. The most important melodic relationships in renaissance and baroque contrapuntal composition are parallel or oblique. The vital structural feature in an invention or a fugue is how the parts fit together on top of one another, how they invert, and how imitation comes into play. Here energy and vital dynamism occur through the interplay of simultaneous melodic parts. In contrast to this, classical homophony often exhibits only one leading melodic part supported by variously arranged chords.

To be sure, the way in which a melody is colored and enhanced by chords is of no small importance. But just as important as the way things *sound together* is the way things *sound side by side.* In other words, the horizontal connection of themes, parts, and sections is the most important principle in classical forms.

Balance, symmetry, and proportion become powerful factors in these forms: four measures balanced by four more; exposition matched by recapitulation;

statement answered by restatement. The most important instrumental genres were those dependent on the Viennese sonata principle: the solo sonata, concerto, symphony, string quartet. Opera and sacred choral music remained important but became less prominent.

THE COMPOSERS

No other period in the history of music is represented by so few major composers as is that of Classicism. Beyond Joseph Haydn (1732–1809), Wolfgang Amadeus Mozart (1756–1791) and Ludwig Van Beethoven (1770–1827), there is only Christopher Willibald Gluck (1714–1787), who revolutionized opera but did not essay very much in other musical forms. But, few though they were, these composers had tremendous impact. The essentials of their art—harmony, form, rhythm, melody—persisted as the foundation of music until the twentieth century.

Chronologically, the adult creative lives of Haydn, Mozart, and Beethoven follow a rather neat line of descent, spanning the whole classical period. Haydn came into his adult artistic powers in the early 1750's, shortly after the death of J. S. Bach. Mozart matured as a creative artist at the apogee of the classical era, in 1776; while Beethoven reached adulthood in 1790. Beethoven's productive days paralleled the final ripening of Classicism, as well as its transition into the romantic century.

The content of their music reflects all this faithfully. Though Haydn's music is sometimes passionate and stormy, it is conditioned somewhat by the pleasantries and mannerisms of the Rococo. It is more often level headed and good humored rather than intensely personal. The gallant style permeates much of his earlier work.

Mozart is often intensely subjective. It often seems that he deliberately plans for a special mood, for a certain melancholy atmosphere. A feeling of unrest, of spiritual travail and personal outpouring, saturates a great number of his mature works—especially the ones in the minor mode. What happens, of course, is that the composer cannot keep from exposing his deepest self. Mozart is very close to Romanticism here.

It is not surprising that Mozart's mature years, 1776–1791, encompassed almost exactly both the American and French revolutions. It was at precisely these portentous years that the new world—built around the new premise of assertion of the self—was wrenching itself from the old. Mozart, the artist and professional, stood in the vortex of vast social dislocations. Small wonder that we feel a curious blend of poignant regret and new adventure in his most personal music.

Beethoven lived to epitomize the very thing that had been passionately sought and finally won—the dignity and unique value of all men. Despite a quality of great tragedy and melancholy throughout Beethoven, there is, even more, exultation and victory. Beethoven, as an artist, symbolizes totally the spiritual charter newly won at the turn of the nineteenth century.

Curiously, little things in the daily lives of these masters corroborate the above. For example, Haydn, who as a young man had brushed the clothes and cleaned the shoes of the composer Nicola Porpora (1686–1766), and who was in the employ of the aristocracy most of his life, seldom, if ever, appeared publicly without donning the formal wig. Mozart often was wigged, but an unfinished portrait of the composer by his brother-in-law, Lange, done in 1791, and others earlier, show him unwigged. Beethoven, whose shaggy mane is well known, was wigged only in his youth.

Mozart, highly dependent on the nobility, chafed constantly under them and was capable of speaking his mind. Once, when the Emperor Joseph spoke of his music being overly refined and containing too many notes, Mozart said, "Just as many notes as are necessary, your Majesty." This, Haydn would never have dared to utter.

Beethoven, himself, had many relationships with the aristocracy—but mostly on his own terms. They were allowed to patronize his work. He came to them as a social equal, a member of what would now be called the "cultural elite."

One does not study the lives of these great men in isolation. They knew and affected each other. Beethoven studied with Haydn and played for Mozart. Haydn and Mozart were quite close. In a sense, they were like spiritual father, son, and grandson. Between Haydn and Mozart, there was certainly a kind of familial affection. Haydn considered the young composer to be the greatest that he knew of. Mozart dedicated six of his finest string quartets to the older man.

Mozart, after hearing the improvisations of the boy Beethoven, recognized his genius and fully prophesied the greatness that was to come.

Haydn, however, thought little of Beethoven's talent and never established close relations with the younger man. The very fact that they were somewhat alien temperamentally and artistically points to Haydn's belonging essentially to the older order of things—to the glittering dignity of a previous age. Beethoven was a child of rebellion, of newness, and of a new century.

Haydn

Joseph Haydn lived a long, fruitful, methodical life. From humble beginnings in a peasant's hut in Austria, he became choir boy at St. Stephen's in Vienna and came under the influence of the poet, Metastasio, and the composer, Porpora. For thirty years he served as Kapellmeister for the noble house of Esterhazy in Hungary. Late in his life there were two trips to London, where he was acclaimed as composer and conductor. His last years were spent in the outskirts of Vienna, where he wrote the great oratorios, *The Creation* and *The Seasons*.

His temperament was benign. When the girl that he loved, the daughter of a wig-maker caller Keller, took the veil and entered a convent, Haydn consented to marry the elder sister due to the entreaties of her father. Though she turned out to be a shrew, it still did not sour his temperament. Altogether he had an extremely even, productive life that was marked by a steady growth of compositional power and technique.

Haydn's output was truly voluminous, numbering many hundreds of compositions. He worked in all the major idioms of the day: opera, oratorio, mass, concerto, sonata, symphony, chamber music, song. But his major contribution was in the symphony and the string quartet; he wrote well over 100 symphonies and 83 quartets. While he did not invent these forms, he did invest them with the structure and scope that was to challenge most of the major composers after him for upwards of 100 years.

With Haydn, the symphony and its performance medium, the full orchestra, became truly modern, capable of expressing a wide gamut of emotion. The forms of the individual movements—sonata-allegro, theme and variation, rondo, song form, minuet with trio—became marvels of studied poise and balance. His development sections—intricate, coherent, logical all at once—were the models for Mozart and Beethoven; they show an uncanny tightness and aptness of individual ideas wedded with an almost blithe naturalness.

Lest we believe that all of this sophistication of form was intuitively grasped by Haydn, one needs to remember his words that his constant concern was "to observe what was good and what was weak in effect, and was consequently in a position to better, to change, to amplify, to curtail."

There is not much doubt that much of the solace in his life came from his work. In his later, honored years he often said that the early years spent in a leaky, freezing garret studying, practicing, and sleeping with his *Gradus ad Parnassum* (a treatise on counterpoint written by J. J. Fux in 1725) under his pillow were the happiest of his life.

Perhaps nowhere can the vivacity and sparkle of Haydn's music be better seen than in the string quartets—especially the late ones. The finale of the *Quartet in G Minor*, Op. 74, No. 3, shows perfectly his wit and lyric power. This movement is typical of the many "gypsy" pieces from his pen. It begins with delightful syncopations. The whole is cast in a mock-serious minor. It is not long, however, before a folk-song-like tune bubbles out from the texture. On perceiving the real charm of this lyric moment we understand what Haydn meant when he told the singer, Michael Kelly, "It is the tune which is the charm of music . . ."

Later, in the development section, the music seems to stumble and hesitate three times. But then it plunges on with incredible zest and brightness. Surely Beethoven admired these pages, so full of the unexpected and of high good spirits.

Figure 22. Mozart performing for Maria Theresa. (Osterreichische Nationalbibliothek)

Mozart

Mozart's life offers contrast to that of Haydn's in several important ways. For one, his background and education were completely different. Mozart's father, Leopold, was a respected and talented composer, the author of a well-known instructional method for the violin. Wolfgang's older sister, Nannerl, was a prodigy like himself; together they toured Europe, astounding the musical world with their musical prowess.

Whereas Haydn worked long and hard for whatever he achieved in composition, Mozart possessed an astonishing facility. At the age of five, he dictated to his father impeccable little minuets.

As a keyboardist, Mozart was supreme, and his improvisations left an indelible impression on his pupils and audiences. He played the violin almost as well as the keyboard. In addition to his native German, he understood English, French, Italian, and Latin. He excelled at dancing, horseback riding, drawing, and billiards. In short, he was supremely gifted.

Whereas Haydn progressed through life ever gaining reputation and material fortune, Mozart often suffered agonies of want and deprivation and died at the age of 35. He died engrossed in the writing of his great *Requiem*, fully realizing that it was as much for himself as for the nobleman who commissioned it.

In some ways, Mozart was not prepared well in his childhood for the trials of adult life. Closely supervised by his father, whom he adored ("next to God is Papa"), adulated by the most brilliant society, he remained nevertheless the child. He was an easy prey for unscrupulous friends like Stadler the clarinetist, lending money which he did not have, while at the same time depriving his family of the bare necessities. The stories of his procrastination and last minute flurries of work are charming but typical of the naïve disorder that afflicted him always. It was not unusual for him to delay writing out orchestral parts to the overtures of his operas almost up to the moment of performance.

At the première of *Don Giovanni*, the orchestra is supposed to have played the overture from music sheets still wet with ink. Mozart's wife, Constanze, plied him with punch and exotic tales the whole night before the day of performance in a desperate attempt to keep him awake and working.

The catalogue of his works is very extensive. Köchel, who catalogued his music, lists over 600 works.* In all major forms that he used, the music is unrivaled for purity, intellectual scope, and passion. Besides succeeding in Haydn's favorite forms, the symphony and quartet, Mozart was the complete master of the concerto. There exist superb concertos for bassoon, horn, clarinet, flute, and violin, the whole collection crowned by more than two dozen for the keyboard. The analysis of the *Piano Concerto in C Minor* at the end of this section shows what unquestionable mastery he ultimately attained over the form.

The operas of Mozart—*The Marriage of Figaro, Idomeneo, The Magic Flute, Don Giovanni*—are superb representations of his best work. *Don Giovanni*, to choose one example, was as fraught with implications for the music of the romantic century as was Beethoven's *"Eroica" Symphony*. Tchaikovsky was smitten by *Don Giovanni*, and Chopin's first important success came with his variations for piano and orchestra on the duet "La ci darem la mano" from Act I. George Bernard Shaw could not keep his piano score of the *Don* on its shelf; he was forever playing it over and singing the parts as well as he could. And small wonder. There is a complete world of expression and mood in the opera.

The opera abounds in exquisite melody. There are moments of great pathos, as at the death of the Commendatore in Act I. The comedy, of course, is superb, as when Leporello reads from the list of the Don's amorous adventures in the "Catalogue Aria." The flute clearly volunteers a kind of "wolf whistle."

---

* The published works of a composer are ordinarily identified by *opus* number. However, Mozart's works are listed by *K.* number—the *K.* standing for "Köchel"—as in the *Symphony in G Minor*, K. 550.

EXAMPLE 6–5   *Don Giovanni*, Act I, Mozart

When in Act II the frightened servant (Leporello) tells his master of the ghostly
statue at the door, the singer imitates the knocking in a delightful way.

EXAMPLE 6–6   *Don Giovanni*, Act II, Mozart

COMMENTARY AND ANALYSIS

Concerto in C Minor for Piano and Orchestra,
K. 491, Movement III, Mozart

Mozart's *Piano Concerto in C Minor* (his twenty-fourth) is one of only two written
by him in the minor mode. (The other is the twentieth, in D minor.) It was greatly
admired by Beethoven, who patterned much of his own *Piano Concerto in C
Minor*, Op. 37, after it. The Mozart concerto is replete with pathos and and drama.
It is a marvel of musical integration, the keyboard part blending naturally with
the orchestra at all times. The virtuosity of the solo part never intrudes upon the
homogeneity and oneness of the whole. All this Beethoven surely admired and
emulated; his work in the concerto form constantly emphasized these virtues.

The opening themes in both works begin in a similar fashion.

EXAMPLE 6–7   *Piano Concerto*, K. 491, Mvt. I, Mozart

EXAMPLE 6–8   *Piano Concerto No. 3*, Op. 37, Mvt. I, Beethoven

Mozart's final movement, an Allegretto in C minor, is cast as a set of eight variations on an original theme. The theme itself is one of rare beauty.

EXAMPLE 6–9   *Piano Concerto*, K. 491, Mvt. III, Mozart

In a miraculous way Mozart managed to capture within this impeccably patterned 16-measure frame a feeling of great poignancy. Its form is regular binary, both parts beginning with different versions of the same motive.

EXAMPLE 6–10

Part A begins: Part B begins:

At the outset, the orchestra presents a complete statement of the theme, without commentary by the piano—as if Mozart had wished to present his theme in all its purity, without filigree or embroidery of any sort. The piano, however, quickly comes into its own. Variation I is entirely given over to embellishing material in the solo part with sparse chordal background in the orchestra.

EXAMPLE 6–11

Two important motives arise. The second, an ascending, tripping figure, will be used as the basis of Variation VI.

EXAMPLE 6–12

The second variation is evenly divided between orchestra and soloist. The orchestra plays part A of the theme through once, after which the piano joins with brilliant scales for its repetition. Part B is treated in the same manner.

EXAMPLE 6–13

In Variation III, things are reversed. The piano sallies forth with quite a stormy idea.

EXAMPLE 6–14

The Sturm und Drang character of this music surely must have thrilled Beethoven. The orchestra answers with fiery material of its own. Then comes a complete change of mood in Variation IV. The winds present a crisp little march in A♭ major, complete with saucy accents at unexpected places.

EXAMPLE 6–15

The piano joins in later, featuring a bouncy rhythmic pattern of its own.

Variation V carries the music back to the original key—C minor. The piano is mostly in charge. It starts in a rather dense, contrapuntal manner.

EXAMPLE 6–16

Shortly afterwards, ascending scales in the left hand underline the right-hand motive heard at the beginning of Variation III.

EXAMPLE 6–17

The tumult of this variation ends with a solid cadence in the tonic minor.

EXAMPLE 6–18

Variation VI enters, this time in the orchestra, suddenly manifesting the warmth and geniality of the parallel key—C major.

EXAMPLE 6–19

Prominently featured is the tiny figure first encountered in Variation I (see Ex. 6–12).

EXAMPLE 6–20

Variation VII reverts back to the tonic minor key. It is shorter than the previous variations and is distinguished by flashing rising scales and glittering arpeggios. All this leads to a cadenza that ushers in the last section, Variation VIII. A very important change occurs in this variation. The meter, instead of continuing in four beats, now is in two—i.e., in six-eight.

EXAMPLE 6-21

At first the music shows a tripping, hesitant mien, but then skyrocketing scales lead to a brilliant, expansive close.

EXAMPLE 6-22

Beethoven

Beethoven's early years and education represent a composite of those of Haydn and Mozart. His father was a musician, as was Mozart's, but of little musical distinction. Beethoven, too, was a prodigy, but did not bud into greatness as easily or as early as Mozart. Like Haydn, he worked very hard to achieve his style. Every new creative advance was marked by enormous labor and spiritual travail —the *Skizzenbücher* (sketch books) attest to this.

Among his teachers were Albertsberger, Neefe, Salieri, and Haydn. It was Neefe who brought him as a young man to Mozart, who is said to have uttered, "Pay attention to this lad; he will make a noise in the world one of these days."

From Haydn and Mozart, Beethoven gained a rigorous sense of the principles of classical form. Indeed, the forms that challenged Beethoven were precisely those brought to such perfection by his two great predecessors: the symphony, sonata, concerto, string quartet and other chamber music, the mass, opera, and song. Indeed, a great body of his early works point in essence and form back to the early classical period.

Like Haydn and Mozart, Beethoven possessed a sense of humor that saturates much of his music. The Scherzo from the *"Spring"* Sonata, Op. 24, for violin and piano, illustrates this quality perfectly. The piano begins with a saucy little tune, which is full of bounce and snap.

EXAMPLE 6–23 *Violin Sonata ("Spring"), Op. 24, Mvt. III, Beethoven*

Then the violin joins in, supposedly doubling the melody. But, somehow, it is always one beat late and never does catch up.

EXAMPLE 6–24

Apparently, Beethoven enjoyed musical frolic so much that he could repeat the same "out of step" process in the Scherzo from his *"Pastorale"* Symphony—this time with the oboe out of step.

Though equanimity, grace, elegance, good humor, balanced structure can be found throughout Beethoven, it is not in this area that he was unique. Rather, it is the energy, dramatic power, exultant majesty, and intensity of mood and passion that distinguish him from his forerunners.

Quite early in life, his sympathies had been given to the forces of democracy and freedom. He devoured Plutarch and Homer. He identified with Napoleon prior to the latter's coronation. Later, Schiller made an enormous impression on him, as did Goethe. Goethe's play *Egmont*—a romanticized expression of the rebellions in the Netherlands of the early sixteenth century—so fired his zeal that he provided it with magnificent incidental music. Schiller's poem to the brotherhood of man, *Ode to Joy*, became the propelling agent and ultimate essence of the *Ninth* (*"Choral"*) *Symphony*.

Throughout his life, there were battles with the world and with himself. In his early thirties he found that he was doomed to deafness. The Heiligenstadt Testament, written in a moment of utter despair, shows the inner struggle that he underwent:

> Yes, the cherished hope—which I brought with me when I came here, of being healed at least to a certain degree, must now abandon me entirely. As the leaves of autumn fall and are withered, so, too—my hope has dried up. Almost as I was when I came here, I leave again—even the courage—which inspired me on lovely summer days—is vanished. O Providence—let a single day of untroubled joy be granted to me! For so long already the resonance of true joy be granted to me! O when—O when, Divine one—may I feel it once more in the temple of Nature and of mankind? Never?—no—that would be too hard! *

Despite constant physical afflictions, disappointments in love, and gross misunderstanding by the public, Beethoven's indomitable will and great faith in the dignity of the human spirit drove him on to ever greater achievments.

His work is generally divided into three periods. The first period covers roughly everything up to 1800, or the music up to the late Op. 40's. This music, though suffused by his unique dynamism, still looks back to Haydn and Mozart. The early works, while often charged with passion and subjective power as in the *"Pathétique"* and *"Moonlight"* sonatas, or the *Quartet in C Minor*, Op. 18, did not really surpass certain works of Haydn and Mozart. Compare the two following passages, one by Mozart and the other by the young Beethoven (p. 193).

With the coming of the second period, inaugurated by works such as the *"Kreutzer"* Sonata, Op. 47, for violin and piano and the *"Eroica"* symphony, Op. 55, Beethoven found his true artistic character. His apprenticeship had ended. The music of this period pulses with power and energy. In it can be heard everything from the solemnity of the Funeral March in the *"Eroica"* to the philosophical de-

---

* Michael Hamburger, ed. and trans., *Beethoven, Letters, Journals and Conversations* (Garden City, N.Y.: Doubleday Anchor Book), p. 34.

Figure 23.   Beethoven, pencil drawing by Klober, 1818. (Beethoven-Haus, Bonn, H. C. Bodnac Collection)

tachment and serenity of the Scene at the Brook from the *"Pastorale" Symphony*, to the almost frenetic fury of the *"Appassionata" Sonata*.

EXAMPLE 6–25   *Piano Sonata*, K. 457, Mvt. II, Mozart

EXAMPLE 6–26   *Sonata ("Pathétique")*, Op. 13, Mvt. II, Beethoven

The last period, beginning with the Op. 100's, also contains some marvelously exciting music: the Gloria from the *Missa Solemnis*, for example, or the Scherzo and the Finale from the *Ninth Symphony*. But still another dimension is present —withdrawal, a searching within. Forms become much freer, more fantasy-like, though solid principles of structure remain in force. There is a decided tendency to play down effect and dazzle. Harmony becomes much more refined, and a deep, searching polyphony often reigns.

The *Quartet in C-Sharp Minor* (see below) illustrates this final renunciation and inner exploration perhaps better than any other late work. Its overall structure, and its content, are revolutionary. There are seven movements, forming a loose but highly cohesive fantasy-like structure. It is as if Beethoven, while composing, remembered the words of his favorite poet, Homer:

"But Fate now conquers; I am hers; and yet not she shall share in my renown."

COMMENTARY AND ANALYSIS

"Leonore" Overture No. 3, Op. 72a, Beethoven

Beethoven's only opera, *Fidelio*, was first performed in November 1805. The *"Leonore" Overture No. 3* is one of four overtures Beethoven wrote for his opera, and it was first performed at a revival of the opera in March 1806. It is now played primarily as a concert overture, whereas the overturn called *Fidelio*, Op. 72b, ordinarily prefaces modern performances of the opera.

The basic idea of the opera concerns the effort of Leonore (disguised as Fidelio, a young man) to rescue her husband, Florestan, from prison. Beethoven was extremely interested in political justice and personal fidelity, themes that form the very core of the opera.

The orchestra consist of two flutes, two oboes, two clarinets, two bassoons, four horns, two trumpets, three trombones, two tympani, and strings. The form of the overture is sonata-allegro with a slow introduction and coda.

The introduction opens in the key of C major in slow majestic style, leading to the Florestan theme (based upon an aria in the second act) beginning in measure 9.

EXAMPLE 6–27

The first theme of the exposition is energetic and exciting. The syncopation in the theme in this first measure becomes a hallmark of the overture.

EXAMPLE 6–28

The second theme contrasts strongly with the first theme in both key and style. A broad lyric theme begins in E major in the French horns, joined quickly by the woodwinds and the strings.

EXAMPLE 6–29

A third energetic theme, also in E major, is characterized by a series of syncopations that are nervous in their insistence:

EXAMPLE 6–30

The development section begins at measure 193 and, after some "busyness" for three measures, is characterized by a rather plaintive theme in the key of F, originally heard in the introduction.

EXAMPLE 6–31

There follows development material based upon Theme 1, and then suddenly a trumpet call

EXAMPLE 6–32

that in the opera itself signals the arrival of the Minister of Justice and the ultimate reunion of Leonore and Florestan. This trumpet call is played offstage. The call that occurs here twice represents a dramatic climax in both the overture and the opera.

The recapitulation puts all three themes introduced in the exposition in the home key of C major. Finally, rushing scale patterns introduce the coda (Presto) as the overture presses on to a rousing close.

COMMENTARY AND ANALYSIS

String Quartet in C♯ Minor, Op. 131, Beethoven

Like Haydn and Mozart, Beethoven wrote string quartets throughout most of his creative life. He found in the string quartet an ultimate creative challenge. This is shown by the fact that he returned to it again and again, producing several of his finest quartets near the end of his life. The *Quartet in C♯ Minor* was written in 1826, a year before the composer's death.

Montaigne (1533–1592), the great French philosopher, once said, ". . . A man must flee from the popular conditions that have taken possession of his soul; he must sequester and come again to himself." This statement applies aptly to Beethoven in the later part of his life. Because of deafness, physical ailments, personal maladjustments, and the public's lack of understanding, Beethoven had largely ceased to look to the external world for inspiration. He increasingly turned to the inner self for the spiritual riches that became manifest in the last string quartets, piano sonatas, the *Ninth Symphony* ("*Choral*"), and the *Missa Solemnis*.

The *C♯ Minor Quartet* is typical of Beethoven's later creative insularity; in atmosphere and meaning it goes beyond mundane beauty, expressing new psychic realities that Beethoven discovered within himself. These new realities are to be felt more than verbalized, but they do have a concrete parallel in Beethoven's original use of form in this quartet. It has seven movements, rather than the usual four, each movement singular in expression and yet functioning as an integral part of the whole.

The seven movements are organized into the following forms:

No. I—Fugue.   Adagio, ma non troppo e molto espressivo (slow and very expressive), leading directly to

No. II—Sonata-allegro form.   Allegro molto vivace (fast and very lively).

No. III—Instrumental recitative.   Allegro moderato (moderately fast), with only a slight break in sound this introduces

No. IV—Theme and seven variations.   Andante, ma non troppo e molto cantabile (slow, but not too much and very singing).

No. V—Scherzo.   Presto (very fast).

No. VI—Binary form (AB).   Adagio quasi un poco andante (very slow somewhat like an andante), leads without pause to

No. VII—Sonata-allegro form.   Allegro (fast).

FUGUE, C♯ MINOR

This fugue sets the mood and atmosphere for the whole quartet. Reflecting Beethoven's spiritual temper in the last years, it has a feeling of regret tempered with acceptance: pain transfigured through philosophical understanding.

The fugue's subject enters successively in all melodic voices, descending from soprano down to bass: first violin, second violin, viola, and violoncello.

EXAMPLE 6–33

As the number of voices increases, the intensity of the chords increases. The dissonance suggests the music of the twentieth century. Compare this fugue with another prophetic work, the opening fugue of Bach's *Mass in B Minor,* "Kyrie Eleison"; then compare both fugues with the opening movement of Bartok's *Music for Strings, Percussion, and Celesta* (1935).

SONATA-ALLEGRO FORM, D MAJOR

This movement has been characterized as "the return to life, to joyful thought and emotion." At the very end of the preceding fugue, look for a long soft C♯ held by all the strings. Although there is no break of sound at this point, you will recognize the second movement's beginning from a striking change of mood. After the intensity of the fugue, the sustained C♯ gives an aura of breathless expectancy. All the strings then move up a half-step to D♮, and the first violin begins a lively tune at a brisk tempo. The key is now a bright D major.

EXAMPLE 6–34

INSTRUMENTAL RECITATIVE, KEY INDETERMINATE

Although there is no fixed key for this section, it does serve as a modulating bridge from the second movement in D major to the fourth movement in A major. The last chord of the recitative is an E chord, the dominant of A major.

In his later work, Beethoven wrote many instrumental passages suggesting vocal recitatives from opera and oratorio. The recitatives in these vocal works prepare for the arias or ensemble pieces that immediately follow. Similarly, Beethoven writes an instrumental recitative here that prepares for the next movement.

Listen for a change of tempo (Adagio, very slow) halfway through this movement (meas. 6), as the first violin takes the lead. A flowing line emerges suggestive of the vocal coloratura heard typically in Italian opera of the time.

THEME AND VARIATIONS, A MAJOR

The theme for these variations was characterized by Richard Wagner as a "blessed incarnation of innocence." A four-note motive is gently passed from first to second violin over quiet repeated notes, played *pizzicato* in the cello. This motive forms the main body of the theme.

EXAMPLE 6–35

Listen carefully to the above theme several times. The variations that follow are subtle, and your ability to trace each variation to its source will depend on knowing the theme well.

SCHERZO, E MAJOR

No scherzo in Beethoven's work is more joyful than this one. The Scherzo in the *Ninth Symphony* may possess more crushing energy but not more zest. What makes this Scherzo particularly exhilarating is Beethoven's use of the unexpected.

Characteristically, he starts out with a joke. The cellist plays four, brusque notes, then abruptly stops, as if he had missed his cue and plunged in alone. After a measure of what might be construed as embarrassed silence, the full quartet proceeds, the motive now in the first violin.

EXAMPLE 6-36

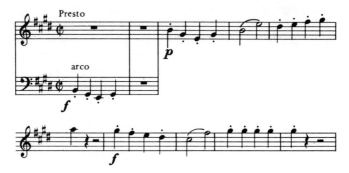

The articulation is mostly detached (*staccato*), and there are many repeated notes. Often the pace slows; forward motion almost ceases. The music catches a breath, then plunges on. Listen for these decelerations throughout the Scherzo—also for the several sudden halts. Expect the unexpected; it is part of the fun.

Besides the opening motive, there are two other themes. You will recognize the second theme (meas. 69), played by the first and second violins, by its folklike simplicity and its smooth articulation (*legato*). Theme 3 (meas. 110) enters shortly after. It sounds similar in expression to Theme 2, except that all four instruments play it together.

Pay close attention to the Scherzo's final section (meas. 470). All strings play high, start very soft, and cross their bows very close to the bridge (*sul ponticello*). You will hear Theme 1 wrapped in a curious, eerie sound. Soon the volume grows, and a bold tonic chord ends the movement as brusquely as it began.

BINARY FORM, G♯ MINOR

This short form is a connecting link between the bright Scherzo and the dark finale. The deep note of melancholy returns from the opening fugue, preparing for the finale's tragic outcome. Out of the dark homophonic sonority, listen for the theme in the viola. This begins Part A.

Part B (meas. 12) is twice the length of Part A and is more contrapuntal, with much close imitation of the second motive of the theme. Notice the first violin's direct motion into the finale.

SONATA-ALLEGRO FORM, C♯ MINOR

This sonata-allegro form is extremely compact. It is like a tight spring that releases its power again and again. At its core are two rhythmic motives heard at the start. Because they will permeate much of the movement, singly and in combination, you should learn them well.

The first motive is heard twice. It outlines essentially the two basic chords in the key, tonic and dominant:

EXAMPLE 6–37

The second motive follows immediately:

EXAMPLE 6–38

Try to follow the development of these motives as Beethoven derives from them many new shapes and meanings.

Beethoven achieves contrast with his next theme, in the key of E major (meas. 56).

EXAMPLE 6–39

Listen for a shift of mood. You will hear flowing scale figures drifting down successively in the three upper strings. This theme appears twice: once in the exposition and once in the recapitulation (meas. 216).

Although many commentators have called this quartet a fantasy-like form in seven movements, there are essentially just four movements. The second, fourth, fifth, and seventh movements are genuine sonata movements, while the other three movements serve as psychological preparation and connection. The following reorganization of the structural scheme presented above (p. 197) will make this clear:

Movement I   No. 1—Fugue (introduction)
              No. 2—Sonata-allegro form

Movement II	No. 3—Recitative (bridge)
	No. 4—Theme with variations
Movement III	No. 5—Scherzo
Movement IV	No. 6—Binary form (bridge)
	No. 7—Sonata-allegro form

In effect, then, the quartet represents an expanded, four-movement sonata.

No matter how revolutionary a work of Beethoven's may at first seem, it is based nonetheless on artistic principles from his immediate cultural tradition. Beethoven did not abandon the forms of his masters, Haydn and Mozart; he expanded and transformed them. All successful revolutions in the arts retain much that is still alive and matters from the past.

The C♯ Minor Quartet, reduced now to four large movements, allows us a possible interpretation of its meaning. The pattern of moods is faithful to that seen in many of Beethoven's larger works. Movement I (fugue plus sonata-allegro form) symbolizes the fundamental duality of man in nature: the solitude of the individual human spirit facing the multiplicity and beauty of nature.

Movement II (recitative plus theme and variations) symbolizes the peace attained through acceptance and understanding. The Scherzo, Movement III, is like a chortling of the gods over the human comedy. With the finale, Movement IV, Beethoven reminds us that personal peace is never assured; that the battles within and without the self must be continually fought.

Each listener, of course, must find in this work his own emotional reaction and understanding.

Gluck

Christopher Willibald Gluck (1714–1787) was an important transitional figure. As early as 1742, he was in London writing operas in opposition to Handel. Later, in Paris, he produced great masterworks in the field, including *Iphigénie en Aulide* and *Orphée et Eurydice*. There was a fierce polemic with the followers of Piccinni (1728–1800) and the Italian school of opera, including a bitter war of pamphlets. Gluck's operatic technique emphasized dramatic consistency and a psychologically true setting of music to text. This was in stark contrast to the Italian style, espoused by Handel, featuring rigidly constructed series of arias, duets, choruses, cadenzas, etc. Gluck's operatic reforms exerted a profound and lasting influence on Mozart, Weber, and the later Romantics.

Other composers

Other important figures of the period are Muzio Clementi (1752–1832), fashion-able concert pianist, composer, and manufacturer of pianos; Luigi Boccherini (1743–1805), cellist and composer of elegant, sparkling music including twenty symphonies; Antonio Salieri (1750–1825), the rival of Mozart and sometime teacher of Beethoven, who was known primarily as a composer of opera; and Karl von Dittersdorf (1739–1799), another composer of symphonies.

Figure 24. Paganini, 1819, by Ingres. (Musée du Louvre, photograph Giraudon)

Chapter seven

ROMANTICISM

"I understand that you are fond of music that does not distract your mind from affairs of state." This comment is said to have been made by the composer Luigi Cherubini during a conversation with Napoleon. The veiled sarcasm of the remark helps us to understand the import and impact of romantic composers and their music. One cannot imagine Haydn, a few years before, addressing the nobility with anything but profound respect. The written terms of his appointment at Esterhazy attests to the menial position of composers and musicians in the centuries before the nineteenth. Haydn must ". . . be temperate; must abstain from vulgarity in eating and drinking and conversation; must take care of all the music and the musical instruments, and be answerable for any injury they may suffer from carelessness or neglect; . . . that when summoned to perform before company he shall take care that he and all members of his orchestra do follow the instructions given and appear in white stockings, white linen, powder, and with either a pig-tail or a tie-wig."*

The nineteenth-century composer assumed a different role from his counterpart of the seventeenth and eighteenth centuries. Beethoven, giving lessons, rapped the knuckles of his aristocratic pupils. The talents of Beethoven and those who followed were for hire—but now mostly on their own terms.

The great Romantics, Cherubini, Beethoven, Rossini, Berlioz, Mendelssohn, Wagner, and others, were mostly of high social position. Each man was independent in a way that his predecessors could only have envied, as can be plainly seen from Wagner's comments:

> . . . The world owes me what I require! I cannot live on a miserable post of organist like your master Bach! Is it such an unheard of demand when I ask that the little bit of luxury that I enjoy be given to me? I, who hold a thousand enjoyments in store for the world! †

---

* Thomas, Paine, and Klauser, eds., *Famous Composers and Their Works*, Vol. II (Boston, Mass.: J. B. Millet Co., 1891), p. 252. © by J. B. Millet Co.

† Jacques Barzun, *Darwin, Marx, Wagner* (Boston, Mass.: Atlantic-Little, Brown and Company, 1941).

Whereas the majority of the baroque and classical masters were directly dependent on either the church or aristocracy for their very bread, the Romantics frequently dealt with the public directly. They realized income from concerts and from the publication of their works. Now they were dignified professionals with a clear, independent social position.

Though he was often materially sustained by interested nobles such as Prince Lichnowsky or the Archduke Rudolf, Beethoven also realized substantial income from his compositions. In fact, Beethoven acquired considerable expertise in his business dealings. At his death, the equivalent of $15,000 was found in a drawer of his desk.

Cherubini, mentioned earlier, ultimately rose to the directorship of the Paris Conservatoire. Mendelssohn, the son of a wealthy banker and born as it were with a silver tuning fork in his mouth, early achieved fame to match his fortune. Berlioz attained partial independance through his compositions and conducting but more especially through his position as a music critic for the Parisian journals. Rossini, after assailing and conquering the musical world with upwards of three dozen operas, ceased altogether to write opera although there are some charming trifles later in his life. For his remaining thirty-nine years, he lived in retirement in the comfort of both his laurels *and* profits. Paganini, the "Devil of the Violin," became affluent enough to present Berlioz with a gift of 20,000 francs after hearing *Harold in Italy*.

We do not mean to suggest that the path to material security for composers had become easy in the early 1800's. For many, it was still a very cruel fight for bare existence. But the composer now had a voice that was heard; the world noticed, took him into account, and was moved. Thus Cherubini could speak to Napoleon on somewhat equal terms. Napoleon had conquered one world, Cherubini another.

With the composer's new-found independence and dignity his music took on a new cast. It now became loosened, freer, expansive. Above all, it expressed deeply and tellingly the subjective state of the composer himself. The music unashamedly expressed *him* directly and without reserve.

There were musical explorations into areas of human experience never before attempted. Berlioz produced a dazzling first symphony, the *Symphonie fantastique*, in 1830. The composer tells us that its intense passions and reveries are those of a young hero who has taken an overdose of opium. The symphony displays a great scenic panorama. In its five movements Berlioz joyfully leaps about from the yearnings of a young man in love, to an elegant ball, to a rustic scene in the country, to the guillotine, and finally, to a sulphuric scene somewhere near hell, replete with witches and the death knell.

In *The Damnation of Faust* the hero literally falls screaming into hell and is greeted by a chorus of demons for which Berlioz invents a barbaric, hideous language. All this tonal agony, represented by groaning dissonances and macabre orchestration, is directly followed by a seraphic chorus telling of Marguerite's salvation. Berlioz, like many Romantics, constantly exulted in the violent juxtaposition of opposites.

But in the piano works of his contemporary, Chopin, we hear a refined, sensitive musical language depicting in minute detail the composer's many fine shades of sentiment. Mendelssohn traveled much and gave to the world musical "souvenirs" of great charm and polish: The *"Hebrides" Overture,* and the *"Italian"* and *"Scotch"* symphonies. And folk songs cropped up everywhere: in symphony, opera, sonata, and other major forms.

Nationalism became very important. Many composers occupied themselves primarily with trying to capture the spirit of their native lands. Edvard Grieg (1843–1907) advanced the cause of Norwegian music with compositions such as *Peer Gynt* (after Ibsen). Smetana wrote the first Czech nationalistic opera, *The Bartered Bride.* His compatriot Dvorak not only produced a great many Czech-oriented works, but during his stay in America in the 1890's was influential in making Americans aware of their native music. Later, Sibelius became a strong spiritual voice for Finland.

Program music—a major concern with the Romantics—not only represented various scenes and situations, but led to the depiction of the character of different countries and peoples.

Late in the century musical realism took hold—especially in opera where it was known as *verismo.* Richard Strauss boasted that he could represent anything with tones—even the shine of a silver teaspoon.

Thus, the Romantics constantly searched within and without themselves for new things to express. Because of this, new technical means had to be created in order to arrive at the desired musical ends. New forms evolved, and old ones were transformed. Melody, rhythm, harmony, orchestration, dynamics, performance: all were profoundly affected.

Of course, as we have seen before, changes of attitude and of expression from period to period do not occur in an environmental vacuum. A composer and his work reflect and complement the total web and texture of his time. The Age of Romanticism saw unique developments in many areas.

Jacques Barzun, in *Darwin, Marx, Wagner* defines Romanticism as "... a constructive effort after a great revolution which had leveled off old institutions and old nations—including the mechanical materialism of the eighteenth century. Romanticism ... valued individual freedom, subjective feelings, human reason, social purpose, and above all, Art."*

Individual freedom was indeed a leading motive in the nineteenth century. The French and American revolutions had occurred in its name.

---

* Ibid., p. 17.

The everyday worker, who had been little more than a drudge for many centuries, now began to be valued as a human being. Enlightened industrialists such as Robert Owen in England began to ease the load of their employees. Trade unions, arising first in Britain and America, spread slowly to other westernized countries. Engels and Marx began to rally the "proletariat" against their "capitalist oppressors." Communism crystallized.

And along with a new-found freedom, man's control over his environment increased tremendously. Watt had already adapted the steam engine to the driving of machinery. This helped to relieve man's burden in industry. The steam engine also led to the railroad. From the time of the Greek civilization 2000 years before, the maximum average traveling speed was approximately five miles per hour. Thus, in Napoleon's headlong retreat from Russia to Paris, a distance of approximately 1,400 miles, he traveled for thirteen days. With the opening of the first railroad in Britain, man would one day be able to cover the same distance in less than two days.

The steam boat achieved comparable results on water, and, in 1835, the telegraph was developed through the efforts of Volta, Galvani, Faraday, and Morse. The blast furnace, according to H. G. Wells, came into being resulting in ". . . tons of incandescent steel swirling about like boiling milk in a saucepan."

The electric light was invented; man's life-span increased; his general health improved; the stethoscope and anesthesia came into use; Pasteur established the relationship between bacteria and disease; Lister showed how to kill bacteria.

Man in the nineteenth century thus found himself freer, healthier, with more leisure than his predecessors, and in better control over his environment. He now had dominion over material things as never before, and he could communicate with a large segment of the world with increasing speed. His horizons were expanding at an increasing rate, on all levels.

Romanticism as an era was a time of expansion. For music it was a time of heightened intensity and expression. In order to express and communicate more of himself the nineteenth-century composer looked to his musical materials and changed them. What had served admirably for Haydn, Mozart, and Clementi would no longer do.

GENERAL CHARACTERISTICS

Melody

Throughout the baroque and classical periods melodic elements were chosen primarily for their potential in compositional development. Fugue subjects tended to be graphic, clear, and plain, as in Example 7–1.

EXAMPLE 7-1   *Ariadne Musica*, Fugue No. 10, J. K. F. Fischer

They usually became charged with emotional or intellectual meaning after they were expanded, combined with other melodic elements. In short, they became interesting only after they had undergone musical growth.

In the romantic period, melodies also were created for their utility. But more commonly, they were shaped for immediate, memorable tunefulness, for innate beauty. In other words, melody attained a primacy over other elements such as rhythm and harmony.

Romantic melody is striking and immediate, often extremely lyric and song-like. It tends also to span larger segments in composition than in previous periods. Because of the attention given to folk and dance music in general, romantic melody frequently takes on a nationalistic or regional tinge.

Rhythm

Flexibility is a major characteristic of romantic rhythm. This shows itself strongly in the area of tempo. In previous periods tempos tended to be uniform, the beat steady and unflagging. Restraint in tempo—as in nearly everything else—was primary. But the personal expressions of the Romanticists could not be stated within strict tempos. Rubato was used for emphasis and to intensify the emotional impact. Individual movements often exhibited substantial tempo changes. Tchaikovsky, in the finale of his *Symphony No. 5*, utilizes no fewer than nine tempos. They are: Andante maestoso, Allegro vivace, Poco piu animato, Tempo I, Poco meno mosso, Molto vivace, Moderato assai e molto maestoso, Presto, and Molto meno mosso.

In contrast, baroque masters often gave absolutely no tempo indications not even at the beginning of a work. Tempo was deduced by the performer from the configuration of the notes on the page, from the time signature, and from the style of the music in general.

Harmony

Providing color and depth, vertical sonority particularly challenged and fascinated the romantic composer. He explored new sounds, vibrant chords, and striking instrumental textures—sounds that would touch and impress the listener and delight his ear.

Dissonance, which in the past resolved to consonance as a matter of rule, now often was suspended in air only to move to another dissonance. Any key could lead to any other; and the transition from any key to another was looser, fluid, unexpected, and colorful.

The net emotional result of this loosening of harmonic fiber for the listener was a feeling of questing and probing. This searching is expressed by the words of the seventeenth century mystic poet, Henry Vaughan, "I cannot reach it; and my straining eye dazzles at it, as at eternity."

Dynamics and register

Expansion is the keynote in both of these areas. Extreme louds and softs and sudden shifts from one to the other were common. The sudden explosion from a sextuple piano to a double forte in this example is typical.

EXAMPLE 7–2   *Symphony No. 6*, Op. 74, Mvt. I, Tchaikovsky

In Tchaikovsky's *Symphony No. 5*, Mvt. II, the spectrum of dynamic color is very wide indeed, from *pppp* to *ffff*, with a great many levels in between. Berlioz, in his *Symphonie fantastique*, Mvt. III, asks the strings to play *ppp*, the slightest musical whisper, and adds the words *quasi niente* (almost nothing).

In range, romantic music shows many extreme highs and lows. Each register is fully explored for its potential. Leading melodic elements might be located in the lower reaches of the bass, then suddenly heard at the top of the soprano register.

In this connection, it is interesting to note that a favorite register is the tenor. Both cello and French horn are entrusted with some of the loveliest lyric moments of the period.

Instruments and performance

The nineteenth-century concert artist, lionized by an adoring public, was a symbol of everything that is uniquely personal in romantic music. Through their magnetic presence on stage, Paganini and Liszt represented to the masses the quintessence of imagination and creative power.

As in previous centuries, many performing artists were also famous composers, including Paganini, Weber, Mendelssohn, Chopin, Brahms, and Liszt. Weber, Mendelssohn, and Wagner were famous as conductors. Sometimes, when native genius was immense, as with Mendelssohn or Liszt, the composer matched the performer. Other virtuosos on the piano such as Herz, Kalkbrenner, and Dreyschock spewed forth garish and tasteless compositions in the form of potpourris, variations on popular themes, and salon pieces.

Harold Schonberg in his book, *The Great Pianists*, tells about the herculean virtuosity of Dreyschock:

> Dreyschock would practice sixteen hours a day with the left hand alone, and got to the point where he could play octaves as fast and as smoothly as single-note passages. Heine once said that "when Dreyschock played in Munich and the wind was right, you could hear him in Paris." *

Many instruments in use developed in quality, power, and flexibility. New ones, such as the saxophone, tuba, and celeste were invented. The orchestra expanded, both in size and in variety of instruments. English horn, bass clarinet, cornet, trombone, bass drum, and cymbals became increasingly common.

The concert artist and conductor became important members of society. Their skills were often prodigious, and the instruments that they played developed accordingly. Romantic music found adequate media for its expression.

Forms

It would be an error to think that romantic forms were entirely new and unique. Although the fugue was a major compositional vehicle in the Baroque, it continued to arouse only sporadic interest in nineteenth-century masters. The symphony, concerto, opera, and sonata, magnificently developed in the classical period, continued to occupy a commanding position.

The solo concerto, which stemmed from those of Mozart, Haydn, and Beethoven, continued forcefully in the nineteenth century. Cadenzas in the concerto remained important structural units.

---

* Harold C. Schonberg, *The Great Pianists.* Copyright © by Harold C. Schonberg. Published by Simon and Schuster, Inc., and Littauer and Wilkinson.

Although basic structural principles from the eighteenth-century concerto remained, refinements abounded. The soloist's part became vastly more demanding. The dramatic power at his command now very nearly matched that of the collective orchestra. Because of this, a dramatic juxtaposition often occurred between soloist and orchestra. Here again, the soloist symbolized the new-found romantic subjectivity.

Among the many smaller forms that were particularly associated with the romantic century, the lied and the character piece for piano were prominent. The lied appealed especially to the romantic composer because of the opportunity to set to music poetry of the highest order. Since the time of Beethoven, the romantic composer had considered himself a tone poet (*Tondichter*). He felt that, like the poet, he could express definite things and feelings. The poems of Schiller, Goethe, Heine, Eichendorf, and Müller, accordingly, were matched by the superlative music of Schubert, Mendelssohn, Schumann, Brahms, Wolf, Mahler, and others. One need only listen to lieder cycles such as Schumann's *Dichterliebe* on poems of Heine to witness the very pinnacle of excellence in word-with-tone.

Because of their potential for intimate mood and atmosphere, *nocturnes, intermezzi, ballades, novelettes, album leaves,* etc., held popular throughout the century. These occasionally appear alone, but more often they are grouped into suites, like Schumann's *Papillons*, Op. 2, or *Carnaval*, Op. 9, for piano.

Of particular note among the larger forms was the tone poem, or symphonic poem. In this the composer attempted to depict poetic scenes or pictures with tone only. Typical of these are: *Battle of the Huns, Mazeppa,* and *Les Préludes* by Liszt, *Manfred* and *Francesca da Rimini* by Tchaikovsky, and *Don Juan* by Richard Strauss.

Permeating a great many of these forms are two important developments: program music and musical nationalism.

The nineteenth-century composer, ever interested in expressing a broader spectrum of human experience, was very much taken with the idea of imagery. Frequently he converted typically classical forms into vehicles for tone painting. The *Harold in Italy Symphony* by Berlioz is a case in point. So are the *Dante* and *Faust* symphonies by Liszt. The *Mephisto Waltz* by Liszt, the *Invitation to the Waltz* by Weber, and the waltz, "Chiarina," from Schumann's *Carnaval* all show an abstract dance transformed into a fanciful vehicle.

Subjects for musical imagery were nearly unlimited, even to the description of split personalities. Schumann, one of the earliest to explore program music for piano, interpreted in tone different facets of his own personality. "Eusebius" and "Florestan," in the *Carnaval*, represent the opposed sides of his psyche. "Eusebius," a limpid, dreamy piece, depicts the gentle, sensitive side of Schumann, the tone poet. "Florestan," volcanic and fiery, suggest the other tempestuous side of Schumann's nature.

The romantic composer was also strongly attracted to ethnic elements found in folk song and folk dance. Here was an opportunity to capture and perhaps to elevate to highest art the musical traces of the sorrows and exultations of generations.

Sometimes composers would quote briefly from actual folk sources, as in the Tchaikovsky symphonies; other times they would polish them to a high gloss, as in the twenty-six arrangements of German folk songs for unaccompanied chorus by Brahms. More often, though, only the spirit of folk literature permeated these works. For example, the symphonies of Dvorak, the Czech, and Sibelius, the Finn, give strong ethnic impressions without quoting at all from actual songs or dances of the people. Other composers who particularly emphasized nationalism in their works were Smetana, Grieg, Glinka, Liszt, Chopin, Mussorgsky, and Rimsky-Korsakov.

The influence of Beethoven

Beethoven, really a composer of the classical period, anticipated nearly every major musical innovation of the Romantics.

The *Pastoral Symphony* pointed the way for innumerable romantic program pieces of a bucolic nature including the excellent "Scenes in the Country" portion of the *Symphony fantastique* by Berlioz.

The parts for chorus in the *Ninth Symphony* influenced Berlioz in his *Roméo et Juliette Symphonie* and *Symphonie funebre et triomphale*, both of which use voices. Beethoven's only opera, *Fidelio*, significantly influenced Wagner.

The remarkable integration of soloist with orchestra in both the *Fourth Piano Concerto* and in the *Violin Concerto* pointed to similar efforts in the same form by Mendelssohn, Schumann, and Brahms.

Incredible harmonic progressions such as those in the 20th variation from the *Diabelli Variations*, though perhaps used as daringly in late Wagner or Liszt, were seldom surpassed. Beethoven, through rhythms and harmonies, rhapsodic forms, and strong emphasis on the passionate and grand, was the catalyst that made all Romanticism possible.

The Romantics themselves were very conscious of the great master; some, like Brahms, painfully so. Brahms' *Symphony No. 1* was immediately dubbed the "Tenth." But when an admirer mentioned the similarity of themes in the finales of Beethoven's *Ninth* and his own, Brahms is reported to have said "Any ass can see that."

EXAMPLE 7–3   (a) *Symphony No. 9*, Finale, Beethoven

(b) *Symphony No. 1*, Finale, Brahms

THE COMPOSERS

Weber and Schubert

Two important composers living and writing during Beethoven's lifetime were Carl Maria Weber (1786–1826) and Franz Schubert (1797–1828).

Weber and Schubert were active as composers at a time when Classicism was still strong. Weber, writing as critic as late as 1809, severely castigated Beethoven's *Third* and *Fourth* symphonies. Weber's ideal was still Mozart. Though Weber was a prolific composer of sonatas, concertos, occasional pieces, and the fine *Konzertstück* for the piano, his major contribution was in opera. He is considered to be the founder of German romantic opera. *Der Freischütz, Euryanthe,* and *Oberon,* through their beauty of characterization, great dramatic power, and superb orchestration, laid the foundation for Wagner and other operatic composers.

Franz Schubert is called by Alfred Einstein the "Romantic-Classicist." Listening to his *Fifth Symphony*, we feel that the music indeed is as lucid and as symmetrical as that of Haydn or Mozart. In the short thirty-one years of his life Schubert wrote an astonishing number of compositions, including nearly 600 songs. The best of the songs, as well as the chamber works, piano pieces, and larger works, show one supreme quality—spontaneous lyricism.

Most of Schubert's works are saturated with memorable melody. It is as if the music's center of gravity were in the melody itself, with other musical elements—rhythm, harmony, and form—revolving around and existing for it. It was Felix Mendelssohn who invented the title "song without words" for some of his smaller piano pieces, but the term can apply to many of Schubert's instrumental compositions as well. With Schubert, the concept of song was never distant. Several of his instrumental works were based on his own lieder: the *"Trout" Quintet;* the quartet, *Death and the Maiden,* the *Wanderer Fantasy* for piano.

Even though lyricism is the major characteristic in his music, Schubert cannot be considered simply a purveyor of astonishingly good tunes. Some of his works possess such dramatic force and piercing intensity of feeling that they truly would do justice to Beethoven. For example, the song, "Der Doppelgänger" ("The Double"), establishes an eerie mood—one that is so psychologically true that it is almost frightening. The poem by Heine tells of a lover standing in a square gazing at the house of his loved one. Before it, in the murk of the night, also stands a lonely figure of a man, the lover's double. The mood is perfectly established by barren chords in the piano and hypnotic stillness in the voice.

The lover peers intently to see who the man is. The expression becomes more taut. Finally, a startling chord *fff* accompanying a high note for the voice communicates the horror of the protagonist as he recognizes the face in the gloom as his own.

The tremendous harmonic power heard throughout the song is typical of Schubert's work. There almost always exists rich chordal color supporting simple, yet vital melody.

Weber lived to be forty: Schubert, thirty-one. It astonishes us to consider what they accomplished within so few years. Schubert is known to have dashed off six songs at one sitting. Schumann sketched the piano version of his first symphony, the *Spring,* in four brief but ecstatic days. These are incredible feats, only to be explained by the compulsive creative drive that dominated the early Romantics.

COMMENTARY AND ANALYSIS

"Der Leiermann," from Winterreise, Op. 89, No. 24, Schubert

Winterreise (Winter's Journey) is a cycle of twenty-four lieder (art songs) written in the last part of the composer's life. It is one of Schubert's highest achievements, occupying a similar place in the development of his style to that of the *Art of the Fugue* in J. S. Bach's or the *"Choral" Symphony* in Beethoven's.

Based on a set of poems by Wilhelm Müller, the cycle deals with frustrated love and alienation. The dark mood of despair is established from the very beginning in the opening song, "Gute Nacht" (*Good Night*).

> *Fremd bin ich eingezogen,*
> *Fremd zieh' ich wieder aus.*
>
> *I came as a stranger,*
> *And as a stranger I leave.*

The journey of the rejected lover carries him near a linden tree (No. 5, "Der Lindenbaum") that reminds him of a happier time. He dreams of spring (No. 11, "Frühlingstraum") but wakens to the cold and gloom of winter, ravens croaking on the rooftop and frost upon the window. He asks:

> *Wann grünt ihr Blätter am Fenster?*
> *Wann halt' ich mein Liebchen im Arm?*
>
> *When will the frost-leaves on my window turn green?*
> *When will my love be in my arms again?*

He does not give up hope. He hears the posthorn blown by the postman (No. 13, "Die Post"). When the postman rides up the street, his heart jumps with excitement for he knows the mail comes from *her* town. But later he gives in to despair; "The Inn" (No. 21, "Das Wirtshaus") shows him stopping at a graveyard—described ironically as an inn—seeking for ultimate rest. All the same, he resumes his journey.

With the song "The Organ Grinder" (No. 24, "Der Leiermann"), the lover has reached ultimate spiritual desolation, wishing now to join his destiny with that of the hapless organ grinder. A free prose translation of Müller's poem follows:

> *Up near the village stands an organ grinder cranking with*
> *cold fingers as well as he can. He is barefoot on the cold*
> *ground, without a coin in his cup. No one notices the*
> *little old man but the snarling dogs. He doesn't complain*
> *but keeps turning and turning.*
> *Oh, wonderful old man, shall I join you? Will you grind out my songs?*

Schubert projects a mood of despair and melancholy with economy and simplicity. The harmonic texture is thin, the melodic materials spare. Repetition pervades. The bare interval of the perfect fifth forms the bass pedal point throughout the piano part, suggesting the drone of a small hurdy-gurdy. Through its cold, near-hypnotic repetition, the drone expresses the numb, defeated state of mind of the spurned lover. A forlorn melody in the piano part returns throughout, with slight variations. In near mechanical fashion, it alternates with short, two-measure phrases in the voice part. The pathos expressed by the poem is so great that a sustained lyric line would not be feasible. The accented dissonances in the keyboard (meas. 4–5) anticipate the feeling of anguish and desolation.

At measures 56–57 the vocal line rises to an agonized cry of remorse at the words, "Willst zu meinem Liedern deine Leier drehn?" ("Will you play your organ for my songs?")

The bare loneliness in "Der Leiermann" manifests a quality that we now think of as existentialist. The same sense of alienation is found in Ingmar Bergman's film *The Seventh Seal,* where the world has gone away and life is bare. We are reminded also of the work of Albert Camus and of Samuel Beckett's existentialist drama *Waiting for Godot.*

EXAMPLE 7–4   "Der Leiermann," Schubert

Und er lässt es ge - hen al - les, wie es will,

dreht, und sei - ne Lei - er steht ihm nim - mer still,

dreht, und sei - ne Lei - er steht ihm nim - mer still.

Wun - der - li - cher Al - te,

soll ich mit dir gehn? Willst zu mei - nen Lie - dern

dei - ne Lei - er drehn?

Mendelssohn and Chopin

Felix Mendelssohn (1809–1847) is a fascinating figure of early Romanticism, both for his music and his personality. His life was completely opposite to the romantic image of the harried, starving composer in a garret, scratching out noble compositions with numb fingers by a flickering penny-candle. His family was as cultured and honored as it was affluent. His grandfather, Moses Mendelssohn, a German-Jewish philosopher, was called "the German Socrates." His father Abraham was a wealthy banker. From his mother he took his first music lessons and imbibed his early love of music.

His natural gifts were immense. Along with a fine appearance and evenness of temper came a natural aptitude for nearly everything he took an interest in. He spoke several languages and was a brilliant conversationalist. His wit was remarkable. He was a classical scholar, could draw very well, and was attracted to chess. Swimming, riding, and dancing came naturally.

His influence in the world around him and after him was great. He revived and performed the works of J. S. Bach, including the *St. Matthew Passion*, which had lain fallow since Bach's death nearly 100 years earlier. He helped to found the

Figure 25.   Drawing of Bach's St. Thomas Church and St. Thomas School at Leipzig, by Felix Mendelssohn. (The Bettmann Archive, Inc.)

Bach Gesellschaft, a society for the publication of the complete works of Bach in an authentic edition.

He not only inaugurated the famous Gewandhaus Concerts but in the same year founded and directed the Leipzig Conservatory. The Conservatory faculty boasted Robert Schumann and the violin virtuoso, Ferdinand David. Mendelssohn's influence as a conductor and pianist was great, and he helped a large number of composers, including Schumann, Berlioz, and Chopin. His gifts matched his material fortune and superior environment. But all this was surpassed by his industry, good will, and modesty.

What, then, about his creative work: the concertos, sonatas, oratorios, and symphonies? The music is refined and polished; the orchestration is superb, with a transparency of texture reminiscent of Mozart. Works like the *"Italian" Symphony,* the last movement of the *Violin Concerto,* and the *G Minor Piano Concerto* have rarely been surpassed for sparkle and luminosity.

Mendelssohn was always careful when it came to writing parts for others to play or sing. Ferdinand David was consulted about the *Violin Concerto* to ensure that the writing for violin was idiomatic and playable. The vocal parts in his oratorio *Elijah* are well within the capability of the average community chorister.

Mendelssohn never would have written the larynx-tearing choruses found in Beethoven's *Ninth Symphony* and *Missa Solemnis*.

"Everything in good measure, nothing in excess," well describes Mendelssohn's music. Everything is clear, rational, and well mannered.

Mendelssohn's music makes good listening. The sounds are always pleasant. But one is seldom if ever shaken and stirred, as by Bach or Beethoven. Perhaps with Mendelssohn music came so easily that it could not become sublime. Or perhaps Mendelssohn revered the great masters too much:

> Don't you agree with me, that the first condition for an artist is, that he have respect for the great ones, and do not try to blow out the great flames, in order that the petty tallow candle may shine a little brighter? *

Frederic Chopin (1810–1849) did not possess the breadth of culture and universal interest of Mendelssohn. He wrote almost exclusively for the piano, at which he excelled. His father was a French tutor who had settled in Poland, and married a Polish girl. Frederick Chopin himself was educated in Poland, but he spent his mature life in Paris and other important cultural centers.

His music as a whole is a compelling composite of Slavic passion and French sophistication. Pieces such as the *"Minute" Waltz* or the *"Black Key" Étude* show the utmost in refined grace and gentility. They are salon pieces pure and simple, glib but impeccably crafted, and very sensitive.

Chopin contributed enormously to the development of piano idioms and of piano technique. In fact, the new role that he established for the piano set a precedent that was to remain until Debussy completely refashioned piano technique in the early twentieth century.

Before Chopin, the literature for solo piano was considerably influenced by that of its forerunner, the harpsichord. Much keyboard figuration in the later piano sonatas of Haydn and Mozart, as well as in the early sonatas of Beethoven, was taken directly from the harpsichord styles. The *Alberti bass*, four-voiced contrapuntal textures, staccato articulations—devices that sound good on the harpsichord—continued as the foundation of much piano figuration and technique in the early decades of the nineteenth century. In fact, there exists a considerable number of keyboard pieces by Mozart, Haydn, and others from the late 1700's that sound good on either the harpsichord or the piano. These were likely performed on whatever keyboard instrument was available at any given time.

The legacy of harpsichord figuration remained until the piano evolved technologically into the paramount keyboard instrument of the nineteenth century. The sustaining pedal had been added as early as 1783, and after 1800 more strings were added, giving the piano greater range. In 1825, the piano's iron frame was

---

* Thomas, Paine, and Klauser, eds., *Famous Composers and Their Works*, Vol. II (Boston, Mass.: J. B. Millet Co., 1891), p. 422. © J. B. Millet Co.

patented by Alpheus Babcock of Boston, Massachusetts, a development that was to lead to an increase in the dynamic power of the piano.

The early Romantics—Schubert, Weber, Mendelssohn, Chopin, and Schumann, along with the mature Beethoven—began to explore the rapidly improving piano in terms of its unique tone color. Beethoven's dynamically surging *Sonata in F Minor, Op. 57, "Appassionata,"* was written in 1804 exclusively for the piano *qua* piano; its textures are thoroughly pianistic. Several of Schubert's *impromptus* and *moments musicaux* require the pianist to produce a "singing" tone, a quality possible on the piano but not on the harpsichord. And many of Schumann's piano works figure among the basic building blocks of the concert pianist's repertoire.

But it was Chopin who most fully tapped the piano's coloristic potential—a potential that was to make the piano the most popular instrument of the nineteenth century both on the concert stage and in the home. Chopin wrote little else but piano music. That he could devote a creative lifetime to piano music alone attests to the technological sufficiency of that instrument at that time.

Chopin matured early, both as a player and composer. The *Piano Concerto in F Minor* (1829), written and performed by him at the conclusion of his studies at the Warsaw Conservatory (just before he left Poland permanently), reveals to the full Chopin's newly evolved pianistic idiom. The 19 year old had already found his style, and he now wrote music that nurtured the emerging voice of the piano.

Of the many pianistic innovations that Chopin introduced into the repertoire, none is more characteristic than his treatment of lyric melody. The solo piano's opening statement in the second movement of the *F Minor Concerto* is typical. High in the piano's upper register the melodic contour shows delicate embellishments. Note how the accompanying harmonies give complimentary support to

EXAMPLE 7–5

the *cantilena* line above; deep single bass tones in the piano provide a reverberant cushion for the melody.

The twenty-four *Études* (1832–1836) of Chopin are amazing in that they provide the utmost technical challenge for the pianist—indeed they are virtually a complete school of pianism—and are at the same time superb compositions in their own right. Useful as they are for instructional purposes, their aesthetic value far outweighs their utilitarian value. The twenty-four *Préludes* (1836–1839), along with the *Études*, represent a compendium of Chopinesque stylistic traits. In the analyses below, note particularly the relationship between accompaniment and lyric melody.

COMMENTARY AND ANALYSIS

Préludes, Op. 28, Nos. 4, 15, 16, 20, and 24, Chopin

Chopin's preludes were composed shortly after his melancholy stay on the island of Majorca with the celebrated woman novelist, George Sand. Schumann admiringly called these preludes "eagle's feathers." Each is independent in mood and expression, yet fits into an ordered plan governing the entire collection. Chopin composed one prelude for each of the twelve major and minor keys. Each major key prelude is paired with a prelude in the key of its relative minor. Thus, the first prelude, in C major, is followed by the second prelude in A minor. The next pair begins a fifth higher—G major and E minor—and so on. Although each prelude is complete in expression and mood, the whole collection is neatly stitched together through the circle of fifths.

PRÉLUDE NO. 4, E MINOR, LARGO (VERY SLOW)

This brief gem is a favorite of the amateur pianist. Easily played, it exhibits the mood of intense pathos that is characteristic of Chopin's later music. Its texture is strictly homophonic: a single-voice melody in the right hand is supported by repeated chords in the left hand.

First listen to the melody throughout. Notice that much of it is repetitive. The first nine notes, for example, use only two basic tones: B and C. Why then is the melody so expressive? It is because of the rich chord progressions in the left hand that add depth and color to the single line above.

EXAMPLE 7-6

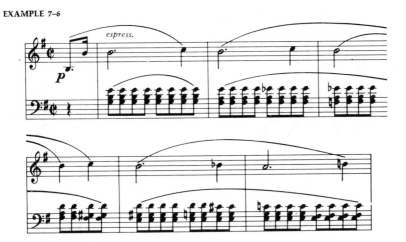

Listen again, this time noting how each successive note in the melody is illuminated by the harmonies beneath it. Watch for the expressive climax that occurs approximately three-quarters of the way through the piece (meas. 17). Here tension builds as the melody stretches itself, hastening its pace to reach the high, climactic note C^2. Near the end, a long rest interrupts the flow, followed by three soft, somber final chords. These chords suggest that the mood need not be over but can echo on and on.

> *Music, when soft voices die,*
> *Vibrates in the memory;*
>
> —Shelley

PRÉLUDE NO. 15, D♭ MAJOR, SOSTENUTO (SUSTAINED)

This prelude is in a simple, ternary (ABA) form. Listen all the way through and notice where each of the three parts begins and ends.

Part A (meas. 1–27)—A lovely melodic line in the right hand is supported by gentle chords in the left. Texture, melodic profile, and the major mode suggest a pastel coloration.

EXAMPLE 7-7

Part B (meas. 28–75)—Key change to C sharp minor darkens the mood.

EXAMPLE 7-8

The melody shifts to the left hand and suggests an ancient modal chant. Two strong climaxes are heard.

Part A^1 (meas. 76–89)—A shortened version of Part A. Back to the major key.

Once you can follow this basic formal scheme, listen for interesting details: for example, the repeated notes in the accompaniment to the melody in both Part A and Part B. Note how in Part A the soft repeated A flat in the left hand is interrupted; its repetitions are irregular, not consistent. By contrast, the same repeated note (now notated as G♯) at the beginning of Part B is repeated in eighth-notes for twelve full measures in the right hand. These hypnotic repetitions, growing in volume, serve to intensify the tragic mood.

PRÉLUDE NO. 16, Bb MINOR, PRESTO CON FUOCO (FIERY AND FAST)

Six strong, dissonant chords, followed by a rest, put the listener immediately on guard; something exciting is about to happen. This prelude creates a single mood of demonic abandon. There are no moments of peace, no contrasts. Do not expect to hear a conventional single-line melody. The pianist's right hand plays nothing but rapid sixteenth-notes, up and down the keyboard, looping in and out. The left hand has a single rhythmic figure that provides tremendous driving force:

EXAMPLE 7-9

Unlike many pieces in which the climax occurs near the three-quarter mark, the climax occurs here only at the very end. As a signal that this climax is near, the left hand stops its gallop-like figure and suddenly joins the right, playing sixteenth-notes. Together, starting very low on the keyboard, both hands climb to the top of the keyboard and then snap off two final chords—dominant to tonic in the middle register.

PRÉLUDE NO. 20, C MINOR, LARGO (VERY SLOW)

Epigrammatic, pithy and bold, this thirteen-measure prelude echoes both Beehoven and J. S. Bach. If there were arpeggiated triplets supporting each melody note, the C minor prelude would resemble the first movement of Beethoven's *"Moonlight" Sonata*. But, whatever its kinship with earlier styles, *Prélude No. 20*, with its sonorous, rich harmony, is pure Chopin. To experience this work fully, one must listen vertically—straight down to the bass line. At measure five, when the music softens for the first time, the bass line becomes particularly interesting. It slips down the chromatic scale, then stretches out for a gentle drop to the tonic note, C, resting quietly in the deepest bass.

The structural pattern of this miniature is simple; there is only one part. The motivic structure is also of the simplest: A five-note rhythmic motive in the soprano is repeated, once for each measure to the end.

EXAMPLE 7–10

PRÉLUDE NO. 24, D MINOR, ALLEGRO APPASSIONATO (FAST AND PASSIONATE)

In this final prelude you should expect to hear a dramatic sweep similar to that of *Prélude No. 16* above. As in No. 16, forward motion is provided by a rhythmic figure in the left hand. This time it looks like this:

EXAMPLE 7–11

These tones outline a spread-out chord. The figure continues throughout the entire prelude. Above it, a clarion-like theme is heard again and again. Scales and arpeggios move up and down the keyboard. Listen for the theme as it enters in several different keys, growing in intensity each time.

Even though Chopin was very careful to allow only his most polished works to be printed, his improvisations for himself or for friends were remarkable. The following passage from *Impressions and Souvenirs* by George Sand shows what one of these improvisations—perhaps the genesis of a masterpiece—was like. Among the listeners was the painter Eugène Delacroix:

> "Go on, go on," exclaims Delacroix, "That's not the end!" "It's not even a beginning. Nothing will come . . . nothing but reflections, shadows, shapes that won't stay fixed. I'm trying to find the right colour, but I can't even get the form. . . ."
> "You won't find the one without the other" says Delacroix, "and both will come together."
> "What if I find nothing but moonlight?"
> "Then you will have found the reflection of a reflection."
> The ideas seem to please the divine artist. He begins again without seeming so, so uncertain is the shape. Gradually quiet colours begin to show, corresponding to the suave modulations sounding in our ears. Suddenly the note of blue sings out, and the night is all around us, azure and transparent. Light clouds take on fantastic shapes and fill the sky. They gather about the moon which casts upon them a great opalescent disc, and wakes the sleeping colours. We dream of a summer night, and sit there waiting for the song of the nightingale. . . .

Schumann

Robert Schumann (1810–1856), in a sense, exemplified traits seen in both Mendelssohn and Chopin. Like Mendelssohn, he was a positive force in musical society. His writing and crusading for better music and performance, his championing of composers with promise such as Brahms and Chopin, and his wit and eloquence remind us very much of Mendelssohn. Like Mendelssohn, he also tried his hand at a wide gamut of compositions: chamber music for many combinations, concerto, opera, symphony, sonata, program music, lieder.

He married the most famous female concert pianist of her century, Clara Wieck. With her and on his own he traveled and brushed elbows with the most important people of his time.

The daughter of the pianist-teacher, Friedrich Wieck, who for several years adamantly opposed her marriage to Robert, Clara was talented both as a pianist and as a composer. Her compositions, extending to twenty-three opus numbers, while consisting mostly of lieder and character pieces for piano, show an astute sense of harmony and a fine ear for pianistic detail. The two scherzos for piano, Op. 10 and Op. 14, exemplify her masterful knowledge of the keyboard; both dazzle technically while avoiding technical display for its own sake—an ideal also held high by Robert Schumann in his own keyboard works.

Clara possessed outstanding creative gifts, but after her marriage in 1840 she used these gifts primarily to further Robert's career. Her immense reputation as pianist helped to gain a sympathetic hearing for her husband's keyboard compositions. Clara premiered the superb *Piano Concerto in A Minor*, Op. 54, as well as the *Piano Quintet in Eb Major*, Op. 44.

In the first year of their marriage, Schumann wrote the incredible number of 121 songs, the finest of these grouped in the cycles: *Liederkreis* (Eichendorff), *Frauenliebe und -leben* (Chamisso), and the *Dichterliebe* (Heine). Such an outpouring of intense composition must be attributed to the long-sought marriage and to the influence of Clara who gave her husband far more than the comforts of the hearth. She eventually bore him eight children and provided the volatile Robert with a much needed steadying force. Her complete faith in his music, her revealing performances of his works, the power of her intellect and creative ability, all these spurred Schumann to great efforts. The two symphonies of 1841, the *"Spring" Symphony* and the first version of the *D Minor Symphony*, Schumann's first important orchestral compositions, were written directly at Clara's urging.

Schumann was extremely emotional and passionate, and his music, like Chopin's, is always pervaded by his personality. The Apollonian reserve of Men-

Figure 26.   Joseph Joachim and Clara Schumann playing a concert in Berlin, by Adolph Menzel. (The Bettmann Archive, Inc.)

delssohn is seldom apparent with Schumann. The prevailing characteristics of his music are intense subjectivity and great diversity of mood. His harmonic vocabulary is much more original and daring than Mendelssohn's. The best work is in the smaller pieces, the short character pieces such as those in the *Carnaval*, Op. 9, the *Kinderscenen*, Op. 15, for piano, or the individual lieder of the cycles *Liederkreis* and *Dichterliebe*. It was in these shorter pieces that the sudden flooding of inspiration that seized Schumann could best be captured. The large musical canvasses, such as the four symphonies, the concertos, and the choral works, suffer somewhat from a certain lack of proportion and sustained intellectual interest. Unlike Mendelssohn, who was at his best in marshalling the components of large works into cohesive, balanced structures, Schumann frequently foundered in large works. Success in large works, where what is done to an idea is more important than the idea itself, requires detachment. This Schumann lacked. For him the ecstasy of the creative moment was supreme.

In this connection it is fruitful to compare Schumann and Brahms relative to their symphonies. We mentioned earlier that Schumann wrote the piano score of the *First Symphony* in four days. Brahms worked on his *Symphony in C Minor* upwards of fifteen years.

Berlioz

The comment about Delacroix, that he was "passionately in love with passion," applies as well to Hector Berlioz (1803–1869). He was a man who could burst into tears at the beauty of a page of his own music, just finished. Here was a man who felt, felt, and then felt some more, always with an ardor and vehemence that was controlled only by his superior intellectual gifts.

No effect was too sensational, no combination of instruments too unusual, if it served to express the volcanic musical ideas that were his. For his *Requiem* he required not only a large symphony orchestra, and a full chorus with soloists, but four extra brass bands placed at the four points of the compass. Obvious in any of his music is the predominance of passion and color.

Like Schumann, Berlioz married a renowned personality, in this case, the Shakespearian actress, Harriet Smithson. Unlike the match of Robert and Clara, however, this marriage was unsuccessful.

His writings were as influential as were Schumann's, and his book on orchestration, *Traité de l'instrumentation*, is still very important and useful.

Berlioz was one of the few romantic composers who was not a virtuoso on any instrument. But he, like Mendelssohn and Wagner, was one of the century's great conductors.

COMMENTARY AND ANALYSIS

Symphonie fantastique, Op. 14, Movements IV and V, Berlioz

This work at times attains huge proportions; the volume of sound generated by the massive orchestra is stupendous. Yet in some sections Berlioz achieves an almost chamber-music-like transparency. The second movement, "A Ball," is the extra movement in the symphony; without it the symphony would follow the usual four-movement scheme. Berlioz wrote the *Fantastique* while in the throes of an undeclared love for the Shakespearean actress, Harriet Smithson. Obviously the symphony is autobiographical, the "young musician of extraordinary sensibility and abundant imagination" being Berlioz himself, and the *idée fixe* (see below) representing Harriet.

The extraordinary feature of the symphony is its prophetic, albeit unconscious, projection of what Freud was to describe seventy years later as wish fulfillment: "If the dream, as this theory defines it, represents a fulfilled wish, what is the cause of the striking and unfamiliar manner in which this fulfillment is expressed? Whence comes the material that is worked up into the dream? What causes many of the peculiarities which are to be observed in our dream thoughts; for example, how is it that they are able to contradict one another?"* In the *Fantastique*, as we experience the psychological dream-saga of the young man, who seeks his beloved, kills her, and suffers the horror of the guillotine and the torments of hell, we feel the peculiarities and contradictions of wish fulfillment as described by Freud. This music makes sense only if we forget previous symphonic models predicated on the conscious, rational mind, and see it as an intuitional probing into the very stuff of the unconscious dream world.

PROGRAMME OF THE SYMPHONY

A young musician of unhealthily sensitive nature and endowed with vivid imagination has poisoned himself with opium in a paroxysm of love-sick despair. The narcotic dose he had taken was too weak to cause death, but it has thrown him into a long sleep accompanied by the most extraordinary visions. In this condition his sensations, feelings, and memories find utterance in his sick brain in the form of melody, like a fixed idea that is ever returning and that he hears everywhere.

MOVEMENT IV—MARCH TO THE GALLOWS

Fourth Movement. The procession to the stake (Allegretto non troppo) He dreams that he had murdered his beloved, that he has been condemned to death

* Freud, Sigmund, *The Interpretation of Dreams*, in *Great Books of the Western World*, Vol. 54 (Chicago, Ill.: Encyclopedia Britannica, Inc.), p. 189.

and is being led to the stake. A march that is alternately sombre and wild, brilliant and solemn, accompanies the procession. . . . The tumultuous outbursts are followed without modulation, by measured steps. At last the fixed idea returns; for a moment a last thought of love is revived—which is cut short by the death-blow.

Introduction (meas. 1–17)   Pizzicato chords in the low strings, ominous rumbles in the timpani, and gutteral sounds in the muted horns immediately plunge the listener into an atmosphere of dread. A portentous crescendo in the sixteenth measure ushers in Section 1 with its macabre first theme.

Section 1 (meas. 17–61)   Although Theme 1 (Ex. 7–12) is extremely simple in intervallic structure, outlining the descending G minor scale, it is nevertheless permeated with a sense of doom.

EXAMPLE 7–12

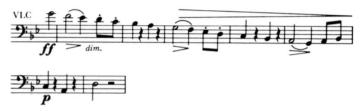

At measure 25 the theme is repeated to the accompaniment of a sardonic *obbligato* in the solo bassoon. The intensity builds and builds until at one point the brass interject a shrieking dissonance.

Section 2 (meas. 62–77)   Ascending scales in bassoons and strings introduce Theme 2 (Ex. 7–13). This theme, carried by the winds and giving a strong impression of the military, perhaps suggests the triumphant march of the forces of political power. We are reminded of the gleeful mobs following the tumbrels as they carried the condemned aristocracy to the guillotine during the French Revolution.

EXAMPLE 7–13

Section 3 (meas. 78–123)   Elements of Theme 2 begin this section. But soon a bizarre version of Theme 1 is heard. Notice how the orchestra chops the theme into little bits, each choir sharing in its descent. Theme 2 returns with increased fury, as does Theme 1. At this point the whole orchestra mounts a cosmic crescendo that crests over into Section 4.

Section 4 (meas. 123–178) The full orchestra, except for percussion, strides majestically down the scale with Theme 1 in the tonic key, G minor. But at measure 130 there is a violent harmonic wrench as Theme 1, in the exotic key of D-flat major, is turned completely about to ascend up the scale in inversion. The feeling of crushing dread continues until a powerful half cadence is heard. Then, in total contrast, the solo clarinet gives out the motive from the *idée fixe*. The head rolls.

EXAMPLE 7–14

The recurrence of the *idée fixe* leaves no doubt that the poet's last thought has been of the loved one.

MOVEMENT V—DREAM OF A WITCHES' SABBATH— WITCHES' ROUND DANCE

Fifth Movement: The Witches' Sabbath (Larghetto, allegro)
He dreams that he is present at a witches' dance, surrounded by horrible spirits, amidst sorcerers and monsters in many fearful forms, who have come to assist at his funeral. There are strange sounds, groans, shrill laughter, and distant yells, which other cries seem to answer. The beloved melody is heard again, but it has its noble and shy character no longer; it has become a vulgar, trivial, and grotesque kind of dance. She it is who comes to attend the witches' meeting. Friendly howls and shouts greet her arrival.... She joins the infernal orgy.... Bells toll for the dead.... A burlesque parody of the *Dies Irae*... is heard at the same time.

This diabolical, maniacal tone-scene is the touchstone for many like pieces of later years. To name a few: Liszt, *Totentanz, Mephisto Waltz*; Tchaikovsky, *Francesca Da Rimini*; Saint-Saëns, *Dance macabre*; Gounod, "Walpurgis Night" from the opera *Faust*; Mussorgsky, *Night on Bald Mountain*; MacDowell, *The Witches' Dance*.

The themes associated with the hellish situation are: first, the *idée fixe*, transformed into a caricature of itself (Ex. 7–15); the theme associated with the Witches' Dance (Ex. 7–16); and a medieval liturgical chant, *Dies Irae* (*Day of Wrath*) (Ex. 7–17).

EXAMPLE 7–15

EXAMPLE 7–16

EXAMPLE 7–17

The *idée fixe* is heard twice and only in the first section. But the Witches' Dance and the *Dies Irae* are scattered throughout, undergoing constant transformation.

Section 1 (meas. 1–39)   The orchestration at the beginning is highly original, setting a mood of leering evil. The muted violins and violas are dispersed through a dissonant chord, while the lower strings play a rising motive. At measure 4, the divided strings slither down a scale to be answered by grumblings in the cellos and basses and *pizzicato* broken chords in the other strings. Later the tempo changes and the disguised *idée fixe* lurches in, madly played by a solo clarinet. As it is about to complete its second phrase, a cataclysmic shout erupts in the full orchestra, as if all hell were egging on the witches with high glee.

Section 2 (meas. 40–126)   It is here that the transformed *idée fixe* sounds complete. The orchestration paints the picture of a hideous, cackling witch. The high Eb clarinet leads (Ex. 7–14). Once the *idée fixe* has run its course, wild chromatic scales in the woodwinds and strings finally plunge down and pause on a half cadence in C minor, the key of the next section. Shooting out of the strings comes the motive soon to be associated with the Witches' Dance (Ex. 7–16). Then cellos, basses, and bassoons fall into the lower depths and pause on a low C.

Section 3 (meas. 127–240)   Bells sound from off stage. The *Dies Irae* theme enters, sounded by low bassoons doubled by tubas. At first it is heard in long note values, but successive repetitions find the chant played by the horns and trombones in shorter note values, then by the woodwinds and *pizzicato* strings in still shorter values. Over a bass drumroll, the Witches' Dance motive returns (Ex. 7–16).

Section 4 (meas. 241–413)   The Witches' Dance is presented as a fugato, with a violent syncopated measure after each entrance of the subject. Later another gigantic buildup leads to what will be one of the main events of the movement: the combination of the Witches' Dance theme with the *Dies Irae*. Transformed versions of the dance sound over and around mysterious harmonies. Much imitation is heard. The crescendo begins at measure 363, and what a crescendo it is! At the peak of its fire, the whole orchestra grinds against itself with a dissonant chord that audaciously anticipates twentieth-century harmony.

Section 5 (meas. 414–524)   Example 7–18 shows how Berlioz combines his two main themes.

EXAMPLE 7–18

Once this has run its course, a much noted passage for the string choir occurs: The violins and violas turn their bows and strike the strings with the wood in a style of playing called *col legno*. The resulting twittering provides background for a new entrance of the Round Dance theme, this time in minor and with trills. Once the Round Dance has finished, we are prepared for the final surging close, but not before the abbreviated *Dies Irae* injects itself into the wild melee once more. For sheer orgiastic abandon these concluding pages of the *Fantastique* have few equals in any art form. One thinks perhaps of the fifteen prints for the *Apocalypse* by Dürer three centuries before or the *Guernica* of Picasso in our time. The end of the movement comes with the whole orchestra stamping and screaming out a new version of the Round Dance.*

* © Copyright 1973, 1974 by Roland Nadeau. All rights reserved. Text reprinted by permission of Crescendo Publishing Co., Boston.

> *Not green leaves were there, but of a dusky color,*
> *Not smooth boughs but gnarled and tangled,*
> *Not fruits but thorns with poison.*
> Dante, *Divine Comedy*, Canto XIV

Other composers

"... *William Tell* is the work of an enormous talent, so much like genius that it might easily be mistaken for it." Thus did Berlioz, the critic, impale Gioacchino Rossini (1792–1868) with his pen. We have already mentioned this enormously successful composer. His many operas are utterly winning, and the best of his comic operas, such as *The Barber of Seville* and *Cinderella*, have all the effervescence of champagne.

The fine *bel canto* operas of Vincenzo Bellini (1801–1835), including the perennial favorite, *Norma,* are distinguished for purity of melodic line and considerable power of characterization.

Gaetano Donizetti's (1797–1848) operas are similar to Bellini's. *Lucia di Lammermoor* is still very popular. The comic opera *Don Pasquale* is all froth and compares very favorably with Rossini's work in a similar vein.

Before moving on to later developments in romantic music we will mention two other Italians and one French composer of considerable influence. Nicolo Paganini (1782–1840) was a concert violinist and competent composer of dazzling concertos for the violin. The high standards that he achieved as a player profoundly affected many Romantics, including Schumann, who, on hearing one of his concerts, resolved to become a virtuoso on the piano.

Luigi Cherubini (1760–1842) worked mostly in Paris, where he was much admired. Beethoven considered him the finest writer for the stage then living. Because his long life straddled rather neatly most of the classical period and nearly half of the romantic century, his music is particularly instructive. Basically, it is classical, with structure and balance primary. But there is also dramatic power and rich harmonic and orchestral color. Among his best works are the *Requiem in C Minor* and the opera *Medea.*

Bizet

Georges Bizet (1838–1875), although best known for his superb opera *Carmen,* produced in the last year of his short life, was responsible for a surprisingly large catalogue of works. The training ground for *Carmen* occurred over a period of nearly twenty years during which he made upwards of two dozen forays into the operatic field. *The Pearl Fishers* (1862–1863) contains charming music, although in it he had not yet attained the dramatic power that was to suffuse *Carmen*.

The *Symphony in C* was written when Bizet was seventeen. Obviously derived stylistically from Mendelssohn and Rossini, and cast in clear classical sonata form, Bizet's youthful fire infused it with the sparkling freshness of invention. The work stands as a masterpiece of its kind. The exotic element later to be found throughout *Carmen* was foreshadowed not only in the third movement of this symphony, but saturated much of his other music, especially the *L'Arlésienne Suite* for orchestra.

COMMENTARY AND ANALYSIS

Carmen, Act 2, Duet, Bizet

Georges Bizet finished his last and ultimately most successful opera, *Carmen*, in 1875, the year of his death. Although he thought it a failure, it was to become an extraordinarily popular work and is now recognized as a masterpiece.

The opera's libretto, done by Meilhac and Halévy from Mérimée's short novel of 1845, *Carmen*, was sensational for its time. The stark realism of the story, rather than the quality of the score, caused early audiences to miss its greatness.

The plot of the opera is simple: Carmen, a seductive Spanish Gipsy, pursues a life of uninhibited pleasure through a philosophy of complete personal freedom. Her flirtation with a young corporal, Don José, leads to his falling madly in love. He deserts from the army, and they become lovers.

Carmen, in the meantime, has caught the fancy of the popular bullfighter, Escamillo, and in turn is increasingly attracted to his glamorous orbit. Finally, when she refuses to go away with Don José, asserting her freedom to love whom she chooses, the corporal kills her.

The scene analyzed below between Carmen and Don José was suggested by the following extracts from Mérimée's novel:

CHAPTER III

I told her I wanted to see her dance; but where are the castanets? At once she took the old woman's only plate, broke it in pieces, and there she was, dancing the *romalis,* clacking the pieces of the plate together as well as if she had castanets of ebony or ivory. One would never be bored with her, I guarantee. . . .

Evening fell, and I heard drums beating retreat. "I must go back to quarters for roll call," I said. "To your quarters!" she cried with an air of contempt. "Are you, then, a slave to let yourself be driven by the whip? You are a real canary in dress and character. Go, you have a chicken's heart!"

Libretto, Act II, Duet   Carmen and Don José at Lillas Pastia's Inn (Free translation by the authors)

Carmen   Je vais danser en votre honneur,
Et vous verrez, Seigneur,
Comment je sais moi-même
Accompagner ma danse!
Mettez-vous là, Don José, je commence.
Lalalala

Carmen   Sit down, Don José. I will dance for you, and I will set the beat myself.
Lalalala (with castanets)

EXAMPLE 7–19   Carmen's Dance Song

José   Attends un peu, Carmen,
Rien qu'un moment, arrête.

Carmen   Et pourquoi, s'il te plaît?

José   Il me semble, là-bas
Oui, ce sont nos clairons
Qui sonnent la retraite;
Ne les entends-tu pas?

Carmen   Bravo! Bravo! j'avais beau faire; il est mélancolique
De danser sans orchestre.
Et vive la musique
Qui nous tombe du ciel!

José   Tu ne m'as pas compris, Carmen,
C'est la retraite.
Il faut que moi,
Je rentre au quartier pour l'appel!

José   Wait, Carmen. Stop for a moment.

Carmen   Please tell me why?

José   I almost think I hear our buglers there—calling us to barracks. Hear them?

Carmen   Bravo for the buglers. I tried hard, but it's frustrating dancing without instruments. Heaven has sent me an orchestra!

José   But Carmen, you don't understand. I have to return to quarters for the roll call.

EXAMPLE 7–20   The Bugle Call

Carmen Au quartier! pour l'appel!
Ah! j'étais vraiment trop bête!
Je me mettais en quatre, et je
Faisais des frais,
Oui, je faisais des frais,
Pour amuser monsieur!
Je chantais! Je dansais!
Je crois, Dieu me pardonne,
Qu'un peu plus, je l'aimais!
Taratata!
C'est le clairon qui sonne!
Taratata!
Il part! il est parti!
Va't'en donc, canari!
Tiens! prends ton shako,
Ton sabre, ta giberne,
Et va't'en, mon garçon; va-t'en!
Retourne à ta caserne!

José C'est mal à toi, Carmen, de te
Moquer de moi!
Je souffre de partir, car jamais,
Jamais femme avant toi,
Aussi profondément n'avait troublé
Mon âme!

Carmen Taratata, mon Dieu! c'est la
Retraite!
Taratata, je vais être en retard!
Ô mon Dieu! Ô mon Dieu! c'est
La retraite!
Je vais être en retard!
Il perd la tête, il court!
Et voilà son amour!

José Ainsi, tu ne crois pas à mon
Amour!

Carmen Mai non!

Carmen Roll call! How stupid I am
to dance for your pleasure! I sang, I
danced, I even think I loved you!
Taratata!
The bugles are calling; run back! Run,
stand and be counted, foot soldier!
Taratata!
Here, don't forget your helmet and your
sword.
Get out boy! Back to your barracks!

José Don't mock me Carmen. It's
cruel. I don't want to leave. No
woman has ever stirred me the way
you do.

Carmen Taratata, O God, it's retreat!
Taratata. I'll be late! He loses his head
and runs. That's how he loves!

José You don't think I can love you?

Carmen No, you can't.

José Eh bien, tu m'entendras!

Carmen Je ne veux rien entendre!

José Tu m'entendras!

Carmen Tu vas te faire attendre!
Non! non! non! non!

José Oui, tu m'entendras!

José Then listen to me!

Carmen I don't want to hear!

José You will listen!

Carmen You'll be late

José Listen!

EXAMPLE 7–21   The "fate" motive is heard as introduction to José's love song
("Flower Song")

English Horn

EXAMPLE 7–22   The "Flower Song"

La fleur que tu m'avais je- té - e

José La fleur que tu m'avais jetée,
Dans ma prison m'était restée.
Flétrie et sèche, cette fleur
Gardait toujours sa douce odeur;
Et pendant des heures entières,
Sur mes yeux, fermant mes paupières,
De cette odeur je m'enivrais
Et dans la nuit je te voyais!
Je me prenais à te maudire,
À te détester, à me dire:
Pourquoi faut-il que le destin
L'ait mise là sur mon chemin?
Puis, je m'accusais de blasphème,
Et je ne sentais en moi-même,
Je ne sentais qu'un seul désir,
Un seul désir, un seul espoir:
Te revoir, ô Carmen, oui, te revoir!

José In prison I kept close to me the
flower that you threw me. Even when
it was dry and shrunken, it kept its
sweet fragrance. For long hours I
closed my eyes, and yet thrilled to
its scent.
And at night I saw you!
I wanted to damn you, to hate you; I
asked: Why had fate thrown you in
my path? I thought I had blasphemed.
But I felt only one desire, one hope
—to see you again! All you need have
done was to look at me to possess me.
Carmen, I was yours. Carmen, I
love you!

Car tu n'avais eu qu'à paraître
Qu'à jeter un regard sur moi,
Pour t'emparer de tout mon être,
Ô ma Carmen!
Et j'étais une chose à toi!
Carmen, je t'aime!

Carmen   Non, tu ne m'aimes pas.

José   Que dis-tu?

Carmen   Non, tu ne m'aimes pas!
Non, car si tu m'aimais,
Là-bas, là-bas,
Tu me suivrais.
Oui, là-bas, là-bas, dans la montagne.
Là-bas, là-bas, tu me suivrais.
Sur ton cheval tu me prendrais,
Et comme un brave à travers la cam-
   pagne,
En croupe, tu m'emporterais!
Là-bas, là-bas, dans la montagne!

Carmen   No, you don't love me.

José   What?

Carmen   No. You can't love me. If you
   did you would come live with me.
   There. Yes, there in the mountains.
   You'd put me on your horse and run
   through the country till we reached
   there, the mountains.

Bizet's setting of the portion of the libretto given above is masterful and inge-
nious. As you listen, be sure to notice, for example, the simplicity of the music for
Carmen's dance—a folk-like melody, an intriguing rhythmic pattern in the castanets, and sparse simple chords in the orchestra (see Ex. 7–19). This effect was
created purposely and for important reasons—Bizet kept it simple in order to
leave space for an important melody that is soon to be added to what is now heard.
Very softly two trumpets (bugles) sound from afar, adding their melody to that
of Carmen's dance (see Ex. 7–20). By combining these two melodies, Bizet juxta-
poses the call of duty with the call of love. José's grappling with the clash of love
versus duty is a dramatic theme, central to the opera; and here it is given explicit
musical expression.

When José is about to heed the call of duty, Carmen becomes furious and the
music for a moment mirrors her anger:

EXAMPLE 7–23

After this listen for the ironic quality of Carmen's melody as it alternates with the pleading tones of Don José's music.

Finally, after a tremendous emotional climax (José's "Listen"), the English horn gives out a melancholy melody (see Ex. 7–21), the opera's fate motive, and José sings the beautiful love aria, "La fleur que tu m'avais jeté" (see Ex. 7–22). The "Flower Song" is lyrical, passionate, and exquisitely scored.

José's final words in the "Flower Song" are: "Carmen, je t'aime." But Carmen's whispered response is: "No, you don't love me!" Again the musical mood must change. Listen for a new rhythmic idea in the orchestra:

EXAMPLE 7–24

This figure generates a gently "cantering" accompaniment to Carmen's melody as she entices José with the prospect of an immediate run to the mountains.

EXAMPLE 7–25

THE LATE ROMANTICS

Liszt

Franz Liszt (1811–1886) is a composer of great importance. He was present and active at the beginnings of Romanticism. At one of his concerts, when he was only twelve years old, he was kissed on the forehead by Beethoven. His first published piece was the "24th variation" from the collection of variations by eminent composers on a theme by Diabelli. This was the same theme that occasioned the masterly effort by Beethoven, *Variations on a Theme by Diabelli,* Op. 120. Liszt later was also square in the middle of the exciting happenings in the time of Wagner, Brahms, and Tchaikovsky.

He was as brilliant a virtuoso on the piano as Paganini was on the violin and as popular a composer as Rossini.

As with Mendelssohn, his was a catholic view; he championed many composers especially Wagner, Chopin, and Berlioz. His personality was pleasant and his intellectual gifts not slight. His music could be as subjective as that of Chopin or Schumann, but it was as brilliant and successful as Mendelssohn's.

His works number into the seven hundreds but are uneven in quality. Pieces of matchless beauty such as the *"Faust" Symphony* and the *B Minor Piano Sonata* are joined by dozens of glittering, depthless potpourris and transcriptions.

Liszt's music had great significance for his day and for later developments. For one thing, his grasp of harmony and form was impressive. With him we find the same richness of modulation and chordal sound as with Wagner. But this is balanced by compression and unity. His large instrumental works often combined all movements into one, as in the *Piano Concerto No. 1. Thematic transformation* was tremendously effective in his hands. The tone poem was developed to perfection by Liszt. Pieces such as *Les Préludes* are highly original and point to Richard Strauss.

Also of importance was his work in national idioms such as the *Hungarian Rhapsodies* and the various pieces with Spanish, Italian, Polish, and Russian flavors. There are curious piano transcriptions of "God Save the Queen" and "La Marseillaise."

In addition to Liszt, there are four other masters of first importance in late Romanticism. They are Richard Wagner (1813–1883), Peter Tchaikovsky (1840–1893), Johannes Brahms (1833–1897), and Giuseppe Verdi (1813–1901).

In discussing the essence of late Romanticism, it is customary to contrast the work of Wagner and Brahms. And it is true that each represented an opposite point of view; the conservative Brahms espoused "Classicism," while Wagner championed the "music of the future."

A bitter controversy in musical aesthetics occurred in the second half of the nineteenth century. The "modernists" on one side espoused the broadening of musical expression to depict ideas, plots, natural phenomena, characterization, etc. Central in this position were Wagner and Liszt. To these men the instrumental tone poem and the music drama for the stage represented the music of the future, an art that would expand its purview until nothing in human experience could withstand its creative power.

At an opposite side were Brahms—the composer of absolute symphonies, concertos, and sonatas—and his powerful supporter, Eduard Hanslick, the Viennese music critic and historian. Hanslick engaged in fierce polemics with the Wagnerites, espousing the cause of "pure" music with words such as: "Music consists of successions and forms of sound, and these alone constitute the subject. . . . whatever be the effect of a piece of music on the individual mind, and howsoever it be interpreted, it has no subject beyond the combinations of notes we hear, for music speaks not only by means of sounds, it speaks nothing but sound."*

While Brahms did not write operas and although Wagner wrote little else, an imaginative juxtaposition of their lives and work is fruitful. It is especially rewarding to compare compositions typical of their individual styles, such as the Brahms *Double Concerto*, an absolute work, and Wagner's *Siegfried Idyll*, a work saturated with poetic reference. Both of these works are analyzed in the commentaries and analyses below.

While a comparison of Wagner and Brahms is fruitful, it is even more valuable to compare Wagner and Verdi as composers of opera and Brahms and Tchaikovsky as symphonists.

Wagner and Verdi

Wagner was a product of the great German operatic tradition by way of Gluck, Beethoven, and Weber. The Italian Verdi followed in the footsteps of Rossini, Bellini, and Donizetti. Both summed up and brought to maturity the respective operatic traditions of their land. Each was an innovator, Wagner in particular scattering significant clues to be followed by Richard Strauss, Mahler, Bruckner, Franck, and the young Schoenberg.

Wagner's career was checked by fantastic turbulence. He considered that it was the greatest of privileges for anybody to know him—and to aid him. He ran up huge debts, seldom if ever paying them back. He was eternally out of funds. He seduced many women, including Cosima, the wife of one of his strongest supporters, Hans Von Bülow. Cosima, whom he eventually married, revered him despite his constant unfaithfulness. He was exiled from Germany because of his overt anti-monarchist revolutionary actions. These included the promulgation of an essay, "The Revolution," an intimate acquaintance with the Russian nihilist revolutionary, Bakunin, and a public declaration asking the king to ". . . declare Saxony to be a free state." His personal and business relationships, in short, were odious, and he got himself constantly caught up in unpopular schemes and ven-

---

* Eduard Hanslick, *The Beautiful in Music*, trans. by Gustav Cohen, ed. Morris Weitz (Indianapolis: The Bobbs-Merrill Company, Inc. The Library of Liberal Arts).

tures. But despite this, such was the power of his personality and genius that many of his intimates stood behind him through every outrage. Ludwig II, king of Bavaria, subsidized him and especially helped in the great venture of the opera house at Bayreuth, all with full knowledge of Wagner's deficiencies. Cosima was so under his spell that she would not leave his body for twenty-four hours after his death.

Besides the magnetic appeal of this narcissist, and besides the immense power of his musical ideas, his idealism must have attracted many to him. His constant championing of better performance standards, especially in singing, his drive for the new opera house, his work with orchestras, and his constant aim to "reform" opera must have appealed greatly. For one performance of *Tannhäuser* he insisted on 164 rehearsals. Such was his perfection and idealism in performance.

Verdi's personal life contrasts vividly with Wagner's. Financial success came rather early, as did fame. Imbroglio was uncommon, although Verdi's republican sympathies did lead him to some political action in his native Italy. After his first wife died, he found a lifemate in his beloved Giuseppina, whom he eventually married. She was a strong force in his life, contributing to the ever deepening current of his creative life. His whole life, though occasionally steeped in shadow, as when his first wife and two children died, was one of steady artistic growth.

What, then, about the music of these two giants, so dissimilar in personality but comparable in genius? Wagner's music clearly follows in the German tradition. The great German masters of the baroque, classical, and early romantic eras had always leaned towards "idea" music, towards what could be done with a theme or a motive. What happened to a melodic idea was more important to them than its own immediate appeal or innate beauty. In the operas of Wagner we see short, trenchant themes—*leitmotifs*—"treated" in the same way that they are in Beethoven symphonies. Tunefulness, of itself, is not the point. Harmony, both in beauty of individual chordal sounds and in scheme of modulation, is emphasized. The harmonic setting of the *leitmotifs* is of paramount importance for the development of the character of the idea. The orchestra becomes symphonic and is often entrusted with melodic elements as important as those heard in the voices. So vital and important is the orchestral part in some of Wagner's works that one sometimes hears portions of these operas in orchestra concerts with the voice part omitted—e.g., the "Liebestod" from *Tristan und Isolde*.

The later operas become more and more homogeneous and organic. Continuous melody supersedes the old division of recitative and aria. The music never seems to end. Cadences do not lead to terminating tonics; instead the music slips on and on. In this continuous, organic aspect of the operas after 1850, such as *Tristan*, the *Ring* Cycle, and *Parsifal*, we are reminded of the "unifying" theories of Darwin and Wallace, who in the 1850's were saying that all life is biologically related and stems from common origins. Jacques Barzun in his book, *Darwin, Marx, Wagner*, says:

...Wagner's pretensions as a dramatist, his friendships with Nietzsche and Gobineau, place him at the heart of the biological and sociological theorizing which sprang from the idea of Evolution.*

In short, Wagner's music is as passionate as it is intellectual, reflecting perfectly Wagner the thinker and Wagner the poet.

COMMENTARY AND ANALYSIS

Siegfried Idyll, Wagner

Dedication to Cosima:
It was your high design, your sacrifice
That gave my work an ample place to grow,
Blessed by you to world-removed silence,
Where now my work's strength has steadily gained,
Transporting hero-world into an idyll,
From distant myths to the beloved homeland.
And now, a call of joy resounded through my songs:
"A son is born"—and Siegfried was his name.

For him and you I could give thanks in music,
Is there a lovelier prize for what you've done?
We always cherished within our home's confines
The quiet joy that now has turned into music.
Unmixed, this joy proved true to us,
Now may it smile friendly on our son,
Whatever we enjoyed in sounding bliss,
May, with your love, to him be open.

(translated by Martin Robbins)

This poem by Wagner showed his deep love and devotion for Cosima, the mother of his infant son, Siegfried. The *Idyll* was first performed on Cosima's birthday, the morning of 25 December 1870, on the staircase of their home in Triebschen bei Luzern. Wagner included several motives from his *Ring* opera, *Siegfried*. As the intertwined themes floated up the staircase to her bedroom, Cosima's recognition of these motives must have affected her deeply. Indeed, the musical quality of the *Idyll* may have pleased her as much as her husband's

---

* Jacques Barzun, *Darwin, Marx, Wagner* (Boston, Mass.: Atlantic-Little, Brown and Company, 1941).

thoughtfulness. The motives selected by Wagner are from the third act of *Siegfried,* the passionate love scene of Siegfried and Brunnhilde; in the *Idyll* they served to express Wagner's loving feelings toward Cosima.*

The orchestra for the *Siegfried Idyll* is modest, especially in the winds. Except for a second clarinet and second French horn, all the winds are single; moreover, there is no percussion. This suggests chamber music, where great volume is not to the point and where the identity of the individual players is more obvious than in the full orchestra.

As you proceed through this work, watch for the many solo passages in the winds and for the clarity of the intertwined melodic lines throughout. The opening idea is presented by the strings, consisting of a cradle-song-like melody in the violins with a second melody in the violas and cellos joining in almost immediately.

EXAMPLE 7-26

---

* Based in part on and reprinted by special permission from Roland Nadeau and William Tesson, *Scores and Sketches: An Anthology for the Listener* (Reading, Mass.: Addison-Wesley, 1971), p. 124.

The winds do not enter until measure 36, when first the flute, then the oboe, and finally the first clarinet add this quiet idea to the melodic materials in the strings:

EXAMPLE 7–27

The music surges and ebbs; new ideas are introduced and briefly explored until measure 91, when the oboe plays an important new theme:

EXAMPLE 7–28

As in the opening theme of the *Idyll,* this melody has the simplicity of a folk song. The next new melodic idea sounds in the first clarinet part:

EXAMPLE 7–29

This theme is developed, and at several points is combined with the first theme.

A climax is reached at measure 255, followed by a quiet and lovely example of tonal imagery, suggestive of a pastoral atmosphere. The second horn holds a long pedal tone in the bass while the first horn plays a new theme, with the clarinet supplying an occasional chirruping motive:

EXAMPLE 7–30

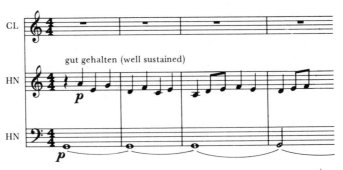

The remainder of the *Idyll* shows melodic ideas, separately introduced, made to blend together, to coalesce. It is in this combining of independent melodic parts that the chamber music quality of the score becomes most apparent.

The *Siegfried Idyll* ends quietly, as it began, with dreamy echoes of previous themes.

EXAMPLE 7–31

Like Wagner, Verdi was also a thinker and he achieved magnificent drama through the force and sweep of his music. The power and dramatic unity of *Rigoletto*, *La Traviata*, *Aida*, and especially *Otello* certainly equal those of Wagner's operas but are arrived at from another direction, that of lyric melody. Whereas Wagner completely transformed opera into music drama, Verdi still worked within the concept of traditional opera and gave it new substance and meaning. It is Wagner's music, not Verdi's, that was called the music of the future, *Zukunftsmusik*.

Italian opera as Verdi found it consisted of a string of lyric numbers—arias, duets, and ensembles—connected by musically static recitatives. The emphases were on tunefulness and display of the bel canto voice. In the hands of masters like Rossini and Bellini, number opera was compelling despite the music's center of gravity unmistakably placed squarely on the vocal line. In the hands of lesser composers, number opera degenerated into showpieces for prominent singers of the time—full of high notes, fury, and spectacle—but signifying little. Verdi took the form as it was, and gradually enriched and ennobled it. His method was simple. Beautiful melody, display of voice, scintillating ensembles, spectacle—all were abundantly present—but the composer never used them at the expense of dramatic truth.

This can be seen clearly in the opera *La Traviata*. Essentially it is a number opera including the basic ingredients found in Italian opera for many years before. The renunciation aria sung by Violetta (Act II, Scene II) displays a kind of sparse, functional accompaniment that served Italian opera well for decades. However, here its simplicity is perfectly fitted to the tragic poignancy heard in the voice part. The aria, "Dite alla giovine" begins with a melody of great purity. When the melody becomes intense with grief, the cellos, playing but two notes below, underline the pathos of the moment. And when the voice part reaches the climactic high note, it is not solely for effect and vocal brilliance, but is a logical culmination of the music.

Verdi never abandoned his emphasis on melody, but the later operas, such as *Aida, Otello*, and *Falstaff*, display a fuller use of the orchestra and an increase in dramatic power.

COMMENTARY AND ANALYSIS

La Traviata, Act III, Verdi

Verdi's drawing-room opera, *La Traviata (The Wayward Woman)*, was written in 1853; it was first performed the same year at Venice. The libretto, by Piave, was based on a novel, *The Lady of the Camelias (Camille)* by Alexander Dumas, son of the celebrated author of *The Count of Monte Cristo* and *The Three Musketeers*. Perhaps because the opera utilized a text reflecting the manners and morals of the urban life of the time (the story was supposedly based on fact), it at first failed with the conservative audiences of the time; only later did it became a standard fixture of the repertory.

La Traviata is the story of Violetta, a young and beautiful courtesan, in the sophisticated Paris of the 1850's. At a party given by Violetta, Alfredo—of the noted Germont family—falls in love with her. Ultimately he takes her away to a small country house outside of Paris. Here they can start a new life, secure in their love.

Giorgio Germont, the father, learns of his son's liaison and visits Violetta while Alfredo is away, pleading with her to give him up. All arguments fail until Germont points out how their liaison can only bring unhappiness to the man she loves in later years; her beauty will fade, love will wane, and no children will bless a union that cannot be blessed by God. Violetta realizes that she stands in the way of Alfredo's ultimate happiness. Desolate, she flees the cottage, leaving a note telling Alfredo that she has gone to her former lover, Baron Douphol.

Later, at a party given by Violetta's friend, Flora, Alfredo confronts Violetta, insults her in front of all, and challenges Douphol, but he is rebuked by his father, Germont, for his conduct.

ACT III

Setting: Violetta's apartment in Paris some time later

The prelude to Act III establishes a melancholy atmosphere appropriate to Violetta's state of mind. As the curtain rises, Violetta, whose health has long been poor, is now very ill. The loss of Alfredo has drastically worsened her condition and she is dying. During a long recitative passage interspersed with orchestral references to the prelude to Act III, the doctor arrives. On leaving, he tells the maid, Annina, that Violetta will live only a few more hours.

A message comes from the senior Germont, telling her that Alfredo now knows of her sacrifice and will soon return to beg her forgiveness. All will be well. She reads his letter aloud.

"Tenesta la promessa . . . La disfida ebbe luogo . . .
Il barone fu ferito, pero mighiora . . ."

"You kept your promise . . . The duel took place . . .
The Baron was wounded, but is improving . . ."

The orchestra plays very softly a melody remembered from the love duet in Act I:

EXAMPLE 7–32

Violetta then says, "It is too late." She looks at the wasted reflection in the mirror, realizes that it is indeed too late for her, and sings the aria, "Addio del passato."

EXAMPLE 7–33

Free translation:

Farewell, happy dreams of yesteryear—already the color in my cheeks is fading. Oh how I miss Alfredo, the love and comfort he gave me! Oh God, forgive me! Grant that I may see you! Now all is ended.

As Violetta's last poignant cry fades, festive music is heard through her window.

EXAMPLE 7–34

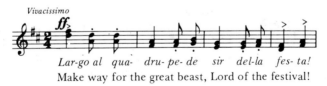

Lar-go al qua- dru- pe- de sir del-la fes- ta!
Make way for the great beast, Lord of the festival!

Revellers enjoying the carnival season pass by on a note of festive joy. Then the orchestra becomes quiet, yet nervous, anticipating Annina's announcement of the arrival of Alfredo. Violetta musters the strength to throw herself into the arms of her lover.

EXAMPLE 7–35

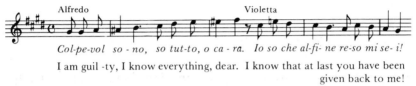

Col-pe-vol so - no, so tut-to, o ca - ra.   Io so che al-fi- ne re-so mi se- i!
I am guil -ty, I know everything, dear. I know that at last you have been
given back to me!

Later, in the tender and lyric duet, *Parigi, o cara,* Alfredo tells Violetta how happy they will be again, away from Paris.

EXAMPLE 7–36

Pa —— ri –gi,o   ca —— ra,   noi la–sce ——re–mo,
Dear, away from Paris   we will find happiness together,

But the excitement is too much for Violetta. She calls for the doctor and in great despair sings, "God! To die so young when I have known such sorrow and when happiness is now so near."

EXAMPLE 7–37

Gran Dio! mo-rir si   gio-vi-ne, io   che pe-na—to ho tan-to!
Oh God!   to die   so young,   I who have suffered so much!

Germont, Alfredo's father, arrives only in time to see that the end is very near for Violetta. His remorse is intense as she sings her farewell.

EXAMPLE 7–38

Se u–na   pu——di—ca   ver—gi——ne,
If   a   lovely   young virgin,   of   your   age,

Violetta continues, "If such a woman, in the full flower of life, gives you her heart, let her be your bride. This is my wish." As the muted strains of the love motive sound in the orchestra (see Ex. 7–32, above), Violetta suddenly revives. But it is only the last surge of life. She dies, joyous, in the hope that salvation is near.

Tchaikovsky and Brahms

A comparison of the work of Brahms and Tchaikovsky is particularly rewarding, especially in the field of the symphony. Both wrote only a few symphonies: Brahms, four (plus two "practice" symphonies, the *Serenades*); Tchaikovsky, six. (The Tchaikovsky *Seventh* is only a reconstruction from very incomplete sketches and should not be used for comparison.) Both lavished their most penetrating musical thoughts on these works, although they followed standard formal procedure with very little exception. The orchestra used by each is also very similar —the cello and French horn figuring prominently in the symphonies of both composers—with Tchaikovsky's being somewhat larger and more colorful.

Each of these composers was strongly influenced by composers of the classical period. Beethoven cast his shadow on both, of course. But with Tchaikovsky, Mozart was of equal importance. A performance of Mozart's opera *Don Giovanni*, heard by the Russian when he was a young man, profoundly influenced him.

> . . . my worship for Mozart is quite contrary to my musical nature. But perhaps it is just because . . . I feel broken and spiritually out of joint, that I find consolation and rest in Mozart's music, wherein he gives expression to that joy of life which was part of his sane and wholesome temperament . . .*

Italian music moved him strongly, too. "There are melodies of Bellini which I can never hear without the tears rushing to my eyes."

---

* Catherine Drinker Bowen and Barbara Von Meck, *Beloved Friend* (Boston, Mass., Toronto, Ont.: Little, Brown and Co., 1937), p. 233.

Beyond a magnetic attraction to the music of Beethoven, Brahms was also influenced by the great baroque masters, Bach and Handel. The many glorious contrapuntal portions in most of his major works attest to this. One need only listen to the finale of the *Fourth Symphony*—said to be based on a passacaglia of Handel—the last portions of both sets of variations on themes of Handel and Haydn, and the magnificent fugues in the *German Requiem* to see this at once.

Figure 27.   Johann Strauss and Johannes Brahms. (The Bettmann Archive, Inc.)

The importance of the influence of early masters becomes clear when we see that both symphonists were concerned with preserving the essence and spirit of absolutism in their symphonies. Tchaikovsky did inject an element of Russian nationalism in his symphonies, and there is a suggested, but very tenuous program in No. 4. But all ten symphonies—Russian and German—use strong classical forms. Occasionally, cyclic technique was used (Tchaikovsky, Nos. 4 and 5; Brahms, No. 3), but this was not entirely original; Beethoven had experimented with cyclic form in Nos. 5 and 9.

The basic problem that both masters faced was in keeping to the classical principles of form while taking advantage of new developments in harmony, instrumentation, rhythm, etc. They had to find new ways to breathe life into the old forms.

The Brahms symphonic style is really leagues away from that of Tchaikovsky, who preferred to dazzle his audience with an impressive array of instrumental color and orchestral gymnastics. Lyric melody as such, often at the expense of other musical factors, is greatly emphasized. This last factor undoubtedly explains Tchaikovsky's great popularity with concert audiences and the ease with which his music wins new friends among the uninitiated. As mentioned above, Tchaikovsky took full advantage of the rising tide of Russian nationalism that occurred in the latter half of the nineteenth century and wrote into his symphonies either real folk songs and dances or simulated ones.

Brahms occasionally dazzles, but only incidentally. Whereas Tchaikovsky arouses emotions rather easily through the means mentioned above, Brahms seems to invite thought first, which then leads to emotional response. He therefore concerns himself very little with sheer sound for its own sake or with striking instrumental combinations. What he is interested in is musical idea, beauty of form, evolution of idea, depth and richness of textures. On first hearing a Brahms symphony, the neophyte often is puzzled; there is so much to hear all at once that he tends to hear little. Overall patterns are so masterfully woven and on such a titanic scale that the beginning listener is lost. Brahms is a great master of musical understatement, while Tchaikovsky appeals directly to the listener with either high rhetorical flourish or hypersensitive lyricism.

Brahms' music makes friends slowly but surely. His style is oblique, reserved, and thoughtful. The style of Brahms is like the discourse of a great philosopher-orator who rises to the heights of passion through the accumulating force of his ideas and the fervor of his idealism. Tchaikovsky's music wins rapport immediately. His symphonic style is brilliant, hotly emotional, passionate in the immediate sense. The sounds pour out of a Tchaikovsky symphony like lava spurting from a crater.

COMMENTARY AND ANALYSIS

Concerto for Violin and Violoncello in A Minor,
Op. 102, Brahms

MOVEMENT I.   SONATA-ALLEGRO FORM, ALLEGRO

Listen all the way through once or twice for continuity before listening for details. Your overall reaction may well be that here we have important serious music expressed through a logical structure. Individual themes, harmonies, and rhythmic ideas create an aura of romantic subjectivity, but they are nevertheless always subject to the requirements of structure.

This is characteristic of Brahms. Writing at a time when subjective romanticism was predominant, he wished to apply the still-living principles of classical form to advances in subjective content. There is no doubt that Apollo reigns; musical reason prevails. Perhaps this is what Clara Schumann felt when she wrote in her diary on September 20, 1887, ". . . it often seems as though he [Brahms] took delight in depriving the listener of absolute enjoyment."

After a short, strong statement in the orchestra, a cadenza is heard. Cello and violin enter successively, each stating highly idiomatic ideas before combining. Thus opposition between the powerful mass of the orchestra and the individuality of the soloist is established early, and this concept is used throughout.

Listen again to the orchestral opening followed by the cadenza. Is there not passion in the solo parts? Does not the emotional sweep of the cello and violin represent the essence of romantic subjectivity? Yet Brahms with this cadenza adheres faithfully to formal principles of the classical concerto. Solo cadenzas are normal in the first movements in concertos by Mozart, Haydn, and Beethoven. But they occur at the end of the movement, showing the performer's technical brilliance and providing a dramatic peak. Subsequently, early romantic composers—Schumann and Mendelssohn—experimented significantly with classical first movement form in certain solo concertos. For one thing, they eliminated the classical double exposition in which the orchestra stated all the themes first, then being joined by the soloist for a second presentation of this material. Instead, both orchestra and soloist now presented the exposition material together, just once. In addition, these composers were dissatisfied with placing the cadenza at the end, perhaps because its showy brilliance tended to break apart the unity of the whole movement.

As we have seen, Brahms introduces his soloists in a cadenza after just four measures of strong orchestral statement. Thus, the expressive power of the solo violin and cello immediately confronts the massed orchestra—after which they proceed in dramatic interplay.

Theme 1 is fully stated only after the soloists' cadenza. It is shaped from strong, short Beethoven-like motives. It is played by the orchestra alone, i.e., without the soloists.

EXAMPLE 7–39

A transitional idea in a contrasting key (F major) appears in the strings. You can recognize it by the syncopated, repeated notes of its motive.

EXAMPLE 7–40

The second theme is lyric and graceful.

EXAMPLE 7–41

The development (meas. 218) chiefly uses elements from Theme 1 and from Examples 7–39 and 7–40 above. Theme 1 complete, in the tonic (A minor), in full orchestra, signals the recapitulation (meas. 290).

MOVEMENT II.   TERNARY FORM (ABA), ANDANTE, D MAJOR

This is Brahms at his warmest. There is a mellow quality to the easy flowing principal melody. But, as always, Brahms' emotion is tempered by the philosophical detachment of the composer/scholar, whose destiny was to carry on the classical tradition. Brahms said, "If we cannot write as beautifully as Mozart and Haydn, let us at least write as purely."

The movement begins with a halting, two-note motive played twice by the winds (Part A). These are the first four notes of the main theme. Violin and cello play it together, backed by the string choir, then by the woodwinds.

EXAMPLE 7–42

Part B (meas. 30) displays a new melody, gentle and chorale-like, initiated by the woodwinds. There is a crescendo towards the close of Part B leading to a brief cadenza in both solo instruments. Note the double stops that enrich the sound of the solo violin.

Part A returns (meas. 79), but modified. Watch for subtle changes in the profile of Theme 1, as well as a changed accompaniment in the orchestra. About half way through this return, a suggestion of the materials from Part B effects a thematic synthesis.

MOVEMENT III.   RONDO FORM, VIVACE NON TROPPO, A MINOR

The rondo follows this structural pattern: A-B-A-C-A-B-A (coda).

A—*Refrain*   The cello leads with a lively "Gipsy" tune. A little later the violin plays it, and later still the full orchestra does it, *fortissimo* (meas. 40).

EXAMPLE 7–43

B—*Episode 1*   (meas. 69) The cello leads with a new theme (C major) featuring double stops. Shortly the violin enters, imitating this theme.

A—*Refrain*   (meas. 101) Variation of the "Gipsy" tune. Bassoon and oboe join in.

C—*Episode*   (meas. 98) Quite long, featuring two new themes in the "Gipsy" style. The first (meas. 98) is dance-like and fiery, while the second (meas. 148) is lyrical.

A—*Refrain*   (meas. 218) Similar to the initial refrain, but with modifications near its end.

B—*Episode*   (meas. 273) Varied, and now in the tonic major (A major).

A—*(Coda)*   (meas. 297) A disguised version of the "Gipsy" tune begins in the woodwinds, while the soloists provide florid figures for background. The end is very bold, the soloists clearly in the lead.

Brahms liked Hungarian music. The *Hungarian Dances* for piano duet (later transcribed for orchestra) rival the *Hungarian Rhapsodies* of Franz Liszt for dash and brilliance. His early *Variations on a Hungarian Theme*, Op. 21, for piano and the late *Gipsy Songs*, Op. 103, attest to a lifelong interest in Hungarian music. That his interest ran very deep is shown by his devoting whole movements in some of his most serious works to the "Gipsy" style. The finales to his *Second Piano Concerto*, to the *Violin Concerto*, and to the *Double Concerto*, all are written in this style.

Characteristic of Brahms is that he yokes the volatile tunes and harmonies of the *Double Concerto* to a traditional form, the classical rondo. Although the content is light and colorful, a firm musical logic prevails.

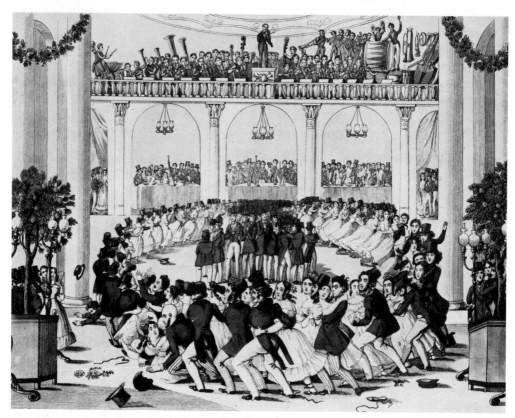

Figure 28. *The Great Gallop by Johann Strauss,* by Johann C. Scholler. (Osterreichische Nationalbibliothek)

Johann Strauss, Jr.

The life of Johann Strauss the younger (1825–1899) is interesting not only because of his music, but because he was part of a musical family important to the development of nineteenth-century music. His father, the composer Johann Strauss the elder (1804–1849), had popularized the Viennese waltz genre; and his two brothers, Josef and Eduard, were also well-known composers.

The waltzes, polkas, galops, quadrilles, and mazurkas of the several Strausses were heard at a time of splendor and prosperity in imperial Vienna, reflecting the brilliance of the later Hapsburg court. Elegant and charming waltzes by Johann Strauss, Jr., such as *The Blue Danube,* Op. 314, and *Wine, Women and Song,* Op. 333, reflected the hedonism of the Viennese public. Great numbers of the Viennese danced to the intoxicating sounds of the Strauss orchestra. A century before, in the day of Haydn and Mozart, cultivated music was practiced and appreciated mostly by the educated nobility. In Vienna in the 1800's, good music could now be enjoyed by a prosperous and pleasure-seeking middle class. And precisely because this was a pleasure-seeking public, the music of the Strausses was light and entertaining. The waltzes and polkas were danced through the night, always with great enjoyment. The Viennese enjoyed their dance evenings and operetta outings in the same spirit as they took coffee and cake at favorite coffee houses.

Although the Strausses produced exactly what the public wanted—light, happy music—a close look at much of this music, especially that of Johann Strauss, Jr., shows high standards of musical taste and craftsmanship. His best music shows sophisticated rhythmic accents, subtle harmony, exquisite orchestration, and a charming melodic lilt. Strauss's operettas, *Die Fledermaus* (*The Bat*) and *Der Zigeunerbaron* (*The Gipsy Baron*), two of his finest scores, remain staples of the repertory to this day.

The mighty handful—"The Five"

Mikhail Glinka (1804–1857), the composer of the opera *A Life for the Tsar*, was the founder of the Russian nationalist school that was to inspire *The Five*.

The Five were a group of Russian composers who worked to create a National Russian School of music. They were: Alexander Borodin (1833–1887), Cesar Cui (1835–1918), Mily Balakirev (1837–1910), Modest Mussorgsky (1839–1881), and Nicolai Rimsky-Korsakov (1844–1908). Together they sought a new way in Russian music. Through their compositions, published articles, and teaching they fought the conservative academic establishment and resisted mightly all European musical influences that they deemed inappropriate. This European musical ethic was well represented by the brothers Anton and Nicholas Rubenstein, composer/pianists and educators. The music of *The Five* was saturated with Russian historical themes and myths as well as with folk song, folk dance, and Orthodox chant. The Russian peasant figured strongly in their works as in the literary works of the novelists Gogol and Tolstoy. All were intensely interested in Russian political life, especially as it pertained to reform. The liberation of the serfs in 1861 affected them profoundly. And their sympathies were not passive. For example, Rimsky-Korsakov published a letter criticizing the too stringent police supervision of his students at the St. Petersburg Conservatory and, because of this, was dismissed from the faculty.

Balakirev was the group's spiritual leader and mentor; his was the catalystic personality around which the others gathered. Balakirev had known Glinka, and was intimately acquainted with his music, spending several years editing the older master's works. Through his travels to the Caucasus, Tiflis, and Baku, he collected many folk songs and later built colorful compositions around them. Many of these, for example the piano piece titled *Islamey* and the symphonic poem *Tamar*, show a decided oriental cast, a characteristic which often appeared in the music of the members of the Mighty Handful.

Balakirev's personality was very strong, perhaps even overbearing. He not only encouraged his nationalistic disciples in their new directions but involved himself in their actual compositions—rewriting, correcting, approving, disapproving. Though this inevitably led to friction, the artistic autocracy of Balakirev was beneficial. This was especially so in the early stages of the group's association when he was the only one with something like professional credentials. For Cui, Borodin, Mussorgsky, and Rimsky-Korsakov music at that time was little more than a passionate avocation. Cui, Rimsky-Korsakov, and Mussorgsky were in the military, while Borodin was a scientist. These gentlemen-composers, involved professionally in the non-musical social fabric of their day, gifted musically but unrefined technically, drew their inspiration from the mind and hand of the better trained Balakirev. Two of them, Cui and Borodin, attained eminence in the non-musical world. Borodin became a professor of chemistry and did important research in this field producing a treatise called *Researches on the Fluoride of Benzol*. When away from the lectern or laboratory, or when on summer vacation, he developed a rich lyric style of composition. In the larger works such as the *Symphony No. 2 in B Minor*, and the opera *Prince Igor*, he attained considerable dramatic power. *Prince Igor*, along with Glinka's *A Life for the Tsar* and Mussorgsky's *Boris Godunov*, form a great triptych of Russian nationalistic opera, each based on early Russian historical themes. In scope, and in their illumination of Russian character, they are comparable to the novels *Dead Souls* by Gogol, *War and Peace* by Tolstoy, and *The Brothers Karamazov* by Dostoevsky. Cui was an army officer, and became an authority on military fortifications, lecturing on the subject at the Artillery School and the Staff College. (One of his charges was the Emperor Nicholas II.) Cui is generally considered to have been the least gifted, musically, of *The Five*. His articles for periodicals both in Russia and in Western Europe brought attention to the work of the Nationalists. Thus both Borodin and Cui led polarized professional lives, attaining considerable influence in the academic sciences as well as in the world of music. In the following chapter, the life and work of the pioneer American composer Charles Ives will offer an interesting parallel. Of *The Five*, the name most familiar to the layman is that of Rimsky-Korsakov. Of aristocratic birth, he spent 7 years at the Naval College in St. Petersburg and became an officer. In 1861 he met Balakirev and resolved to improve his talents in composition. His first symphony was written during a three-year naval cruise (with the constant supervision by mail of Balakirev) and was performed to considerable public acclaim in St. Peterburg in 1865. On his return, Rimsky-Korsakov resumed his musical studies and, several years later, was appointed professor of composition and instrumentation at the St. Petersburg Conservatory.

Despite his late start, Rimsky-Korsakov ultimately became the finest craftsman among the Nationalists, excelling particularly in the art of orchestration. The canvas of his orchestra abounds in a riot of exotic coloration. His *Principles of Orchestration* (1896–1898) is still valuable for students of that art.

The *Russian Easter Overture, Scheherazade* and the *Spanish Capriccio* are familiar and much applauded by concert audiences. In them is found an artful and exotic mixture of melodic, rhythmic, and harmonic elements ensconced in a lush instrumental setting. Less well known, but deserving of attention are his several operas. Certain portions of these, such as "Hymn to the Sun" from *The Golden Cockerel* or the "Flight of the Bumblebee" from *Tsar Saltan*, are well known. But *The Golden Cockerel*, based on a fairy tale by Pushkin, and the little known opera *Mozart and Salieri* are seldom heard in the West.

Without question, the composer among *The Five* with the most impressive gifts was Modest Mussorgsky. He must rank as a major figure in romantic music, especially in the areas of musical irony and realism.

Mussorgsky's life was often in disarray, his personality disordered and unbalanced. As a young man he was a member of the Regiment of the Guards, and later entered the Civil Service, progressing fitfully through its ranks. As were the other disciples of Balakirev, he was largely self-taught. His music is thoroughly original, often twentieth century in its use of fresh sounds. Because his harmony, rhythm, and melody are often deliberately inelegant and primitivistic—strongly anti-Western—many believed his work to be uncouth and crude. In fact, it was Rimsky-Korsakov who "refinished" Mussorgsky's powerful opera *Boris Godunov*, and it was in that revised version that most of the western world first heard it. But his music is not crude. Rough hewn, realistic, yes; but not crude. In 1863 he and several young intellectuals shared a "commune" apartment in St. Petersburg where they ardently discussed artistic, political, and religious ideas. Mussorgsky's later artistic credo, formed in part through his years in the "commune," contained within it a disdain for surface polish and formal beauty in musical forms; a total repudiation of art for art's sake. He said, ". . . art is a means of communicating with people, not an aim in itself." With some peasant blood in his veins, he identified strongly with the peasants' aspirations. The massed peasant scenes in *Boris Godunov* form a powerful social undercurrent to the drama, symbolizing the composer's awareness of the incipient power and drama to be found in the masses. Among his popular works is a programmatic suite for piano entitled *Pictures at an Exhibition*, often heard in the orchestral transcription by Ravel. Suggested to the composer by a posthumous exhibition of the drawings and water colors of his friend, the architect Victor Hartmann, the individual items of the suite typify Mussorgsky's artistic stance. They communicate easily; they are vividly ironic and very naturalistic. Several of the "pictures" are introduced by little transition pieces called "Promenades," representing the composer in his tour of the exhibition. Subject matter of the pictures varies considerably: There is the sinister "The Hut of Baba Yaga," a sentimental love ballad, "The Old Castle," a tender scene of French children at play called "Tuileries," and the superb finale, "The Great Gate of Kiev." The songs cycles, *Songs and Dances of Death, Sunless,* and *The Nursery,* show Mussorgsky to have had tremendous psychological insight in areas highly diverse in mood and content. *Night on Bald Mountain* for orchestra is craggy and uncompromising in its exploration of the bizarre.

Chapter eight

EARLY TWENTIETH CENTURY

IN TRANSITION: POST-ROMANTICS, IMPRESSIONISTS, PRE-MODERNS

The music produced in the waning years of the nineteenth century until the close of World War I is marked by diversity and flux. These few years linked two periods strongly contrasted in essence and manner—the Romantic and the Contemporary. In this time can be seen the dying yet still glowing embers of true Romanticism itself. Post-Romantics such as Mahler, Richard Strauss, the young Schoenberg, Sibelius, and Rachmaninoff gazed back to an ebbing age and refused to let it die. Much of their music is possessed of a ripeness very near decay.

During these years Impressionism arrived on the musical scene. Its prime mover was a genuine master, Claude Debussy. But Impressionism as a movement was short lived. Its concern with and constant search for fresh sound was soon trampled under by the strident, urgent outcries of contemporary music.

While the fruit of Romanticism had ripened on the bough and Impressionism was briefly flowering, contemporary music had actually germinated and its new growth could plainly be seen. Very early, even before Impressionism, the Connecticut iconoclast Charles Ives, with works such as the *Variations on "America" for Organ* (1891), anticipated by thirty years important techniques of composition. In this particular piece Ives wrote a perfect example of polytonality. Here the composer foreshadowed a technique that was to be explored by Milhaud and others much later.

Schoenberg's *String Quartet No. 2* (1907–1908) featured a finale almost completely atonal. Tonality, the bed rock of all music for hundreds of years, was all but banished in this movement.

Stravinsky, in the years 1910–1913, electrified the world with three ballets:

Firebird, Petrouchka, and *The Rite of Spring.* The powerful dissonances and nervous rhythmic patterns were in stark contrast to the shimmering sounds of Debussy and Ravel.

The whole period is remarkable because of this overlap of styles.

Late Romantics, such as Puccini and Rachmaninoff, lived through the two decades of Impressionism and well into the contemporary period while retaining the essential musical elements of a perished romantic age. Simultaneously, as early as the 1890's, the seeds for contemporary music were slowly but firmly taking root.

Post-Romanticism

Four post-Romantic composers must be discussed when considering the transitional period from romantic music to contemporary music. They are Richard Strauss (1864–1949), Giacomo Puccini (1858–1924), Gustav Mahler (1860–1911), and Jan Sibelius (1865–1957). Each wrote important works in the late nineteenth century, yet lived well into the twentieth century. And though certain aspects in their music are contemporary—for example, the realism in the operas of Puccini and Strauss—their basic outlook is that of the nineteenth century. We find again the emphasis on beauty of melody and sound. We find also the grand, sometimes bombastic, gesture. We find the same concern for the subjective, personal, passionate, and intimate. Strauss and Puccini achieved notable success with opera; Mahler and Sibelius concerned themselves chiefly with symphony.

Richard Strauss

It was perfectly natural that Richard Strauss, the son of a leading horn player in the Munich opera, should have taken to opera. His father had known and worked with Wagner. It was inevitable that the creator of *Tristan und Isolde* and *Die Meistersinger* would cast his shadow over the young man. At any rate, his three best-known operas, *Salome, Elektra,* and *Der Rosenkavalier,* carry on the Wagnerian tradition through the dramatic use of voices, the large symphonic orchestra, and the use of the continuous style of melody.

An added element in these works, not usually found in Wagner, is the hyper-realism of the score. *Salome,* for example, originally a play by Oscar Wilde, is set with every detail of its gory plot minutely described by the music. When Salome offers the "Dance of the Seven Veils" for Herod, the music builds to an orgiastic frenzy, giving an insight into her thinking. A theme associated with John the Baptist is suddenly heard. After the dance, Salome asks for his head on a silver platter. The orchestra then glimmers with a macabre silvery sheen.

Besides opera, Strauss also wrote stunning, extravagantly detailed tone poems.

Figure 29.   Richard Strauss (left) in Bavarian Alps, 1903. (Culver)

Till Eulenspiegel is a humorous musical tale based on an early German fable. *Don Juan* and *Don Quixote*, though less uproarious, are similar in concept, while *Death and Transfiguration* and *Also sprach Zarathustra* are deeply philosophical.

Puccini

While Strauss followed in the steps of Wagner, Puccini carried on in the tradition of Verdi. Unlike Wagner, who stressed the role of the orchestra in his operas, Verdi took the typical Italian view that voice and melody are primary. All Verdi, then, is a glorious manifestation of how well the human voice can sound and how beautiful melody can be. Puccini, like his great predecessor, revered melody and the voice. His highly effective operas, including *La Bohème, Tosca,* and *Madama Butterfly,* are redolent with the melodic fragrance that has always permeated musical Italy. As in Strauss, there is great realism, a tremendous feeling for effective dramatic theater.

The Puccini orchestra is always colorful, full, luxuriant. While never impinging on the primacy of the voice parts, Puccini's harmony is highly refined, often suggesting French impressionistic coloring and sensitivity. Because Puccini often used the *leit-motif* technique, his operatic style can be regarded as a synthesis of Italian, French, and German traditions.

Mahler

In the nine titanic symphonies of Mahler can be seen the last fruit of the German symphonic tradition. This tradition began in the later 1700's and brought forth such supreme masters of the form as Haydn, Mozart, Beethoven, Schubert, Mendelssohn, Schumann, Bruckner, and Brahms.

A deep, soul-searing musical sentiment organized through grand, cohesive structural design permeates the Mahler symphony. The tonal canvas is almost always massive. Not only are these works very long, but the forces used are sometimes enormous. For example, the *Symphony No. 8,* the "Symphony of a Thousand," employed at its first performance a chorus of 850 voices, 8 soloists, and an orchestra of 146.

Mahler, like Berlioz, was enchanted with the sound of the human voice in the symphony. In the words of Salazar, "Mahler moved from song to symphony, just as the acorn engenders the oak. In a simple melody, in a children's popular song, Mahler heard the musical murmurings of the cosmos."[*] The *Symphony No. 1* contains folk-like melodies taken from his earlier song cycle, *Songs of a Wayfarer,* while the *Second, Third, Fourth,* and *Eighth* symphonies all employ vocal forces— chorus and/or soloists. There was precedent for this: We have already mentioned the voices in Beethoven's *Ninth.* Even Mendelssohn had contributed a sort of hybrid symphony-cantata, the *Hymn of Praise;* and Berlioz used chorus and soloists in his *Romeo and Juliet Symphony.* But there is a significant difference between Mahler's use of the human voice within the vast panorama of his symphonic thought and its use by his predecessors. Beethoven in the *Ninth* saw the voice as the necessary intensifying medium for the achievement of the ultimate statement of his philosophy. The human quality of the voice was a perfect tool to express the sentiments of brotherhood, love, and universality found in the Schiller

---

[*] Adolfo Salazar, *Music in Our Time* (New York: W. W. Norton and Company, Inc., 1946), p. 55.

text. Berlioz' use of chorus and soloists in the *Romeo and Juliet Symphony* stems from his concern with dramatic content. What better plan than to use important sections of Shakespeare's play in a thoroughgoing integration with symphonic style?

With Mahler, however, it is the microcosmic lied itself that provides spiritual motivation. Unlike these other masters, Mahler came on the scene after a large body of lieder had developed. Schubert, Schumann, and Brahms had evolved the lieder cycle to the point where it had become one of the major forms of the romantic century. These songs represent the very quintessence of the personal and subjective. They directly embody the intimate, poetic, and lyric—traits of basic importance to Romanticism as a whole. Mahler, whose primary characteristic in his music is that of intense subjective statement—the total expression of the self —grasped the importance of the folk and art song as the agent for "humanizing" the symphony. His extraordinarily agonized personal involvement in the very web of the music can best be understood by his own words written on the score of the unfinished *Tenth Symphony*, "Madness seizes me, accursed that I am— annihilates me, so that I forget that I exist, so that I cease to be. . . ." As one listens to the symphonies, shot through with tortured, spasmodic passages, searing climaxes, frenetic exultations, and mystic murmurings, these words come true. And always, song is very near, not only actual quotations, but in the very heart of all his lyric moments. The first melody from the Adagietto movement of the *Fifth Symphony* is a perfect example of the pervading lyricism in the symphonies. It throbs with the bittersweet poignancy of old Vienna and the travail of a troubled soul.

Sibelius

Jean Sibelius, another post-Romantic whose major contribution has been in the symphony, is different. Whereas Mahler is ultra-passionate, super-emotional, Sibelius is spare, incisive, granitic, frequently sober. Mahler's music occasionally makes jokes, especially in the scherzo movements and in the delicious Finale of the *Fourth Symphony*. Sibelius's music never laughs.

The prevailing spirit comes about through a blend of Finnish nationalism with powerful classical structures, the whole tempered by a romantic sensitivity to sound and texture. While Sibelius denied using actual folk songs in his symphonies, melodies such as the one below strongly suggest the hardiness and sturdiness of north European folk song and dance.

EXAMPLE 8-1 OB CL. *Symphony No. 2, Mvt. I, Sibelius*

One does not find extreme modernity in the basic structural elements of the music of Sibelius; melodic, harmonic, and rhythmic materials are within the romantic idiom already explored. Certainly Berlioz and Mussorgsky had handled rhythm much more freely. Wagner's modulations are vastly more adventuresome than those of Sibelius; and the fresh vertical sonorities of his contemporaries, Debussy, Ravel, Mahler, R. Strauss, far outstrip anything from his pen. As noted above, his forms were those from the past: symphony, symphonic poem, concerto, chamber music, and the song. But, despite Sibelius' non-innovative approach to both inner materials and overall form, there is a very special quality in his work. The unique Sibelius mix of musical elements results in high originality: the way in which the forms are handled. No matter what the overall structure at hand, sonata-allegro, ternary part form, rondo, etc., he achieves something different, something entirely viable and logical.

The manner in which the composer manages motives and themes within developmental structures will illustrate this. Like Beethoven and Brahms, Sibelius does the most with the least. His melodic materials within the sonata pattern tend to be incisive and sparse. It is what they ultimately become that makes them interesting. Through a rigorous logical procedure Sibelius makes these ideas grow, burgeon, catch fire. But his musical logic is not "classical." Rather than present an ordered sequence of themes, separated by fluid transitional passages and followed by a development section as in the symphonies of Haydn, Mozart, Schubert, and Mendelssohn, Sibelius follows the lead of Beethoven in the first movement of the "Eroica" Symphony. Transitions are vitalized and expanded, becoming much more melodic so that the distinction between transition and theme is blurred. One is hard put to segmentize these forms into themes, transitions, expositions, codas, etc. Relations are totally organic; all elements are vital. There is no padding. In the process of achieving this logical mix of organically related structural materials, Sibelius often reversed the traditional developmental procedure. His method is deductive rather than inductive. Rather than present a well ordered succession of full-blown themes, then proceed to explore their inner motivic structure, Sibelius first exposes plain, concise thematic ideas which ultimately are transformed into themes of high lyric intensity. The emotional climate established at the outset is one of expectancy: Something is being groped after, something will unquestionably be grasped, stated, and understood in proper time. The structural method of Sibelius does suggest Beethoven and Brahms, but the sound and texture is utterly different from that of any previous composer. It is unique.

Perhaps in no other way is it more unique than in orchestral timbre. The instruments used, both in kind and number, are not different from what came before, in the romantic period. Sibelius' instrumentation is standard, but his orchestration is not. Orchestral coloring is of a somewhat dark, somber cast, yet it is clear and bold. The low winds in choir are much in evidence giving the texture an organ-like solidity. And it is not only the bass and tenor winds that heavily anchor the total sound; soprano instruments such as the oboe and clarinet often are made to plunge to the lower limits of their range. In these lower registers they give out a plaintive, nostalgic sound suggestive of the dark forests and somber landscape of Finland. Thus the structural materials of Sibelius' craft are traditional while the resulting sound and sense of the music in fresh and unique. What were the forces in the composer's life that helped to shape his powerful, introspective musical personality?

Sibelius was born at Tavastehus, Finland, in 1865. Born to a well-to-do family, he was given a classical education. He studied law at Helsingfors University, but like Schumann and Tchaikovsky who had also studied law, the magnetism of music soon drew him away from a career in the safe professions. He studied music with Wegelius in Finland, and with Carl Goldmark, the Viennese composer of the well-known *Rustic Wedding Symphony*. In 1897, Finland, at that time under the domination of Russia, keenly aspired for national independence, and recognizing in the young artist a strong voice for cultural selfhood, gave him a life grant. Appropriately enough, Sibelius is probably best known today for his nationalistic tone poem, *Finlandia*.

Except for sorties abroad and to other parts of Finland, Sibelius spent many of his creative years with his family at his country home in Jarvenpää. He held great veneration for the Finnish national epic, the *Kalevala*. Within the seclusion of the hardy but idyllic countryside, it was natural that the twilight moods of this immense saga should permeate his music. Among his works directly suggested by the *Kalevala* are: The *Kullervo Symphony*, *The Swan of Tuonela*, *Pohjola's Daughter*, and *Lemminkainen's Journey*.

> *In the cold my song was resting,*
> *Long remained in darkness hidden.*
> *I must draw the songs from Coldness,*
> *From the Frost must I withdraw them.**

COMMENTARY AND ANALYSIS

Symphony No. 2 in D Major, Op. 43, Sibelius

The *Second Symphony* was written in 1902 while Sibelius was on an extended trip to Italy. There is a pastoral quality in much of this work, perhaps reflecting the

---

* W. F. Kirby, trans., *Kalevala or Land of Heroes* (New York: E. P. Dutton & Co. Inc., Everyman's Library Edition). Reprinted with permission.

composer's stay in sunny Mediterranean climes. Certainly the outer movements (I and IV) project an expansive, relaxed feeling. But the geographical locale suggested is less that of Italy than his well-remembered homeland, Finland.

For several years Sibelius had written orchestral tone poems reflecting the folk-lore of his native land. With the *Second Symphony*, an absolute work, he goes beyond specific literary reference. Here the composer achieves synthesis: an application of traditional sonata principles to a melodic, rhythmic, harmonic content abstracted from Finnish folk sources. As you hear this symphony you will experience a feeling of structural strength and logical progression, as strong as any since Beethoven. Yet themes and overall orchestral color will turn your imagination to the northern terrain: the people of Finland and the poetry of their history.

The *Second Symphony* is divided into four movements, following the normal tempo plan:

Movement I — Allegretto	Movement III — Vivacissimo
Movement II — Andante	Movement IV — Allegro moderato

The orchestra is modest for 1902: two flutes, two oboes, two clarinets, two bassoons, four horns, three trombones, tuba, timpani, and strings.

MOVEMENT I

Movement I begins with soft, repeated chords in the strings.

EXAMPLE 8–2

The strings continue their quiet pulsations, accompanying a folk-like theme in the oboes and clarinets (see Ex. 8–1, above). Later on, another important theme is heard, also in the woodwinds, with pulsating chords in the strings.

EXAMPLE 8–3

Unlike Theme 1, this idea has no suggestion of the folk. Its shape is typical of Sibelius: a long, single tone intensifying through crescendo, finally dropping by a single skip. These contrasted first and second themes symbolize the polarity of content throughout the symphony. There is an interaction from theme to theme, and movement to movement—between folk-like expression and the composer's more personal expression derived from his European symphonic heritage.

Sibelius chose sonata-allegro form (without slow introduction) for this first movement. The form is very economical; nothing is wasted; every moment is filled with precisely enough sound and idea to complete the total pattern.

While Sibelius' ideas develop, in steady but inevitable progression, all is enveloped in unique orchestral color.

MOVEMENT II

Nowhere in the symphony does the "somber cast" of Sibelius' orchestra sound more effective than at the beginning of the second movement in D minor. The movement begins with the low strings playing a steady, pizzicato bass line. There is a primeval loneliness to the sound recalling perhaps the sight of craggy rocks, mists, and vapors. As it turns out, this pizzicato passage is a preparation for the entrance of Theme 1. Two bassoons, an octave apart, play a dark, chant-like theme.

EXAMPLE 8–4

Although the remainder of this movement contains passionate outbursts of great intensity and much diversity of mood, it is the dark first theme that sets the mood for the whole.

MOVEMENT III

Movement III is a Scherzo following the pattern, ABAB. Two moods are present. The first, in Part A, is wild and impetuous. The following motive moves through the orchestra at a furious pace,

EXAMPLE 8–5

Above it, Theme 1 enters in the woodwinds.

EXAMPLE 8–6

Throughout Part A, a mixture of sudden dissonant stabs, unexpected modulations, climaxes and quick dynamic drops, shows that Sibelius need not be regarded exclusively as a conservative Romantic. In fact, for its time (1902), this portion of the Scherzo anticipates a true twentieth-century musical temper.

The mood of the Scherzo changes in Part B. Here is Sibelius at his lyric best, providing genial country atmosphere.

EXAMPLE 8–7

Note here the repeated tones intensifying to an interval drop; compare it to Theme 2 in Movement I (Ex. 8–4).

There is no break between the Scherzo and the Finale. Instead, Sibelius writes a bridge that grows in volume leading directly into the Finale.

MOVEMENT IV

The Finale, as is Movement I, is in sonata-allegro form. Theme 1 is ponderous and majestic. It moves strongly, propelled by a kind of grinding rhythmic pattern in the trombones, tuba, and timpani.

EXAMPLE 8–8

Theme 1 is built up of four, seminal motives: the first in the strings, the next in the trumpets, the following in the horns, and the last back in the strings. There is then a brief episode in the violins, after which a crescendo builds and Theme 1 returns, considerably transformed. But the first motive is now used. Richer harmonies and full support in the winds give it a feeling of spiritual fervor. The atmosphere then gradually becomes quiet and the lower strings play a scale-like, circling idea in eighth-notes. This is a preparation and background for Theme 2.

EXAMPLE 8–9

Again Sibelius presents a theme forged from a short, simple motive in the oboe and clarinet. The effect of the woodwinds sounding in their low registers over the circling figure in the bass is uncanny. As he does so often, Sibelius gives the impression of time and motion held back and suspended. We are brought back to a primeval earth where the measure of time is slow and still.

The development section is constructed chiefly of explorations of the first motive from Theme 1 (Ex. 8–8) and of a herald motive in the brass. Ultimately, the three-note motive from Theme 1, repeated over and over again with crescendo, leads to a resplendent statement of Theme 1, complete.

The Finale's end is approached with the swirling scale idea from above, gradually intensifying to a huge climax. The herald motive is heard four times in the brass, followed by another short crescendo, leading to the beginning of the coda (molto largamente). The sonority is tremendous, all choirs full blown and rich. For this massive conclusion Sibelius has saved up a final, chorale-like theme in the oboe and brass.*

EXAMPLE 8–10

OB, TR, TB

Other post-Romantics

Of perhaps less stature, but nevertheless of considerable value are the works of several other post-Romantics: Elgar (1857–1934) in Victorian England; Fauré, d'Indy, and Saint-Saëns in France; Wolf in Germany; MacDowell in America; Rachmaninoff in Russia; and Dohnányi in Hungary.

Sir Edward Elgar, in the *"Enigma" Variations* and the fine oratorio, *The Dream of Gerontius,* was often content to repeat harmonic and melodic formulas from the early 1800's, albeit with great refinement and elegance.

The music of Fauré (1845–1924) and d'Indy (1851–1931) has overtones of Impressionism. It has little of the robust quality found in German and Italian Romanticism but displays very subtle harmonic shading and effective orchestration. The suite, *Pelléas et Mélisande* and the *Requiem* are well known.

Saint-Saëns (1835–1921) wrote polished, elegant works, often in classical forms. The five piano concertos reflect his own immense virtuosity at the keyboard. In this respect he resembles Liszt, whom he knew and admired. His four

* Examples 8–2 to 8–10 are from Jean Sibelius, *Symphony No. 2, Op. 43.* © Copyright 1903, 1931 by Breitkopf & Haertel. Used by permission of Associated Music Publishers, Inc. Text reprinted by permission of Crescendo Publishing Co., Boston. © Copyright 1973, 1974 by Roland Nadeau. All rights reserved.

symphonic poems, including the well-known *Danse macabre*, also point to Liszt. Among his best work is the massive *Organ Symphony*, Op. 78, and the slight but charming *Carnival of the Animals: Zoological Fantasy*.

Hugo Wolf (1860–1903) is best known for his lieder, many of which are equal in quality to the songs of Schubert, Schumann, and Brahms. Throughout the evolution of the nineteenth-century lied, the piano part became more and more important. With Schumann and Brahms it frequently carries as much melodic interest as the voice part, in addition to setting the mood and atmosphere in general. With the lieder of Wolf, such as those in the *Goethe Lieder* and the *Michelangelo Lieder*, the piano part is not only equivalent to the voice but sometimes predominates. As in the operas of Wagner, where all substance and energy seem to swell up from within the orchestra, the piano part in many of the songs of Wolf is central.

The American composer Edward MacDowell (1861–1908) at one time was considered by many in the United States as a kind of musical messiah, one who would kindle the flame of adventure and originality in young American composers while showing the way to a true school of American music. However, the effect of his music on our time has not been deep or lasting. Gilbert Chase, in *America's Music*, says:

> . . . MacDowell was not a great composer. At his best he was a gifted miniaturist with an individual manner. Creatively, he looked toward the past, not toward the future.*

Despite the modest position that he holds among post-Romantics, there is much charm among his smaller compositions, especially those for piano. Among these engaging pieces are *To a Wild Rose, From Uncle Remus, From a Wandering Iceberg* and *To an Old White Pine*. The large works, such as the *"Keltic" Sonata* for the piano and the piano concertos, are completely Europe-oriented but seldom fail to make their effect in concert.

Sergei Rachmaninoff's (1873–1943) work has had enormous success ever since the writing of his *Second Piano Concerto* in 1901. The public has always responded strongly to this composer's way with melody and to the smouldering, cresting passion of the music. Rachmaninoff was one of the world's great pianists, and his playing of his own compositions on the stages of many continents contributed to the enormous popularity of his music. Looked at objectively, the music is very solid; obvious Russian nationalistic elements are subtly blended with formal and melodic characteristics seen previously in Chopin, Schumann, and Liszt. The harmony is especially luxuriant, and there is considerable polyphonic ingenuity, especially in certain of the piano preludes and the four piano concertos.

---

* Gilbert Chase, *America's Music* (New York: McGraw-Hill Book Company, Inc., 1955), p. 364.

Ernst von Dohnányi (1877–1960), the Hungarian composer, had a broad career in music. He taught throughout his life both in his native land and elsewhere. In 1919 he directed the Music Conservatory in Budapest; in 1949 he became composer-in-residence at Florida State University. As a fine pianist and an able conductor, he toured extensively and first visited the United States in 1899.

Dohnányi was a conservative Romantic, composing felicitously in absolute instrumental forms such as the sonata, concerto, and theme with variations. The logic of his forms at once suggests the music of Brahms, a composer much admired by Dohnányi. The harmony is richly chromatic and the writing for instruments is deft and colorful. This last is especially true in piano works such as the *Four Rhapsodies*, Op. 11, where Lisztian keyboard heroics are tempered by the logic of structural design.

The composition analyzed below, *Variations on a Nursery Song*, Op. 25, for piano and orchestra, represents Dohnányi's best work as a thorough-going post-Romantic. In one sense the variations are a compendium of Dohnányi's eclectic style of composition. Successive variations pay hommage to the formative influences in the composer's style. There are subtle references to the music of Wagner, Brahms, Mahler, Bach, Johann Strauss, Jr., and others. Dohnányi has transformed these remembered influences and with them has woven a work permeated by his creative personality.

COMMENTARY AND ANALYSIS

Variations on a Nursery Song, Op. 25, Dohnányi

The tune for these variations is familiar. It has been known and sung as "Mark My Alford," "The Alphabet Song," and "Twinkle, Twinkle, Little Star" in English, but originally was known as "Ah! Vous Dirai-je, Maman" in French. Mozart wrote twelve variations on the song while in Paris in 1778; and the tune is found in Camille Saint-Saëns' *The Carnival of the Animals* in the tone portrait called "Fossils."

Here the Hungarian composer-pianist Ernst von Dohnányi uses a large symphony orchestra with a virtuoso solo part to create music that often sparkles with musical witticisms and caricatures.

INTRODUCTION, MAESTOSO, C MINOR

Although the point is long in coming, the first joke is well worth the waiting. The introduction spans eighteen pages in full score, all of it heavy and dramatic. The Hungarian Dohnányi is spoofing the German "serious" style of Richard Wagner, Richard Strauss, and Gustav Mahler. The atmosphere is heavy with expectancy. The orchestra groans and soars. Near the end listen for four soft, pizzicato notes in the low strings, repeated over and over again under a *leit-motif*, suggesting Wagner's opera, *Tristan und Isolde*. All this fades away and dramatic pauses are suddenly followed by a tremendous clap of sound in the orchestra, on the dominant chord. We are now ready for the grand musical event that has been so carefully prepared; we expect a passionate flood of dramatic expression. But no, the balloon suddenly deflates and we hear, simply and quietly, in the solo piano "Twinkle, Twinkle, Little Star."

EXAMPLE 8–11

At first the theme is played by the pianist, bare and unadorned. In the fifth measure the strings play soft harmonies, pizzicato, to accompany the piano, and, near the end, the solo bassoon joins in with a bouncy countermelody.

VARIATION I. POCO PIÙ MOSSO, C MAJOR

The tune, its individual tones separated by rests, appears in the strings, while the background is provided by the pianist scampering up and down the keyboard.

VARIATION II. RISOLUTO, C MAJOR

The horns start with a Wagnerian, herald-like motive derived from "Twinkle, Twinkle."

EXAMPLE 8–12

The piano answers with a capricious staccato figure going down the chromatic scale. This dialogue continues to the variation's end.

VARIATION III. (SAME TEMPO AND KEY AS VARIATION II)

A gentle lampoon of Brahm's warmest, most sentimental style. The languorous melody in the strings closely resembles a lyric theme from Brahms' *Piano Con-*

certo No. 2 (fourth movement). The nursery tune is barely discernible, yet it hovers about here and there within the Brahms-like melody.

VARIATION IV. ALLEGRO MODERATO, C MAJOR

Bassoons take the lead in this variation, suggesting a Cossack dance. The piano accompanies throughout with staccato chords such as those often heard in the Rachmaninoff piano concertos. (Listen to the third movement of Rachmaninoff's *Second Piano Concerto*.)

VARIATION V. PIÙ MOSSO, C MAJOR

The writing for piano and its joining with the harp suggest the delicate sounds of a music box. This is a gossamer variation featuring atmospheric harmonies and unusual tone color.

VARIATION VI. ALLEGRO, C MAJOR

This is a scherzo with the piano constantly moving in tricky sixteenth-note motion. Watch for the pianist's glissando abruptly ending the variation with a wisp of sound.

VARIATION VII. WALTZ, TEMPO GIUSTO, C MAJOR

Timpani and low strings set the beat for an elegant waltz.

EXAMPLE 8–13

The waltz tune is then played by the piano soloist. Later the strings take over the tune, after which it goes back to the piano. The original nursery tune now seems very distant, but it is recognizable nonetheless.

VARIATION VIII. ALLA MARCIA, ALLEGRO MODERATO, C MAJOR/MINOR

The figure that introduced the piano waltz (Ex. 8–13) now introduces a slow march in the style of the symphonist, Gustav Mahler. Chunks of the tune crop up here and there—in the oboe near the beginning and in the flutes a little later.

EXAMPLE 8–14

VARIATION IX. PRESTO, C MINOR

Again, the introductory figure in the timpani (Ex. 8–13) begins the variation, now a Scherzo in the style of Camille Saint-Saëns. The bassoons start out with a staccato version of the tune. The solo piano plays only background figures. Watch for two short entrances of the xylophone that plays the line previously heard in the bassoons. Is this a reference to Saint-Saëns' "Fossils" from *Carnival of the Animals,* which contains a similar passage for xylophone?

VARIATION X. PASSACAGLIA, ADAGIO NON TROPPO, C MINOR

A somber and melancholy mood prevails throughout this variation. Listen for the nursery tune's first phrase as it is transformed into a ground bass repeated throughout the entire variation.

EXAMPLE 8–15

For a time the tune will sound only in the bass. When you hear the tempo quicken slightly, the ground appears in the solo horn and, later, higher in other instruments.

Now listen again for the highly expressive, interwoven melodic lines accompanying the ground. Towards the close of the variation watch for a further acceleration of tempo and a massive crescendo leading directly to Variation XI.

VARIATION XI. CHORALE, MAESTOSO, C MAJOR

The ground bass from the passacaglia is now back in the major and is harmonized in block chords to become a study chorale. Trumpets and trombones lead. Between the phrases of this chorale, the piano and harp play a florid idea, itself derived from the nursery song.

FINALE: FUGATO, ALLEGRO VIVACE, C MAJOR

The fugato does not begin at once. First, uprushing scales, reaching a high trill on the dominant, prepare for the excitement to come. The fugato's subject, clearly

EXAMPLE 8–16

derived from "Twinkle, Twinkle," is given an academic treatment: It enters successively in all four strings beginning with the viola and ending with the cellos and basses. A little later the woodwinds have a turn at it—but they play it upside down (inversion).

Listen for powerful octaves in the solo part, fortissimo, near the end. A roll in the timpani, followed by a crash and long pause, prepares the final joke. The nursery tune returns in the piano, as if starting over. But soon various solo instruments take their turn at giving it piquant little melodic twists. A final rush by all players closes the work on a note of jubilation.*

Other important post-Romantics include Mascagni, Dukas, Glazounov, Pfitzner, Glière, and Reger.

In our discussion of the post-Romantics we have emphasized their *fin de siècle* orientation: each extended, stretched out, and ended an era that had run its course.

Because most of these masters lived well into the twentieth century, they must be considered as transitional. Though their musical aesthetics were derived from a past century, they continued to write and were themselves physically active and influential while newer musical styles were developing. They affected a necessary overlay, a stabilizing effect, while newer musical attitudes were in the making.

Impressionism

Impressionism owed much to the romantic century. For one, it is in direct descent from nineteenth-century program music. But it emphasizes imagery of nature rather than the tonal representation of plot, drama, or personal characterization as in the typically romantic *Ein Heldenleben* by Richard Strauss or *The Battle of the Huns* by Liszt.

Second, Impressionism is firmly based on tonality, in spite of the new use of principles of key, relationships of consonance-dissonance, and modulation.

In a similar way, representation is present in the impressionistic painters Manet, Monet, and Renoir just as in the romantic school of painters. We can as plainly recognize the subject—a pretty girl, a field of flowers, a cathedral—with the Impressionists as we do with romantic painters, but there is no doubt that the treatment of the subject differs. So tonality, like representation in painting, is always present but subtly transformed. While Impressionism is clearly rooted in Ro-

---

* Examples 8–11 to 8–16 are from Ernst von Dohnányi, *Variations on a Nursery Song.* ©
Copyright 1922, 1950 by N. Simrock. Used by permission of Associated Music Publishers, Inc.

manticism, it also points to contemporary music. Its primary concern and search for unique, original sound as such is modern. Debussy always looked for *le ton juste*, the precise sound, that would make an original effect. This foreshadows the experimental approach of contemporary composers.

In their search for a fresh, unique sound, the Impressionists developed new instrumental techniques. Their orchestra became a highly flexible instrument, pregnant with coloristic potential. It still is the basis for much orchestral writing today.

Also strongly suggestive of contemporary music is the objective semidetachment of Impressionism. In its shift away from the Romantic's tonal depiction of states of subjectivity, in its moving away from psychically generated emotion, it concerned itself almost exclusively with the world outside of man—the world of nature, of things. This very de-emphasis of the emotional, personal, subjective contributed greatly to the geometrical, cerebral element in contemporary music.

A particularly curious facet of Impressionism is its brief span: from about 1892 to perhaps 1918, a little over 25 years. After that there were no significant Impressionists, though impressionist techniques were often used in combination with others. This, of course, points to impressionism's transitory role; it unquestionably bridged the gap from the idealistic, subjective, powerfully humanistic music of Romanticism to the detached, "cooler," experimental realism of our time.

If, then, Impressionism contained within itself the seed and promise of the music of our day while resting solidly on the musical ground gained in the century before, the question may be asked: What gives it its unique character? Despite its dealing with objects and things in nature—rain-drenched gardens, exotic temples in the light of the moon, footsteps in the snow, the sea in its myriad moods, girls with hair like silk, rag dolls, toy elephants, regal peacocks—it ordinarily does not attempt to represent these objects directly in any way. Rather, the impressionist composer presents to us in musical terms sensations, moods, and emotional reactions that external objects in nature have evoked from him. "Nuages," for example, is the musical response in the heart and soul of Debussy to his impressions of the particular phenomenon in nature called a cloud. A different impressionist composer would undoubtedly produce a cloud piece with a completely different sound.

Descriptive titles, of course, do head most impressionistic pieces. But enjoyment of the music is not at all dependent on a preknowledge of the title. Debussy, who insisted that his music was solid enough to be enjoyed without knowing what it was about, inserted titles only at the end of each of his *24 Preludes for Piano* and discreetly in parentheses.

Impressionism, in a way, is also a very simple kind of music. In technical structure it is ultra-sophisticated, but in effect and in what it tries to do for the listener it is plain and simple. Debussy said, "Music should seek humbly to please . . . extreme complication is contrary to art." A piece such as Ravel's *Rhapsodie es-*

pagnole, or Delius' *On Hearing the First Cuckoo in Spring*, appeals directly to our senses. It aims to please, to entertain. It does not preach or try to stir us up.

The artist/hero, the artist/prophet, and the artist/teacher are foreign to the Impressionist. Frankly autobiographical and sensational pieces such as Berlioz' *Symphonie fantastique* or R. Strauss's *Ein Heldenleben* were totally foreign to Debussy and Ravel who both lived rather retired, secluded lives.

And because Impressionism aims directly and unabashedly to gratify our aural sense, it is permeated and saturated with the most sensuous combinations of sounds, presented to our ears with the subtlest use of instruments and voices. Of paramount concern is the immediate beauty and effect of the sound. Thus does the Impressionist combine his instrumental colors, with a view to the utmost voluptuous quality.

Harmony is the area where this sensuous quality becomes most obvious. In fact it can be said that much of the interest in impressionistic music is generated through novel chords, and especially in the novel juxtaposition of chords. Sam Hunter, in his book, *Modern French Painting,* says of the work of the impressionistic painter Monet ". . . he had discovered that the most intense optical sensations were obtained when colors were mixed by the eye."* In similar fashion, the novel effect produced in musical Impressionism comes about when the ear mixes adjacent chordal colors that in past periods did not "go well" together.

EXAMPLE 8–17 *Préludes,* "Danseuses de Delphes," Debussy

---

* Sam Hunter, *Modern French Painting, Fifty Artists from Manet to Picasso* (New York: Dell Publishing Co., Inc., 1956), p. 91.

Another characteristic of impressionistic music is its scant use of brio sound. Rather than overwhelm, the Impressionist insinuates and suggests. Much of his music begins with a whisper and ends with the tiniest tremor of sound.

Marked, biting accents are also scantily used, though they occasionally arise, as in the "Dialogue of the wind and sea" portion of Debussy's *La Mer* or in the "General Dance" in Ravel's *Daphnis and Chloé*, Suite No. 2. Because of the lack of both rhythmic bite and obvious melody, the music seems to some at first like an amorphous mixture of musical tremors, trills, and gurgles. With the master Impressionists, however, repeated listening reveals magnificent design and direction.

Devices of impressionism

1. *Parallelism.* The chordal thickening of a melodic contour (see Ex. 8–17, meas. 1).

2. *Pedal point.* This is not new, but Debussy uses it extensively to serve as an anchor for "wandering" harmonies.

3. *Ostinato.* This is not new either, but like pedal point it serves as an anchor, and as well acts as an "intensifier." An example occurs in the piano prelude, *Footsteps in the Snow,* in which the ostinato occurs throughout the entire work, with the exception of the three measures that include the climax. Debussy's comment about the rhythm of the ostinato stresses its expression of a "mournful, icy sound."

4. *Added notes.* To a chord built in 3rds, added notes lessen its original clarity, giving it a denser texture and a more diffuse color. They also produce harmonic intervals of a 2nd. The stressing of these lends "bite" to a passage. They are not treated as dissonances, but rather as "color."

5. *Tone clusters.* Any vertical structure that consists of two or more adjacent intervals of a 2nd.

6. *Cross relation.* This refers to a chromatic semitone change that normally had occurred in the same voice, but now crosses over into another voice.

7. *Pan-diatonicism.* The use of several tones of a scale or mode melodically and/or harmonically as if the use were indiscriminate. Actually, great care is taken in the choice of tones.

8. *Whole-tone scale.* In the piano prelude, *Voiles,* we find Debussy's most extensive use of the whole-tone scale as the basis for a work.

9. *Pentatonic scale.* The use of a five-note pattern such as CDEGA.

10. *Modal scale.* The main melody of the piano prelude, *The Sunken Cathedral,* uses the tones of the mixolydian mode on C (C D E F G A B♭).

11. *Tritone switch.* Alternation of chordal structures with roots a tritone apart.

12. *Evaporation.* The piano prelude, *Voiles,* uses a B-flat pedal point throughout

nearly the entire prelude as an anchor. However, it is not present in the opening four measures, and in the 4th measure from the end it is allowed to vanish or "evaporate," the final sound being a major 3rd on C.

Debussy

Without question, the two most successful impressionist composers were Claude Debussy (1862–1918) and Maurice Ravel (1875–1937). Though Debussy is credited with the first truly impressionist work, *Prelude to the Afternoon of a Faun* (1894), it should be remembered that Ravel composed the piano version of the *Rhapsodie espagnole* only one year later. It is true, however, that Debussy from 1894 wrote almost exclusively in the impressionistic manner, while Ravel frequently concerned himself with other styles and compositional techniques. Of the two, Debussy is the typically impressionistic composer and Ravel, the occasional one.

Debussy was born early enough (1862) to have been strongly influenced by Romanticism, and wrote several early works in the late romantic idiom. Music such as the *Deux Arabesques* and the *Rêverie* for piano are suave, elegant, melodious, sentimental almost to excess—clearly in the romantic tradition. "Clair de Lune," from the *Suite Bergamasque*, is typical.

Despite the obvious eclecticism of these early pieces, they are immaculate in design while seldom failing to please. The superior workmanship points to the finesse and the incredible sophistication heard in the mature Debussy.

The later works of Debussy are typified by such works as the *Nocturnes*, *La Mer*, and *Iberia* for orchestra; *Chansons de Bilitis* for voice and piano; the *Images* and *24 Préludes* for piano; and the opera *Pelléas et Mélisande*. They are completely original and magnificent in conception. Their subject matter is far-ranging, geographically and pictorially.

The color and character of many lands is fair game for Debussy's Impressionism. There is the suggestion of an early American dance in the "Golliwog's Cakewalk," and a Frenchman's view of British pomposity in the piano prelude, *Hommage à S. Pickwick Esq., P.P.M.P.C.* An ancient Egyptian burial urn, Greek Delphic dancers, and the hills of Anacapri in Italy are all in the piano preludes. *Iberia* is a smouldering portrait of Spain. *Poisson d'or* represents the brilliant sheen of goldfish on a Japanese vase, while *Pagodas* reflects the composer's interest in Javanese music that he heard at the Paris Exhibition in 1889.

Subject matter itself varies greatly: anything from *Footsteps in the Snow* to *Sounds and Perfume Turning in the Evening Air*.

The tendency of Debussy to communicate his aesthetic responses to outside scenes of nature is remarkably similar to the *plein air* school of painting typified by Manet. Here the painter strapped his easel to his shoulder, went out into the fields and woods to work, and captured an immediate impression. But, in addition to Debussy's obvious power to evoke atmosphere and mood, the music is saturated with mellow melancholy. In the phrase of André Suarès, it is "la douleur qui parle" (sorrow speaking). The music frequently is as warm as it is sensuous and colorful.

COMMENTARY AND ANALYSIS

Prélude à "L'Après-midi d'un faune," Debussy

Debussy's *L'Après-midi d'un faune* (1894), his second orchestral work, became one of the great landmarks in the history of music. Preceding Stravinsky's *Le Sacre du printemps* by nearly twenty years, it paved the way for *Le Sacre* through a novel treatment of sound as color—an effect that had never before been achieved. Debussy stretched the bounds—or rather enlarged the scope—of tonality; nevertheless he always retained tonality as an anchor to his work. Much tonal straying and returning may be heard in this work.

In the opening two measures we hear a flute solo as it outlines the tritone interval, C♯–G♮, suggesting vagueness and instability. In the traditional tonal sense this interval *could* suggest a resolution in the key of D.

EXAMPLE 8–18

However, in measure 3 the G natural is cancelled and Debussy makes the first reference to E, which is the tonal center of the work.

When the chromatic figure of the opening measures is restated throughout the work, listen for new harmonizations. For example, notice the harmonic color Debussy uses at measure 11.

EXAMPLE 8–19

An appreciation of this aspect of Debussy's treatment of a single figure—not developing it but coloring it differently each time—is the beginning of an appreciation of Debussy's approach to composition.

The middle part of the work strongly contrasts with the first section through a change of key and the introduction of an expansive new theme in the woodwinds. This theme is initially pentatonic in structure and quickly covers the range of nearly an octave and a half. Under this theme you will hear a rhythmic thrust in the strings through the use of energizing syncopation.

You will next hear a brief woodwind melody, at measure 62, built upon the whole-tone scale. With its sense of tonal vagueness, this passage is a counterpoise (on the opposite side of the color spectrum) to the solidity of the pentatonic theme that begins again in measure 63 and goes on, this time for four measures.

EXAMPLE 8–20

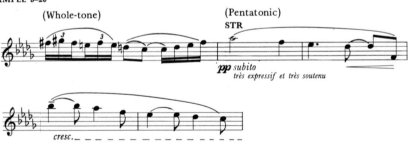

The return of materials from Part I begins in the second half of measure 79, again in the flute, again chromatic, but now in longer note values (augmentation), and now firmly rooted in the key of E.

EXAMPLE 8–21

However, Debussy disturbs this seeming placidity by abruptly switching to a new key color with nervous trilling sounds followed by quick staccato sounds heard first in high woodwind territory, then descending through the oboe and clarinet in quick succession, and concluding in the middle register with the French horn.

EXAMPLE 8–22

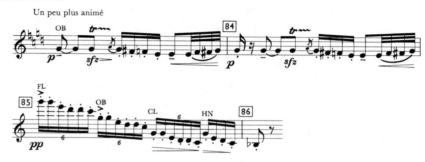

The final statement of Theme 1 (measure 100) is again somewhat varied as the musical materials gradually thin out. In this final section special color effects still prevail (note especially the harp); the French horn and violin suggest Theme 1 again; the faint sound of the very small antique cymbal enters; and the music—getting ever softer—concludes on a quiet E major triad. A final pizzicato in the lower strings returns us to silence.

L'APRÈS–MIDI D'UN FAUNE

Eclogue

Le Faune

Ces nymphes, je les veux perpétuer.

Si clair,

Leur incarnat léger, qu'il voltige dans l'air
Assoupi de sommeiles touffus.

Aimai-je un rêve? . . .

"Que je coupais ici les creux roseaux domptés
"Par le talent; quand, sur l'or glauqe de lointaines
"Verdures dédiant leur vigne à des fontaines,
"Ondoie une blancheur animale au repos:
"Et qu'au prélude lent où naissent les pipeaux,
"Ce vol de cygnes, non! de naïades se sauve
"Ou plonge. . . ."

—Mallarmé

Free Synopsis:
The Faun

Nymphs, do not go, you who float in air
drowsy with deep sleep—has this been a dream?

Upon a cut-reed I bestow the gift of sound;
in the green and gold of the distant fountains
a white flesh rests. The swans—no! naiads—
run or plunge at the sound of my air.

COMMENTARY AND ANALYSIS

Fêtes, Debussy

Fêtes (*Holidays*) is the second of three *Nocturnes* for orchestra written by Debussy in the late 1890's. The translation given here, "Holidays" rather than the usual "Festivals," is given because of Debussy's own description of the piece presented in *Achille-Claude Debussy* by Vallas. "*Fêtes* had been inspired by a recollection of old-time public rejoicings in the Bois de Boulogne attended by happy, thronging crowds; the trio with its fanfare of muted trumpets suggests the former drum and bugle band of the Garde Nationale, beating the tattoo as it approached from afar and passed out of sight."

Swirling, sweeping music illustrates that Debussy is not all vapour and mist. Indeed, some of his more rhythmic pieces are as springy as the luminous ballerinas in the paintings by Degas. Besides the rhythmic vitality and drive in *Fêtes*, there is a stunning use of climax. The fantastic, almost orgiastic climax achieved by the fanfare-march in the middle section shows that Debussy sometimes loved great splashes of sound as well as delicate nuances.

The orchestra is large: three flutes, two oboes, English horn, two clarinets, three bassoons, four horns, three trumpets, three trombones, tuba, two harps, timpani, cymbals, snare drum, and strings.

The piece's form is very simple: ternary, ABA. It starts with a brusque figure in open intervals for the violins, *ff*. This serves to introduce the first theme, played by the clarinets and English horn.

EXAMPLE 8–23

Figure 30. *Musicians in the Orchestra* by Degas. (Musée du Louvre, photograph Giraudon)

All this is loud. Suddenly the dynamic level drops to a hushed *pp* and the accompaniment figure now appears fleshed out in parallel ninth chords.

EXAMPLE 8–24

Above this, the first theme is handed down from treble to bass in crescendo leading to a brilliant but brief heraldic statement in the brass, *ff*.

EXAMPLE 8–25

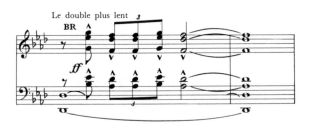

Note the 3rd measure in Example 8–26, which is now different from Example 8–23.

EXAMPLE 8–26

This comes twice. Then, a rough figure in the horns backed by bassoons

EXAMPLE 8–27

is answered by a blithe idea, *piano* and staccato, in the clarinets and English horn.

EXAMPLE 8–28

Examples 8–26 and 8–27 are both heard again. Then the first lyric theme of the piece occurs, in the solo oboe.

EXAMPLE 8–29

Example 8–29 soon is heard again, but this time with flutes added, the whole set higher in the soprano, and again in crescendo. Ultimately, the oboe and flutes joined by the clarinet give out a new idea, which is accompanied by the strings playing a staccato figure derived from earlier materials.

EXAMPLE 8–30

Examples 8–29 and 8–30 alternate for the remainder of the A section, the whole finally building towards a climax.

EXAMPLE 8–31

However, just before the expected crest, the music suddenly drops to a hypnotic, eerie march rhythm, ultra soft.

EXAMPLE 8–32

This signals the beginning of the B section. Above the shuffling march rhythm and above an A♭ in the bass that remains throughout the section, three muted trumpets —as if out of nowhere—give out a fanfare theme, *pp*.

EXAMPLE 8–33

Later the woodwinds take up the fanfare. The horns sally forth with the basic motive of the fanfare rising,

EXAMPLE 8–34

to be answered by the falling winds.

EXAMPLE 8–35

When the trumpets, buttressed by trombones, reiterate the complete fanfare theme (Ex. 8–33), the strings play a version of the first theme (Ex. 8–23). Thus, the leading melodic idea from Section A joins with the theme from Section B to provide a synthesis of disparate elements. The A section then returns but with many changes of orchestration.

Instead of the original heraldic statement of Example 8–25, followed closely by the harp glissandi, the composer now writes a broad figure in the strings,

EXAMPLE 8–36

followed immediately by this passage in the trumpets.

EXAMPLE 8–37

The other themes—except for Example 8–30—come back in order and the music gradually becomes more and more quiet, terminating in the pianissimo tremors of the last measure. But before the music fades away, echoes of the fanfare theme of the B section

EXAMPLE 8–38

and a strange, new melodic fragment

EXAMPLE 8–39

glow quietly through the gathering stillness.

Ravel

Ravel also possessed a gift for musical imagery, but he did not use it as often as Debussy. Nor is his Impressionism as sweet and warm. Stravinsky called Ravel the "Swiss watchmaker." Indeed, his music is fastidiously put together, as neat and ordered as a French formal garden.

To know the essential difference between the two Impressionists one need only compare Ravel's *Pavane pour une infante défunte*

EXAMPLE 8–40   *Pavane pour une infante défunte*, Ravel

with Debussy's "Sarabande" from *Pour le piano*.

EXAMPLE 8–41   *Pour le piano*, "Sarabande," Debussy

Both were written in the late 1890's and are re-creations of early court dances. The Ravel is tender, yet somehow cool and reserved. Its harmonies are sometimes frosty. The Debussy, on the other hand, pulses every moment with a warm, romantic glow. It is more relaxed, freer, less formal.

On listening to the music of Ravel, the listener is much more conscious of structure and a clear beat. Typical are the *Valses nobles et sentimentales, Daphnis and Chloé,* and *La Valse.* The *Bolero,* of course, is well known. *Le Tombeau de Couperin* includes three dances from the Baroque, a "forlane," a "menuet," and a "rigaudon."

Ravel's feeling for Spanish music is perhaps superior to that of Debussy. The *Rapsodie espagnole* and the one-act comic opera *L'Heure espagnole* capture every nuance and all of the excitement of Spanish music. The composer's mother was descended from a Basque family. His later compositions, particularly those after World War I, show little of the impressionistic style. The *Piano Concerto in G* shows the influence of American jazz, as does the *Violin Sonata*.

The opera *L'Enfant et les sortilèges* is remarkable. The "Duet of the Cats," for example, and the "Insect Music" are remarkably realistic. There is a clear use of polytonality near the beginning of the piece, as can be seen from the differing key signatures.

EXAMPLE 8-42   *L'Enfant et les sortilèges*, Ravel

Reproduced with permission of Durand & Cie, Editeurs-propriétaire Paris.

Other impressionists

Among several others writing with impressionistic techniques is the Russian, Alexander Scriabin (1872–1915), whose exotic, almost mystic music is a curious blend of late romantic expressivity and French color. Among his best work is the *Poem of Ecstasy* for orchestra and the sonatas for piano—especially the *Sonata No. 5 in F-Sharp Major*.

Works such as *Nights in the Garden of Spain* for piano and orchestra by Manuel de Falla (1876–1946) show an interesting blend of Impressionism with indigenous Spanish musical elements. Falla was acquainted with Debussy in Paris. In fact, it was a postcard sent from Spain by Falla to Debussy picturing a gate of the Alhambra that inspired the piano prelude, *La puerta del Vino* by the Frenchman.

Figure 31. *Mlle. Marcelle Lender Dancing the Bolero,* by Toulouse-Lautrec, 1896. (From the collection of Mr. and Mrs. John Hay Whitney)

Frederick Delius (1862–1934), wrote many compositions in the impressionistic style. They are lusciously vaporous, sometimes overripe; but pieces such as *Brigg Fair* and *Walk to the Paradise Garden* are nevertheless charming.

Charles Griffes (1884–1920) was an American Impressionist whose untimely death at the age of thirty-six cut off a very promising career. His *Poem for Flute and Orchestra* is effective.

The pre-moderns—satire and the experimental attitude

As mentioned earlier, the period we are now examining produced a tremendous overlap of styles. We have seen that post-Romantics such as Sibelius and Rachmaninoff continued to write many years after the establishment of the contemporary idioms. Rachmaninoff wrote the frankly romantic *Rhapsody on a Theme of Paganini* fully twenty-one years after the riotous premiere of Stravinsky's *Le Sacre du printemps*. Two important figures anticipated contemporary musical idioms and attitudes by at least twenty years. They were the French iconoclast, Erik Satie (1866–1925), and the American iconoclast, Charles Ives (1874–1954). Satie was perhaps the first to revolt against romantic "expressivity" and bombast. His music is rather ascetic, often mordantly witty. The *Gymnopédies* are chaste, objective, and detached. Titles of many of his works are highly ironic, meant to arrest the attention and to pique the curiosity; for example, *Desiccated Embryos* and *Cold Pieces*, both for piano. Satie's playing directions are outrageously humorous: "Play like a nightingale with a toothache," or, for the "Tango" in his *Sports and Diversions for Piano*, "Play in moderate tempo and very bored."

Satie's attitude affected Debussy, who himself had a rather caustic sense of humor. It also influenced later French composers such as Poulenc, Milhaud, and Auric. His non-sentimental approach is similar to that of Stravinsky, who in the twenties and thirties ruthlessly resisted all "expression" in music. "For I consider that music is, by its very nature, essentially powerless to express anything at all...." These words by Stravinsky could well have been uttered by Satie, who resisted all expressionistic or impressionistic suggestions in his own music. *Socrate*, a symphonic drama based on Plato for soprano with chamber orchestra, is considered to be Satie's most important work. In its pale simplicity and homely, non-coloristic mien, it symbolizes the anti-romantic outlook of many twentieth-century composers.

In many ways, Satie's ballet *Parade* exemplifies his position as precursor of the experimental attitude in composition. This playfully sardonic work, conceived in part in the spirit of Dadaism, was the result of the touching of minds of five of the most fecund, adventuresome figures of this century. Produced by Diaghilev for the Ballets Russes, its scenario was written by Cocteau and it was choreo-

Figure 32. Drop curtain by Picasso for ballet *Parade*, by Erik Satie. (Musée National d'Art Moderne, Paris, Editions Cercle d'Art, photograph Masson)

graphed by Massine. Sets and costumes were done by Picasso. The score itself anticipates certain important trends to be seen several years later. Satie's use in the music of strange "instruments" such as the typewriter and the siren suggests the organized sound of Varèse in the 1930's. Moreover, the use of elements from ragtime in *Parade* predated that in Stravinsky's *L'Histoire du soldat*, making *Parade* one of the first pieces of art music to come to terms with the indigenous popular music of the USA.

In contrast to Satie, who was at the center of the fluid, exciting developments in Paris at the turn of the century, Charles Ives was a musically isolated figure whose originality has only recently been recognized. He was little touched by European artistic currents but was saturated with the folk, popular, and church music of his own land. The New England transcendentalists, especially Emerson, influenced him. These, added to a natural inclination to experiment with tone, strongly encouraged by his bandmaster father, led to some incredibly prophetic work.

One of the masterpieces of Ives is the orchestral work *Three Places in New*

England. This is the work of an ecstatic visionary with musical roots deep in his land, and it set the stage for many of the younger men of contemporary music to come.

Unique among composers, Ives stands to this day as one of the most original minds in music. Unfettered by tradition, he wrote often in a daring manner that included devices or techniques of composition that predated their use by such composers as Stravinsky, Schoenberg, Milhaud, Varèse, Hába, Cage, and others.

To merely read the list of devices explored by Ives is to be struck by the scope of his originality: chord clusters, polytonality, polymeter, polyrhythm, constantly changing time signatures, the use of quarter-tones, pan diatonicism, and pan pentatonicism.

Ives was born in Danbury, Connecticut, and early on was exposed to small-town band music. Ives was especially fortunate to have a father who was not only the town band master, but also a musician with a daring and original mind. From the fecund mind of the small-town bandmaster came the spark that was to lead to the international renown of Charles Ives. Ives was exposed to the European masters, including Bach, Beethoven, and others, but most importantly he was constantly urged by his father to "stretch" his ears. All the sounds that were heard in his daily travels were considered by the senior Ives to be possible sources for musical inspiration. The elder Ives constantly experimented with synthetic scales, including quarter-tone scales. Such experiments included the stretching of twenty-four or more violin strings and tuning them in various ways. He also experimented with water glasses to produce new scales and even attempted to reproduce the sounds of church bells on the piano. These experiments definitely left their mark on the younger Ives.

Charles Ives learned about instruments from his father's band. At the age of twelve he played drums in the band; at the age of fourteen *Holiday Quick Step*, his first composition, was performed by the band. He had meanwhile received training in cornet and piano and had begun playing organ at a Danbury church.

In the late 1800's music was much more of an outdoors affair than it is today. Ives heard the music of country fiddlers, outdoor camp meeting services, barn dances, outdoor political gatherings (with the musicians on trucks and the trombonist tailgating), and of course the outdoor concerts that would include the perennial Fourth of July festivities.

There are two fundamental aspects to the music of Charles Ives: the outdoors aspect and the philosophical aspect. Both of these were conditioned by Ives's interest in Transcendentalism.

Many titles of Ives's works specifically refer to the outdoors both in and out of town. *Three Places in New England*, already mentioned, is a musical description of "The St. Gauden's in Boston Common (Col. Shaw and his Colored Regiment)"; "Putnam's Camp, Redding, Connecticut"; and "The Housatonic at Stockbridge."

Other works include *Central Park in the Dark; The Gong on the Hook and Ladder,* or *Firemen's Parade on Main Street,* for chamber orchestra; *Over the Pavements,* for chamber orchestra; *Violin Sonata No. 4,* subtitled "Children's Day at the Camp Meeting"; *Piano Sonata No. 2,* subtitled "Concord, Mass., 1840–1860"; and *From the Steeples and the Mountains,* for brass and chimes.

As the *plein-air* painters in France left the artificial atmosphere of the studio to paint outdoors, and as Winslow Homer, a New Englander, filled his canvases with the ruggedness and vitality of shore and sea, of wind and wave, so too did Charles Ives in many of his works seek to represent in music his response to the outdoors.

The aspect of Ives as a composer of the outdoors is substantiated by these comments of his on the score of his *First Piano Sonata:* "What is it all about—Dan S. asks. Mostly about the outdoor life in Conn[ecticut] villages in the '80's and '90's.... In the Summer times, the Hymns were sung outdoors, Folk songs ... and the people like things as they wanted...." The final phrase of the portion quoted is also indicative of Ives's attitude toward his own compositions: He composed things as he wanted, without regard to the so-called established rules or traditions of composition. As Debussy abandoned the structural principles of sonata-form, so, independently, did Ives; as Stranvinsky used constantly changing time-signatures, so, independently, did Ives; and apart from the convention of the time, Ives, when he chose, abandoned bar lines.

The philosophical aspect of Ives is represented in many of his works, including the *Concord Sonata (Piano Sonata No. 2),* the four movements of which are subtitled "Emerson," "Hawthorne," "The Alcotts," and "Thoreau"—a work unprecedented for its innovations in harmony, rhythm, tonality, and form.

But perhaps most representative of Ive's philosophical side is the work *The Unanswered Question* for solo trumpet and four flutes, with a string orchestra playing in a different meter and tempo. The trumpet states "The Perennial Question of Existence," and in the music of the flutes is "The Invisible Answer."

Ives—through his rugged individualism, his iconoclasm, and his constant experimentation, and the incorporation in his music of references to the hymns, the popular music, and the patriotic songs that were commonly heard—was the most "American" of composers.

There is an ironic twist that is part of the Ives story. He knew nearly from the first that his music would not gain easy or early acceptance. He entered the field of insurance in order to provide himself with financial security. The irony includes the fact that he became one of the most successful insurance men in America; the irony continues in the fact that his music did not receive any acclaim until three decades after he had stopped composing.

He was awarded the Pulitzer Prize in 1947 for his *Symphony No. 3,* thirty-six years after it was written. His *Fourth Symphony,* a monumental work for large orchestra and chorus plus a "distant choir" of strings and harps and a special percussion group, was completed in 1916; but not until 1965 was it given a complete performance under the baton of Leopold Stokowski and two assistant conductors.

As the first important American experimentalist, Ives was the fountainhead in this country of an attitude that resulted in what has been called "The American Experimental Tradition." There are a number of composers who followed in this tradition. They include Edgard Varèse, Henry Cowell, Carl Ruggles, and many others, but most especially John Cage.

Figure 33.   Charles Ives, and Claude Debussy and Igor Stravinsky. (The Bettmann Archive, Inc.)

Ives wrote over 200 songs, in a multiplicity of styles, textures, and lengths. He printed at his own expense a collection entitled *114 Songs*. "Cradle Song" (1919), 9 measures long, is a simple tune over sonorous harmonies that include bi-chords, chords built in ascending fifths, and other devices of chord-building based upon a pan-diatonic approach.

There is also the song, "Charlie Rutledge" (1914 or 1915), which is in essence a cowboy ballad that includes unpitched rhythmic declamation.

The boldest song of all is "General Booth Enters into Heaven" (1914) based upon a poem of Vachel Lindsay. It opens as a heavy-footed march akin to "Onward Christian Soldiers" as sung at a revival meeting led by a hearty evangelist. The melody is developed in various ways, including quotations from various sources, such as hymns and the minstrel-show tune "Oh, Dem Golden Slippers."

Debussy was the first important composer in the twentieth century to point the way to the detached experimental attitude. In his way of synthesizing and combining, in his use of the whole-tone scale and of chords as color rather than function, he set the stage for all future experiments in music. We have already seen the structural devices of Impressionism that include new uses of harmony pointing away from Romanticism. But Debussy's roots lay very deeply in the music of Romanticism and before. Though he did point to new directions he did not intentionally subvert the romantic style. It is with Satie and Ives that we see an overt effort to reject the aesthetics of the immediate past. Their method was that of satire and irony.

The titles of many of Satie's works are obviously satirical, while the music is primitive as well as sophisticated and fresh. An iconoclasm similar to Satie's may be seen in the social satire of the playwright G. B. Shaw, in the barbed shafts of the critic H. L. Mencken, in the flamboyant posters of Toulouse-Lautrec. A like raucousness was found in the impudence of the brash Dixieland style. In items such as the *Livery Stable Blues* as played by the Original Dixieland Jazz Band can be seen an intention parallel to that of Satie in his *Three Flabby Preludes for a Dog*.

Ives, under the influence of his father, and with his own fresh approach, was afraid of neither tradition nor dissonance. The final blurting chord of his *Symphony No. 2*, containing all but one of the tones of the chromatic scale, is as irreverent as the W. C. Fields remark, "A man who hates dogs and children can't be all bad."

When Duchamp, the French cubist, painted a mustache on the Mona Lisa in 1920, or when Picabia in the same year put a monkey in a frame and called it a portrait of Cézanne, they, with Satie and Ives, were serving notice that the old ways would no longer do.

AFTER DEBUSSY—EXPRESSIONISM

Stravinsky

The work of this century that had the most far-reaching, as well as the most immediate effect, was *Le Sacre du printemps* (*The Rite of Spring*). Igor Stravinsky (1882–1971) was born into a musical family in Russia, began piano lessons at the

Figure 34. Nureyev as the puppet Petrouchka. (Authenticated News International, N.Y.)

age of nine, and thereafter began to compose. He was self-taught with the exception of two years of study in orchestration with Rimsky-Korsakov.

Before *Le Sacre*, Stravinsky already had two large works to his credit, both of which had achieved success; he had written *The Firebird* and *Petrouchka* for Diaghilev's Ballets Russes in Paris. But where "*Petrouchka* had shaken the musical art of the period," according to Alexandre Tansman, "*The Rite of Spring* delivered a blow from which it was never again to recover. . . ." Stravinsky's concept of rhythm seemed to the audience barbaric and relentless, after the "loveliness" of most romantic and impressionistic music. Stravinsky's tonal concepts were basically those of the impressionist school. But whereas Debussy had been criticized for the vagueness of his melody, Stravinsky was attacked for its absence. It was even said by some musical reactionaries that Stravinsky was incapable of writing a melody. Where Debussy had alternated chord structures to blur the tonality, Stravinsky combined them. What the critics could not comprehend in the music of Stravinsky was no more than what had dumbfounded them in the music of Debussy: originality. They constantly tried to assess the new against what they were familiar with in the old.

Stravinsky was to influence two generations of composers with his harmonic procedure and his exposure of the "raw nerve" of rhythm.

Petrouchka   In the opening measures of *Pethouchka*, "Shrove-Tide Fair" (1947 revision), there is a 41-measure ostinato begun by the clarinets. The peculiar repetitive treatment of the melody is uniquely Stravinsky's—a technique that may be seen in many places throughout his works. In this instance, it consists of repeating a short fragment of melodic material but changing the accent or adding or subtracting a note during the course of the repetition. This treatment gives the melody a rhythmic force that propels it forward; it might almost be described as a "darting" melody: short thrusts forward, differing slightly in length and in direction, but constantly moving ahead, while at the same time imparting a nervous, kinetic energy to the texture.

The opening of the next section of *Petrouchka*, the "Danse Russe," shows us, in addition to the use of parallel chords, an example of the modal influence in Stravinsky's writing.

It is of interest to note that Stravinsky disagreed with the terms "revolution" and "revolutionary" as applied to his music and to the general thought of the times in the first years of this century. In his "Poetics of Music," he had this to say:

> Let us not forget that *Petrouchka, The Rite of Spring,* and *The Nightingale* appeared at a time characterized by profound changes that dislocated many things and troubled many minds ... I am well aware that there is a point of view that regards the period in which *The Rite of Spring* appeared as one that witnessed a revolution, a revolution whose conquests are said to be in the process of assimilation today. I deny the validity of that opinion. I hold that it was wrong to have considered me a revolutionary. When *The Rite* appeared, many opinions were advanced concerning it. In the tumult of contradictory opinions my friend Maurice Ravel intervened practically alone to set matters right. He was able to see, and he said, that the novelty of *The Rite* consisted, not in the "writing," not in the orchestration, not in the technical apparatus of the work, but in the musical entity.*

* Igor Stravinsky, *Poetics of Music,* trans. Arthur Knodel and Ingolf Dahl (Cambridge, Mass.: Harvard University Press. 1947), p. 9. © Harvard University Press. Reprinted by permission.

Now what of *Le Sacre?* Does it logically follow *Petrouchka?* Is it a development of a musical philosophy, or is it an upheaval in musical thinking?

Le Sacre du printemps   The bassoon solo that opens *Le Sacre du printemps* is an excellent example of Stravinsky's melodic style. The constantly high *tessitura* of the solo is unique, but this aspect is one of tone color which rightfully falls within the art of orchestration. More to the point, the solo is an example of Stravinsky's individual way with a melody. The limited range, the rhythmic exploration of a limited number of notes, the careful addition of new notes, the constant repetition of melodic patterns combined with rhythmic alterations—they are all there.

We might describe this individual melodic style of Stravinsky's with the phrase, "a constantly evolving ostinato." Paradoxical though the phrase may seem to be it does describe the *yielding obstinacy* of this kind of a melody.

An analogy comes to mind. It is as if Stravinsky were looking at a gem, turning it over in the palm of his hand, at first slowly, and catching only a few of the different glints of its facets in the light; then turning it more quickly, and at the same time seeing a new glint, and then turning it to his first view of it again, but at a slightly different angle.

The rhythmic heart of the matter is found in the "Danses des Adolescentes" that follows the "Introduction." The throbbing, elemental rhythm with its sporadic accents takes us back to a primitive form of expression. The rhythm is seen in a $\frac{2}{4}$ meter, but the listener hears this:

1 2 3 4 5 6 7 8 9 / 1 2 / 1 2 3 4 5 6 / 1 2 3 / 1 2 3 4 / 1 2 3 4 5 / 1 2 3 /

Stravinsky had in essence removed the bar line, which for ever two hundred years had indicated the metrical accents inherent in a piece of music. The bar line appears in the music only as a convenience for rehearsal purposes.

Stravinsky, having achieved international recognition, next surprised the world by turning away from the orchestra of symphonic proportions, and in 1918 he presented *L'Histoire du soldat* written for seven instruments—a work for the stage, "told, acted, and danced." The new sparse and ascerbic style confounded many listeners, but this change of direction was only the first of many that Stravinsky would take. He has often been likened to Picasso; each of these two artists never let himself be put in a special category, but constantly sought for unique ways of expression.

With his ballet *Pulcinella* (1920) Stravinsky entered a phase designated as *neoclassicism*. In this and later works such as the austere *Octet* (1923) and the *Capriccio* for piano and orchestra (1929) he went back to the music of earlier times as a source of new inspiration. With the *Symphony of Psalms*, for chorus and orchestra (1930), Stravinsky turned again to large forces. This work with Latin

Figure 35.   Picasso's drawing of Stravinsky, 1920. (Giraudon)

text shows Stravinsky's interest in the words not for their meaning so much as for their particular sound. A later work, the *Cantata* for soprano and tenor and a small chorus (1952), illustrates the same interest.

Perhaps the most striking thing about Stravinsky is his diversity of styles. He differs from many composers who have evolved slowly into what is considered their mature style. Aside from what has already been mentioned, Stravinsky's output has included *Ragtime* for eleven instruments (1918), an arrangement of the *Star-Spangled Banner* in 1941 (which was literally banned in Boston), *Ebony Concerto* for the clarinetist Woody Herman and his orchestra, and a ballet for elephants and ballerinas of the Ringling Brothers, Barnum and Bailey Circus (1942).

Stravinsky remained a dominant and constant force throughout his life, not only in his music, but also in his many appearances as conductor and through writings such as *The Poetics of Music* and *Conversations with Stravinsky*. At several points in his career it was thought by many that the well-spring had dried up, but Stravinsky continued to produce music, undaunted and uninfluenced by opinion, picking his own path in his constant search for expression, *his expression*. The opera *The Rake's Progress*, written in 1951 when the composer was nearly seventy, shows Stravinsky in complete possession of his creative powers. After *The Rake*, he astonished the world—along with the newest generation of composers— by espousing the twelve-tone method of composition (see pp. 313–314).

COMMENTARY AND ANALYSIS

L'Histoire du soldat, Stravinsky

The outbreak of World War I in Europe in 1914 caused many changes in the large world of music and, more specifically, in the personal world of the musician. Large orchestras diminished in size, concerts became fewer. No longer was it easy to present full-blown symphonic, operatic, or balletic works.

Stravinsky, who settled for a while in Switzerland, went on composing, and his Switzerland interlude resulted in several notable works for smaller forces. In addition to *Renard*, a folk tale about animals, and most of *Les Noces*, a cantata based upon a Russian peasant wedding, Stravinsky produced *L'Histoire du soldat*, the story of a soldier—any soldier—in any war.

Based upon an old Russian folk tale, the story begins with a soldier on his way back home for a ten-day leave, trudging the last few miles to his hometown to meet his mother and seek out his sweetheart. He is carrying a violin in his kitbag, and he occasionally interrupts his journey to play it. On the way he meets a stranger who says that in trade for the violin he will give him a magic book—a book that promises wealth and happiness. The soldier trades his violin and his soul for the false promise. He has traded with the devil.

The score is written for six solo instruments and a battery of percussion. The score states that the work is "To be Read, Played, and Danced." Thus, there is a narrator and actors who speak, mime, or dance, and a chamber ensemble that consists of violin, clarinet, trumpet, trombone, bassoon, double bass, and percussion. All participants are to be on the stage. The work is a suite of short characteristic pieces as follows.

Part I: "The Soldier's March," (introductory), "Music to Scene I," "Music to Scene II," "Music to Scene III";

Part II: "The Soldier's March," "The Royal March," "The Little Concert," Three Dances ("Tango," "Waltz," "Ragtime"), "The Devil's Dance," "The Little Chorale," "The Devil's Song," "Great Chorale," "Triumphal March of the Devil."

The duration of the work is approximately thirty-five to forty minutes.

L'Histoire du soldat begins with a brief introduction, "The Soldier's March," during which the narrator speaks of the soldier trudging homeward. The opening musical figure in the trumpet and trombone is plain and march-like enough,

EXAMPLE 8–43

but note that the instruments play in different keys. However, in this march and later in the three dances—"Tango," "Waltz," and "Ragtime"—the traditional titles are not to be taken literally. We have already encountered the idealized dance forms of the baroque period; these pieces do not represent ordinary dance music. And later, in the romantic period, the Chopin waltzes were not designed to accompany ballroom dancing. The tango, waltz, and ragtime in *L'Histoire* passed through a process of refraction in Stravinsky's mind, and then were projected into their present style as a way to tell a story—in this case, a fairy tale. Thus, especially in the "Ragtime," you will hear only slight suggestions of actual ragtime.

Although the contrabass plays a march-like figure,

EXAMPLE 8–44

most of the first movement ("The Soldier's March") involves simultaneous conflicting rhythmic patterns in other instruments. Measures 64–69 illustrate this combination—see Example 8–45. (Only the trombone and bass are shown, but all the instruments are playing.)

EXAMPLE 8–45

The curtain opens at the end of the "March" and we see the soldier sitting by a stream. He takes out his fiddle and the "Music to Scene I" begins.

The following violin figure enters in measure 2 over the pizzicato bass

EXAMPLE 8–46

and continues in this vein. The violin figure continues as a prominent part of the musical fabric, and it may be regarded as a representation of the aimlessness of the soldier's thinking—other than to just get home—thus leaving him vulnerable to the offer of trading his violin for the magic book.

The stranger appears during the "Music to Scene I," but at first hides himself to observe the soldier as he plays. Near the end of the scene he steps up to the soldier. The soldier, startled, stops playing and springs up in alarm.

As the soldier and the devil barter over trading the violin for the magic book, the "Music to Scene II" begins. After a brief opening clarinet figure in the first measure, there begins a slow, plaintive solo, played in the upper register of the bassoon.

EXAMPLE 8–47

During the "Music to Scene III," the soldier, having traded his violin, finds that the magic book is a false promise. The disenchantment of the soldier is underscored by the music as it brings back the general musical style and mood of the *Music to Scene I*. The soldier hears this music as a reminiscence of a happier time, but then the cloud of memory begins to dissolve.

Part II begins like Part I, with "The Soldier's March." He is still a soldier on his way home, but his life has changed. The opening musical materials of Part I (see Ex. 8–43, above) now undergo a process of contraction, making the "March" shorter. The narrator recites, sometimes rhythmically, sometimes freely, and occasionally talks to the actors.

> *Somewhere twixt Rock-hill and Lode*
> *Tramping straight along the road,*
> *Where's he going? Who can say?*
> *Walking, trudging all the day.*
> *Past the brook and bridge he goes.*
> *Where's he off to?*
> *No one knows.*

The soldier, after spending three days living in luxury with the devil, returns to the normal world only to discover that three years have passed. When he arrives at his village, his mother doesn't recognize him, and his former sweetheart is married and has children. He now realizes he had been consorting with the devil.

The soldier hears that the king's daughter is ill. The king has offered her in marriage to the man who can cure her. The soldier heads for the palace. The first few measures of "The Royal March" express the soldier's newly found jauntiness, with the trombone leading the way.

EXAMPLE 8–48

At the palace he is confronted by the devil, now in the guise of a violin virtuoso. In a card game with the devil, the soldier—now wise—purposely loses his money, thereby freeing himself from the devil's control. He gets his violin back and cures the princess with his playing.

In "The Little Concert," the opening measures prominently feature a repeated one-measure motive in the cornet part, played against strong brusque downbows in the violin. It is possible to consider this passage as combining the characteristics of soldier and violinist in a new spirit of confidence.

EXAMPLE 8–49

After this piece, the princess, now cured and smiling, rises up to embrace the soldier in happiness and gratitude. The "Tango" has begun and the opening measures fall to the violin.

EXAMPLE 8–50

She dances. Then they both dance. Like the "Tango," the "Waltz" and the "Ragtime" both emphasize the role of the violin.

EXAMPLE 8–51

EXAMPLE 8–52

The prominence of the violin in all three of these dances underscores the force of the soldier's personality. Stravinsky imbues these dances with a certain wit and irony that are fitting in the light of the situation. While the couple dances, however, the devil appears again, now in true guise. The soldier picks up his fiddle anew. In his new found power he makes the devil dance. The devil cannot resist the power and dances to exhaustion.

"The Devil's Dance" uses the full forces of the orchestral group and is assertive, demanding, and relentless in it's rhythmic accentuation. At the end of this dance the devil is dragged out of the room by the now happy couple. They return, fall into each others arms, and "The Little Chorale" begins. It is extremely brief, consisting of only eight measures, which even at a very low tempo last less than a minute. The new prince and his princess are still embracing as the devil reappears to state, in "The Devil's Song":

> *Now the luck is on your side,*
> *But the Kingdom's not so great and wide.*
> *Who tries the frontiers to traverse,*
> *Recaught by me, his fate is worse.*
> *So don't attempt to do what's not allow'd,*
> *Or back again to bed you'll go, my Princess proud;*
> *And as to that young Prince, your plighted spouse,*
> *Let him beware, lest he my anger should arouse.*
> *I'll hand him to my demon hosts,*
> *Who'll see that all alive he r(rr)oasts!*

The "Great Chorale" follows, during which the prince and princess reflects on several things. She wants to know about his past, and he would like to see his native village again; but "one joy at a time, two cancel one another." All the same, he cannot restrain himself and crosses the frontier. The "Triumphal March of the Devil" opens in strident tones. The soldier wanted all happiness, but the devil takes possession of him—and his violin, his soul. The princess stands with vainly outstretched arms. The texture of the music thins out, and the lights fade on the plaintive figure of the princess.*

One definition of *Expressionism* speaks of it as a "revolution from the 'superficial' . . . to a style directly expressive of the artist's soul in all its hidden depth and with as little interference as possible from formal and compositional elements." In further explanation, "The artist paints the expressive character of the object. Instead of painting a tree, he paints its convulsiveness or its strength." †

---

* Narrator's dialogue and "The Devil's Song" plus examples 8–43 to 8–52 by the kind permission of the copyright owners, J. & W. Chester Ltd., London.

† D. D. Runes and H. G. Schrickel, ed., *Encyclopedia of the Arts* (New York: Philosophical Library, 1946), p. 340.

The term *Expressionism* did not come into use until 1911, but we see convulsiveness in the late paintings of Van Gogh, who was a forerunner of both the expressionist and Fauvist movements. In 1900 Sigmund Freud published *Interpretation of Dreams*, the first public statement of his theories. Met at first by incredulity and scorn, during the first decade of the twentieth century his doctrine gained wider and wider acceptance. The theories of Freud were not without their effect in contributing to the dominant thought of the time. The exploration of the subconscious helped to lay bare man's inner nature. The probing into innermost thoughts was equated with the removal of a mask. The original shock that met the exposures of the inner self in Freud's writings was not too different from the shock that the audience felt at the first performance of *Le Sacre*.

Schoenberg

Arnold Schoenberg, even more than Stravinsky, shows the influence of the expressionist movement. An early work, *Pierrot Lunaire*, reflects this in its choice of subject and the treatment of that subject.

Sprechstimme is notated so that it indicates a pitch that is not maintained by the singer but is barely suggested and immediately moved away from. It is half singing, half speaking. It is ideally suited to express Pierrot in the moon-struck night, to depict his mind-wanderings, and his sense of futility. For voice and only five performers using seven instruments, *Pierrot Lunaire* pictures the convulsiveness that can lie under the innocent mask. Although the impact of his music was less immediate than that of Stravinsky's, Schoenberg's ultimate rejection of the old was even more complete than that of Stravinsky. His search for a new means of expression finally turned him completely away from tonality.

Schoenberg (1874–1951) was born in Vienna. In addition to his studies, which included violin, cello, and counterpoint, he gained practical experience in orchestration through arranging music for popular consumption.

In view of his later rejection of nineteenth-century Romanticism and its tonal system, it is somewhat ironic that Schoenberg's first successful work, written in 1899, is one of his best known and perhaps the most played of his entire output. This is *Verklärte Nacht* (*Transfigured Night*), written originally as a string sextet. It is usually heard in its later arrangement for string orchestra, and it is this arrangement also that provided the music for the ballet, *The Pillar of Fire*. The work is in the full romantic tradition.

Schoenberg's super-romantic style was carried to its extreme in his work, *Gurre-Lieder* (1901–1913). In addition to five solo voices and a speaker, the score calls for four separate choruses, and a very large orchestra. It is a massive work in the tradition of Mahler.

Debussy had pointed the way to the use of dissonance for color rather than tension; the natural extension of this concept led Schoenberg to the idea that no dissonance need be resolved. His *Three Piano Pieces*, Op. 11, written in 1908, are important pivotal works in his progress towards the "emancipation of dissonance." They also illustrate the angularity of melodic design that was to characterize many of his later works.

The twelve-tone method

Schoenberg's constant search for new modes of expression gradually turned him away from all previous methods of composition, and in 1923 he initiated the serial technique of composing with twelve tones. In this system, the tones represented by the seven white notes and five black notes are treated as completely equal. The *Five Piano Pieces*, Op. 23 (1923), show Schoenberg first arriving at the twelve-tone system. Important works that are fully twelve-tone are the *Third String Quartet* (1926), *Variations for Orchestra* (1928), and the *Violin Concerto* (1936).

Schoenberg abandoned the idea of diatonic scales with "coloring" chromatic tones, the concept of tonal centers and keys, the idea of tendencies of tones inherent in all previous scale patterns, and the idea of tonality affirmed by the root progression of chords. The basic concept of twelve-tone writing is the establishment of a *row*, placing all the twelve different tones in an order that uses each and all of them just once. Both melody and harmony arise out of the order of the tones in the row. When the tones are used melodically, the approach is similar to the statement of a subject in contrapuntal writing, and thus it is natural to the system to use the devices of counterpoint: imitation, transposition, retrograde motion, inversion, and so on. When the row is used chordally, dissonance and spacing are completely at the discretion of the composer. Writing in the system of twelve tones does not *necessarily* abrogate the use of tonality, but Schoenberg's use of it was certainly a rejection of tonality in the traditional sense. Although Schoenberg disliked the use of the term *atonal*, it has been consistently applied to his twelve-tone compositions.

The possibilities inherent in *serial writing* attracted wide attention and influenced composers throughout most of the Western world. The system of writing with twelve tones can be at once the most abstract and yet the most personal. That it yet leaves the rhythmic aspect, chordal spacing, orchestral color, and all the other aspects of composition to the composer still puts the burden of choice on the shoulders of the composer. This is as it should be.

The twelve-tone system was at one and the same time hailed as the solution of all compositional problems and condemned as an artificial straitjacket that strangled imagination. It was also described by some as an easy way out for composers with no talent and by others as the only way in which to achieve a new freedom. It is but a system, and like all systems it is only a means to an end. Like the earlier contrapuntal style, twelve-tone writing could be—and was for some— merely an exercise in the mathematics of relations of tones. For others, the system opened the way toward great, truly musical compositional achievement.

Schoenberg's influence through his music and his teaching was worldwide, and the twelve-tone system has spread throughout the musical world. Some composers have adopted it completely, while others have used its techniques as part of a larger, overall system. Two outstanding composers who used the system were Alban Berg and Anton Webern.

Berg

Alban Berg (1885–1935) was born in Vienna. After some untutored music study he began the study of composition with Schoenberg, who became not only teacher but friend. Berg aligned himself with the private performances of new music that had been organized by Schoenberg and supervised by Webern. He taught, lectured, and wrote articles on new music for magazines.

Berg's adoption of Schoenberg's twelve-tone method, in contrast to that of Webern's, allowed for a freer use of the disciplines of serial technique. Whereas the writing of Webern has been considered pointillistic, or dry and acerbic, Berg did not deny himself a lyricism that many listeners readily identify with. This lyricism, as well as the occasional use of tonality, have allowed for a readier acceptance of Berg's music than is true in the case of both Schoenberg and Webern.

Two important works that illustrate these qualities are the *Lyric Suite* for string quartet (1926) and the *Violin Concerto* (1935), which is discussed in some detail below. Berg also contributed two operas, *Wozzeck* (1921) and *Lulu* (1935). *Lulu* was never completed but is performed nonetheless. Both of those works are highly expressionistic.

COMMENTARY AND ANALYSIS

Concerto for Violin and Orchestra, Berg

One of the most felicitous works written in the twelve-tone system, Berg's *Violin Concerto* is a work that we shall look at in some detail. We shall examine Berg's use of the twelve-tone system and concurrently observe that Berg was unwilling to abandon all implications of tonality.

Dem Andenken eines Engels—thus is the work dedicated—"In remembrance of an angel." Berg had been approached in 1934 by the American violinist Louis Krasner to write a violin concerto. The project for the concerto lay dormant in Berg's mind until a close friend—an *intime* in Berg's circle—died in the spring of 1935. This was Manon Gropius, the 18-year-old daughter of Alma Mahler Gropius, the widow of Gustav Mahler. Berg decided that the concerto would stand as a memorial to Manon's memory. It was to be his last work, for he himself died later in the same year.

Although a memorial, the *Violin Concerto* is not a brooding work, nor does it restrict itself to an attitude of resignation. It has rather an aura of quiet reflection, an intellectual contemplation, as it were, on the mystery of life and death. Although we shall discuss the work with these ideas in mind, the listener should seek his own personal relation to the work.

The *Violin Concerto* is in two movements. The movements are further divided as shown in the table below.

Movement I

TIME SIGNATURE		MEASURES
$\frac{4}{4}$	Introduction: Andante	1–10
$\frac{2}{4}$	Section I Improvisatory style (ruminative)	11–103
$\frac{6}{8}$	Section II Scherzando: Allegretto Trio I Trio II	104–136 137–154 155–175
$\frac{3}{8}$	Scherzando (like a waltz) Folk song	176–213 213

Movement II

TIME SIGNATURE		MEASURES
	Section I	
$\frac{3}{4}$	Allegro (like a cadenza)	1–62
$\frac{4}{4}$	Written cadenza Pedal point on F	63–96 97–135
	Section II	
$\frac{4}{4}$	Adagio (chorale)	136–200
$\frac{3}{4}$	Folk song	201–213
$\frac{4}{4}$	Coda (chorale)	214–230

In the *Violin Concerto* there are tonal implications both within and without the twelve-tone row. In the opening measure of the work (Ex. 8–53) we hear pyramiding perfect fifths over a pedal B-flat sustained by the bass clarinet, providing

EXAMPLE 8-53

an implication of tonality that is later clarified in the chorale setting found in the final pages of the work. The solo violin enters in the second measure, imitating the bare fifths of the first measure, and establishing G as a second important tonal "root." The bass clarinet B-flat continues during this measure.

EXAMPLE 8-54

We first see the tone row that is basic to the work dispersed throughout the harmony in measures 11 to 15:

EXAMPLE 8-55   *Violin Concerto,* Berg

The row is then clearly seen in melodic order in the solo violin entrance that begins in measure 15.

EXAMPLE 8-56   *Violin Concerto,* Berg

Music on this page is used by permission of the Theodore Presser Company and Universal Edition A. G. Vienna, 1936.

While the row is being played *in toto* by the solo violin, the notes of the row are also being scattered throughout the accompanying instruments to form chordal structures. You can observe in measures 11–15 (see Ex. 8–55) that the composer has considerable freedom, even within the row, in choosing the notes to form a chord and in choosing their specific position within a chord.

Let us "step aside" for a moment to emphasize that the twelve-tone system is only a method of organization of sound. Whether the basis of a piece of music is pentatonic, modal, tonal, twelve-tone, or otherwise, the amount of consonance or dissonance is but a means to an end. What is most important is the composer's ability to handle his materials within the all-encompassing concept of music as existing in time. It is the rhythmic movement of the work that is primary. The rhythmic movement—in all its diversity of tension and release, climax and calm, ebb and the flow—is the *sine qua non.*

There are several ways in which Berg's row may be grouped. It may be thought of primarily as a series of ascending thirds from (1) through (9) and of major seconds from (9) through (12).

EXAMPLE 8-57

It may be considered for its possibilities of forming triads.

EXAMPLE 8-58

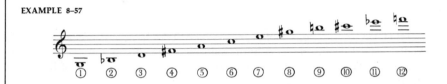

And it may also be thought of as three four-note groupings, in which the first two groups form identical chord structures, with the third group being the whole-tone tetrachord that is the hallmark of the Bach chorale, *Es ist Genug* (*It is enough*), which concludes the work.

EXAMPLE 8-59

Examples 8–57 and 8–58 are used by permission of the Theodore Presser Company and Universal Edition A. G. Vienna, 1936.

But note that the Bach chorale, *Es ist Genug,* is not only the goal of the entire work. It lies at the very heart of it. The twelve-tone row that is the basis of the work is so designed that the end of the row and the opening of the chorale consist of the same four notes (transposed).

MOVEMENT I

Berg divides the first movement into two main sections, the first ruminative, or reflecting, in its quasi-improvisatory style. The contrasting second section, marked *Allegretto,* is freely based upon the traditional Scherzo form with trio.

EXAMPLE 8–60

Berg marks the sections *Scherzando,* Quasi Trio I, Trio II, *Scherzando* (like a waltz); and towards the end he introduces a Carpathian folk song. At the beginning of Trio I, a Viennese waltz flavor is suggested by the use of broadly lyric major sixths in the strings.

EXAMPLE 8–61

Shortly after the beginning of the second *Scherzando,* the solo violin plays a theme that, by virtue of the parallel thirds and the melodic contour, is again suggestive of a Viennese waltz.

EXAMPLE 8–62

This is immediately echoed in the woodwinds. Shortly thereafter, Berg brings back the theme of the first *Scherzando,* as first heard in measure 104 (Ex. 8–60).

EXAMPLE 8–63

The horn now introduces the folk song, which may be thought of as representing the simple joys of everyday life.

EXAMPLE 8–64

MOVEMENT II

The second movement may be divided into two sections, the first of which is in the manner of an accompanied cadenza. The improvisatory style of the first section leads to the Bach chorale. Out of the randomness that often seems to be true of everyday existence emerges the clarity of thought and the peace of mind that *Es ist Genug* exemplifies.

In the second measure of the second movement the solo violin enters in an arpeggiation of the first four notes of the row and establishes G as the axis tone during the next few measures. During this section the four notes of the tritone tetrachord, and the logical extension of this, the whole-tone scales, are explored in the devices of inversion, retrograde motion, and so on. At measure 97 Berg establishes a pedal-point on F that lasts for 39 measures. At measure 136, the chorale, which has been alluded to in fragments, emerges in the solo violin part. It is alternately stated by the solo violin and the woodwind section. The woodwind section plays the Bach harmonization. The chorale becomes the summation of the work, and although it is briefly transformed and overshadowed by the folk song in measures 196–213, it reassumes its rock-like symbolization of stability at the coda, measure 214, to conclude the work.

In the following example, the particular sections that Berg quoted literally—in alternation with the solo violin—are bracketed.

EXAMPLE 8–65   *Es ist Genug*, J. S. Bach

Es ist genug!
So nimm, Herr, meinen Geist
Zu Zions Geistern hin.
Lös auf das Band das allgemächtlich reisst,
Befreie diesen Sinn, der sich nach seinem Gotte sehnet,
Der täglich klagt und nächtlich thränet:
Es ist genug! Es ist genug!

Free translation:

It is enough!
So take, oh Lord, my soul
To Zion on high.
Dissolve the bond that constantly is rent,
Free this mind that is longing for God,
That daily laments and nightly cries:
It is enough! It is enough!

Webern

Anton Webern (1883–1945), born in Vienna, studied at the University of Vienna. He conducted theater orchestras, taught composition and became actively involved in a series of performances organized by Schoenberg for the purpose of presenting new musical works. In his adoption of the twelve-tone method he extended the idea of row technique into the area of tone color, so that there is a constantly changing "wheel of color" as it were. His output was not large and, at first, acceptance of his work was tentative; since his death the circle of appreciation has been growing larger and larger. It was Webern, finally, more than Schoenberg and Berg, who was to be the strongest influence on many composers today. This influence has been international.

Webern was strongly impressed with the compactness and brevity of Schoenberg's *Three Piano Pieces*, Op. 11. They became for him an ideal, and in following this ideal Webern went even further in the concentration of materials. Webern's music is not exploratory or developmental; his method is not to be thought of as an essay or a journey. It is epigrammatic: An idea's first statement is its final statement. The conciseness of Webern's musical thought—adhering to the belief that something need be said only once—demands great concentration on the part of the listener. Webern's *Five Pieces for Orchestra* (1911–1913) are but one example of his concise style of writing. The five pieces take a total of about ten minutes to play. The shortest, the fourth piece, is six measures long and takes under twenty seconds to play. Webern had already abandoned tonality, and we see in these pieces the looking forward to the twelve-tone method that he turned to in 1924 with his *Three Songs*, Op. 17. Webern's innate sense of rhythmic flow is not always readily apparent to the listener, but it is there, nonetheless, as a unifying factor in the music. His attitude of meticulous concern for the placement of every tone with respect to rhythm and pitch make it easy to understand why he did not employ the use of *Sprechstimme*, where pitches are only approximated. His total output is contained on four discs. Other important works are: *Symphony for Chamber Orchestra*, Op. 21 (1928); *Das Augenlicht* for mixed chorus and orchestra (1935); *Variations for Orchestra*, Op. 30 (1940); and *Cantata No. 2*, for soprano and bass soloists, chorus and orchestra (1943).

It has been stated that "Webern's music often seems to be on the verge of silence"—rests play a major role in his music—and it is in this area, too, that he paved the way for later and bolder experiments.

Hindemith

Paul Hindemith (1895–1963), born in Germany, attained early proficiency on several musical instruments. His main instrument was the violin, and his ability was such that he became concertmaster of the Frankfort Opera. His interest then turned to the viola, and it is this instrument that he played in quartet tours of Europe. He later maintained that a composer should be able to play, at least a little, any instrument that he wrote for. This is an interesting ideal, and there is certainly nothing that can be said against it. But by no means has it been effectively demonstrated in practice.

Hindemith began in Berlin what was to be a long career in teaching, a career he pursued in addition to his composing. His differences with the new political regime resulted in his leaving Germany in 1935. He toured as violist in the United States in 1937 and at later times, but it was through his teaching of composition in this country after 1940 that he exerted the most influence. It was in the summer of that year that he taught at the Berkshire Music Center, and in the same year he was appointed to the faculty of Yale University.

Hindemith, along with Stravinsky, Schoenberg, and Bartók, was one of the dominant forces in musical thought in the United States until at least the middle of the twentieth century. Hindemith enhanced his influence further through several books that he wrote. *The Craft of Musical Composition* is a standard work, along with his *Elementary Training for Musicians*. *A Composer's World* is a collection of essays delivered at Harvard University in 1949.

Hindemith composed some of the most important works of our day. The amount of music he wrote was not only prodigious but much of it gained immediate acceptance and was performed regularly in the leading musical centers. He wrote for all instruments and in every genre. And he conducted performances of his own works along with those of other composers in the major capitals of the world.

His style was his own. His technique, as expounded in *The Craft of Musical Composition*, was a careful construction that included a contemporary way of approaching music, which, nevertheless, had in its roots in tradition. His melodies, which often seem both to evade and to suggest tonality, are sometimes modal in flavor but spiked with jagged contours that temporarily disguise the mode. His harmonies are based upon a system of comparative tension of vertical structures.

A humorous short opera, *Hin und Zurück* (*There and Back*), showed the use of a basic contrapuntal retrograde device applied to a total work. The story and the music having proceeded about half the way, each thereupon goes backward until the end, which is to say, the beginning.

Hindemith also believed, contrary to most contemporary composers, in practical music, *Gebrauchsmusik*—music that may be performed by amateur groups. A concert of his music at Harvard University in 1949 exemplified this interest. The concert was given on the occasion of the birthday of Mrs. Elizabeth Sprague Coolidge, a great patroness of music. Hindemith composed a round especially for this event, and he taught it to the audience so that they could serenade Mrs. Coolidge.

In line with the idea of *Gebrauchsmusik*, Hindemith set for himself the task of writing a sonata for each orchestral instrument.

Among his outstanding works are the opera, *Mathis der Maler*, from which he later extracted a symphony; *Nobilissima Visione*, originally a ballet; *Symphonic Metamorphosis of Themes by Weber* for orchestra; *Der Schwanendreher* for viola and small orchestra; and *Das Marienleben*, a cycle of songs.

Bartók

Of all the outstanding composers active in the first half of the twentieth century, Béla Bartók (1881–1945) received the least general recognition while alive.

Figure 36.   Béla Bartók. (Courtesy, M. Schwald)

Financial rewards as well as the plaudits were minimal and performances were few. His death in New York City in 1945 released the floodgates, however, and his music began to be played, published, recorded, and discussed in a surge of belated recognition.

Bartók was born in Hungary. His father died when he was seven, and there developed between mother and son a close bond. It was she who gave him his first piano lessons when he was five, and it was she who discovered that he not only had perfect pitch, but a Mozartean faculty for remembering a tune he had composed, not needing to write it down until some time later. At the age of 11, Bartók made his first public appearance as both pianist and composer, a dual role he was to maintain throughout his life. Perhaps the most important phase of his career was entered when he notated a Hungarian peasant song, taking it down from the singing of a young peasant girl. This brought him to the realization that there was a vast native music of which he was unaware. He began a study of peasant music, and with Zoltán Kodály he spent about two years recording the native music not only of Hungarians, but also of Rumanians, Slovakians, Walachians, Turks, and Arabs. The peasant folk song became central to Bartók's compositional style, and examples of this influence may be found on many pages of his work.

Whereas Hindemith had a system that encompassed all his writings, Bartók had no general system, but rather approached each work anew. The system for that work would arise out of the composition itself. Thus, when harmonizing a Hungarian folk song, he might find the harmony from the melody itself, by "verticalizing" the melody.

Bartók's manner of approaching each work may be seen most conveniently in his six volumes for piano, *Mikrokosmos*. The title is indicative of his intent. Within a specific small world of a certain number of tones Bartók will explore and probe every corner. This small world is sufficient unto itself. It desires no other world, nor does it need one. What this technique does require, however, is a special kind of composer, because this way of writing can lead the composer into the trap of monotony. For each piece Bartók sets the problem and finds the solution, a solution that is unique for each piece. This approach may be seen in Bartók's last large work, the *Concerto for Orchestra*, written under a commission from Serge Koussevitzky. The entire first movement has as its seed and its defining feature the interval of a perfect fourth.

Prokofiev and Shostakovich

Sergei Prokofiev (1891–1953) began composing at the age of nine, and before he graduated from the St. Petersburg Conservatory he had become an excellent pianist and was performing his own works. He later traveled extensively as a concert pianist, including trips to America. His biting, ironic style of writing produced *Diabolical Suggestion* and *Sarcasms* for piano and earned him a reputation as a "futurist." *Scythian Suite* was his first important orchestral composition and is an example of a barbaric, primitive style, somewhat similar to that of Stravinsky in *The Rite of Spring*.

He also wrote music that is simple, charming, and naïve. *Peter and the Wolf* was written for a children's theater and his since attained great popularity. Although Prokofiev's music contains sudden juxtapositions of keys, polytonality, and other contemporary practices, it is rooted in the tonal system. In his music may be found a mixture of Russian nationalism, neo-Classicism, and French colorism. He was a prolific composer and wrote in all idioms, including music for a film, *Alexander Nevsky*. His *"Classical"* Symphony is a superb example of sophisticated wit, concise form, and clear, sparkling orchestration.

Dimitri Shostakovich, who was born in 1906, is best known in this country for his symphonies. His *First Symphony*, composed when he was 18, is still popular, and the *Fifth Symphony* is also often performed. His "Polka" from *The Golden Age*, a ballet, is exceedingly well known. After World War II he was in great favor in both his own country and the United States, and the completion of his new symphony in 1942, the *Seventh*, set off a flurry in the world press. Known popularly as the *"Leningrad"* Symphony, it was wildly hailed. As a representative composer of Russia, Shostakovich, like Prokofiev, often found himself in a precarious position. Several times he was denounced by the Russian government as leaning towards the "decadence" of capitalism and each time he had to admit his "fault." During a visit to New York in 1949 he tried—somewhat unsuccessfully—to expound to the press why a composer must be guided by political and national ties.

His symphonies are large in scope, somewhat bombastic and militaristic, but well-knit and appealing.

Other important composers

Ralph Vaughan Williams

Vaughan Williams (1872–1958), the elder statesman of twentieth-century English composers, may be understood most immediately by making reference to two of his most familiar works, *Fantasia on a Theme of Tallis* (1910) for orchestra and his arrangement of the rugged church tune *Old Hundredth*. In each, the choice of materials and harmonic setting springs out of traditionalism, the mark of the Englishman. We find influences of the English renaissance polyphonic style as well.

His texts show a very strong preference for English writers, from Chaucer to

Hardy, with the Bible being a pervading influence. Vaughan Williams wrote in all forms. His output included operas, choral works, chamber works, and nine symphonies.

Gustav Holst

Although not as dominant a force in the resurgence of English music as Vaughan Williams, Gustav Holst (1874–1934) was nevertheless an important part of the musical scene in England in the early twentieth century. Holst wrote in all forms, with choral works forming the largest part of his catalogue, and an interest in Eastern literature and in astrology produced a number of works of unique appeal. One of the most important works resulting from this interest, *The Planets*, a suite for orchestra in seven movements, was first presented in a semi-private concert in 1919. Holst's interest in text in his choral writings led him to the use of uneven time-signatures and changing time-signatures in order to produce a freedom and elasticity of rhythm that would enhance the text.

William Walton

A generation later than Vaughan Williams, and a child of the twentieth century, William Walton (1902–   ) nevertheless retains in his work some elements of Romanticism. In a time which brought forth Bartók's *Allegro Barbaro* (1911), Schoenberg's *Pierrot Lunaire* (1912), Stravinsky's *Le Sacre du printemps* (1913), and Berg's *Wozzeck* (1914–1923), Walton retained the restraint typical of the English. His *Belshazzar's Feast* of 1931 is representative. A large choral work, it is colorful and theatrical, and based on the book of Psalms and the book of Daniel. The orchestra is large and the score also calls for two extra brass bands. A charmingly ironic setting for small chamber orchestra of Dame Edith Sitwell's set of poems, *Façade*, written when he was twenty, was the first work to bring him considerable attention.

Benjamin Britten

A prolific composer who has assayed music in all forms, Benjamin Britten (1913–   ) is perhaps best known for his operas. For a while—from the year 1945 on—Britten turned out a new opera each year. *Peter Grimes*, in 1945, was followed by the *Rape of Lucretia, Albert Herring*, a new version of John Gay's *The Beggar's Opera*, and in 1949, *Let's Make an Opera*. This last is a chamber opera that begins as a play and shortly involves the audience in the performance.

Britten's first opera, *Peter Grimes*, was such a success that it soon was produced on the stages of famous opera houses throughout the world. Britten had, prior to this, written the scores to over a dozen films, and had also written an operetta, *Paul Bunyan*, produced in New York at Columbia University in 1941. His first important work was *Variations on a Theme of Frank Bridge* (1937) for string orchestra. Britten's compass is large, evidenced not only by the variety of his works, but by the scope of his musical thought within a work. He is also an accomplished pianist. Most recently he has been the fountainhead for an opera house at Aldeburgh where he keeps fresh the stream of live performance, often including his own works. He is producer, manager, money-raiser, and conductor. The works best known in America are the operas *Peter Grimes*, *Albert Herring*, *Billy Budd*, and the more recent *Turn of the Screw* which effectively adapts Henry James' chilling psychological novel for the operatic stage. His *Serenade* for tenor, horn, and strings, identified with the superb artistry of the late eminent French horn player, Dennis Brain, shows Britten's felicitous use of smaller forces. His *Young Person's Guide to the Orchestra: Variations and Fugue on a Theme of Purcell*, was written in 1945 as the score to an educational film. Both witty and robust in its presentation of the instruments, it is a uniquely refreshing work, and has become Britten's most recorded work in America. Grandiose and well-wrought, the *War Requiem*, written in 1962 to commemorate the rebuilding of Coventry Cathedral, is a dramatic composition based on the English poems of Wilfred Owen and the liturgical requiem mass.

Heitor Villa-Lobos

The leading Brazilian composer, Heitor Villa-Lobos (1887–1959), was one of the most prolific of twentieth-century composers. Filled with boundless energy, he not only wrote hundreds of works in every genre, but also was internationally active as a conductor, and in addition found time to become one of the leading educationists in his native country. His efforts in this last area resulted in the establishment of his own National Conservatory in 1942; he had already been appointed Superintendent of Musical Education in Rio de Janeiro. His musical life was influenced by two opposing factors. As a youth he made several forays into various interior parts of Brazil, usually as an itinerant musician, and in this way became well acquainted with the various kinds of folk music and popular music that was his heritage. In later years he spent some time in Europe, much of it in Paris where the influence of Ravel was important. His music displays these two seemingly opposing factors. It is both nationalist and international. One of his most endearing and well-known works, *Bachianas Brasileiras No. 5* for voice and eight cellos, exhibits both his national and personal emotional expression combined with his love for the objectivity of the music of a composer (Bach) much removed from him in distance and time.

Carl Nielsen

The strongest voice in the music of Denmark has been that of Carl Nielsen (1865–1931). Somewhat overshadowed for many years by his fellow Scandinavian, Sibelius, he began to be noticed in America about mid-century, and now a good body of his works are available on recordings, including several concertos, much chamber music, and his six·symphonies. Nielsen writes in a broad, expansive style that combines uses of modality and chromaticism, and often he uses conflicting tonalities in a unique way to achieve a tension that is resolved sometimes with the simplest of harmonies. His work is easily assimilated and his audience, while still small, is growing ever larger.

Les Six

In the Paris of post-World War I, the names of six composers were grouped together by Henri Collet in a newspaper article as representative of the new expression in French music. Known as "Les Six," and with Satie as their "spiritual" leader, they made a strong impact. Only three of these six composers moved forward to take their places in the main stream of twentieth-century music.

Arthur Honegger (1892–1955) symbolized the machine age with *Pacific 231*, a musical "imitation" of a locomotive. This attracted much attention, but Honegger moved away from this "representational tone-painting." A prolific composer, he wrote five symphonies, as well as operas, choral works, ballets, chamber music, piano music, and songs. He also composed for film and radio. His large choral work, *King David*, is representative. His chamber work, *Sonatine*, shows the influence of jazz. Although he used devices such as polytonality and suggestions of atonality, his music was tonally based and lyrically melodic.

Darius Milhaud (1892–1974) wrote a steady stream of music from his student days in Paris. One of the first to exploit polytonality, a pianist, conductor, and teacher, an experimenter in forms as well as means, he wrote in every important genre in interesting styles that encompassed the lyrical and the rhythmical, the dramatic and the playful. He exerted a great influence on young American composers through his teaching in the United States. One of his earliest works is still the best known: the ballet *La Création du monde*. Written for a small orchestra, the musical idiom suggests not so much jazz, as is often stated, as the music of the night-club of the 1920's.

Francis Poulenc (1899–1963), the last of the three composers to be discussed here, represents in his music a certain delightful kind of Gallic wit and charm. His style is eclectic, but a certain tongue-in-cheek approach often adds a distinct individuality to his scores. His work covers satirical chamber works, concertos and ballets, large choral works both secular and sacred, and opera. The opera *La Voix*

Figure 37.   "Les Six."   (Bulloz)

humaine, is a splendid example of his ability to impart a compelling immediacy to his work in its portrayal of a woman at the telephone in a farewell outburst to a faithless lover.

The other three of Les Six—Georges Auric, Louis Durey, and Germaine Tailleferre—did not go on to fulfill the promise that seemed to be theirs as members of an elite group. Auric is best known as the composer of scores for several successful films, among them: *Caesar and Cleopatra* (1945), *The Queen of Spades* (1948), and *Lavender Hill Mob* (1951).

Copland

Aaron Copland, born in 1900 in Brooklyn, was one of the first American composers to study in Paris with Nadia Boulanger, an important French teacher. The "trek" had begun, and many young American composers after Copland were to come under her wing. Growing up in an America that was seeking to find itself musically, Copland was energized by the cosmopolitan exchange of ideas among the artists there. He purposely sought to become an "American composer," and in so doing we find the influence of jazz in some of his early works. His *Piano Concerto* (1927) reflects this. He then turned to the music of an earlier America, and the barn dance and the hoedown became prominent in his music. In *Rodeo, Billy the Kid, Appalachian Spring,* all ballets, we find the "prairie" style in the homely dance rhythms and simple folk tunes.

Copland has sometimes been referred to as the "dean of American composers," not so much for the Americanism of his music as for his constantly active life as a composer, conductor, author, lecturer, and teacher. He has written several books, among them *Our New Music,* which have had wide dissemination. He has always pleaded the work of the American composer—calling attention to it, discussing it, analyzing it, performing it, and conducting it. For many years his influence was strong in his position as head of the composition department at the Berkshire Music Center at Tanglewood.

Other Americans

Roger Sessions, born in 1896 in Brooklyn, was influenced early by Ernest Bloch, with whom he studied, and later to some extent by Stravinsky. His writing is highly individual, with emphasis on a tight contrapuntal style and uncompromising dissonance, with the result that his work has not gained wide public acceptance. His thoughtful, probing approach has not produced a large number of works, but among his works there are four symphonies, a variety of chamber works, some concertos and choral works, and an opera, *Montezuma.* As a teacher at Smith College, Princeton University, and other institutions, he has had widespread influence extended by a text on harmony, as well as other writings.

Walter Piston, born in 1894, was handily served during thirty-six years of teaching at Harvard University by the proximity of the Boston Symphony Orchestra, for which he wrote many works. In his music we find a workmanlike approach, a sense of craftsmanship and a careful concern for design. There are six symphonies to his credit and much delightful chamber music, but his most played work has been the ballet *The Incredible Flutist*, introduced by Arthur Fiedler and the Boston Pops Orchestra in 1938. His teaching resulted in three important texts, each of which is widely known and widely used: *Harmony*, *Counterpoint*, and *Orchestration*.

Samuel Barber has received many commissions and honors. Born in 1910, and considered by some to be American to the core, his work nevertheless has its roots in Europe. His diatonic style is easy to listen to. His *Essay for Orchestra* is one of his most played works, and his *Overture to the School for Scandal* is also well known.

Elliott Carter studied with Piston and Nadia Boulanger. He was born in 1908 into a well-to-do family in New York, and acquired a leisurely, thorough education. Some of his early works show influences of Stravinsky and Copland, but his style was constantly developing towards a rhythmic concept that is uniquely his own. His *Piano Sonata* of 1945–1946 is considered his first outstanding work. Although his work was largely unknown before 1950, it has been gaining much notice and far wider acceptance in the last few years. Perhaps Carter's most important achievement has been what he calls "metrical modulation," in which the speed is carefully adjusted by special metronomic designations for successive note values.

Underlining the strong Americanism of William Schuman (born 1910) is his *Chester Overture* for band, based upon a hymn tune by William Billings, a composer of American revolutionary times. Among others writing in this pleasing, colloquial style are Douglas Moore (1893–1969), Howard Hanson (1896–   ), Virgil Thomson (1896–   ), Roy Harris (1898–   ), Paul Creston (1906–   ), and Randall Thompson (1899–   ).

Gunther Schuller (1925–   ) is one of the recent lights on the musical scene in America. His activities are many and varied, and in this respect he may be considered a latter-day Aaron Copland. He has written much for small groups. He also has to his credit a *Symphony for Brass and Percussion*, which is an exceedingly well wrought piece, one of the few works written for brass by a composer who knows how to handle these instruments from practical experience (as a professional French horn player). His best-known work is *Seven Studies of Paul Klee*, and it takes its place beside a work written well over a half-century before—Mussorgsky's *Pictures at an Exhibition*—as a composer's reaction to a graphic expression. Schuller has not only been active in the music of the concert hall, but has concerned himself with the most serious personal expression of the times—jazz. Originator of the phrase, "Third Stream," which refers to the blending of

Figure 38. "La Creation du Monde," sets and costumes by Leger, 1923. (Danmuseet, Stockholm)

jazz and art music, he has been intimately involved as composer, conductor, and promulgator of these apparently opposite expressions in an attempt to find a new expression for our times.

Gian-Carlo Menotti (1911–   ) has been a somewhat controversial figure in this country. Commissioned to write a short opera for television in 1951, he was thrust into immediate renown and, as well, into the forum of discussion regarding his merits as a composer. The opera, *Amahl and the Night Visitors*, has been a staple on television during the Christmas season for a number of years. Its commercial success, and the commercial success of the operas which followed, produced in the manner of Broadway plays rather than by the Metropolitan Opera Company, were part of the reason for the criticism. The criticism was also directed toward his writing obviously for the people, his eclecticism—especially his musical style as reminiscent of Puccini—and his dramatic approach, which some thought to be too ebullient for the twentieth century. Nevertheless, in his operas —perhaps most notably in *The Saint of Bleeker Street*—he has shown that he has the capacity to do what every successful operatic composer must do: write a musico-dramatic work which not only exists in the mind of the composer but is a complete, well-wrought work on the stage, ultimately becoming a complete expression for the opera-goer. That he achieved these aims is beyond question. Whether he has written works of enduring quality is something for the future to ascertain.

Gershwin and Bernstein

Two composers, some distance apart and of rather opposite backgrounds, are responsible for two of the most important works of the musical theater: George Gershwin and Leonard Bernstein. They had been preceded by Kurt Weill, who in 1933 brought over from Germany *The Threepenny Opera*, a modern adaptation of *The Beggar's Opera*. In its social satire the popular song style is purposely used to illustrate social decadence. It is used so well that one of the songs, "Mack the Knife," has become an American popular song. Weill settled in America in 1935 and thereafter produced several successful musical plays, among them *Knicker-bocker Holiday, Lost in the Stars*, and a folk opera, *Down in the Valley*.

Gershwin grew up in the world of popular music. Born in Brooklyn in 1898, he began playing piano in music stores at the age of sixteen to demonstrate current songs for buyers of sheet music. Gershwin was not a jazz musician, as has been so often claimed. This confusion on the part of many writers arises from the fact that in the twenties, known as "The Jazz Age," popular music was called jazz and all orchestras of the time that played for dancing were referred to as "jazz" orchestras. Gershwin was, rather, a high gifted composer of popular songs, and in turning his talents to works in larger forms successfully synthesized the popular music element with the aims of these large dramatic forms. This is apparent in his *Rhapsody in Blue*, the *Piano Concerto*, and *An American in Paris*. His supreme achievement, however, was his folk opera *Porgy and Bess*.

Gershwin had already become extremely familiar with the multitudinous problems of producing successful musical theater while writing many musical comedies. Gershwin brought into this field his unique approach to writing popular music.

Popular music is, in certain ways, a folk music. It is not written for the concert hall, and it is not usually written for instruments; it is written to be sung. It is similar to true folk music in that it is for an individual singer with or without accompaniment. That it is often trite or insipid is true but unimportant. And the fact that jazz has often absorbed popular materials into its modes of expression has no bearing except perhaps to show how much difference there is between popular music and jazz.

Gershwin's contributions to popular music were of the highest order. His most important work, *Porgy and Bess*, is a mixture of popular styles, the blues, and the Negro spiritual. For example, the opening song, "Summertime," in its almost totally pentatonic usage, is reminiscent of the spiritual. No single one of these elements in itself makes a successful work, but in *Porgy and Bess* they all contribute to its importance.

Leonard Bernstein's musical background was the antithesis of George Gershwin's. Born in Lawrence, Massachusetts, he studied music at Harvard University and went on to study further at the Curtis Institute in Philadelphia, where,

Figure 39.   Leonard Bernstein with Serge Koussevitzsky. (Orkin, N.Y.)

in addition to piano, he studied orchestration and conducting. At the Berkshire Music Center he became first a protégé of and then an assistant to Serge Koussevitsky, music director of the Boston Symphony Orchestra. In 1943, Bruno Walter, conductor of the New York Philharmonic, fell ill, and on short notice Bernstein filled in. His achievement was noted in the press, and he went on to conducting engagements with major symphony orchestras throughout the world.

He wrote symphonies and chamber works, ballets and vocal works. Of importance to his ultimate contribution to the theater were *On the Town* in 1944 and *Wonderful Town* in 1952, both extremely successful musical comedies. In *Trouble in Tahiti*, a one-act opera, and *Candide*, a rather "serious" musical comedy, he received further experience in the theater, culminating in 1957 with *West Side Story*, which successfully reflected the issues of contemporary America.

Gershwin began as a composer of popular music and finally broadened the scope of his talents through constant study until he finally embraced the larger forms. Bernstein learned the formal aspects of music first, and thoroughly, and then allowed the popular music idiom to permeate his work for the theater.

It is important to stress that in each of these composers—Gershwin and Bernstein—the ultimate expression, which embraced both popular music and the larger dramatic concept, was not a forced expression. The fusion was the natural result of an honest appreciation of both types of expression. Neither had to search to *be* an "American composer." Each *was*.

COMMENTARY AND ANALYSIS

Rhapsody in Blue, Gershwin

This pioneer work was written for the Paul Whiteman Band in 1924. It was the first product of Gershwin's deep interest in the larger forms of music, an interest which developed after his early success as a composer of popular songs and show tunes. (*La La Lucille*, 1919, had 104 performances.) He continued in this more serious vein with works such as the *Concerto in F* for piano and orchestra (1925); *American in Paris* (1928); and the superb folk opera, *Porgy and Bess* (1935).

Each of these works shows the influence of the popular/jazz idiom, but each also represents more than that influence. Gershwin achieved a remarkable synthesis of popular American musical expression with forms previously developed in Europe. His larger works represent neither popular music, nor classical music; they are rather anticipations of the concept of Third Stream Music in the 1950's (see above). Gershwin's part in broadening the stream of American music cannot be overemphasized.

Theme 1, following the famous clarinet trill and glissando, is bluesy and syncopated. It will reappear in many guises.

EXAMPLE 8–66

After Theme 1 is given a leisurely presentation by the orchestra, a new idea—built on accented repeated notes—appears about half way through the first section.

EXAMPLE 8–67

The role of this new melodic idea is subsidiary for now; later it will take a leading part. After a quiet entrance of the solo piano followed by brilliant technical heroics, Theme 1 makes a strong re-entry in the orchestra. The faster tempo and bright orchestration make it now sound exciting—almost raucous.

Soon a new theme appears (Theme 2). Introduced by a dissonant trill in the trumpet, it possesses great rhythmic drive; the piano accompanies it with light, decorative figures.

EXAMPLE 8–68

Next, bold and brash, Theme 3 enters:

EXAMPLE 8–69

Though it sounds brand new, it has been heard previously. Compare it with Example 8–67, above; it is now simply a full statement of what had been hinted at before. Gershwin has used the idea of thematic transformation, so prominent in the tone poems of Liszt and other romantic composers.

Still Theme 4 arrives, again in the orchestra. It is highly syncopated, beginning in the bass, but later it is carried through into other parts of the orchestra.

EXAMPLE 8–70

At the end of this theme the piano plays alone for a considerable time, presenting a variant of the repeated-note idea seen in Example 8–69.

Theme 1 now returns, *fortissimo*, first in the piano and then in the orchestra. The piano again is given a long solo section that develops Theme 4 (Ex. 8–70). This then turns into a short cadenza that ends on a quiet note of preparation.

It is now time for the Rhapsody's "hit tune" to enter: Theme 5. Theme 5 is presented quietly, first by the orchestra, then by the soloist. Except for the syncopations cropping up in the third measure, one might think it was written by Rachmaninoff.

After a pause, the piano plunges into a new idea (Agitato e misterioso) suggesting the baroque toccata style. Soon, slipping in underneath, the basic motive from Theme 5 (Ex. 8–71) takes over again.

EXAMPLE 8–71

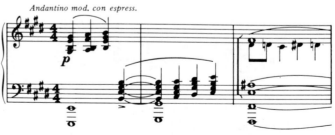

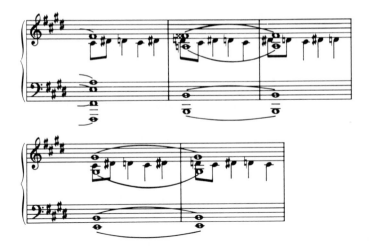

Powerful rising octaves in the piano, a pause, and a dissonant chord prepare for the conclusion. The piano, *agitato*, plunges ahead and finally ushers in a full statement of Theme 3 (Ex. 8–69). In its turn, this leads to the final *molto allargando* (very broad), an exultant entrance of Theme 1.*

* Examples 8–66 to 8–71 are from George Gershwin, *Rhapsody in Blue,* Version: Four Hands, Two Piano Score. © 1924 Harms, Inc. Copyright renewed and assigned to New World Music Corporation. All rights reserved. Used by permission of Warner Bros. Music.

Chapter nine

THE OTHER SIDE: FOLK, JAZZ, AND POP

FOLK MUSIC

There has always been the other side; that side of music—sounding not in gilded court or bourgeois salon but in the field, hut, barge, and tavern. Folk music, both song and dance, not only has expressed man's deepest joys and agonies, but also has been a vital thread within the fabric of the human community. The fishmonger chanted his wares before the walled courtyards in great Chinese cities; blacks moaned their spirituals and later their blues to lessen their pain; and many a colonial maiden in 1776 sang of her absent love:

> O Johnny dear has gone away,
> He has gone far across the bay,
> O my heart is sad and weary today,
> Johnny has gone for a soldier.

Although the physical part of common man more often than not has been abused and debased, that human portion of his being, that part which is at the core of music, has never been touched. Man sings so as never to lose his human selfhood.

Throughout this book we have referred to folk music, though we have not emphasized it as such. One cannot speak of the masters and their times without taking into account how folklore has touched and stimulated their creative lives. We have seen a humorous quodlibet at the hands of J. S. Bach where two German folk songs are intertwined within a most sophisticated contrapuntal texture. Brahms' *Academic Festival Overture* is a well-known composition that is based on four German student songs. We have seen how the "Mighty Handful" in nineteenth-century Russia were sparked by folk music and dance to contribute a superb body of music strongly suggestive of the rich earth and the people closest to it (see Chapter 7). In the preceding chapter it was shown how a folk song may crop up in a serial work, the first movement of Berg's *Violin Concerto*. And Copland's ballet *Appalachian Spring* features an American Shaker song, "Simple Gifts."

Folk music research

It was in the nineteenth century that music historians and musicians first took serious account of the creative musical voice of the people. But as early as 1778, the philosopher/critic Johann Herder pointed the way to the rediscovery and utilization of folk art with literary works such as *Volkslieder* (*Folk Songs*). Early in this century Bartók and Kodály scoured mideastern Europe, compiling large collections of folk songs and dances and assimilating them into their own personal musical styles. Vaughan Williams in England, Villa-Lobos in Brazil, and Carlos Chávez (1899–   ) in Mexico experienced a similar folk "enlightenment." Not only did the music of the people enter the domain of the concert hall, but it also became the object of careful research and philosophical speculation. If folk music pervades the life of man, what makes it so vital? What is its essence?

The essentials

For a music to be of the folk it must have simplicity and immediacy. It must be easily understood and savored by the masses and be simple enough technically to be played or sung by anyone with a desire to do so. Its harmony, if present, is uncomplicated and its formal structure is often plain. Many folk songs from the Western World can be set to elementary harmony consisting of just a few chords. Much of the time its structure is *strophic:* a tune repeated several times to changing text. Also, it must have permanence and universality; it must have been fired and toughened by the collective life experience of a people until it endures. The universality of all folk music lies in its reflection of the emotional identity common to all mankind. Just as joy, grief, love, hate, resignation, aspiration reside everywhere, so do these emotions underlie the folk music of the world. This universal emotion in all folk music persists even though the exterior musical shape varies from people to people, from land to land.

One should not be hampered with fruitless speculations on the validity of folk music relative to its anonymity. There have been many who held that to be truly of the folk, music must spring from the anonymous masses. The French critic Tiersot thought that, "There is no such thing as a folk song whose composer is known, not only by his name but even approximately by his place of origin or the period of his life." And Carl Sandburg suggests the same thing speaking of his superb collection of folk songs: "*The American Songbag* comes from the hearts and voices of thousands of men and women. They made new songs, they changed old songs, they carried songs from place to place, they resurrected and kept alive dying and forgotten songs." What really matters is not so much the folk song's origin—individual or collective—but its acceptance, molding, and transmission by the masses. Once a people is moved by what Sandburg calls, "strips, stripes, and streaks of color," over the years they gradually give it a contour and atmosphere that is uniquely theirs. The music then becomes of the folk; it has acquired a patina, a durability that transforms it into a cherished item of human culture. Once the idea is accepted that a folk music is selected, refined, and transmitted by the masses, there is little difficulty in understanding why certain popular items, no matter what their source, are a true folk music. The French tune, "Au Clair de la lune" certainly must be seen as a folk expression. Yet it was written by Lully, the court composer to Louis XIV. Many of the popular songs of Stephen Foster, and songs such as Daniel Emmett's minstrel tune, *Dixie*, became folk music. A broadened view of folk music to include much composed or improvised music makes it easier to see the role of jazz as lying somewhere within the purview of folk music. The jazz critic Nat Hentoff calls for a broader concept in this way: ". . . if 'folk' as a term is to have any operative (rather than merely promotional) meaning, it will have to be redefined. And considerably elasticized. It will have to allow for broad heterogeneity of material and musical interests in a single performer, united by a firmly personal stamp of conception and style."* Folk music need not be anonymous, and it need not be unlettered. Some of it originated in musical notation, and much of it has been handed down this way. Actually, a notated folk song can no more lose its plasticity than a country yarn can lose its punch by appearing in a newspaper or magazine. It is the special manner in which folk music is performed each time that keeps it fresh.

Folk/art music

A serious question arises concerning folk songs and dances transcribed or arranged by modern composers. The collections, *Old American Songs* by Copland, Britten's arrangements of *Songs of the British Isles*, Falla's *Seven Popular Spanish Songs*, Bartók's *Roumanian Folk Dances*, are but a few. Here, already well-formed expressions of the people have been polished, honed, and adjusted to the composer's highly personal musical language. Though tune and text are left close to the origi-

---

* David A. De Turk and A. Poulin, Jr., ed., *The American Folk Scene: Dimensions of the Folk Song Revival*, "The Future of the Folk Renascence," by Nat Hentoff (New York: Dell, 1965), p. 328.

Figure 40. Negro slaves in early nineteenth-century America, dancing. (Abbey Aldrich Rockefeller Folk Art Collection)

nal, the sophisticated harmony in the accompaniment devised by the composer transforms the music into a kind of hybrid folk/art music. These settings result in valid works to the degree that the composer identifies with and sublimates the simplicity and universality of his folk material.

Modern folk: USA

There has been a resurgence of folk music in recent years. What about it? Does it contribute to the cultural climate of the world? Is it true folk? Does its unabashed commercialism reflect in any way on its validity and integrity? In the rural areas of the USA, folk music has always been a pervasive force. Through the process of acculturation a polyglot music from many corners of the world became American-ized. In the "culturally deprived" countryside and among the working class in general it waxed true and strong. In the fields of the South the black slave sang

> Bendin' knees a achin',
> Body racked wid pain.
> I wish I was a child of God,
> I'd git home bimeby.

to music that would ultimately suffuse the blues, ragtime, and then jazz. The colonial maid, singing forlornly the words

> *Shule, shule, shule agrah,*
> *Time can only heal my woe,*

from "Johnny Has Gone for a Soldier," cared little that the song was of Irish import. Alan Lomax tells that this soldier tune was used as well for a lumberman's complaint and a sea chantey. America's truly indigenous Indian music had little impact on the broad current of folk music. But various folk expressions reflecting immigrant ethnic sub-cultures did have great impact. The two most powerful influences on the development of folk music USA were those musical elements coming from black Africa and from Anglo-Saxon Europe. In the early twentieth century, folk scholars such as John A. Lomax and Cecil Sharp, the Englishman, combed the land, collecting large numbers of authentic songs. In the 1930's and 1940's these found their way into many printed collections. In the 1930's John and Alan Lomax, using primitive recording instruments, captured the actual sound of many native songs. But it was when they introduced the great blues singer, Leadbelly (Huddie Ledbetter) to large urban centers that the folk "arrival" really began. This was a significant moment. Modern folk music as we know it today is essentially a big-city, college-campus music. Only when the hardy stock of traditional countryside music became leavened by urban intellectual curiosity and ferment did it burgeon into the pervasive force that it has become. What it has become in the last decade is of a perplexing variety and quality. Robert S. Whitman and Sheldon S. Kagan list modern folk as falling into several basic categories: traditional as practiced by Texas Gladden; interpretive—Peggy Seeger; straight —Joan Baez; pop—Kingston Trio; art—Richard Dyer-Bennet; parody—the Smothers Brothers. Today our culture is flooded with enormous activity in this field, buttressed by powerful commercial interests. Folk and rock-pop have virtually elbowed jazz out of the popular marketplace. There are some who abhor the commercialization of folk. G. Legman, for example, cries out, "One of the most encouraging signs in the present development of the folk song fad is the overcrowding of the field. This will inevitably result in the driving out of a sizeable group of folklore fakers, Johnny-come-latelys, city-billies, folkniks, folksongsters, and other opportunists who have been attracted by the tales of a quick buck, plenty of beer, girls, and public acclaim . . ."* But whether or not modern folk will ultimately join the body of permanent folk music, its cultural effect has been and will perhaps continue to be significant. This cultural effect may well be positive, if only for the reason that such great numbers of young people are now actively involved in *making* music, not just hearing it. In a sense this involvement,

---

* Ibid., G. Legman, "Folksongs, Fakelore, and Cash," p. 314.

made possible by the mass production of recordings, folk instruments, and concerts, may have a comparable effect to that of the mass production of Henry Ford's flivver. The flivver led to our being a highly elastic, mobile society. Today's young folk songster-player may well be led through the "now" sound of modern folk into a love of the superb body of traditional folk music. From this he will grasp the pulse and essence of the human identity. Perhaps he will move on to an appreciation of those "classical" masters who were steeped in the music of the people. This is not to say that the only desirable end is the progressive assimilation of ever finer music by young people. Rather, we suggest that a serious personal involvement in folk music could lead to a significant broadening of musical perception and could contribute to a new attitude toward musical culture: one that is catholic, discriminating, and inclusive. Alan Lomax, speaking of the recent surge of folk music in his book, *The Folk Songs of North America*, puts it this way:

> What is more important, however, is that a whole generation of creative young people are becoming expert practitioners of our native folk song and thus are coming to grips with the profoundest American emotional problems ... In them the young people discover the source of their own malaise and by singing them, they begin to face these problems with increased maturity ... So long as these keys to our past lie rusty and unused we will repeat the old stereotypes and half-truths in glossy and increasingly superficial guises—in comic books, records, films and advertisements; new legends and new art forms will not arise and we will continue to play, like children, in the sunny forecourt of creation.*

Ethnomusicology

The new science of ethnomusicology is of fairly recent development. Since World War II several centers for this work have been established, such as that at the University of California, Los Angeles. Ethnomusicology is the systematic, inclusive study of present or past music throughout the world. The origin, development, and present state of a single strain of music within a culture may be examined. Or this strain may be compared with other strains within that or other cultures. Thus, the ethnomusicologist may collect and analyze the indigenous music of a region—say that of a particular tribe of American Indians in a particular locale. He will not only study the history of their traditional music, but also examine all other music present within that locale. He will want to know, for example, how traditional tribal music, rock, jazz, "the classics," commercial—the total music used—affects life within that tribe.

Man's power of communication steadily expands as he now can quickly reach

---

* Alan Lomax, *The Folk Songs of North America* (New York: Doubleday and Company, Inc., 1960), p. xxviii.

every corner of the globe. Telstar begins to tell. The world is shrinking and the musics of the world are coming together. People in one culture now experience much music from other cultures. The ethnic folkster may pack in his tune bag traditional songs from Japan, Ghana, Appalachia, Ireland, or anywhere. The youngster in a Tokyo classroom will sing songs from Canada, Uganda, and South America, along with those from his own home. Students in the ethnomusicology center at UCLA perform on the Balinese quartet of instruments known as *gendèr wajang*. Composers increasingly use ethnically mixed musical sources in their compositions. To this musical mix the ethnomusicologist brings new understanding.

JAZZ

The seeming paradox of jazz is that it is both a personal expression and a group expression. On the one hand, it is the highly subjective, spontaneous personal expression of the jazz soloist; on the other, it is the constant group expression of the other players that seeks to align itself with the soloist and support him. There is ever-present, in good jazz, an "electric current" connecting the soloist and the group. Each of these two expressions—that of the soloist and that of the group—is sparked by, and sparks, the other. Thus there is a constant cross-reaction. To put it another way, the soloist is part of a "performing collective."

The performance of symphonic music, to take one kind of art-music, seems to be a large group effort. But each player does not so much seek to spark and be sparked by his fellow player as to perform his individual part as well as possible. The playing of a symphonic composition is in reality a one-man operation in spite of all the words that have been written to the contrary. The one man is the composer. And everyone from the conductor to the back-chair player bears one obligation: to carry out the composer's wishes. This is how it should be. However, except where the composer himself is the conductor, this kind of performing can be exceedingly impersonal.

The important thing about jazz is its immediacy. The composing soloist—the improviser—is right there, on the spot. It all happens in the here and now. This is the excitement of it. Whether jazz was born in New Orleans is not pertinent to our discussion here, but New Orleans certainly nurtured it through its first years and sent it out into the world. Jazz at various times has been described as an unhealthy, and even wicked, offspring of music, but it has shown an amazing vitality through the years, and the diatribes against it have abated. Indeed, jazz has even made its appearance in the church (e.g., Ellington's *A Concert of Sacred Music*). The result of a fusion of the culture of the African Negro, European harmonies, and some American folk idioms, early jazz also contains traces of Creole French and West Indian. It has always borrowed and absorbed whatever seemed interesting or pertinent to its expression, but it has never lost its own individual personality. It is recognized throughout the world as America's unique contribution to music. But critical and academic recognition has come slowly in America.

Jazz is an Afro-American contribution. When the black slave first put his feet on American soil, American music was mostly European music. Since the time of Stephen Foster jazz has changed the course of American popular music so that it finally is no longer dominated by European traditions.

Jazz has also changed theater music from the operetta in the style of European opera to the musical comedy, which is America's other unique contribution to music. But the acculturation of the black slave—the blending of his African musical heritage with the European harmonies of the hymn tunes which he learned in the churches of his masters—resulted in one of the most moving kinds of group vocal expressions. The African rhythms and the African melodic scale fused with the European harmonies to produce the *spiritual*, at once one of the most personal and the most universal expressions of the sorrow and the longing, the suffering and the hope of a people. It may be said that white America could not truly understand the expression-through-music of the black American, but this new African-American expression was absorbed by white America, even though the black himself was not. The early "hollers" and shouts, the work songs of the field and the boat and the barge, the improvisation that was inherent in the call and response pattern, the rhythmic dynamism, the pentatonic basis of much African melody—somehow all these (containing both secular and sacred elements) were refined in the crucible of the spiritual and became solidified as the blues. Out of a music that was originally functional (in every aspect of the term) arose an expression that was to become traditional art form. The blues became the heart of jazz. And certain characteristic *blue notes* (resulting in the so-called "blues scale") have infused not only jazz but practically all popular music in America. (See Ex. 9–1, below.)

Whether the slow recognition of jazz was due to the nature of its origin or just the fact that it arose in an America that was trying to acquire its culture from Europe cannot be argued here. But it can at least be pointed out that once again the new, the different, the strange could not be accepted by those attempting to find their social plateau in the comfortable surroundings of the traditional.

The durability of the call and response element of the work song and the slave song was still in evidence in the group singing of the civil rights demonstrations of the 1960's. The spiritual changed the early American hymn-tune into a more spirited affirmation of faith, while at the same time retaining an affinity for the tribulations of the Hebrews of the Old Testament. "Swing Low, Sweet Chariot" and "Nobody Knows the Trouble I've Seen" are representative of the many spirituals that, often pentatonic in structure, are given life by the jabbing accents

Figure 41.   African statue of musicians playing a drum. (Courtesy, Museum of Primitive Art, N.Y.)

of syncopation. The use of the pentatonic scale may be seen in "Swanee River" by Stephen Foster (1826–1864) who attempted to simulate the plantation songs that were the inspiration of much of his writing.

The blues

The origins of the blues are not clear, but somehow out of the work songs, hymns, spirituals, and other sources it developed to become a basic expression in jazz. Its text, almost always secular in its *statement*, *restatement*, and *conclusion*, has a vernacular simplicity that is disarming; within this text may be found plays on words, sophisticated humor, a statement of resignation tinged with hope, and even sexual connotations. The classic blues form is 12 measures long, in three phrases of 4 measures each, matching the three parts of the text.

The blues has had a considerable impact, not only as a basic form of jazz still in use today, but as an influence on all jazz. Its melody contains the contours of the pentatonic spiritual plus the *blue notes*. This term refers primarily to the lowering in pitch of the 3rd and 7th scale steps of the major scale. These lowerings of pitch are superimposed onto the major scale. If we use C major as an example, the blue note E-flat of the melody sounds simultaneously with E-natural of the harmony. The same principle holds for the blue note B-flat.

EXAMPLE 9–1   Blue Notes(*)

The origin of the blues was in vocal expression, but the blue notes may be performed by most instruments of the jazz orchestra. The blues pianist tries to approximate the inconstancy of the blue note by playing the lowered 3rd and the regular 3rd of the major scale simultaneously.

The final cadence of a blues phrase often avoids melodic stepwise motion to the tonic. Thus the tonic may be approached from the 6th scale step below or from the flatted 3rd above. Furthermore, these lowered tones may vary in pitch through distortion. Tone-distortion has become one of the outstanding characteristics of jazz expression and has been applied to other notes of the scale besides the 3rd and 7th; in addition, this distortion has been carried over to the type of sound each instrumentalist produces on his instrument. The distortion is part of the personal expression of each jazz musician. Various mechanical devices are also used as a natural extension of the performer's desire to personalize his sound. Whereas the brass player of the symphony orchestra rarely uses more than one mute, the jazz brass player has a wide assortment of mutes: straight, cup, wow-wow, stem, buzz, and so on; also derby hats, felt hats, buckets, and bathroom plungers. The variety of cymbals and other varying effects used by the drummer are also part of this picture. The saxophone player rarely resorts to mutes since he can get a unique, personal sound simply by his manner of playing.

Ragtime

The *rag* is a syncopated instrumental dance, originally written mainly for piano. Making the perfect foil to pathos-ridden blues, it was a happy music that began in the "gay nineties." Scott Joplin's "The Maple Leaf Rag" (published in 1899), one of the first ragtime "hits," came out of a honky tonk in Sedalia, Missouri, called the Maple Leaf Club. But the rag's jerky syncopations could soon be heard in New Orleans, St. Louis, Little Rock, Nashville, and as far north as Chicago.

It was the white ragtime pianist, Ben R. Harney, billing himself as "author, musician, comedian, and dancer," who claimed to be the originator of ragtime. Harney's successful rag song, "Mr. Johnson, Turn Me Loose," was published in 1896, but it was probably appropriated from a tune already extant and popular.

But much more important than who wrote the first rag was who gave it the spirit and the impetus that caused it to race through this country and Europe. It was the black composer, Scott Joplin, who, with "Maple Leaf" and others, set the style and pace. The rag's influence was strong. It was heard not only in the clubs and bordellos but in the parlors of genteel homes. It even left its mark on "serious" composers. Stravinsky included a pseudo-rag in his *Histoire du soldat* (1918) and, in the same year, wrote a *Ragtime for Eleven Instruments*. The French impressionist, Claude Debussy was charmed by the *cakewalk*, one of the dances that led to the rag, and wrote two little piano pieces patterned after it. One he called the "Golliwog's Cakewalk" and the other, "The Little Negro."

By the early twenties, classic ragtime had about run its course. Jazz began to take over in popularity, as is suggested by the reactionary title of a rag of 1921 by James Scott, "Don't Jazz Me—Rag (I'm Music)." Indeed, jazz took over and raced through the country at this time, but it should not be thought that it was born in the twenties. Jelly Roll Morton claimed to have used the word jazz as early as 1902 in the pristine days of classic ragtime. He tells of his "jazzing" any type of music: quadrilles, Sousa marches, folk songs, operatic selections and even rags. All of this can be verified by listening to the Library of Congress recordings of Jelly Roll's playing.

Figure 42.   Ragtime music cover. (Courtesy, Roger Hankins)

Jazz gradually assimilated certain characteristics from ragtime in the same manner that it absorbed the essence of the blues. The blues, ragtime, and jazz all coexisted for many years at the beginning of the twentieth century before jazz gained ascendancy. Of the three separate forms, only jazz and the blues continued as major factors in American musical life. The blues continues to this day in its classic shape at the hands of singer-instrumentalists such as B. B. King and Otis Spann. And instrumental jazz still holds within its core a strong element of the blues.

Why is it that ragtime in its pure form fell by the wayside while the older blues and the younger jazz continued to develop? Perhaps it was because both of these forms—jazz and the blues—held the possibility for subjective involvement of the performer, and both relied heavily on improvisation.

Gunther Schuller, in his book *Early Jazz*, notes that, "At even the most superficial level of listening it is clear that [Jelly Roll] Morton had moved away from the stiff, 'classically' oriented right hand and the march-like left hand. . . . Morton accomplished this innovation by making improvisation, especially in the right hand, the keynote of his piano style, thus directly opposing it to ragtime, a music largely written down."* And later, ". . . the blues, especially at the turn of the century, was essentially improvised. . . ."†

It was out of improvisation that jazz evolved. And though its increasing sophistication ultimately necessitated its notation and a more "schooled" musician to read this notation, jazz has never to this day lost its inner core of spontaneous and irrespressible improvisation.

One need only compare the playing of a ragtime pianist/composer on a player piano roll with the actual page of music to see that liberties were rarely taken. In fact, Scott Joplin in his *The School of Ragtime—Six Exercises for Piano* (1908) is severe in his demand for a strict realization of the printed page of music, "It is evident that, by giving each note its proper time and by scrupulously observing the ties, you will get the effect." And there is evidence of the influence of the European musical ethic in the rag, too. Some rags show the direct influence of classical compositions or classical styles. Joseph Lamb tells how his "Ragtime Nightingale" was suggested by Ethelbert Nevin's "Nightingale Song." And although Lamb may not have consciously planned it, the first few notes of the left-hand part are identical with the basic accompaniment figure in Chopin's "Revolutionary" Étude.

Rob Hampton's "Cataract Rag" (1914) owes as much to nineteenth-century European virtuosic figuration as to indigenous American influences. Rudi Blesh and Harriet Janis in the book *They All Played Ragtime* put it somewhat laconically in

---

* Gunther Schuller, *Early Jazz* (New York: Oxford University Press, 1968), p. 144.
† Ibid., p. 145.

speaking of "Cataract": "Parts of the third theme, for example, seem to echo a Brahms chamber work of the late Bad Ischl period." Perhaps it was the excessive influence of formal European approaches to composition that led the ragtime composer astray; at any rate the rag perished in the early twenties. In attempting to make ragtime "respectable," the ragtime composer turned too far from those rich springs of musical creativity that had originated in black American acculturation and that had made ragtime possible.

Its sources

What then were the musical sources of ragtime? A formal structure in three or four clearly articulated and contrasted parts, including a trio in the subdominant key, clearly points to the early marches of Sousa and others. But, whatever the effect of the march on ragtime, its real roots lay in the banjo dances and songs of the minstrel show and plantation life. The cakewalk, the buck and wing, the "coon" songs—all contributed to classical ragtime. In New Orleans, at Congo Square, the beating of the drums and the frenzied dancing of the black slaves to the *bamboula* pointed to an even earlier influence, that of Africa. It was in 1847 that the young American composer Louis Moreau Gottschalk attempted to capture the spirit of wild dance in his piano fantasie titled, *La Bamboula-danse des Nègres*.

Its musical elements

Without question those elements at the very heart of ragtime that most clearly define it are in the area of rhythm—tempo, meter, and accentuation. Tempo was rock-solid, motoric, but never very fast. Joplin, in *The School of Ragtime*, admonishes, "Play slowly until you catch the swing, and never play ragtime fast at any time." His tempo indication given for the rag illustrations in this set of études is "Slow march tempo (Count Two)." Thus the tempo was moderate and the meter was duple. (Almost all published rags have a time signature of two-four.) Each beat was strongly marked by the lowest bass notes in the left-hand part. Against this march-like bass, the right hand articulated mostly quarter, eighth, and sixteenth-notes. The triplet is not used. Favored rhythmic figures were: eighth-quarter-eighth; sixteenth-eighth-sixteenth; eight sixteenths beginning on the first beat but with the fourth and fifth sixteenth tied; and several variants of these basic patterns. These figures are arranged in a rhythmic figuration that constantly pulls against the basic beat by providing a nervous, bouncy syncopation. Instrumental ragtime melody, energized by the above syncopated configurations, often outlined chordal shapes, but also made use of scale patterns with dashes of chromatics. The right hand traversed an extensive portion of the keyboard as it traced the melody.

The rag's harmonic scheme was simple, usually incorporating one key change —to the subdominant for the trio. Chords and chord progressions were highly suggestive of "barber-shop" harmony: progressions of linked dominant sevenths at cadence points, sliding diminished seventh chords, and triads with added sixth.

The harmonies of jazz

The harmonies of jazz are essentially composed of what we might term a "cultivated folk music." Originally based on popular materials such as hymn-tunes and marching tunes, the harmonies were traditional European chords plus the colorations of the pentatonic mode. Although it did produce a new kind of dissonance, the effect of the blues was more melodic than harmonic. Later, jazz arrangers picked up some of the harmonic devices of the impressionist composers as well, and this combination became the basis for much big-band jazz harmony until the middle of the century. There were some influences from the music of Stravinsky

Figure 43.   Benny Goodman Quartet, 1937. (Photo Files)

and others, but for the most part the music of jazz maintained its traditional tonal basis, harmonically and melodically, along with the diatonic scale. Such chromaticism as was introduced revolved around the notes of the major scale.

The instruments

The saxophone, which to many is the representative instrument of jazz, did not exist when jazz began. After the Civil War the easiest instruments to obtain were those that were Army surplus. There were many Negro marching bands which played for various public functions. The basic instruments of these early bands were the clarinet, the cornet, the trombone, the brass bass, and the drums; these became the instruments of the early New Orleans jazz bands. When the music moved indoors there was no need to worry about the portability of an instrument, and the bass fiddle began to replace the brass bass that, along with the drums, had supplied the rhythm. To the rhythm section was added the banjo (of African origin), which was later to be replaced by the guitar. And the piano, which had been the chief instrument for the immediate progenitor of jazz (ragtime), joined forces with the other rhythm instruments.

Louis Armstrong

This is the way it was when Louis Armstrong was born in New Orleans on July 4, 1900. He learned to play bugle and cornet in a waif's home, and after that he learned by listening to the sounds around him, especially to those of King Oliver. King Oliver went up the Mississippi River to Chicago, and he sent for Armstrong in 1922. Jazz had left the cradle of New Orleans and was taking its first steps in a society that would greet it alternately with enthusiasm and surprise; that would dance and drink to it but not respect it; that would embrace it or treat it with scorn; and that finally might learn to love but never really understand it.

The first recording of a jazz group was made in 1917. The Original Dixieland Band was a group of five white musicians playing clarinet, trumpet, trombone, piano, and drums. With the exception of the piano, these are the instruments that came out of the marching bands. You can hear the 2-beat accent of the march, as well as the pattern of the blues and distorted tones—and also special effects, such as the horse whinney. We have mentioned that the blues contained elements of humor—an ironic humor. For years jazz retained this element of humor and entertainment. However, jazz has never been cute; in its best moments it has always been a serious personal expression.

While the Dixieland groups were making recordings, Armstrong began to carve out a technique and a style that was to be admired by jazz musicians the country

over for more than two decades. Armstrong was not a Dixieland player. Whatever kind of a band that he led or played in over the years, his was a solo style.

A man of tremendous endurance, with an exceptionally well-controlled high
register for his day, and a phenomenal feeling for the beat—on it or between it—
Armstrong set the standard for years. He became and remained an international
figure until his death in 1971.

Louis Armstrong spent his early years in New Orleans absorbing the sights and
sounds of this wonderfully diverse city—diverse in that it contained a conglom-
erate of various cultures, and also cultures within cultures. The city had been a
major port for export and import since the days of Jean Lafitte, the early nineteenth-century French-American pirate. It was also a stopover for those coming
from other lands who were heading north for New York or west to California.
Foreign strains were mixed here as in no other city in America. The mixture in
New Orleans called Creole was a blend of African and Spanish or French blood.
This was very apparent in the music that Armstrong was exposed to as he roamed
the streets as a child. What Jelly Roll Morton called "The Spanish tinge" was
apparent in such dance forms as the tango and the habanera.

In the French Quarter could be heard the quadrille, "Tiger Rag." And in Congo
Square there were rhythms of the African drums. Add to this the sound of the
marching bands: on festive occasions bright and happy, on the way to the cemetery
a muffled drum and "Nearer, My God to Thee," on the way back from the cemetery
a happy and often improvised version of "Didn't He Ramble." With obvious relish
Louis Armstrong paints an exciting picture of his early years in New Orleans in
his autobiography, *Satchmo.*

Armstrong, who had heard King Oliver playing a music that was becoming
jazz, later joined Oliver's band in Chicago. In 1924, he joined Fletcher Henderson,
getting experience in ensemble orchestral playing. His Henderson period also included recordings with Bessie Smith, the first great urban blues singer.

COMMENTARY AND ANALYSIS

Heebie Jeebies, Armstrong

In 1925, Armstrong made a series of recordings that are known as *Louis Armstrong
and His Hot Five;* these recordings number among those most respected by con-
noisseurs. While playing mainly in the New Orleans style, Armstrong nevertheless

broke away from the contrapuntal style of Dixieland to establish a solo trumpet style that has evoked the admiration of jazz musicians ever since. One of these remarkable *Hot Five* recordings was *Heebie Jeebies,* in which Louis introduced *scat* singing—which has since been demonstrated most notably by Sarah Vaughn and Ella Fitzgerald. *Scat* singing is the use of meaningless syllables sung in the style of a jazz musician improvising on an instrument.

HEEBIE JEEBIES—*The Louis Armstrong Story, Vol. 1—Louis Armstrong and His Hot Five* (1925–1926), Album: Columbia, CL 851

Heebie jeebies, *pl. n. Slang.* A feeling of uneasiness or nervousness; the jitters. [Coined by Billy De Beck (1890–1942), American cartoonist, in his comic strip, *Barney Google.*]—*American Heritage Dictionary.*

PERSONNEL:

Trumpet	Louis Armstrong
Clarinet	Johnny Dodds
Trombone	Kid Ory
Piano	Lil Hardin
Banjo	Johnny St. Cyr

Verse (12 bars) and chorus
The tune: (18 bars)   16 bars plus a 2-bar tag
Key: A-flat major
Introduction: 8 measures   Piano (like a vamp)

CHORUS	MEASURES	
I	18	Ensemble, trumpet lead
	12	Verse — trumpet
II	18	Clarinet solo
III	18	Vocal — Louis Armstrong
IV	18	Vocal — scat chorus—Louis Armstrong
V	18	8 bars — Trombone;
		8 bars — Trumpet
		2 bars — Trumpet (Dixieland style)
Tag	8	

Bix Beiderbecke

Bix Beiderbecke (1903–1931) may perhaps be considered the founder of the second school of trumpet playing that was to influence many a jazz musician. Whereas Armstrong had an extremely high range, a powerful, vibrant sound, and a feeling for the beat as if it were an entity in itself, Beiderbecke played in the middle register with a cooler sound and a different feeling for the beat. Beiderbecke's rhythmic style was influenced by the recordings of the Dixieland Jazz Band, and his style followed in the tradition of what was to become known as Dixieland. The influence of Louis Armstrong may be seen later in Bunny Berigan's high soaring lines; that of Beiderbecke showed up in the playing of Red Nichols and later Bobby Hackett.

The legend of Beiderbecke—as is true of most legends—has become somewhat larger than life. His short life of twenty-eight years was the propellant of the legend.

Beiderbecke made his first recordings in 1924 with the Wolverines, including *Davenport Blues,* named for his home town in Iowa. His recordings have become record collectors' items, and include those made with his own group, as well as with Frankie Trumbauer, the Wolverines, Gene Goldkette, and even Paul Whiteman. In the large bands he suffered the same as Bobby Hackett later in Glenn Miller's band: He was mostly buried in the band, and only occasionally could be heard in a short solo. But the brief solo is often the highlight of the recording.

Beiderbecke also played piano, and wrote several pieces that distinctly show the influence of the impressionist school. *In a Mist* is the best-known example.

Art Tatum

Art Tatum was considered by all jazz musicians, and by some other musicians as well, the greatest pianist to play in the jazz idiom. He rose to prominence during the thirties, most often playing as a single performer in clubs and on recordings. Nearly blind, he was his own man, playing as he chose, and not necessarily answering requests from the patrons. His command of the instrument was considered to be unsurpassable, and the story among musicians of the time was that he spent most of his spare time practicing Bach. Apocryphal though this may be, it is certainly true that he could carry off roulades, cascades, and cadenza-like material of the utmost difficulty with aplomb.

His technique was immense in scope, sure and clean, and when he played within the confines of a steady tempo, breathtaking in his sense of the beat. This has been true of other great jazz musicians but is all the more to be wondered at in Tatum's case because he attempted so much.

Often, as may be noted on his recording of *Body and Soul* (see below), he went out of a strict tempo into rubato, and in that sense his playing is more like cocktail piano playing than jazz; but in his own time, no cocktail pianist could have approached his sound at all.

Nearly every jazz musician admired Tatum's work, and the great majority of jazz pianists tried to absorb some of his style.

COMMENTARY AND ANALYSIS

Body and Soul, Tatum

Album: *The Genius of Art Tatum*
Art Tatum: Piano (b. Toledo, Ohio, 1910; d. Los Angeles, Calif., 1956)
Cut: *Body and Soul* (c. by Green, Heyman, Sour)
Personnel: Art Tatum, solo piano

Time Signature: $\frac{4}{4}$ (four beats to the measure)

Tempo: When *free* $\quad \downarrow = 60$ to 120; when *a tempo* $\downarrow = 100$ (walking)
Key (or Tonality): D♭
The original tune: 32 meas.; a a b a (8 meas. ea.)
Form: Tune and improvisations
  Note: Each presentation of the tune or improvisation is called a *chorus* and is
     numbered below by Roman numerals.

CHORUS	MEASURES		
I	8	a	D♭ (Free tempo $\downarrow = 60$–120)
	8	a	D♭
	8	b	D and Dm and modulating
	6	a	D♭
	2		(in tempo $\downarrow = 100$)
II	8	a	
	8	a	
	8	b	first 4 measures quote ("Nobody Knows the Trouble . . .") slightly slower
	8	a	
III	8	a	Double-time (original tune stays original length)
	8	a	
	8	b	
	6	a	
	2		Single-time
IV	8	b	Still in tempo $\downarrow = 100$
	8	a	Free tempo
			Slight extension—free, about two measures, accel., rit., hold

Fletcher Henderson

In 1919 the Fletcher Henderson orchestra went into the Roseland Ballroom in New York for the first time and made appearances there until the mid-thirties. Henderson was a pianist, but his greatest influence has been as an arranger-composer. It was he who was the first to produce a big band with a drive and a sophistication that was to set the tone for big-band writing to the present day. His writing shows a feeling for the effect of *tutti* ensemble writing,—the antiphony of brass section against sax section against rhythm section. His band was the first to exhibit a polish of performance that had previously not even been considered necessary. Among the musicians in the orchestra, the "sidemen," there were many with highly individual talent as expressive solo players. One of the chief of these was Coleman Hawkins, whose later recording of "Body and Soul" became an all-time classic.

Henderson's influence extended further when his arrangements became the basis of the "book" for the Benny Goodman orchestra, which came to high notice in the mid-thirties.

Swing

In the early thirties the American public was seeking entertainment wherever it could be found. The financial disaster of 1929 was now in the past, and the only direction the economy could take was up. The public danced as it had never danced before. Big bands—jazz bands and commercial bands, black and white—were constantly on the road touring from one end of the country to the other. And on the radio, late at night, many of them could be heard live from the ballrooms, from the hotels, from the nightclubs, on coast-to-coast hook-ups. The names of Don Redman, Fletcher Henderson, Duke Ellington, the Dorsey Brothers, Glen Gay, Isham Jones, and many more became household names. The big band era was in. In 1935 Benny Goodman came riding in on this wave with a band of polished performers. His theme song, "Let's Dance," was the motto for the spirit of the times.

Goodman's facile technique on the clarinet was the beginning of a new expression in jazz that had less of the heart and more of the mind in it. The precision of the tight-sounding brass, the exploitation of the "saxophone chorus"—a display of the saxophones as a section—the drum solo as an expression of its own, these all came to a peak. For some musicians it was too organized, too neat. The Fletcher Henderson arrangements for Goodman seemed to lose some of their personality. Some musicians preferred them as played originally by Henderson.

But the wave was not to be stopped. The big bands multiplied and some became permanent fixtures on sponsored radio shows.

Goodman was the first to successfully integrate white and black musicians. He brought Teddy Wilson in on piano, and Lionel Hampton on vibraphone to become part of the Benny Goodman trio or quartet.

Artie Shaw as a clarinetist competed with Goodman for a while and was preferred by many musicians, but his more volatile temperament, which accounted for his more flexible clarinet style, also contributed to the impermanency of his organization. Goodman remained to rule the scene until the break-up of the big bands during World War II.

Lester Young

The tenor saxophone playing of Lester Young first came to national attention during his four years with Count Basie at the end of the thirties. His style established a new ideal, not only for saxophonists, but for all jazz musicians. Influenced by Frankie Trumbauer of the Bix Beiderbecke years, Lester Young set an ideal of improvisation that was dynamic but controlled. Other tenor saxophonists of the time often played the instrument more than they played the music, resorting too often to honks and squawks to the detriment of melodic line. Young was either ahead of his time, or if he was just right, then time would catch up to him. His playing was emotional, yet controlled, and had a rhythmic drive capped by a feeling for creative continuity that still stands as an ideal. Young antedated not only the entire cool school of playing that was to come after Bop, but also the life-style of the generation coming to maturity in the late 1950's. A representative recording to listen to is "Lester Leaps In" (which also includes Charlie Parker), in the album *The Essential Lester Young*.

Duke Ellington

Before, during, and after Goodman and the swing era there was Duke Ellington. It almost seems as if there was always Duke Ellington. Born in Washington, D.C., he was more truly a New Yorker with all the sense of sophistication that being a New Yorker implies.

His first successes were in New York, the first big one as a result of his opening at the Cotton Club. Ellington's style of writing was one of the most distinctly individual of all jazz composers. Most jazz musicians, whether in small groups or in big bands—from the 1920's to the 1950's—have drawn heavily upon popular music. This might consist of songs clearly current and "commercial," or of the quality products of Jerome Kern, George Gershwin, or Cole Porter. Ellington also used popular music as source material but only for a minor part of his output. Ellington's contribution lay in his completely original writing. And in many cases, with lyrics added later by a professional lyricist, this "became" popular music.

Ellington had the feeling for orchestration that only comes from living with an orchestra and knowing each player's abilities intimately. Some of the freshest sounds in jazz came from his pen. Ellington's music often included the inspirations and the suggestions of individual musicians during rehearsal, and thus many of the works were a joint effort of Ellington and the men of his orchestra. It would be impractical to list Ellington's important works here—there are too many—but they range from "Ebony Rhapsody" (from the music of Liszt) and with the voice of Ivie Anderson, through works like "Sophisticated Lady," "Mood Indigo," "Reminiscing in Tempo," and "Solitude" to his more recent album *Far East Suite*.

Ellington always tried to reach his audience, but he rarely followed the musical trends of the times. In fact for many years he set the trend himself. He was playing with a "swing" before it became a label for an era, and his unique approach to the organization of sound will probably last for many years to come.

The kid from Red Bank

This is the title of one of the works played by Count Basie and his orchestra. It refers not only to his place of origin, Red Bank, New Jersey, but to the spirit of his pianism. The essential characteristic of youth is its curiosity. This characteristic remains, not changed in its essence but expanded, in the inquiring mind of the artist. This combination of "youth and artistry" is true of Basie as of all jazz musicians and flows over into the playing of the musicians. Not a composer-arranger like Ellington, Basie is nevertheless the guiding force. His orchestra has a vital drive and constant awareness of the beat *as a group* that is hard to match. Like Ellington, the Basie band has had many imitators, but unlike Ellington it has never been as experimental. It has a record for a polished presentation which for those who seek the delights of Ellington at his best consider "mechanized." For others it is like drinking cream from the top of the bottle.

Bop

During the World War II years, 1942–1946, the big band era came to an end. Charlie Parker, Dizzy Gillespie, and a few others brought in the new era with a return to small groups. The hard, clean, jagged lines of bop were the reaction to what had become almost a national fetish: The big band had become a large well-oiled machine that left, in many cases, small room for the jazz soloist. This reaction resulted in a single melodic line with supporting percussion. The percussion now became free-wheeling, doing away with the steady four beats to the bar that had been the beat for swing. The piano was no longer just a rhythm instrument, but also a solo instrument. The bass fiddle proceeded in this direction as well.

Parker and Gillespie introduced a technique heretofore unheard of for its agility. Their fresh version of the tune at the beginning and the end, but more especially their individual solos, confused many listeners who asked the same old question, "Where is the melody?" The bop musicians were employing a form that goes back to Haydn, Mozart, and Beethoven: *theme and variations*. This form had been the accepted one for most jazz since its inception. But in bop the stated theme itself was often a variation to begin with. The best-known example of this is "Lullaby of Birdland," based on an old "standard," "Love Me or Leave Me."

In spite of much chromaticism in many of the melodies, with an especial emphasis on the flatted 5th, the basic harmony of bop was traditional.

The "cool" school came on the heels of bop and with it brought jazz to an about-face. Where once "hot" was the adjective that denoted an excellent improvisational performance, "cool" was now the term, and in addition somehow implied an even closer involvement with the problem of personal expression. It connoted an intellectual reserve in contrast to the emotionalism that was the aura of hot playing. And it suggested control.

But the big bands had not died out completely, and two that attracted a large following in the 1940's and 1950's were Woody Herman and Stan Kenton.

Woody Herman had begun in 1936 at the Roseland Ballroom in New York City with some of the musicians and even some of the music of the disbanded Isham Jones orchestra. It soon became billed as "The Band That Plays the Blues." But Woody's best and best-known group has been what is called "The First Herd." As a clarinetist Herman was never outstanding, but he knew how to pick men and how to make a band. The First Herd had an excitement in its playing that has rarely been equalled.

Stan Kenton's approach to the sound of the big band—at one point in his career—was a precursor of the idea of Third Stream music, which was to come in the late 1950's. After his popular "Artistry" phase (*Artistry in Rhythm*, etc.) of the late 1940's, he encouraged composers to experiment with new ways of writing that extended beyond the jazz beat as the central core. For example, *City of Glass*, by Bob Graettinger, non-motoric in beat, shows a structured concept of composition that lay more in the realm of art music than in jazz.

Third Stream

In the late 1950's there began a more serious effort to fuse jazz with "serious" non-jazz. One definite result of this was a recording of Gunther Schuller's *Symphony for Brass*, coupled with works by J. J. Johnson (*Poem—Jazz Suite for Brass*) and others, in which jazz and non-jazz techniques were combined. And a concert at Brandeis University in 1957 presented works by jazz-oriented composers George Russell, Jimmy Guiffre, and their non-jazz contemporaries, Harold Shapero and Milton Babbitt. Schuller later gave the name "Third Stream" to this fusion of the two musics.

Many people regard the fusion of jazz and serious music an impossibility. But this has not stopped others from searching for a solution. The use of the term *Third Stream* has faded but the search for the fusion has not. Eddie Sauter wrote a non-jazz set of backgrounds specifically as a vehicle for Stan Getz's improvisation in an album titled *Focus,* and Sauter and Getz collaborated in a similar effort for a film score, *Mickey One.*

Dizzy Gillespie

Dizzy Gillespie stands with Charlie Parker as one of the innovators of bop. The results of their efforts changed the face of jazz to make it once again a more personal expression. The angularity of melodic line, the chromaticism, the advanced technical facility, the expansion of range, and the rhythmic loosening—all these had the most profound effect and made possible the burgeoning of a talent such as Coltrane's.

John Coltrane

The powerful voice of the New Wave of expression that occurred in the 1960's was that of John Coltrane. He was first influenced by Lester Young, but later he was attracted by the styles of Johnny Hodges and Charlie Parker. He played at various times with the bands of Dizzy Gillespie, Johnny Hodges, Miles Davis, and Thelonious Monk. This was the best kind of training that could be had since each of these men was an outstanding figure in the development of jazz. Coltrane began to come into his own when he formed his own quartet in 1961. Constantly searching, constantly becoming aware, he does not arrive at a certain point, but keeps searching for a new solution. The extent of the unique contribution of John Coltrane may be seen in the diverse approaches that he took in the explorations of expressions by briefly scanning some of his albums: 1961 *My Favorite Things;* 1964 *A Love Supreme;* 1965 *Ascension*—(total improvisation), preceded by Ornette Coleman's important *Free Jazz;* 1967 *Kulu Sé Mama.*

Miles Davis

Miles Davis is a very special figure in jazz. He was responsible for the reaction to bop—in some ways it was an expansion of bop—by making recordings in the late 1940's and early 1950's that expanded the size of the bop combo. His album *The Birth of the Cool* is typical. Consisting of nine to ten musicians, the size of the group necessitated more orchestration, but nevertheless left more room for improvisation than during the big band era. Important figures associated with Miles Davis were: J. J. Johnson, who was to become a leading trombonist and composer; Gerry Mulligan, baritone saxophonist, who was later to form a quartet without piano; and John Lewis, who went on to form The Modern Jazz Quartet, that was to represent the essence of cool, and make important contributions to adventures in Third Stream music. Miles Davis has consistently searched for new ways of expression, always remaining himself but constantly synthesizing, absorbing, and experimenting. His album *Sketches of Spain* is a notable example in which he tries to fuse the Spanish idiom and his reaction to it into a new expression. A more recent album, *Filles de Kilimanjaro*, shows him with a deepening maturity which has resulted in a wider but more personal expression. This is evidenced, not only in his own trumpet sound, but also in that of the group. The rhythmic and harmonic concept encompasses both a new improvisatory freedom and the purposeful boundaries of repetitive ideas. The scope is ever broader.

COMMENTARY AND ANALYSIS

Godchild, Davis

Miles Davis has been a constantly growing force in jazz since his appearances on recordings with Charlie Parker in the middle 1940's. In 1949 and 1950 he produced a series of recordings under his own name that represent an important milestone in his career.

The recordings did not make a large impact on the record-buying public when they first appeared, but ultimately their importance was recognized, and these recordings are now considered to be a major landmark in the history of jazz.

The recordings, originally issued on 78 rpm discs, were re-issued as an LP entitled, *Birth of the Cool*. The concept was a step away from the bop concept of small groups—often four or five performers—playing without written arrangements. The new concept was to keep improvisation, yes, but to incorporate it within compositional writing that was in no way a return to the sound of the big bands of the Swing Era. "Cool" is a reasonably apt label as labels go, and it does define the ensemble playing and the improvisation. The playing, whether ensemble or solo, was distinguished by a lack of vibrato, an avoidance of sudden louds and softs, an avoidance of heavy rhythmic effects, and a melodic style that might best be described as suave. However, listening will tell you more than words.

Godchild, which was composed by George Wallington and arranged by Gerry Mulligan, adheres to certain elements that were traditional in 1949—namely, the setting of a tune in a 32-measure frame and the use of four beats to the measure. However, when listening to the recording note that in the first statement of the tune, measures 8 and 16 are each extended by 2 beats. The remainder of the arrangement keeps to the traditional 4 beats to the measure.

Godchild from album—*Miles Davis—Birth of the Cool*, Capitol T 1974 (Mono)

Composed by George Wallington
Arranged by Gerry Mulligan, recorded January 21, 1949, New York
Personnel:
  Trumpet—Miles Davis
  French horn—Junior Collins
  Trombone—Kai Winding
  Tuba—John Barber
  Alto sax—Lee Konitz
  Baritone sax—Gerry Mulligan
  Piano—Al Haig
  Bass tuba—Joe Shulman
  Drums—Max Roach

Note the presence, unusual at the time, of the French horn and the tuba. Both had been previously "introduced" by the Claude Thornhill Orchestra as a source of new sonorities. (Gerry Mulligan had made arrangements for Thornhill.)

Form of the original tune:

	A	A	B	A
meas.	8	8	8	8

Form of the arrangement:
      Tune and improvisations (four choruses plus 4-bar coda)
Each setting of the tune is called a "chorus" and is represented in the schema below by a Roman numeral.

CHORUS	MEASURES	INSTRUMENT(S) PLAYING MELODY
I	8	Ensemble
	8	Ensemble
	8	Trumpet ad lib
	8	Ensemble
II	32	Trumpet ad lib
III	4	Ensemble
	4	Baritone sax
	8	Baritone sax
	8	Baritone sax
	4	Ensemble
	4	Ensemble plus baritone sax
IV	8	Ensemble
	8	Ensemble
	8	Trombone ad lib
	8	Ensemble
Coda	4	Ensemble

Art Blakey

We have already spoken of roots of jazz being in Africa, and jazzmen have always been aware of this. But in the 1960's there was a more conscious effort to connect the new expression in jazz with its African expression. Black musicians in both jazz and popular music have been consciously seeking to reaffirm their heritage. This means not only the African heritage, but includes the American experience as well. John Coltrane made the connection in his album *Africa Brass*. But let us turn to Blakey. Art Blakey and the Jazz Messengers have had many successful albums and he, as a percussionist, had a strong influence all through the 1960's.

Particularly pertinent to our discussion here is his album, made in 1962, *The African Beat*, in which the personnel consisted of Blakey and seven other percussionists on a large variety of percussion instruments (the majority African) plus a bass fiddle, and Yusef Lateef on various melodic instruments, including oboe, flute, and tenor saxophone. Blakey was looking not only for a new fusion of African music and jazz, but also to "new ways in which African and American musicians can enrich each other." This effort seemed to be more successful than most of the Third Stream attempts at fusion thus far.

Jazz—in conclusion

There is a certain distinction—a dichotomy, perhaps—that may be discerned between the jazzmen of the 1930's to 1940's, and those of the 1950's to 1960's. Jazzmen of the earlier period had a certain naïveté. Although artists in every field begin by copying the earlier masters whom they admire, they do so with the full awareness that after they have mastered the techniques and probed the minds of those who are their idols, they must go beyond this to attain—each in his own way—their own personal manner of expression. The earlier jazzman did not necessarily believe that he had to overthrow what he had learned but should rather add to it. The later musicians, in what seems to be a more feverish search for identity, also had their masters. But it seems that from the bop period on this search for identity could not rest in development but must be accompanied by an explicit desire to turn off the old in order to find the new. We spoke of the naïveté of the earlier jazz musician. What we mean is that he was aware of his heritage, of the influences around him, and of the musicians he idolized. He let these influences permeate his being and then took it from there, believing that if the talent were there it would be expressed in a new and wonderful way. The later jazz musician specifically looked for roots—this is especially true of the black musician —and in seeking them he has sometimes denied his correspondence with the

world about him, the world (especially the world of music) in which he grew up—
that world of music that was his milieu, that formed his life-style.

Whether one is aware of the music of Schoenberg or not, its impact on the
music world makes ripples which affect everyone's existence.* The earlier jazz
musician may not have been aware of the ripples, but they were there. The later
jazz musician is not only aware of the ripples but is consciously turning these
ripples into waves. In doing so he may be looking for the wrong thing. Duke Ellington was always aware of his heritage, and he often spoke of his music as representing the jungle of Africa. But he didn't mean this. His jungle music—with brass
plungers and growls and the saxophone and clarinet wails—was always filtered
through the sophistication of Ellington, the urbanite. Perhaps it is the wrong point
of view to wed African music to the jazz of today. Perhaps it is somewhat similar
to Aaron Copland searching for American roots in prairie music, although he was
a Brooklyn Jew. George Gershwin was not so misled. Also a Brooklyn Jew, his
roots were imbedded in the music of New York—popular and jazz. Understanding
this, his greatest achievement, the folk opera *Porgy and Bess*, utilized everything
he knew as a sophisticated musician in the New York world of popular music. He
did not have to search for his identity. He knew what it was. He knew that he was
a sophisticate; he knew that he had written scores of successful musical comedies.
He knew that the strongest influence of popular music in America had been the
contribution of the black man. He put them all together, and added to it the dedication of the artist, which in this case took him to South Carolina to study the life-
style and the music of a black community. He came up with an opera that is not
Jewish or African, or anything else alien to George Gershwin as a New York
musician and composer. He came up with an extremely credible work that represented what he knew through a musical idiom that was natural to him. This is
what Aaron Copland did not achieve. This is what Milhaud and others did not
achieve. The jazz that Milhaud and Honegger and others tried to put into their
music was more in the way of a novelty rather than a feeling for the idiom itself.
Never really understanding the jazz idiom, they used it for effect. Stravinsky
seemed to understand jazz better. His various works that utilize jazz effects do
not so much seem to *use* jazz as to *look* at jazz.

The leading members of the avant-garde, both in jazz and in non-jazz, more
and more have been getting together in New York and other major centers—
listening to each other, talking to each other, and writing. The search continues.
It is *not* like the efforts of Copland (in his *Piano Concerto*, 1927) to absorb jazz
into art-music; and, on the opposite side, the borrowing by jazz musicians, such
as Paul Whiteman, from European composers to become a kind of "symphonic
jazz." Both efforts are equally in vain.

---

* Le Roi Jones spoke of this subject very aptly in *Black Music* (New York: William Morrow
& Co., Inc., 1967), p. 70.

AMERICA'S MUSICAL THEATER

Where it came from

Early in the twentieth century, the American musical was defined as a *musical comedy*. It had one foot in Europe, home of the operetta, and the other foot in America, the home of minstrel shows, vaudeville, and burlesque shows. *The Black Crook*, a stage spectacular of almost six hours, was mounted at Niblos Garden in New York on 12 September 1866. It was America's first musical comedy. Songs from many composers were patched together to form this extravaganza, which was neither totally European nor American. Never before had American theater-goers been treated to the French ballet while getting their usual dose of melodrama and barroom songs such as "You Naughty, Naughty Men."

The first composers of American musical theater

Musical theater continued to expand in this early period with foreign imports, such as those of Gilbert and Sullivan. European operettas, such as Franz Lehar's *Merry Widow*, flourished in New York. However, three composers led to the crystallization of American musical theater as it was to appear in the 1920's. They were Victor Herbert, a serious composer with European training; George M. Cohan, an American song-and-dance man who composed, directed, and produced many musicals; and Jerome Kern, equally adept in European and American styles. The music of Victor Herbert (as well as that of Sigmund Romberg and Rudolph Friml) has remained popular. Cohan's musicals, however, faded from view early in the 1920's. Jerome Kern had a long and successful career in the American musical theater, not only composing original material, but assisting in the adaptation of European operettas to American tastes. Kern was an important talent for the musical theater, representing the best of the European and American styles.

Words and music

As we have seen in studying opera and lieder, great poets and dramatists have always contributed to the history of vocal music. However, the lyricist in American musical theater is more than a mere contributor; he is first and foremost a collaborator with the composer. For example, the music of Richard Rodgers, one of the great musical theater composers, was influenced greatly by two of his lyricists, Lorenz Hart and Oscar Hammerstein II. Hart was a whimsical, risqué lyricist who evoked from Rodgers the simple, lilting melodies of the 1920's and 1930's, such as "My Heart Stood Still," "Bewitched, Bothered and Bewildered," "Mountain Greenery," and "Johnny One Note." Hammerstein, on the other hand, was a serious writer whose lyrics had deeper overtones. Upon working with Hammerstein, Rodgers seemed to change style overnight in such songs as "You'll Never Walk Alone," "You've Got to Be Carefully Taught," "We Kiss in a Shadow," and "Something Wonderful."

Some musical theater composers wrote their own lyrics. Irving Berlin, Frank Loesser, Cole Porter, and, more recently, Stephen Sondheim, are but a few who have shown this special ability.

The roaring '20's—the composers' era

The Broadway composers of the 1920's sound like a "Who's Who" in American musical theater. George and Ira Gershwin were in their early twenties when the decade started. Richard Rodgers, Oscar Hammerstein II, Larry Hart, and Cole Porter were there, as was Irving Berlin. The musical theater of the 1920's offered composers many chances to compose new shows each year, *every* year. For example, George Gershwin composed music for *George White's Scandals* each year from 1920 to 1925. This allowed him a special opportunity to try out new approaches for his uniquely rhythmic and melodic compositions. Irving Berlin had the same opportunity in the *Music Box Revues* from 1921 to 1926. Rodgers and Hart were provided their opportunity in the *Garrick Gaieties* in the middle 1920's.

Although many of the songs of the 1920's appear to be dated by today's standards, songs like "Blue Room," "Tea for Two," "Bill," and other 1920's show tunes have lasted through the years. One show of the 1920's bears special mention: *Show Boat*, written by Jerome Kern and Oscar Hammerstein II in 1927, is one that played two Broadway theaters (in the same block) concurrently. The show was ahead of its time in its commentary on the plight of the southern Negro and, again, shows the kind of meaningful composition a lyricist like Oscar Hammerstein II can elicit from a composer like Jerome Kern. "Ol' Man River," "You Are Love," "Make Believe," and "Can't Help Lovin' Dat Man" are some of the great American songs from that show.

The '30's—musicals become a forum

The same composers who had made such a major contribution in the 1920's were still with us in the 1930's. The composers, the lyricists, and the librettists had evolved artistically to the point of making serious commentary about the social and political situation in America. George and Ira Gershwin were in the vanguard with *Of Thee I Sing* in 1931, which included some of the greatest Gershwin songs. This show won the Pulitzer Prize for the best play in 1931, but George Gershwin, himself, was excluded. (When *South Pacific* won a Pulitzer Prize in 1949, Richard Rodgers was *not* excluded.) Irving Berlin wrote *Face the Music* in 1932 with such songs as "Let's Have Another Cup o' Coffee" and "Soft Lights and Sweet Music." His was a very traditional style of popular song. The depression was in full swing and *Face the Music* was all about the actuality of the economic situation that existed in America. Audiences—who had come to the musicals of the 1920's to escape—now had to "face the music."

There were still escapist shows such as *Roberta* by Jerome Kern, with such beautiful songs as "Smoke Gets in Your Eyes," but new influences, such as *Three Penny Opera*, by Kurt Weill, a German composer, and *The Cradle Will Rock*, by Marc Blitzstein, showed that even Socialist commentary was possible in the musicals of the 1930's. Meanwhile, Rodgers and Hart were still writing beautiful musicals reminiscent of the 1920's like *Babes in Arms* and *I Married an Angel*, featuring songs such as "My Funny Valentine" and "Spring Is Here."

George Gershwin's *Porgy and Bess* literally jarred the critics in 1935. Although it is classified as an opera, the work was composed by a man whose early success lay in composing Broadway musicals. *Porgy and Bess* is now widely accepted by a great, diverse American audience as both serious music and as Broadway musical theater. It has also reached a world audience through its performances abroad in the 1950's.

The '40's—musical theater's golden age

The Theater Guild was nearly bankrupt when Rodgers and Hammerstein agreed to make a musical adaptation of *Green Grow the Lilacs*, a play by Lynn Riggs. The resulting show, *Oklahoma!*, ran for 2,248 performances and musical theater was transformed. There were no more opening numbers with kicking chorus girls. Dance and scenery were integrated into the total concept, becoming as important to the show as its tunes.

Some of the songs from *Oklahoma!* were "Surry with the Fringe on Top," "People Will Say We're In Love" and "Oh, What a Beautiful Mornin.' " *Carousel*, a musical adaptation of the play *Liliom*, by Ferenc Molnar, was presented by Rodgers and Hammerstein in 1945. Like *Oklahoma!*, it was excellent musical theater. *Carousel* included such important songs as "If I Loved You," "June Is Bustin' Out All Over," and "Soliloquy." The rest is history: *South Pacific*, *The King and I*, and *The Sound of Music* are some of the works that followed from the pens of Rodgers and Hammerstein.

Other composers came along. Cole Porter wrote *Kiss Me Kate,* an adaptation of Shakespeare's *The Taming of the Shrew.* Porter's sophisticated music showed firm musical training. In addition, he was one of the better lyricists. Alan J. Lerner and Frederick Loewe, who began their careers with *Brigadoon* in 1947, later composed *My Fair Lady* and *Camelot.* Leonard Bernstein, Irving Berlin, Jule Styne, and Kurt Weill all were strong contributors to the musical theater of the 1940's.

The '50's and '60's—continued evolution

Many new musical appeared in the 1950's and 1960's. Some of the more noted composers were Frank Loesser with *Guys and Dolls, The Most Happy Fella,* and *How to Succeed in Business Without Really Trying;* Leonard Bernstein with *On the Town, West Side Story,* and *Candide;* and Cy Coleman with *Little Me, Wildcat,* and *Sweet Charity.*

Stephen Sondheim, who wrote both lyrics and music, established an unusually creative, diverse, and sophisticated style that began to look like the wave of the future. Having begun with a collaboration with Bernstein on the lyrics of *West Side Story,* Sondheim soon developed musically with shows like *A Funny Thing Happened on the Way to the Forum,* for which he wrote book, lyrics, and music. More recent works include *Company* and the highly innovative *A Little Night Music.*

A new trend in modern musical theater emerged with the advent of such works as *Hair, Godspell,* and the theater-related *Tommy* and *Jesus Christ Superstar.* At this writing it is difficult to say whether this mixture of rock music and contemporary social commentary adequately mirrors the changes that are evident now in the same way that the musicals of the 1930's reflected their decade.

POP

Leonard Bernstein with his musical, *West Side Story* (1957), introduced into popular music the concept of unusual time signatures. Jazz musicians also experimented with time signatures hitherto uncommon to popular music and jazz; Dave Brubeck's *Take Five* in $\frac{5}{4}$ meter is well known.

As jazz reached further and further into the realm of art music, its rock-solid beat—one of its most defining aspects—became less important. Jazz became less easy to listen to, less easy to snap fingers to. With the appearance in the first half of the 1960's of Ornette Coleman's album *Free Jazz* and John Coltrane's *Ascension* the general listening audience could understand very little of these new musical expressions.

Rhythm & blues

While jazz musicians were searching out the possibilities of Third Stream music, and certain others were reacting to the diffusion and watering down of the cool approach, a new expression developed that employed a harder driving style, termed either *funky* or *hard-bop*. The blues combined its vocal origins and instrumental uses to become *rhythm & blues*. The pulse of $\frac{12}{8}$, implicit in jazz from the middle 1930's into the 1950's now became an explicit pounding out of 12 beats to the bar. While jazz itself was becoming more and more avant-garde—and losing its audience along with its beat—rhythm & blues was capturing audiences with its overwhelming rock-solid beat. Here was something you could snap your fingers to. Here was something you could dance to.

The history of rhythm & blues goes back to the early 1950's, when it was first heard on a few radio stations. At that time the large commercial radio stations would not play the music. They catered to middle-class tastes that preferred music that didn't disturb, music with lyrics that were pleasant and inoffensive. In 1951, Alan Freed, who had been promoting rhythm & blues groups featuring black musicians but aimed at white audiences, changed the rhythm & blues label to *rock 'n' roll*. The enthusiasm of the young was like that when Benny Goodman caused a near riot at the Paramount Theater in New York in 1938, with teen-agers dancing in the aisles. Rock 'n' roll concerts produced by Alan Freed drew thousands upon thousands wherever they were given. Popular recordings became dominated by the names of soloists or groups of singers backed by a small but loud "rhythm & blues" band. Rock 'n' roll gained the distinction, formerly reserved for jazz, of being denounced in the pulpits of America as an outrageously bad influence on young Americans.

Bill Haley and his Comets

Onto this scene came Bill Haley and his Comets. Nik Cohn, in his book, *Rock from the Beginning*, says

> Bill Haley was large and chubby and baby-faced. He had a kiss-curl like a Big C, slapped down on his forehead with grease and water, and he was paunchy. When he sang, he grinned hugely and endlessly, but his eyes didn't focus on anything. Besides, he was almost thirty, married and the father of five children. Definitely, he was unlikely hero food. Just the same, he was the first boss of rock.*

Haley made many hit singles. He had started in country-and-western music, moved over to rhythm & blues, and in 1951 had success with "Rock the Joint." In

---

* Nik Cohn, *Rock from the Beginning* (New York: Stein and Day, 1969), p. 17.

1954 he had a hit with "Shake, Rattle and Roll." In the same year, his recording of "Rock Around the Clock" established him as an international figure. "Rock Around the Clock," sung by Haley and the Comets, was used in the film that introduced Sydney Poitier, *Blackboard Jungle*. The film went around the world. In 1957, Haley made a tour of England, and it seemed as if there were no stopping his successes. Haley and the Comets depended partly on a quasi vaudeville routine with much stage action. For instance, the bass fiddle player would lay the fiddle down on its side and crawl from the bottom of the instrument up to the neck while he plucked the strings. At the same time, others would run around the stage performing various showbiz antics.

Elvis Presley

In 1956 Elvis Presley made a recording of "Heartbreak Hotel" that was an immediate best-seller. This was the beginning of the end for Haley. Immediately Presley became a national hero for teen-agers. Where Haley had emphasized stage routines, Presley projected a more personal style. His gyrations earned him the name of Elvis the Pelvis, and he began to be denounced by the clergy. When he was signed to appear on the Ed Sullivan Sunday night TV program, Presley was shown on camera only from the waist up.

Many consider Presley, rather than Haley, the true father-figure of rock. He was born in Mississippi and while growing up absorbed the sounds of the music around him—traditional Southern folk song, the authentic blues of the black man, the revival singing of the white fundamentalist church, the country ballads by both black and white. His singing had a raucous earthiness that turned middle America off, but turned the younger people on.

On the Ed Sullivan show Presley sang the song, "Hound Dog," that most identified his style in the early years. The lyrics of "Hound Dog" have the rawness of certain blues lyrics in their reference to the man-woman relationship. His recording of "Blue Suede Shoes" in 1957 in many ways symbolized the new popular music. No longer were the lyrics about boy-and-girl-in-the-moonlight; now they were about clothes, cars, money, motorbikes: things that symbolized pleasure-objects of a new life-style.

The Beatles era

In 1964, a group from Liverpool began to appear on the best-seller charts of pop music in America. The Beatles foursome had toured Scotland, played in Germany and recorded there, and by 1963 were the hottest group in Britain. Then they hit

America and they hit it hard. They had listened to the music of America—country music, rhythm & blues, rock 'n' roll—and they added to it their own sound. At first the music was simple, the lyrics unpretentious. "I Want to Hold Your Hand" was typical of their first successes. In their first recordings they still occasionally did American pop tunes in ballad style, such as "Till There Was You" from Meredith Willson's musical, *Music Man*. But mostly they wrote their own material, and the beat was rock. As much as their music, their hairstyle and their mode of dress affected much of the Western world. The young, and not so young, began to let their hair grow, and schools, banks, and the managers of baseball teams had new problems to face: New dress codes had to be formulated. Conformity was being challenged. Nonconformity is a threat to comfortable, traditional ways. It took several years for the turmoil to die down.

The audience for the Beatles grew steadily larger. In 1964 they made their first movie, *Hard Day's Night;* it was a smashing success. Later they made *Help* and *Magical Mystery Tour*. They then moved to a full-length cartoon film, *Yellow Submarine*.

Figure 44.   Cartoon of the Beatles in *Yellow Submarine*. (Culver)

Meanwhile they continued making recordings for an ever-widening audience. Their album, *Sergeant Pepper's Lonely Hearts Club Band* (1967), was a break-through in rock music recording in that it was an album with a total concept: "We are the Lonely Hearts Club Band, everyone is, and these are our songs."* *Sergeant Pepper* moved away from separate pretty little pop tunes. The Beatles' use of imagery and fantasy was flowering. The lyrics started to be taken seriously, to be explored and analyzed. Meanings beyond the words began to be read into the lyrics by record reviewers, columnists, and the everyday listener. One of the tunes from *Sergeant Pepper* was "Lucy in the Sky with Diamonds." Many thought it was about an LSD trip. The plain answer, according to the Beatles (*The Beatles Illustrated Lyrics*, ed. Alan Aldridge) is that John Lennon's son, Julian, did a drawing at school that he brought home. A schoolmate of his was Lucy. John Lennon said, "What's that?" Julian said, "Lucy in the sky with diamonds."

The Beatles became a cult. Their every move was watched. Their clothes, their hair, their life-styles were imitated. When they went to a guru in India to learn about meditation, many other rock groups and many of their followers were in-fluenced to do similar things.

One of their last albums, *Abbey Road*, had a cover that showed them walking across the street in single file. Paul McCartney was the only one out of step, the only one bare-footed, and so on. Speculation rose. What was it about Paul Mc-Cartney? Was he to be dropped from the group? Was he dead? Multiple games were played. Cultism reached a climax. Many searched back through the record-ings of the Beatles for occult readings. It was a little like the Ouija board phase that swept America in the forties—there *was* a destiny that guided the hand. The Beatles were now larger than life.

The Rolling Stones

Jazz and blues and American pop music had gone around the world before World War II. But very few musicians outside the United States could play jazz or blues with authority. By the end of the 1930's Australian music heard over the radio sounded like American popular/jazz of the early 1920's; there was a lag of at least a decade. In England, however, there were bands that emulated the big band style of American jazz. Of these, Ted Heath's band was the most musically successful, although his orchestra did not achieve the natural swing of American jazz. After World War II, however, touring American jazz musicians found more and more European musicians who could play jazz well.

By the late 1950's, American music was beginning to be represented abroad

---

* Ibid., p. 162.

more and more by rhythm & blues, rock 'n' roll. The Beatles had heard this American music and had successfully turned it into a specific English copy. Another group in England, contemporary with the Beatles, also influenced by Amercian rock, ultimately established an authentic style of their own. The Rolling Stones, with Mick Jagger as lead singer, developed their own style of rock: "mean, moody and magnificent."

The Beatles had appealed to adults as well as to the young. In fact, prominent personalities in the overlapping worlds of entertainment and music had accorded them an importance in music that was stronger than fact. However, the outrageous look of the Rolling Stones, unkempt as possible, mean-looking, "ugly but beautiful"—especially appealed to the young. The more the Rolling Stones turned off adults, the more they turned on teen-agers. You didn't have to be "pretty and nice" anymore in order to make a million dollars in the entertainment world. The Rolling Stones mostly had been second in popularity to the Beatles in the 1960's, but finally they became for many "the group." They represented rebellion against a placid style of life. They were loud; you might not hear Jagger's words and you might not hear the melody, but you could feel the noise and the din. Their image was the final image of the 1960's.

Rock festivals

There was a tremendous surge of interest in rock in the late 1960's. Although the Beatles continued in popularity until their breakup in early 1971, other groups were offering various styles—music styles and life-styles—to satisfy tastes that were now more diversified. In fact, the Woodstock Festival of 1969 (at Woodstock, N.Y.) was a culmination of the surge of interest in pop music in America. The music at Woodstock became the public statement of each participating group, a comment on or a protest against things that were as relevant as the day's news or as important as the themes of love or brotherhood. Among the many performers at the festival were Blood, Sweat and Tears; Joni Mitchell; Santana; Crosby, Stills and Nash; Sly and the Family Stone; and Creedence Clearwater Revival.

The Watkin's Glen Festival held in upper state New York in 1972 gained less press coverage than the Woodstock Festival, but it had an attendance which exceeded Woodstock's 500,000 by about 100,000. The Woodstock Festival had been a unique experience of young people coming together for a mass experience unequalled in its style in American History. *Crawdaddy* magazine put it this way:

> Four years before and 160 miles to the East, the Woodstock Festival had become an instant myth on a similar weekend and it was that event and that myth that hovered over Watkin's Glen. Woodstock had ended proclaiming itself a nation, a thing apart from the rest of Amerika, as it was spelled then. That fragile concept had passed, crushed by ugly drugs, by the despair of an unending war . . . Wat-

kin's Glen would be different. . . . Watkin's Glen was not a new event but a ritual recreation of a past event with the sole purpose of providing a good time for its participants.

Music festivals are similar in their magnetic attraction to political rallies, and religious camp meetings. The magnetism of the leader(s) is the foremost concern. Daniel Webster, Billy Graham, Martin Luther King drew audiences of thousands upon thousands because they were compelling, dynamic, magnetic forces.

The Watkin's Glen Festival featured only three rock groups; the Woodstock Festival had more than a dozen. The three groups that appeared at Watkin's Glen were among the most popular in America: The Grateful Dead, The Allman Brothers, and The Band.

Rock in the seventies

Nostalgia is a large part of the mood of the American public in the 1970's. It affects several aspects of the field of entertainment. In musical theater there have been new productions of various earlier successes: *Irene*, originally produced in 1919; *No, No, Nanette* (1925); and a new production of *Good News* (1927), a musical about college life. Nostalgia in music differs from a true appreciation of a great work of the past in that nostalgia is concerned with the private evocation of a former time. Thus nostalgia blurs the sharper edges of the remembered reality and prefers the sunset glow that permeates the atmosphere of recall. Nostalgia has invaded the pop music scene as well. The early 1970's saw Bill Haley and his Comets brought back before the public in various television appearances. More recent groups, such as Shā-na-na, affect the hairstyles, the clothing, the antics— and, oh, yes!—the music, of the 1950's.

And in 1973, the Beach Boys, originally prominent in the middle 1960's, made a concert tour that induced many to hear again their earlier favorites. The following is from a newspaper review of one of the Beach Boys concerts: "The applause was minimal for the new material, but when the Boys broke into an 'oldie' the entire audience rose from their seats as one unity. They clapped, stomped and danced dances that haven't been seen for five years."

There is not only nostalgia; experimentation goes on. The total concept album, as first evidenced in *Sergeant Pepper*, led not only to the rock operas *Tommy* and *Jesus Christ Superstar*, but also affected many other groups that began to deal with the idea of total concept: Emerson, Lake and Palmer with *Tarkus*; Santana with *Santana Abraxus*; War with *Deliver the Word*.

Also, there is constant experiment with the uses of sound, synthetic and other. There are various uses of multilayers of sounds with different textures. *Deliver the Word* contains speech in a separate sound layer against the singing and the musical instruments. This montage effect is but one avenue that is being explored by the more imaginative groups who feel limited by the earlier simplicities of rock.

Diversities and fusions in pop

Ray Charles and James Brown, as the outstanding spokesmen for the young black and the young black's new mood, also have had an impact on the popular music scene. Ray Charles cannot be put into any special category. He is most often called a Soul singer, but his background is broad, including jazz, rock, and popular. Both Charles and Brown are primarily entertainers. But they and other musicians in the forefront today must be considered also for their effect on the social attitudes of the young people of today. Perhaps the most important thing to note is that music is now more than music; it is social and political in its effect. The orbit of popular music today is constantly enlarging. The music is absorbing influences from a variety of sources and transmuting these influences into an ever new expression.

Just as jazz was a fusion of Africa and American/European strains, and later contained within itself such divergent strains as Impressionism and Latin-American rhythms, so popular music today is reaching to the music of India, is dipping back again into jazz (as seen in the Blood, Sweat, and Tears), and is experimenting with large forms.

Imaginative performers and artists, young and old, never stop searching, experimenting, and synthesizing. Duke Ellington, although long recognized throughout the world, never let himself be categorized. Two of his more recent works have been as diverse as the titles of the albums suggest: *Far East Suite* and *Concert of Sacred Music.*

John Coltrane has also searched for the spiritual essence of man and tried to express it through his *Love Supreme* and *Meditations.* His album *Cosmic Music* and Sun-Ra's album *Heliocentric Worlds* suggest an awareness of mysticism.

Henry Pleasants, in *Serious Music—and All That Jazz*, has this to say: "The new younger generation, both black and white, is making its own music on its own terms—not just on the musician's terms, but on terms valid for the entire generation."*

The projection of sound through amplification

During the decade beginning in 1960, the various breakthroughs in electronics opened up myriad possibilities for enhancing or changing the sound of musical

---

* Henry Pleasants, *Serious Music—and All That Jazz* (New York: Simon and Schuster, 1969), p. 198.

instruments and for producing musical sound. The instruments of the jazz band had been limited to those that could be heard above the noise of the crowd; this was one reason for the acceptance of the saxophone into the circles of jazz. Much has been written about what constitutes a jazz instrument. But as now can be seen the matter has been mostly a practical one. Instruments which could not compete in volume with the saxes and the trumpets and trombones—not to mention the percussion—just were not practical as jazz instruments. The only major exception to this was the guitar. However, the guitar's chief role was as a rhythm instrument for the benefit of the men in the orchestra only. It was not until the guitar was amplified that it made a breakthrough as a solo instrument. And the incidences of time and place converged to make the jazz guitarist Charlie Christian, while he was with Benny Goodman, the progenitor of the new, melodic-line solo.

In the 1950's and 1960's other instruments became part of the jazz expression. Even the flute, in spite of its soft tone, could be heard when played at the microphone. In the last few years various instruments have employed electronic devices. Amplifiers are attached directly to the instrument so that the volume can be

Figure 45.   Bernstein's *Mass*, finale. (Courtesy, John F. Kennedy Center for the Performing Arts, photograph Fletcher Drake)

controlled to any degree desired. Thus not only the guitar and flute but also the trombone and other instruments may have the advantages of electronic magnification. An even later device enables an instrument to change its register and timbre. The amplification of the guitar has changed the whole style of popular music. This has led to the electric guitar that is itself an electronic instrument. Both the electric guitar and the amplified acoustic guitar are in common use today.

It is certainly true that much of the popular music of today, with its never-changing, insistent rhythmic pattern and limited harmonic variety, provides little to intrigue the more careful listener. But we must remember that the charge of monotony and ineptness could be levelled at many of the so-called swing bands of the 1930's; for, although inspired by real jazz, they often produced a slick commercial product where the making of money became more important than the making of music. Indeed, the "swing and sway" bands of the 1930's and 1940's —and there were many of them—helped bring on the demise of the big band era.

Imagination and talent are permanent qualities, and the current groups that have these qualities will be remembered.

COMMENTARY AND ANALYSIS

Mass, Bernstein

As we previously noted, Leonard Bernstein's various works—particularly those for the theatre—stem from an American composer who is aware of his heritage.

Bernstein's musical training was formal, which is to say, in the European tradition, but his awareness of the world around him has always been that of an American. He never became a jazz musician, but from his early years he was extremely aware of jazz. His *Symphony No. 1, "Age of Anxiety,"* has a "role" for quasi-jazz piano; his opera *Trouble in Tahiti* gives us jazz-style singing by a night club trio functioning as a Greek chorus. In *West Side Story*, we see eclecticism at its best: Bernstein draws on jazz for its varieties of accent, on Stravinsky for the special rhythmic propulsiveness of changing time signatures, and on the mainstream of American popular music for its melodic charm.

Also, let it be noted that Bernstein's *West Side Story* (1957) made him one of the most successful American composers of popular music. The work was a notable success on Broadway, and as a film it was one of the top dozen financial successes in the history of motion pictures. For the next ten years almost every musical number in the work remained standard fare for professional singers traveling the entertainment circuit or making recordings.

In addition, Bernstein's use of changing time signatures has affected the entire world of theater music and popular music to the present day. And now, in the *Mass*, written in 1971 for the opening of the John F. Kennedy Center for the Performing Arts in Washington, D.C., he added elements of folk and rock to his assimilation of Stravinsky, jazz, and popular music.

There are critics who decry a composer's use of popular materials. Yet the use of popular expressions for serious music has a long and dignified tradition in Western civilization. In the music of the church of the fifteenth and sixteenth centuries, folk or popular music, including dance tunes, became a part of the sacred liturgy. And after the Reformation, the hymns of the Lutheran service contained many tunes that were originally secular in nature.

Bernstein found a direct predecessor in one of the most American of composers, Charles Ives, who incorporated into serious music different kinds of music that he heard around him in Connecticut at the turn of the century: hymns, the music of marching bands, ragtime and/or jazz, and sentimental popular songs. The important question is not whether a composer uses materials from the popular idiom, but what he does with them.

Bernstein's *Mass* is first of all a secular work for the theater. It is described by the composer on the title page of the vocal score as "A Theatre Piece for Singers, Players, and Dancers." The co-author of the *Mass* is Stephen Schwartz, composer of the musical *Godspell*.

The *Mass* explores the everyday interests of human beings in the context of a service of the Mass; it becomes a catalyst and focal point for a rebellion against ritual for the sake of ritual. The problem of ritual losing its meaning and tradition outliving its usefulness was also central to the dramatic tension of the musical, *Fiddler on the Roof*.

Bernstein's *Mass* opens with the traditional opening of the *Mass*, the *Kyrie Eleison* (Lord, have mercy). The soprano voice begins in coloratura style (p. 1)* and is joined sequentially by other voices, but as the music proceeds it soon becomes apparent that no one is "at the controls" and the constant crescendo runs on, ending at a point of "maximum confusion" (p. 17). A young man appears in casual street dress, strikes a chord on his guitar and wipes out the confusion. Thus begins *Hymn and Psalm: "A Simple Song,"*

> *Lauda, Laude . . .*
> Make it up as you go along
> Laude, Laude . . .
> Sing like you like to sing.
> God loves all simple things
> For God is the simplest of all.

He continues with this simple, popular type melody, including some of the text of the 121st Psalm, "I will lift up my eyes to the hills from whence comes my help . . ."

The guitarist, in his middle twenties, is then invested with the robe of a priest, and it is he, as the Celebrant of the Communion, who is the central character of the work.

There is a brief *Alleluia* (Responsory) in jazz-style opening with scat syllables, "Du bing, du bong," etc. (p. 23). The *Kyrie* is then taken out of the church setting

---

* Page references are to the piano-vocal score of Leonard Bernstein's *Mass*.

(Prefatory Prayers, p. 34) and is performed by a street chorus playing as if it were at a political rally, accompanied by a marching band. The street players take over the usually solemn *Kyrie* in a broad, blunt manner, "Lord, have mercy! Christ, have mercy!" is here a shouting chant of desperation.

The rousing march is interrupted by a brief quiet section (p. 46) in which altar boys sing in their naïvely pure voices, "Here I go up to the altar of God." The march resumes without voices, but in the last few measures (p. 53) we hear boys joining in with kazoos. The use of a street instrument like the kazoo is reminiscent of the use of another street instrument, the Jew's harp, in the *Holidays Symphony* of Charles Ives. (The Jew's harp is heard in the barn dance section of the first movement, entitled "Washington's Birthday, 1909.") The Celebrant, the Boys Choir, and a street chorus join in the *Thrice-Triple Canon: Dominus Vobiscum (God Be with You)* (p. 54), which keeps the simple beat of the march. In its canonic style, voices are gradually added until a peak is reached with a total of nine different vocal parts; then the texture begins to unravel, as the number of voices diminishes. Over the fading phrases the Celebrant speaks (p. 58): "In the name of the Father, and the Son, and the Holy Ghost." Acolytes enter with ritual objects, and there is a primitive rhythmic rendering of "In nomine Patris" ("In the Name of the Father"), in the mixed time signature of $\frac{3}{8}$, $\frac{3}{4}$. At the end of this section the celebrant says, "Let us rise and pray. . . . bless and protect all who are assembled" (p. 63). Then follows the *Prayer for the Congregation* in simple and brief chorale style, which leads into the *Epiphany* (p. 66) (a January feast day celebrating the Magi's visit to Bethlehem): a taped oboe solo darting about among four loud speakers.

We now go into Section IV, *Confession* (p. 67), starting with the liturgical *Confiteor Deo Omnipotenti (I Confess to Almighty God)*, which Bernstein sets rhythmically for chorus in somewhat traditional choral style until the words "cogitatione, verbo, et opere" ("thought, word, and deeds") (p. 70). Then, a swinging section in $\frac{5}{4}$ is introduced accompanied by finger snapping, with three guitars (p. 71) playing in a basic jazz rhythmic style; over this the chorus now sings, "Mea culpa, mea maxima culpa" ("My fault, my most grievous fault") (p. 72). This soon leads into the first of two tropes, which are musical and textual insertions in a liturgical service. Tropes have existed since the tenth century. The trope, "I don't Know" (p. 77), specified as in "heavy blues" style, opens with a street chorus of men, accompanied by a rock band, singing *Confiteor*; this serves to introduce a rock singer singing "If I could, I'd confess,"

EXAMPLE 9–2

who then proceeds to tell of his uncertainty with regard to his feelings and his resolutions, ending with "What is real, Lord, I don't know."

The music melds into a "blues combo" on the other side of the stage, and the second trope, "Easy," presents a blues singer stating (p. 82), "Well, I went to the holy man and I confessed."

EXAMPLE 9–3

A female blues singer joins in (p. 85) "If you ask me to love you on a bed of spice, Now that might be nice, Once or twice. But don't look for sacraments or sacrifice, They're not worth the price." A third rock singer and a third blues singer add their voices of discontent and disillusionment, and finally the three rock singers and the three blues singers join in the prevailing message of these tropes, "If I could, I'd confess," and the *Confession* comes to a close with a musical reiteration of the opening (p. 93), but now under the Latin text, "Orare prome," and then a final statement of uncertainty, "I don't know" (p. 95). The Celebrant speaks at the end, "God forgive you . . . Let us pray" (p. 97).

Section V, the orchestral *Meditation No. 1,* follows. The meditative mood is interrupted by strident bursts of sound, as if meditation in this contemporary world of ours were barely possible. The mode of life that includes fast travel and the noise of cars, trains, and jet planes is not conducive to lengthy quiet moments.

Section VI, *Gloria* (p. 101) begins with *Gloria Tibi,* the first of the *Gloria's* four sections, with a brisk, exuberant rhythmic pattern in $\frac{5}{8}$ meter. This is first set by bongos played by the Celebrant, quickly joined by first the Stage Wind Orchestra, and then by the Celebrant singing softly, but excitedly, "Gloria tibi . . ." (Glory to you).

EXAMPLE 9-4

Antiphonal singing between the Celebrant and the Boys Choir dominates the first part of this section. This is followed by a brief instrumental middle section (p. 104) and a final section set in imitative polyphony between the Celebrant and the Boys Choir (p. 105).

The *Gloria in Excelsis* (p. 107) comes next, set in a blunt 2-beat style reminiscent of the rhythmic feeling of Gershwin's "I Got Plenty o' Nothin' " from *Porgy and Bess.* Here there is no subtlety, no veiling of feelings, but an open, high-spirited and joyous statement by the Celebrant: "Glory to God in the highest, and peace on earth to men of good will." The full adult choir immediately joins in with the traditional Latin version of the Celebrant's shout of praise: "Gloria in excelsis Deo, et in terra pax hominibus bonae voluntatis."

A trope follows entitled *Half of the People* (p. 112) sung by the street chorus. It begins with the musical materials of the preceding *Gloria in Excelsis* but with contemporary lyrics. As a matter of fact, Bernstein has inserted a footnote that says: "This quatrain was a Christmas present from Paul Simon [of Simon and Garfunkel fame]. Gratias. L.B."

The Simon quatrain follows (p. 112–114):

> *Half of the people are stoned*
> *And the other half are waiting for the next election.*
>
> *Half of the people are drowned*
> *And the other half are swimming in the wrong direction.*
>
> *They call it Glorious Living,*
> *They call it Glorious Living.*
>
> *And, baby, where does that leave you,*
> *You and your youth and your kind?*
> *You and your youth and your mind?*

The ending of this musical section leads directly into the trope, "Thank You" (p. 116), which is in a more moderate tempo and is correspondingly quiet and graceful. A soprano sings, accompanied by electronic instruments, "There once were days so bright, and nights when every cricket call seemed right, and I sang Gloria," and later she sings (p. 118), "And now, ... I miss the Gloria, ... gone is the thank you." The trope ends softly with words from the quatrain: "the other half are swimming in the wrong direction."

There is a second orchestral meditation (p. 120).

In the *Epistle* that follows (p. 123) the Celebrant begins by reading from one of the letters of St. Paul: "Brothers: This is the gospel I preach; and in its service I have suffered hardship like a criminal; yea, even unto imprisonment; but there is no imprisoning the word of God ..."

The reading of St. Paul's letter serves as a bridge to the world of today. In a montage effect we hear first a male voice reading from a letter (p. 123), "Dearly Beloved: Do not be surprised if the world hates you. We who love our brothers have crossed over to life ..." The voice continues briefly and a second voice supersedes the first. A young man reads from his letter, "Dear Mom and Dad: Nothing will make me change my mind ..." The voice continues reading; the center of attention moves to the Celebrant singing in a simple recitative style, "You can lock up the bold men ..., You can stifle all adventure ..., Smother hope before it's risen ..., But you cannot imprison the Word of the Lord ..." The street chorus joins briefly. The recitative style turns into a decisive rhythmic statement of defiance, "No, they're never gonna scuttle the Word of the Lord!"

A third voice, a young man (p. 128), reads from the Bible, "I think that God has made us apostles the most abject of mankind ..." And then we hear a young woman reading her very personal letter, "Dear Folks: Jim looked very well on my first visit. With his head clean-shaven, he looked about 19 years old. He says the prison food is very good, cafeteria-style ..." And so on. The Celebrant continues with the theme, "You cannot abolish the Word of the Lord." The orchestration becomes thicker, the beat intensifies, and the dynamics increase as the Celebrant says (p. 131): "Oh you people of power, your hour is now ..." The music crescendos to a climax and then, in the ensuing stillness, the Celebrant closes the Bible, and once again sings in recitative style: "So we wait in silent treason until reason is restored, and we wait for the season of the Word of the Lord." The tension subsides, the music softens, the pace slows. Suddenly the Gospel-Sermon, *God Said* (p. 133), begins.

In spite of changing time-signatures of $\frac{2}{4}$ and $\frac{3}{8}$, the mood here is straight out of the revival meetings of the sawdust-floored tents of the white religious experience in early America, as well as the uproarious mood of the dynamic singing in the sanctified churches of black Americans. True, these aspects of our American heritage are distilled and synthesized, but the roots cannot be ignored.

The Celebrant has finished. The Preacher (in contrast to the Celebrant's general dignity) jumps up onto a bench, and—surrounded by his congregants—goes "Old Testament" (p. 133), singing rhythmically, "God said: Let there be light. And there was light." The chorus of congregants joins him, and there follows a good-humored, rhythmically rousing story of the creation, including a few contemporary interpretations of, and answers to, age-old questions that everyone has asked since childhood. As Bernstein gives the answers, he raises the questions again, because the answers have always been simplistic. "Why do we have snakes or rats, Mother?" Mother says, "Each animal has a purpose on earth. The snakes eat the rats." "But what about the rats, Mother?" Well, the rats, er ..." "What about frogs, Mother?" "Well, the frogs eat the flies." "What about the flies, mother?" "Well, the flies ..."

The text continues (p. 137), "God said: let there be gnats. Let there be sprats to gobble the gnats so that the sprats may nourish the rats, making them fat, fine food for the cats ... and God saw it was good ..."

The *Credo*, Section X (p. 146), which contains the traditional *Credo in Unum Deum* (I Believe in One God), is followed by four tropes that in the colloquial language of every day raise various questions about the statement made in *The Credo*. Bernstein sets the Latin text of *Credo in Unum Deum* (sung by the choir in unison and octaves) in syllabic style (one note to each syllable) and exclusively in quarter note values at a rather fast pace. Rigid and declamatory, the effect is of a chanting that allows no breathing places where questions might be asked about this traditional statement of belief: "I believe in one God, the Father Almighty, Maker of heaven and earth, And of all things visible and invisible. And in one Lord, Jesus Christ, the only begotten Son of God ..."

But questions are raised nonetheless. The tropes interrupt (p. 149) in the language of the street and, in terms of disrespect for the traditional church service, state in turn (beginning in the *Non Credo*, p. 150): "You, God, chose to become a man, to pay the earth a small social call. I tell you, sir, you never were a man at all. Why? You had the choice when to live, when to die, and then become a God again."

The choir re-enters, continuing with the *Credo* but is interrupted by another trope: "Hurry" (p. 156): "You said you'd come again. When? When things got really rough ... Well, things are tough enough. So when's your next appearance on the scene? I'm ready. Hurry ..."

The *Credo* is heard briefly again. The next trope: "World without End" picks up from the Latin of the *Credo* (p. 160), "Cujus regni non erit finis ..." ("Whose reign will be without end ...") "World without end spins endlessly on, Only the men who live here are gone, gone on a permanent vacation, . . . Dark are the cities, dead is the ocean, Silent and sickly are the remnants of motion . . ."

Once again the *Credo* is heard but as it concludes, it is pitted against the voices of the street saying, "Hurry and come again . . . Lord, don't you care?"

The next trope, "I Believe in God" (p. 167), introduces a Rock Singer, in a simple four-beat metric pattern with strong off-beats, singing, "I believe in God, but does God believe in me? I'll believe in any God, if any God there be . . ."

There follows *Meditation No. 3 (De Profundis,* part 1) (p. 173) for choir, the *Offertory (De Profundis,* part 2) (p. 182), and *The Lord's Prayer* (p. 191) that includes a trope, "I Go On," sung by the Celebrant.

The Mass continues. As the Boys Choir sings the *Sanctus* (p. 194), the Celebrant prepares the Communion. During this there is an interesting interlude in which the Celebrant receives an acoustic guitar from a choir boy (p. 200). In a contemplative mood he sings an introductory passage containing a play on words. Bernstein borrows the old gag of a non-singer checking out his voice before he really gets started. But this becomes quickly a musical pun in which the "sol-fa" syllables not only represent the notes they stand for, but get turned into a wordplay as well. The Celebrant sings "Mi . . . Mi . . . (p. 200) (third-scale step) *Mi* alone is only me. But *mi* with *sol* (fifth-scale step), Me with soul, *Mi sol* means a song is beginning, . . ." and then the Celebrant goes on lyrically, in full voice.

It is during the *Agnus Dei* that follows (p. 207) that the opposing points of view of the church (symbolized by the Celebrant) versus those of the street people begin to clash. The *Agnus Dei* text ("O Lamb of God, who takest away the sins of the world, have mercy on us") is usually found in a musical setting that is quiet and reverent, perhaps even other-worldly. But that is not the case in this *Agnus Dei,* which is scored in a nervous, rhythmic manner, marked *agitato.* When the street singers shout at the tops of their voices, "Donna nobis pacem!", it is not a plea but a demand.

At the important moment when the Celebrant says, in the commemoration of the Last Supper, "This is My Body, this is the chalice of My Blood" (p. 211), his way is barred as he goes to the altar. *"Pacem! Pacem! Pacem!"* sung by the crowd now becomes a street slogan, a poster in a picket line, a bumper sticker. PEACE NOW!

There ensues a period of push-and-pull, give-and-take, as the service continues. But the stage becomes disorganized (p. 217), the Celebrant is having increasing difficulty maintaining the dignity of his position, and the "Pacem" slogan is reiterated again and again (p. 219).

The choir has been leaving the pews and mixing with the street people (p. 223). There is a confusion of tongues, the street people singing in English, the choir in Latin. The music gets louder, more and more musicians join in, several begin improvising. There is a final *Pacem* by the Celebrant on a long high note, and on his last syllable, he hurls the Sacrament to the floor (p. 237). The chalice and monstrance are shattered.

Silence.

This brings us to the section, *Fraction: Things Get Broken* (p. 237). The Celebrant begins singing in a rigid, sparse, hesitant—at times almost immobile–style: "Look . . . Isn't that . . . odd . . . red wine . . . isn't red at all . . . It's sort of . . . brown . . . brown and blue . . . I never noticed that." And a little later, excitedly, "What are you staring at? Haven't you ever seen an accident before?" He continues singing, meanwhile smashing things on the altar—candles and anything at hand, and also ripping the altar cloth. He finally leaps on the altar, and dances wildly (p. 246). He continues in this manner, gradually quieting down, ending the way he started: "Oh, how easily things get broken."

The *Pax-Communion (Secret Songs)* (p. 255) concludes the work, beginning with a darting flute solo (previously played by the oboe, in the *Epiphany*), moving to a boy soprano singing the simplistic song performed earlier by the Celebrant, "Sing God a simple song, Lauda, laude...." During the praise singing (p. 258), church people and street people begin to recognize that they are all searching for the same thing. A choir boy and a man of the street embrace, leading to a chain of embraces, while the swelling Latin *Lauda, Laude, Laudate Deum* brings all the people together. The Celebrant appears (p. 264), again dressed as he was at the beginning of the work, in simple street clothes.

The work closes with a hymn sung by the entire company (p. 266), starting with the words "Almighty Father, incline thine ear; bless us and all those who have gathered here...." A taped voice declares: "The Mass is ended; go in peace."*

---

* Based in part on Leonard Bernstein, *Mass*, piano vocal score. Copyright 1972 by Leonard Bernstein and Stephen Schwartz. Used by permission.

Chapter ten

SINCE WEBERN

In the early twentieth century certain composers turned away from their romantic heritage and established new modes of musical thought. Debussy, Ravel, Stravinsky, Bartók, and Schoenberg are now considered masters of their time. In whatever idiom they worked, each left a definitive body of music now recognized and revered by a sizeable concert-going public throughout the world.

Through their musical legacy we see a sharp break from traditional concepts of tonality, rhythm, and form. We see a more catholic approach to the selection of materials: new harmonic combinations, new rhythmic concepts, borrowings from the related arts, inclusion of cultural elements from all parts of the globe. We also see the beginnings of a progressive alienation of the mass listening audience and, most important, the firm entrenchment of the attitude of experiment. With the *new* composers now to be examined in this chapter, there is an intensification and acceleration of these trends. New sounds include not only traditional pitch combinations, but also sounds from nature and/or sounds produced synthetically. The alienation of the average concert goer, symbolized by the violent audience reaction to the premiere of Stravinsky's *Le Sacre* (see Chapter 8), has now reached the stage where a gap of gigantic proportions separates audiences and composers. As an example of this problem, symphony orchestras are unable or unwilling to devote sufficient rehearsal time to learning new works, leading many composers to hesitate to allow their works to be performed; indeed, many composers write only for soloists or small ensembles, or else just for electronic media.

One of our leading American composers, Milton Babbitt, has written and spoken frequently about the dilemma facing the serious composer in today's hostile cultural environment. Describing the totally inadequate performance of one of his recent works by one of our major orchestras, Babbitt has said:

> Until, if ever, such an orchestra [i.e., an orchestra willing and able to perform difficult contemporary orchestral works] is formed, few demanding contemporary works will be performed, and fewer still will be accurately performed, and the composers of such works who have access to electronic media will, with fewer and fainter pangs of renunciation, enter their electronic studios with their compositions

in their heads, and leave those studios with their performances on the tapes in their hands.*

This statement echoes a similar view expressed by Babbitt some dozen years earlier:

> And so, I dare suggest that the composer would do himself and his music an immediate and eventual service by total, resolute, and voluntary withdrawal from this public world to one of private performance and electronic media, with its very real possibility of complete elimination of the public and social aspects of musical composition.†

It is clear that Babbitt and others are finding sanctuary within the musical laboratories of the university. How large a percentage of serious composers share Babbitt's views is unclear, but the very fact that any important composer feels as Babbitt does is evidence of the widening chasm.

The earlier twentieth-century composer's tendency towards the universal and inclusive has led to an emphasis on the integration of heterogeneous elements. Works in mixed media are now prominent. The Greek sculptor Takis, for example, has exhibited works activated by electromagnetism, some giving out a musical sound. And Earle Brown has written an aleatory composition called *Calder-Piece*, for four percussionists and "mobile"; the performers take their "chances" with the music according to the speed and position of the mobile by Alexander Calder.

And there are bold, newer departures. Since Webern, there have arisen radical tendencies fraught with both dangers and promise for the future of musical art. These tendencies lie primarily in the essentially opposed areas of predeterminancy and of chance. The move toward total predeterminancy and control comes out of total abstract serialism, its chief progenitor and protagonist being Webern. Ultimately this led to electronic composition where the composer's choice of each sound is preset by mathematical formula and each performance also totally controlled through the elimination of the interpreter/performer. The responsibility is entirely that of the composer. Uniformity of product and faithful reproduction is assured. On the other hand, anti-control is the essence in chance music. Here the final result cannot be planned. The performer has the last say. The responsibility lies less with the composer than with the performer. The music can never be the same. The spontaneous instant is all. The audience must understand and receive the message at once and only once.

Implications arising out of both of these radical philosophies of composition are shattering. A revolution of the whole social basis of artistic communication is

---

* Robert Stephan Hines, ed., *The Orchestral Composer's Point of View: Essays on Twentieth-Century Music by Those Who Wrote It* (Norman, Okla.: University of Oklahoma Press, 1970), p. 38.
† "Who Cares if You Listen?", *High Fidelity* 8 (February 1958): 126.

implied. Added to all this is the accelerated pace of stylistic change and a great diversity of effort on a world-wide stage. New idioms multiply and composers leap over each other in their rush to the future.

CONSTRUCTIVIST CONCEPTS IN THE ARTS

The French painter Cézanne had said, "Deal with nature by means of the cylinder, the sphere, the cube." When the Fauvist painter, Matisse, in a moment of derision, coined the word *cubism* when speaking of the work of Picasso and Braque, he chose an apt term. The cubists transformed traditional elements of perspective into disciplined, mathematical fragments and facets. Through these were projected the inner essence of the object, beyond and deeper than that given by a representative reproduction. When one sees Picasso's *The Ladies of Avignon* (1906–1907), or Duchamp's *Nude Descending a Staircase* (1912), the first impression might be that of overlapping images as seen through a prism. But one ultimately sees the texture of inner life, shorn of unessentials. There is motion and the raw nerve and heartbeat of what really is. Braque's montage and collage techniques, an outgrowth of cubism, combine assorted mounted materials that are synthesized into an expression emphasizing tactile qualities. So did the work of the constructivists, such as Tatlin and Pevsner, who also dealt with elements of cubic space.

Several composers also investigated the use of mechanical concepts in their compositions. Typical are: Honegger's *Pacific 231*, simulating the rhythmic throb of the locomotive; George Antheil's *Ballet méchanique* (decor by the cubist, Léger) with the use of airplane propellers; Prokofiev's *Leap of Steel*, and Mossolov's *Iron Foundry* (including the sound of shaken sheet metal reflecting the new industrialism of the young Union of Soviet Socialist Republics).

THE EXPERIMENTAL ATTITUDE

The contemporary composer has complete freedom of choice. As a result of this freedom, however, he is much more responsible for his choice. The independence of the individual in his thought and in his action is predominant in the world today as in no other time.

This has been reflected in the arts as well. Andy Warhol's painting of a can of soup—whatever it is of itself—is a statement *against* all preconceived ideas of what art should be. Experiments in music that deny the use of pitch and emphasize noise are statements against all former concepts of music. The emphasis on the random expression, the interest in a "happening," is exactly opposed to the conception that a work of art is a *selection* of materials in an ordered form. All these experiments are a symbol of the search for new stimuli that is prevalent in our society today.

These rejections of previous concepts raise an important point that has been stated very clearly in the writings of Jean-Paul Sartre. Rejection of authority and tradition is not enough. Something must take their place. The establishment of meaning now rests with each individual.

"The existentialist . . . finds it extremely embarrassing that God does not exist, for there disappears with Him all possibility of finding values in an intelligible heaven."* Sartre also says ". . . the first effect of existentialism is that it puts every man in possession of himself as he is, and places the entire responsibility for his existence squarely upon his own shoulders."† And this is the dilemma of the twentieth-century composer. The entire responsibility for a new composition is his. Since every door is open to him, his decision is the more difficult.

There are no rules of composition, but there are principles of organization. Each composer must find these for himself. We have seen, in the evolution of music, in each period, constant searching and constant change. What was accepted at one time is no longer true in a later time. What was true in a later time became superseded itself by a new expression. Each age must find its own expression. This expression—when it is true—does not result from formulas that already exist, but from an inner need to express, and from a seeking of the way to make this expression meaningful.

In light of the above, and later developments in music, it is interesting to note that Edgard Varèse (1883–1965) acquired an engineering degree before becoming fully involved in the intricacies of music. This double interest led him ultimately into electronic music. Even before his involvement with electronic music his inclination towards engineering resulted in works that are partially mathematical in their basis. His *Octandre* may be thought of from at least one point of view as a continuous reshaping of a three-note pattern. This mechanistic piece for eight instruments is in line of succession with the neo-baroque objectivity of Stravinsky's *Octet*. In 1931 came *Ionisation*. Scored for thirty-seven percussion instruments manned by thirteen players, it epitomizes the new search for new sounds. Among the instruments are two sirens, two tam-tams, and two anvils, each pair in two registers, high and low. It was the engineer in Varèse who titled his work for solo flute, *Density 21.5*. The work was written for the debut of George Barrère's platinum flute: 21.5 is the density of platinum. The inherent musical abstraction of the total percussion of *Ionisation* points away from traditional pitch usage. It led the way for later developments in computer music, which also abandoned con-

---

* Jean-Paul Sartre, *Existentialism and Humanism*, translation and introduction by Philip Mairet (London: Methuen & Co., Ltd., 1946, 1948, reprinted 1960), p. 33.
† Ibid., p. 29.

ventional pitch distinctions. Varèse, the first to recognize the possibilities of total percussion, stopped writing in 1937; then he was drawn back to composition, perhaps by the lure of electronics, in the 1950's.

COMMENTARY AND ANALYSIS

Ionisation, Varèse

Edgard Varèse was born in Paris, but he came to the United States in 1915, and all his important writing was done here. He became the most important composer of the new experimental movement in the 1920's.

He wrote six works prior to 1930 and added four more in the following decade. *Ionisation* was one of these four, and it was one of the first works to deal to such a large extent with percussion instruments. To the familiar instruments of the percussion section Varèse added many others, and with this extended battery was able to treat these instruments like a choir, covering the various registers of soprano, alto, tenor, and bass. (These terms refer most commonly to voice registers, but they are used in connection with instrumental registers as well.)

As important as *Ionisation* was when it was written in 1931, it is now seen to have been prophetic of important new directions in music to come. In the emphasis on sound-mass, Varèse's work presaged the advent of electronic music. In addition to sirens, tam-tams, and anvils, this unusual score calls for an amazing complex of instruments. There are three sizes of bass drum, three instruments of the snare-drum type (sometimes without snare), and there is a string-drum, also known as the "Lion's Roar." This instrument consists of "a medium-sized wooden barrel, with parchment head, through which a rosined string is drawn. The sound is produced by rubbing the string with a piece of cloth or leather." The description of this instrument is from the score that contain Varèse's specifications concerning the various instruments and how they are to be played. As an aid to listening to this work, the instruments that the thirteen performers play are listed below:

1. Crash cymbal; Bass drum (very deep); Cow-bell (muffled)
2. Gong; Tam-tam (high); Tam-tam (low)
3. Two Bongos; Side-drum; Two Bass drums (medium size and large)
4. Tambour militaire; Side-drum
5. Siren (high); String-drum (lion's roar)
6. Siren (low); Slapstick; Gourd (with scratcher)
7. Chinese blocks (high, middle register, and low); Claves; Triangle

8.   Snare-drum (with snares relaxed); Maracas (high and low)
9.   Tarole (flat military drum); Snare drum; Suspended cymbal
10.   Cymbals; Sleigh bells; Tubular chimes
11.   Gourd; Castanettes; Glockenspiel
12.   Tambourine; Anvils (high and low); Grand tam-tam (very deep)
13.   Slapstick; Triangle; Sleigh-bells; Piano

Ionisation opens at a leisurely pace, 4 beats to the measure. The opening 8 measures are introductory, however, and are characterized by whirring sounds produced by rolls on a snare drum (with the snares off) and a suspended cymbal, plus the sounds of a high and a low tam-tam (Chinese gong) and a regular gong—with this total effect added to by a 7-measure crescendo-diminuendo on a large siren. The introduction is generally soft, but culminates in a loud climax in measure 8.

At the end of measure 8, the first subject begins softly, played by the tambour militaire. A clearly articulated rhythmic pattern is heard. The 2-bar motive ends with an accentuation—a *sforzando*.

EXAMPLE 10–1

This motive is repeated, followed by a few measures similar to the introduction and a brief reference to the first subject. Then come 3 measures of quicker drum beats plus sounds from Chinese wood blocks. After this, Subject 1 is restated by the tambour militaire, now louder and moving into developmental materials that include the Subject 1 motive and new patterns. Changing time-signatures are introduced, as in measures 27–31:

EXAMPLE 10–2

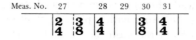

At measure 38, the dynamics change suddenly from soft to loud, and the rhythmic pattern consists of eighth-note triplets. This increased rhythmic intensity continues over 6 measures and leads into the second subject, which begins in measure 44 with a triplet pattern in eighth-notes followed by a quintuplet pattern in sixteenth-notes. The triplet pattern is played simultaneously by a side-drum and two bass drums (middle and low-pitched); the quintuplet pattern occurs simultaneously in five sets of instruments: a high and low bongo, two snare-drums, two Chinese blocks, two maracas (high and low), and two snare-drums.

EXAMPLE 10-3

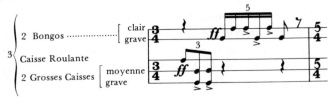

The triplet-quintuplet motive continues with some alterations and embellishments over six measures of varying lengths and can be perceived rather well despite some complexity in the texture. The two bass drums continue as an important part of the texture, which includes various references to subjects 1 and 2, until a fermata (hold) in measure 65. The sound at the fermata is produced by gongs, cymbals, a siren, and anvils.

Beginning at measure 75 Varèse introduces the various *pitched* instruments in quick succession: piano, tubular chimes, glockenspiel (with resonators), plus—for the first time in the work—a very large, deep-sounding tam-tam. With this and other means he creates a sonority that reaches a new plateau of sound—satisfying in its expansiveness.

As the sounds of the instruments of indefinite pitch begin to die away, the sound of the chimes emerges to dominate the texture. The work comes to a soft close.

Henry Cowell (1897–1965) was one of the early experimental composers. He was at first self-taught. At the age of 15 he came upon the idea of playing upon the piano keyboard with his forearm or fist, thereby producing large clusters of sound. This technique may be used to produce percussive sounds or soft "multiple vibrations." This, and a procedure of plucking the piano strings as if it were a harp, opened the way for many younger composers into experiments with sound. With Leon Theremin, Cowell also produced a Rhythmicon, an electronic instrument that could produce multiple rhythms concurrently. The composer of over 500 works, he was constantly active in championing new music. His experiments—including others not mentioned—have been perhaps his outstanding contribution to contemporary music.

Charles Koechlin (1867–1950) only rather recently came to notice; much of his work has been seldom played or published. He was a powerful individualist who drew on all sources to make his own unique statement. Koechlin, in company with Ravel, Milhaud, and Honegger, had been taught by the French pedagogue and theorist, Henri Gedalge. In turn, Poulenc and Sauguet were guided by Koechlin. Koechlin was also a strong influence on Milhaud; Koechlin's approach to the uses of tonality/polytonality was important in the development of Milhaud's extensive utilization of mixed tonalities.

One of the most important and individual of Koechlin's works is the massive, pictorial cycle based upon Kipling's *The Jungle Book*. One section of *Les Bandar-Log*, sub-titled *Scherzo of the Monkeys*, shows the broad spectrum of Koechlin's musical thought. Here we find a melding of diverse sounds. In illuminating the imaginative Kipling text where the monkey-world is perhaps seen as the microcosm of the human situation, Koechlin weds heterogeneous musical styles and techniques: expressionistic, coloristic orchestration and harmony, a serial fantasy, a polytonal invention, and a fugue built on the subject from the French folk song "J'ai du bon tabac." Koechlin's Kipling cycle brings to mind the jungle scenes of the French primitivistic painter, Henri Rousseau. There is a like feeling in both artists for the enigma and mystery of the jungle. Koechlin's identity with, and encouragement of, the fresh and the new accounted for his ever-changing creative vistas. At the age of eighty he wrote orchestral interludes to go with an earlier work, the *Seven Stars Symphony* of 1933. The stars were Charlie Chaplin, Douglas Fairbanks, Emil Jannings, Marlene Dietrich, Clara Bow, Lillian Harvey, and Greta Garbo.

Olivier Messiaen (1908–   ), through his treatise on methods of composition, as a teacher at the Paris Conservatoire, as well as through his association with the group *La Jeune France*, has had considerable influence on younger composers. Some of his works are massive in scope and contain elements of mysticism and oriental influences, using various modes. To enhance his expression he has used unusual percussion instruments, as well as the electronic instrument, the *ondes martenot* (named after its inventor), which produces a sound not unlike a female voice with a tremendous range. *Turangalîla*, his ten-movement work for orchestra, exhibits his full technique, and is a masterful expression, almost hypnotic in its profound probing. From the perspective of our time it may be seen that Messiaen in his role as composer, teacher, and writer was a pervasive influence on the younger avant-garde. He taught, among others, Boulez, Stockhausen, Nono, and Barraqué.

In his credo that "technique serves expression"; in his expression of such diverse elements as angels, birds, the genesis of life, and the mystery of the earth; in his use of Sanskrit and his own pseudo-Sanskrit; in his interest in the ondes martenot—we see a broad-ranging, universal approach to artistic creation. In his later works Messiaen became interested in the actual songs of birds as a basic element in his materials of composition. Here is a catholic fusion of resources—those from nature and those from the most advanced technical developments of our time.

Turangalîla contains rhythmic innovations similar to Schoenberg's use of pitch serialism. This rhythmic serialism was later adopted by Stockhausen.

COMMENTARY AND ANALYSIS

Turangalîla Symphonie, Messiaen

Turangalîla is Messiaen's only symphony. This massive work places the composer within a tradition—that of the French attitude towards creative art. This attitude leads the French composer generally to distrust the possibility that music transmits spiritual states, elevation of the soul, or kindred effects. Rather he takes the position that music ornaments the good life and, as a corollary, that it refines the aural sense through the precise art of composition. As Martin Cooper put it in his book, *French Music*, ". . . to seek in French music primarily for a revelation of the composer's soul or for marks of the sublime is to look for something which the French consider a by-product."

The *Turangalîla Symphonie* is a ten-movement work based on the Sanskrit words *Turanga* (time, movement, rhythm) and *Lîla* (the play of life and death, love). Eight of the ten movements have program titles; two, the first and last, are simply labelled according to their position within the whole:

1. Introduction
2. Chant d'amour 1 (Song of Love 1)
3. Turangalîla 1
4. Chant d'amour 2
5. Joie du sang des étoiles (Joy from the Blood of the Stars)
6. Jardin du sommeil d'amour (Garden of the Dream of Love)
7. Turangalîla 2
8. Développement de l'amour (Development of Love)
9. Turangalîla 3
10. Finale

Turangalîla is a programmed work that emanates from the French tradition in instrumental music. This tradition includes the music of the clavecinists of the late Baroque, such as Daquin, F. Couperin ("Le Grand"), and Rameau; *Harold in Italy*, and the *Symphonie fantastique* by Berlioz; the tone poems of Saint-Saëns, Franck, and Dukas; and the Impressionism of Debussy, Ravel, and others.

Also clearly in the French tradition is Messiaen's search for new orchestral sonorities in *Turangalîla*. The ear feasts on extraordinary tone color that goes even beyond the original orchestral sonorities of Debussy and Ravel, of Stravinsky in the Paris ballets of 1910–1913, and of Koechlin in his *Bandar-log*. This symphony could not have existed without their influence.

A particularly interesting feature of *Turangalîla* is the use of a new instrument, the *ondes martenot* (see above), which plays a leading role (along with the solo piano) throughout. The sound of the ondes martenot is somewhat like that of the soprano voice, disembodied and refined.

EXAMPLE 10–4   Movement II

It lends a mystic quality appropriate to the expressive intentions of the work as they relate to Indian philosophy.

Messiaen scores intentionally to produce sonorities suggestive of the East. In a note on *Turangalîla,* Messiaen states: "The three keyboard instruments, glockenspiel, celesta and vibraphone, have a special part similar to that of an East Indian gamelan as used in the islands of Sonde (Java and Bali)."

EXAMPLE 10–5   Movement III

In addition to the keybroad instruments playing the figure in Example 10–5, the ondes reinforces the Eastern atmosphere with glissandi.

Influences other than from the East are also present. Messiaen has made a special study of bird song, and melodic materials derived from actual bird calls can be heard in many of his works. Movement VI, *Jardin du sommeil d'amour,* finds an extensive exploration of the possibilities of bird song melodic material. The solo piano (later joined by the woodwinds) plays intricate aviary imitations that counterpoint a broad, expressive melodic line in the full strings and ondes martenot.

EXAMPLE 10–6   Movement VI

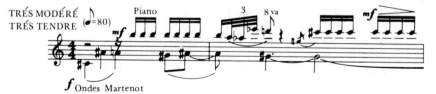

The above characteristics—fresh orchestral sonorities and detailed imagery—relate essentially to *Turangalîla* as a programmed work within the French tradition. But other characteristics link the work to a broader tradition—that of symphonic structure.

One important structural factor is its cyclic form. There are four cyclic themes that bind the symphony together. The first, in the low brass, massive and ponderous, has in Messiaen's words "the terrifying brutality of old Mexican monuments."

EXAMPLE 10–7   Movement I (Introduction)

The third cyclic idea is the "theme of love," thoroughly tonal and lyric (see Ex. 10–4 above).

Each of these cyclic themes enters at important points in the symphony and joins other themes that appear solely in individual movements. This was a common procedure in symphonies by romantic composers such as Berlioz, Franck, Tchaikovsky, Liszt, and Dvorak.*

Movement II, Chant d'amour I (Song of Love I), is shaped from a variety of melodic threads woven into a richly colored musical design. At the same time there is a rigorous logic to the design.

Of far greater importance than its exotic colors and motivic relationships is the sense in this music of charged duality, of action and reaction within a kind of Eastern dialectic. Referring to the presentation of the two most important melodic ideas, Messiaen identifies this duality within the opening section of the movement: "The refrain keeps alternating two elements of totally contrasted tempo, nuance and feeling." After a short bitterly dissonant introduction, followed by a drum roll, Motive I enters in the trumpets (see Ex. 10–8 below). Messiaen indicates that this idea is to be played briskly and with passion. The music suggests a kind of aggressive warmth. Soon, the tempo changes, *un peu lent, tendre* (rather slow, tender), and Motive II, totally contrasted in character, enters in the strings with the ondes (see Ex. 10–4 above). These opposed yet yoked motives provide the most important melodic substance for the first section of this movement.

---

* © Copyright 1973, 1974 by Roland Nadeau. All rights reserved. Reprinted by permission of Crescendo Publishing Co., Boston.

EXAMPLE 10–8

Section II (measure 100) is made up from another encounter of opposing melodic expressions. The first chant-like idea (Motive III) is intoned by the oboes and English horn doubled by violas:

EXAMPLE 10–9

As he did in Section I above, the composer now immediately presents a vividly contrasted melodic idea (Motive IV):

EXAMPLE 10–10

Whereas the motive in Example 10–9 suggests reserve and containment, the idea in Example 10–10 is explosively impetuous.

These deeply contrasted moods alternate throughout this section until a climax is reached. At this point, the drum roll from the beginning returns and leads to the entrance of Motive I (Ex. 10–8), again in the trumpets. An expectation of return is implied, and you could now reasonably look forward to hearing Motive II in the ondes. Instead of this, Motive I is developed intensively and leads to a return of Motive IV, which itself is now developed. Excitement builds until the ultimate climax of the whole movement is reached: an exultant entrance of the ondes.

EXAMPLE 10–11

After a time the ondes leads again, this time with its melodic character very close to that of Motive I—representing a final synthesis of diverse elements.*

Musique concrète

The acceleration of technological evolution and discovery in the twentieth century could not pass unfelt or unnoticed by twentieth-century composers.

It is to be noted that more and more composers are also mathematicians, engineers, and inventors. Austin in his *Music in the Twentieth Century*, in presenting a list of important developments, states: "Varèse made experiment the foundation of all his work, and published only his distilled achievements. The list includes, on the other hand, inventors, some of whom did not compose at all, and most of whom composed pieces that caught attention only briefly. . . ."†

In 1948 in Paris Pierre Schaeffer, the first exponent of *musique concrète*, furthered the attitude of experimentation by recording sounds (not necessarily pitched) and then re-recording them distorted in one way or another—changing the speed of the original recording, repeating and mixing portions of the recording, and otherwise manipulating the original to achieve new effect.

Schaeffer's music was called *musique concrète* because it deals with a collage of concrete sounds and noises, rather than with abstract emotional expression. And it contains the element of chance because it uses an empirical method of trial and error that is diametrically opposed to predetermination. These two concepts—predetermination and chance—were to invade the minds of composers in the years ahead. The first important work of *musique concrète* was that of Schaeffer and Pierre Henry, *Symphony for One Man*, produced in 1949.

Pierre Boulez (1926–   ) has become since Messiaen a dominant figure of the avant-garde, not only in France, but throughout the musical world. Having studied with Messiaen and with Renée Leibowitz, a disciple of Schoenberg, he absorbed Messiaen's searching attitude and combined it with the rigorously mathematical twelve-tone system. He became a leading exponent of the new serialism that has pervaded the thought of principal avant-garde composers. This new serialism, originally suggested by the works of Webern, predicates a through-going serialism including not only the choice of tones but also counterpoint, durational values, choice of instruments, and dynamics.

Boulez has carried the experimental attitude to a near scientific level. Here predeterminism is almost absolute, pointing the way to his later involvement with

---

* Examples 10–4 to 10–11 are from Olivier Messiaen, *Turanglîla Symphonie*. Copyright 1953, Durand et Cie. Used by permission of the publisher. Elkan-Vogel, Inc. sole representative, United States.

† William W. Austin, *Music in the Twentieth Century* (New York: W. W. Norton & Co., Inc., 1966), p. 378. © W. W. Norton & Co., Inc.

electronic music. However, *Grove's Dictionary of Music and Musicians* describes Boulez' workshop as the "adventurous alchemist's rather than the methodical chemist's." Thus, Boulez, regardless of the system and the planning, retains the *sine qua non* of every worthwhile composer, fertility of the spirit.

The Boulez influence has been disseminated through an ever-widening range of activities, such as his appointment as Director of Music at the Jean-Louis Barrault Theatre in Paris in 1948. In recent wears he has done more and more conducting throughout the world, his most recent appointment being Music Director of the New York Philharmonic. In addition to his instrumental works, *Le Soleil des eaux* is one of his more accessible earlier works (1948–1950); this is a cantata based upon two poems of René Char, the surrealist poet. His best-known work is *Le Marteau sans maître*, for soprano and instruments, also based on the work of Char. Heterogeneous in its mixture of severe Webernesque serialism, the dream world of surrealism, the aroma of the Far East, and the sounds and silences of discontinuity, it forms a synthesis that is uniquely Boulez.

Prepared piano

Piano tone is produced by the striking of a felted hammer upon the strings, similar in nature to the manner in which a percussionist strikes a drum. Some percussion instruments are of indefinite pitch, like the cymbals, while others are pitched, like the orchestra bells, the xylophone, the marimba, etc.; the chief point is that they are all struck. But the piano, from Mozart's time to the twentieth century, has been treated by composers and pianists as an instrument that must rise above its most central quality, its percussiveness. Mozart declared that when playing the piano, "it must flow like oil." From Mozart to Chopin, and on to Debussy, composers and pianists sought in the piano a lyricism that would transcend the percussive attributes of the instrument.

But the second decade of the twentieth century saw a new interest in percussive rhythm, which found expression in Stravinsky's *Le Sacre du printemps* and *L'Histoire du soldat*, Bartók's *Allegro Barbaro*, and the rise of jazz. An indelible mark was left that could not be ignored by later composers, even in their writing for piano. The piano's percussive quality became the concern of many composers.

Henry Cowell had devised a way of treating the piano that emphasized its percussive qualities. Cowell, in striking several adjacent keys with fist or forearm produced a dynamic percussive effect verging on noise—the resulting "chords" are known as *tone-clusters*. And in reaching inside the grand piano and dampening the strings by hand, he altered the sound so that it became non-sustaining.

John Cage (1912–   ), who studied with Cowell, picked up from there and developed what became known as *prepared piano*. A prepared piano is one in which the strings are treated in various and sundry ways—as you will see from the discussion of *Amores*, below.

Figure 46. Pierre Boulez in front of Cocteau's caricature of Stravinsky. (J. P. Charbonier, TOP)

COMMENTARY AND ANALYSIS

Amores, Cage

Amores was composed in 1943. It is a work for percussion instruments in four movements: prepared piano in the first and fourth movements with more ordinary instruments employed in the two middle movements. The instructions in the score are like a preface to the work. Here Cage states in considerable detail the manner in which the piano is to be prepared. Screws, bolts, pieces of rubber, and other objects are put between the strings dampening their sound and/or changing their timbre. The result is a new instrument with its own special qualities.

Amores lasts for nine minutes. Its four movements are organized as follows:

I   Solo for prepared piano

II   Trio (9 tom-toms, pod rattle)

III   Trio (7 woodblocks, not Chinese)

IV   Solo for prepared piano

The first movement, which is brief (occupying just one page of piano score), opens with a short, strong chordal sound. It then moves into several measures of what one would be tempted to call "filigree," if one looked at the piano part and expected the usual sounds to come out. But remember that each tone has been subjected to a specific preparation. Also note that the *8va* at the beginning of the righthand part is an abbreviation for *ottava*, meaning that the notes sound an octave higher than written.

EXAMPLE 10-12

The movement continues, with repetition and ostinato, in true percussive style, and ends with a soft resonant figure

EXAMPLE 10-13

to be echoed and somewhat extended near the end of the fourth movement.

The second movement, for three percussion players, is for nine tom-toms (three per player), plus a pod rattle played by the second percussionist. As usual with tom-toms, the pitches are indeterminate. Each player has three different size tom-toms graduated in pitch: low, middle, and high. Each tom-tom has its own further definition of low and high. Thus, there are six pitch areas available to each player.

The movement begins with conventional rhythmic patterns, but measure 4 introduces crossed rhythmic patterns that continue as part of the design of the movement.

EXAMPLE 10–14

The third movement is also performed by three players, with varying numbers of woodblocks each. The instruction "not Chinese" means that the hollow sound of Chinese woodblocks is not desired. (Usually called *Chinese temple-blocks*, these are a normal part of a percussionist's equipment, but Cage does not want their rather dry, sharp sound.)

The movement opens slowly and softly with a simple, repeated figure.

EXAMPLE 10–15

The rhythmic figures never become complex in this movement, but the texture does get thicker. However, as the texture thickens, gradually the volume becomes softer and softer until at the end the sounds are a mere whisper.

The last movement, returning to the prepared piano, is the longest and the most sonorous of the four. Starting thinly in the right hand, a low series of sonorities is added in the left hand in measure 4.

EXAMPLE 10–16

The music continues with alternating tones in the lower part producing an ostinato effect throughout the first quarter of the movement. Repeated patterns of several notes heard above this ostinato create an atmosphere of Oriental contemplation.

The lower part now moves from the alternating tones to a second ostinato containing leaps, and the upper part becomes more spasmodic. There follows an increase in density, intensity, and the rapidity of figuration. The last twenty measures of the movement are based chiefly on the material shown in Example 10–13 (from the first movement). The effect of this closing passage is a non-adventurous, non-developing mood of contemplation and reflection, far removed from the surge of the every day world. These measures remind us of Cage's deep interest in the philosophy of the East.*

It was Cage's attitude and vision, perhaps far more than his results, that were to have a strong and lasting effect on many composers working in new directions in mid-century and thereafter. As early as 1937, Cage was saying that "the use of noise to make music will continue and increase until we reach a music produced through the aid of electrical instruments which will make available for musical purposes any and all sounds that can be heard. . . ."

Chance music

The element of chance has always affected the inspiration of the composer in one way or another. For example, consider the Bach family gatherings at which they

---

* Examples 10–12 to 10–16 are from John Cage, *Amores* (Peters no. 6264). Copyright © 1943 by John Cage. Copyright © assigned in 1960 to Henmar Press Inc. Reprint permission granted by the publisher.

Figure 47. John Cage. (Courtesy, Artservices, Inc.)

improvised *quodlibets* out of whatever melodic materials came to mind. Or a Russian folk song capturing the attention of Balakirev in his travels in the Baku, later sparking a symphonic work. A recent example occurred when the Duke Ellington Orchestra was touring India. As Billy Strayhorn, Ellington's co-composer, sat in his room, the song of a myna bird filtered in through the open window, and this song became the motive for *Bluebird of Delhi*.

But it has been left to the "serious" composer of the twentieth century to systematize chance as a basic element in the compositional process. Chance first appeared intentionally in *musique concrète*. After that it suffused the work of many younger composers, both in Europe and the United States.

Experiments in random composition have included what may be termed a "musical mobile." The mobile effect is achieved through assigning to each performer a certain number of "examples." Each example will contain a certain amount of notated music, from one note to perhaps several measures. Each performer chooses the order in which he will play these examples. In the next performance, either immediately thereafter or at some later time, the order is again chosen by the performer. In other words, the particular "viewing" depends upon the way "the wind blows," as with a mobile.

Random composition bears a resemblance to improvisation, and while this had once been a vital force in music, especially in the Baroque, and also during the classical period, it waned during the nineteenth century. The spirit of improvisation has never died out in folk expression, nor in the great tradition of organ extemporization. Until the advent of jazz, however, it did not contribute again to any growing cultural body of music.

Improvisation, dead in the concert-hall, was brought to life again by jazz in the early twentieth century. Through the entire history of jazz, improvisation has been its life-blood, constantly nurturing it and revitalizing it. Improvisation has always been understood by the jazz musician. It is seriously open to question whether the modern non-jazz oriented composer has known how to handle it.

Aleatoric, or chance, music may include improvisation, but as this includes the possibilities of selection by the performer, there are many experiments that emphasize the aleatoric aspect—that of "gambling" with the results—even more. Such experiments include the throwing of dice to decide the order of tones or sections of music. There are those who have severe reservations about current aleatoric composition. The critic Roy McMullen puts it this way: "The procedure yields nothing more philosophical than the effect of a solemn jam session by a very cool jazz outfit, with perhaps an ultrasophisticated rhythm section. The random elements float, as it were, inside serial or post-serial forms."* Whether or not there is philosophical yield is not so important as whether viable communication is at all possible. Within this new reality is it possible for the performer to be enough aware of compositional procedures to realize the composer's intention? Are the composer's "notational guidelines" enough?

The issue here is not that of the validity of chance elements in music. Music as a time-art has always included the unforeseen as an element of its performance. No two performances of a single work have ever been the same. In the past composers have always known this; often they have deliberately planned for spontaneity. Time left by composers for improvised cadenzas in early concertos illustrates this. And the baroque composer neither expected nor desired that every one of his notes would be performed exactly as penned. Within figured bass parts a wide latitude of options was left to the performer/improviser. But implicit in the baroque master's use of "aleatoric" elements was a trust in the taste and competence of the interpreter. Besides, his musical materials were common enough to all—composer, performer, listener—so that communication of some sort was assured.

---

* Roy McMullen, *The Great Ideas Today*, "Music, Painting, and Sculpture" (Britannica Great Books, 1967), p. 106.

In our day, musical language is extraordinarily complex and heterogeneous. And it changes in style and direction by the decade rather than by the century. Since Webern, its basic thrust has been along mathematical, ultra-technological lines. What is required then is an entirely new breed of performer: one who is utterly dedicated, superbly trained technically, highly aware and conversant with the latest compositional materials, and willing to work out a symbiotic relationship with the composer.

John Cage has been a continuing and ever-more influential force in his exploration of aleatoric music. His book, *Silence,* taken from his lectures and articles from 1939 to 1961, indicates his constant concern with new directions. His well-known attempt to negate the very foundations of composition and performance is embodied in a piece called *4' 33".* During this period of time, precisely clocked with a stopwatch, a person sits at the piano but does not play. Instead he or she opens and shuts the keyboard cover at specified times, dividing the work into three movements. The content of the work is created—by chance—from noises provided by the audience, external street sounds, passing air planes, flies buzzing, and what have you.

Music has come out of "song and dance"—as all music must—to become an exploration in "sound and time." This is the essence of music. When the exploration leaves sound and time—i.e., when it is no longer discernible by even the most astute listener over a reasonable length of time—then it may be a new experience, a new art form, but it is not music. It should then be called something else. Just as the table or the chair is no longer a table or chair when it is chopped up—it is then just wood—so then is music no longer music when it is chopped up beyond recognition. It is then something else; name it what you will. It is debatable whether *4' 33"*—and other works of like ilk—should be regarded as music.

One of the most important figures affected by the new wind blowing across the contemporary scene is Karlheinz Stockhausen (1928–   ). He has aligned himself with all contemporary developments including chance music, the new serialism, and electronic music. He is at the very cutting edge of further new developments. Having begun with works for conventional instruments, his first influence was Webern. Of his works for piano, *Piano Piece XI* (1956) is an interesting experiment in chance. It consists of nineteen fragments that may be played in any order at the whim of the pianist. The pianist also has the choice of any of six different tempos, dynamics, and articulations. Stockhausen specifies that when one fragment is played three times the piece must end. His *Gruppen* (1955) for three orchestras investigates spatial dimensions in the fashion of the antiphonal choirs in Venice in the early Baroque. The three orchestras synthesize their separate strands of orchestral, chamber, and soloistic music. A work similar to *Gruppen* in attempting to capture the spatial relations of sound is *Gesang der Jünglinge* (1956). It is composed for five loudspeaker groups and includes both ordinary vocal and electronically produced sounds. The text, biblical in origin, is partially incomprehensible, for to Stockhausen the sound of the words is more important than their meanings. We are reminded of Stravinsky's use of words for their sound qualities rather than their conceptual meanings.

THE NEW SERIALISM / ELECTRONIC MUSIC

The influence of Webern on various major figures has resulted in an ever more inclusive serial application. We will now discuss composers who have been strongly identified with serial technique of various sorts. The original impetus and influence of the Schoenberg "idea" has been superseded by the differing and unique approaches of his students, Berg and Webern. There are those within the new serialists who retain the lyricism that Berg did not deny himself. Other more radical members of the avant garde take the ascetic purity of Webern's strict serial technique as their ideal. Among those who temper the strictures of serialism by combining it with other approaches are Ernst Krenek (1900–   ), Luigi Dallapiccola (1904–1975), Rolf Liebermann (1910–   ), Mel Powell (1923–   ), and Hans Werner Henze (1926–   ).

Krenek was born in Vienna, and at one time was married to a daughter of Gustav Mahler. It is interesting to note that almost all writings that discuss Krenek speak foremost of his jazz-influenced opera *Jonny spielt auf! (Johnny Plays Out!)* (1927). There is no doubt that this has been his most popular work. It has been translated into eighteen languages and performed in more than 100 opera houses, giving him an international reputation. He emigrated to America in 1937, by which time he had adopted the twelve-tone system. His scores have often included admirably clear explanatory notes.

Dallapiccola, first as a student and then as a teacher at the Conservatory in Florence, combined the Italian love of lyricism with the exactitudes of the procedure of twelve-tone writing without losing the innate Italian flavor. In his work at Tanglewood as teacher at the Berkshire Music Center and as professor at Queens College of the City of New York, his influence was greatly felt by young American composers. Two of his better-known works are: *Il Prigioniero (The Prisoner)*, an opera of 1944–1948; and *Variations for Orchestra*, 1954, commissioned by the Louisville Orchestra.

Liebermann, born in Zurich, at one time was on the musical staff of Radio-Zurich, and in more recent times he has held the post of music director at the Hamburg State Opera. His style is eclectic, embracing twelve-tone techniques that do not deny the use of sonorities more common to earlier styles. His *Concerto for Jazz Band and Symphony Orchestra* of 1954, originally performed in Germany, was recorded in this country by the Chicago Symphony with the Sauter-Finegan Orchestra.

Powell was one of the very few jazz musicians (he was pianist for Benny Goodman) to take the step into serious art music. It is likely true that it is easier for a jazz man to enter the ranks of art music than vice versa, but it has been rare for the jazz composer/arranger to enter the "hallowed halls." Powell is an exception. Formerly professor of music at Yale, Powell's best-known work is *Filigree Setting for String Quartet*. Here he seeks to combine the improvisation of jazz with aspects of the twelve-tone method.

Henze is now coming into prominence on the world stage, not only as one of the few contemporary composers who are writing in the large symphonic style, but as a conductor with broad talents. With five symphonies to his credit, all recorded and conducted by him, he has also been responsible for a revived interest in ballet in Germany with his *Ballet Variations* (1949) and *Ballet Scenes for Orchestra* (1950). Henze had also contributed to the repertoire of opera with works for the opera stage and for radio. Also he has incorporated certain jazz elements into his work, such as his ballet, *Jack Pudding. Undine*, in 1959, received great acclaim from the public and brought knowledge of his work outside of Germany to England and the United States. Henze is able to imbue his work with a lyricism that is not anathematic to his controlled use of the serial idiom.

Liebermann and Powell have each participated in the coming together of avant-gardists in both the jazz and art music fields. Indeed, Liebermann's *Concerto for Jazz Band and Symphony Orchestra* was a forerunner of the concept of Third Stream, and this particular work points up the continuing interest among serious composers in the ever-flowing fresh stream of jazz. Stravinsky showed a renewed interest in 1946, not in the style of jazz per se, but in the use of the jazz instruments in his *Ebony Concerto* (not of serial origin), written for the Woody Herman Orchestra. And later, in 1957, we find another attempt at "fusion" at a Brandeis University concert where the program was divided equally between compositions by jazz-oriented and non-jazz-oriented composers. Among the works represented were Milton Babbitt's *All Set* and George Russell's *All About Rosie*.

One of the more recent attempts at fusion is by Gunther Schuller. His opera, *The Visitation*, dealing with the race problem in America, continues in this trend. There is a jazz band in the pit along with the traditional opera orchestra.

There are four important names that are clearly associated with the severe serialist approach. They are: Bruno Maderna (1920–1973), Iannis Xenakis (1922–   ), Luigi Nono (1924–   ), and Luciano Berio (1925–   ).

In Italy, ironically enough the home of *bel canto*, there now exists a center for electronic music. Maderna was one of the founders of the Studio di Fonologia Musicale at the Milan Radio. In his writings for conventional instruments he already showed the influence of Webern through a preference for restricted combinations of instruments. He was gifted with an Italian lyricism, but in spite of

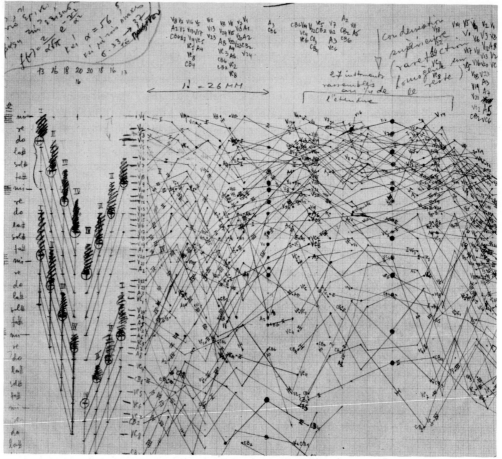

Figure 48.   Xenakis composition. (M. Desjardins, TOP)

this he moved toward a constructivism that included complex serial calculations. Predetermination was primary. One of his earlier works, *Studies for Kafka's "Trial"* (1950), showed an expressionist atmosphere. But more in keeping with his interest in total serialism was the *Serenata No. 2 for 11 instruments* (1955).

Xenakis, born in Roumania, has carried mathematical manipulation to the ultimate degree. He is not only a musician—his teachers included Honegger, Milhaud, and Messiaen—but also an architect, having studied with Le Corbusier. (He participated in the design of the French Pavilion at the Montreal Expo '67.) Messiaen has called Xenakis "an architect, mathematician, logician, poet, and, above all else, a musician." If Messiaen is correct, then Xenakis represents in this day and age the embodiment of the Pythagorean ideal of the oneness of music and mathematics. *Musique stochastique* may or may not become the new term to describe current and future manners in music. This is Xenakis' term used to describe his statistical grouping of masses. His *Atrées* (Hommage à Pascal), performed in Paris in 1962, utilizes a stochastic program.

Nono, a student of Maderna, espoused the twelve-tone system from the beginning. His early pieces were sparse in sound and texture, but he gradually moved to a more Italianate lyricism. At the same time he also moved towards total serialization. The dramatic lyricism found in the *Epitaph for Federico Garcia Lorca* (1952–1954) found its ultimate realization in the opera *Intolleranza*, a work controversial because of its leftist political implications.

Berio was associated with Maderna in the establishment of electronic music in Milan. He also came under the influence of Dallapiccola at the Berkshire Music Center. As with Dallapiccola, there is a certain lyricism in his work. He has a strong feeling for instrumental color, and his interest leans toward strong predetermination affecting not only the selection of sounds but their duration, intensity, and timbre. *Nones* (1954) is a rigidly structured twelve-tone work. In its rigid, mathematical approach it is reminiscent of those academic contrapuntists of the Renaissance who tried to seek perfection within the domain of mathematics.

The dividing line that once existed between composers of twelve-tone persuasion and tonal composers is vanishing, as is the dividing line between adherents of the new serialism and those of electronic music. In fact no longer is it easy to put a contemporary composer under a single classification. Otto Luening (1900–   ), Vladimir Ussachevsky (1911–   ), and Milton Babbitt (1916–   ) are representative figures of the composers whose interest in serialism has carried them well into the mathematical field of electronic music. To these men pure electronic composition has the neat feature of requiring no performing musicians who may get in the way of the production of pure sound. Luening and the engineer/composer Ussachevsky have contributed important works in electronic media. Works jointly composed by Luening and Ussachevsky that have been recorded are *Rhapsodic Variations for Tape Recorder and Orchestra* and *A Poem in Cycles and Bells*.

Babbitt was the first exponent of the new serialism in America. His studies with Roger Sessions were the background for his earlier efforts in conventional pitch composition. But he has moved steadily through exploration of total serialization into electronic works. Now on the faculty at Princeton University, he is one of the Directors of the Electronic Music Center operated jointly by Columbia and Princeton universities. Here resides the RCA Synthesizer that makes it possible for Babbitt to carry out his experiments. Among his more conventional works are *Three Compositions for Piano* (1947) and the song-cycle *Du* (1951).

Babbitt has aroused considerable interest with two works that combine live solo singing with electronic tape accompaniment: *Vision and Prayer* (1961) and *Philomel* (1963–1964). The latter work combines the recorded sound of a soprano voice with the electronically produced sounds in the tape accompaniment. The noted soprano, Bethany Beardslee, premiered both works, and it is her voice that is heard on the original tape of *Philomel* prepared by the composer.

EPILOGUE

In reviewing the material that has been presented in this chapter one is well aware that there has been much discussion of systems (and non-systems) of composition. Important as it is to know something of the methods of a composer in trying to understand what a composer is about—all information about a work helps one to become aware—nevertheless, in the last analysis a composer's methods are important to him only. His achievement must be judged for what it is.

We may find fascinating, in a discussion of American Colonial furniture making, the fact that wooden pegs or dowels were used instead of nails. It is also fascinating to realize that at the heart of a composition lies a mathematical equation that gives it order. Nonetheless we do not need to know the composer's system of order. The order in one way or another, without our knowing it at all, will invade the finished product and will be perhaps a part of its perfection. But the "system of order" will not guarantee the worth of the work anymore than a system of rhymes, rhythms, or meter will guarantee the worth of a poem. This must come from the inspiration of the creator which includes, pervades, and, most of all, goes beyond his system.

It has yet to be established whether Third Stream, chance music, predeterminism, electronic calculations, random treatments of material in either jazz or art music can be meaningful experiences as art. The artist in each of the arts will—and must—constantly search for new means of expression. It is not within the province of this book to discuss a matter that properly belongs to aesthetics. The aesthetics of music has been a vexing philosophical problem in recent times, and we can do no more here than make a few comments. This book has been about the appreciation of music, and about the understanding of music. You may already have found that more understanding can sometimes result in *less* appreciation. Certain works that were once favorites have lost their luster. Like a first love, they are remembered with some nostalgia, but, as understanding develops, tastes broaden. You should not only go back further in time, and dig deeper into certain areas, but keep your eyes—and especially your ears—directed toward the future.

Whether a new work becomes a part of the established literature of the twentieth century only the future can tell. Rebellion is not enough; the rebellion must be successful. Its success depends not only upon the overthrow of the old regime, which is certainly the first step, but most especially in putting in the place of the old authority a new authority. The standards of judging the worth of a work of art in any field have never been set to the satisfaction of the majority. These words of Aldous Huxley are to the point.

The traditional distinction between the crafts and the fine arts is based, among other things, on degrees of complexity. A good picture is a greater work of art than a good bowl or a good vase. Why? Because it unifies in one harmonious whole more, and more diverse, elements of human experience than are or can be unified and harmonized in the pot. Some of the non-representational pictures painted in the course of the last fifty years are very beautiful; but even the best of them are minor works, inasmuch as the number of elements of human experience which they combine and harmonize is pitifully small. In them we look in vain for that ordered profusion, that lavish and yet perfectly controlled display of intellectual wealth, which we discover in the best works of the "literary" painters of the past.*

Whether Huxley's view is valid is something that must be considered seriously. Whether you ultimately accept or reject his premise is your decision. But let us make a final statement to the listener.

With regard to contemporary music, as with all contemporary art, you should have an absolutely open mind; at the same time you must try not to allow yourself to be "taken in." Do not judge new music by the values you have derived from older music; but also do not conclude, as some extremists do, that whatever is new and daring must be good. One of the tests of a work of music is whether you can go back to it again and again. You do not have to be a musician or a critic or a philosopher to make this test. *All you need do is listen.*

---

* Aldous Huxley, *On Art and Artists* (New York: Harper & Row, Publishers, 1960), pp. 301–302.

Figure 49.   Musical knife. (Cliché des Musées Nationaux, Paris)

CHRONOLOGICAL
BIOGRAPHIES OF COMPOSERS

Alphabetical Index of Composers*

*The number following each composer's name indicates that composer's chronological position according to year of birth.

1150   Léonin   1

born circa 1150, birthplace unknown
died late twelfth century, Paris, France

Chapel master (organist and choirmaster) at the cathedral of Beatae Mariae Virginis in Paris, later rebuilt as Notre Dame Cathedral. Léonin was the first great master of the Notre Dame school; he created the *Magnus Liber Organi*, a cycle of two-part organa for the entire ecclesiastical year. These two-part organa (based on Gregorian chant) represent the first development of contrapuntal polyphony.

1190   Pérotin   2

born circa 1190, birthplace unknown
died early thirteenth century, Paris, France

Successor to Léonin as chapel master at Notre Dame in Paris. Active around the turn of, and in the first decades of, the thirteenth century. Pérotin undertook a revision of the work of Léonin, going beyond the two-part organum to add a third, and sometimes a fourth, part to his compositions. This period also saw the rise of more planned rhythmic organization in polyphonic music.

1240   Adam de la Halle   3

born circa 1240, Arras, France
died 1287, Naples, Italy

French comic playwright and trouvère. Living in Arras, a thirteenth-century center of literature and drama, he turned to music and the theater, composing the first-known liturgical drama, *Le Jeu de la feuillée* (*Play of the Leaves*) around 1276. This work, written to honor the coming of spring, includes Celtic myths, political and anticlerical humor, and burlesque. Later he followed Prince Charles d'Anjou to Naples and composed *Le Jeu de Robin et Marion* (*The Game of Robin and Marion*), around 1285, for the French-speaking court established there.

1300   Guillaume de Machaut   4

born circa 1300, Champagne, France
died 1377, Rheims, France

French priest, poet, and musician who is one of the best-known composers of the early fourteenth century. The majority of the musical manuscripts surviving from that century were composed by this one man, who served the kings of Bohemia, Navarre, and France, and who was later a canon at Rheims Cathedral. Most familiar of Machaut's works is the *Messe de Notre Dame* (*Notre Dame Mass*), an outstanding example of Ars Nova composition utilizing the devices of isorhythm and hocket. These same techniques appear in his secular vocal works.

1370   John Dunstable   5

born circa 1370, birthplace unknown
died 24 December 1453, London, England

English composer who carried the English harmonic style to Europe (especially to Burgundy), causing the Franco-Flemish composers to become more aware of harmony as an expressive element.

1400   Guillaume Dufay   6

born circa 1400, probably in Hainaut, Belgium
died 27 November 1474, Cambrai, France

Burgundian composer. Dufay was the most important composer of his time and the leading master of the Burgundian school. Equally at home in church music and secular song, he (along with his contemporary, Binchois) developed a musical language that served as a transition from the music of the Ars Nova to that of Josquin. Dufay was thus the bridge from the music of the Middle Ages to that of the Renaissance.

Many of the compositions of the Burgundian school had elements that were to lead to later developments in harmony: the use of *faux bourdon* (sixth chords, such as triads in first inversion) and melodic and harmonic tendencies pointing the way towards major-minor tonality.

Dufay was trained as a choirboy at Cambrai and later spent some time in Rome at the papal choir, which attracted many musicians from the Netherlands during this period. From about 1440 Dufay lived at Cambrai.

His work includes many masses and motets, as well as French and Italian chansons. Two representative sacred works are Missa *"L'Homme armé"* and Missa *"Se la face ay pale."*

1420   Jan Ockeghem   7

born 1420, Hainaut, Belgium
died 1495, Tours, France

Serving three kings of France as court composer, Ockeghem wrote masses based on secular songs. Unlike Dufay, Ockeghem gave more equal emphasis to all four voices and eventually abandoned cantus firmus style in favor of his own style of imitative counterpoint.

1450   Jacob Obrecht   8

born 1450, Bergen-op-Zoom, Netherlands
died 1505, Ferrara, Italy

Composer of music with new harmonic and rhythmic energy, he enjoyed presenting themes upside-down or backwards; he also explored numerological relations between the intervals of a theme.

1450   Josquin des Prez   9

born circa 1450, Hainaut, Belgium
died 27 August 1521, Conde, France

Generally considered the master of late fourteenth-century style, Josquin des Prez was an exact contemporary of Leonardo da Vinci and worked for a time in the ducal court at the Sistine Chapel. One of the first composers to benefit from movable type and the printing press, Josquin saw many of his works published in his lifetime, including a collection of seventeen of his nineteen masses and several chansons in the volume *Odhecaton A* (1501).

Josquin's motets are written primarily in a melodic style that influenced the development of the Italian madrigal. Josquin also composed in Spanish and French song forms, including a chanson *Adieu mes amours* (*Goodbye My Loves*), which is believed to have been his reminder to his employer, Louis XII of France, that his salary was overdue. Josquin also worked in Milan, Ferrara, and Rome.

1500   Cristobal de Morales   10

born circa 1500, Seville, Spain
died 1553, Málaga, Spain

Morales is considered one of the most important Spanish composers of the sixteenth century. His music embodies the passionate religious emotion characteristic of the people of Spain. As a singer in the papal choir (1535–1545) he traveled extensively, and his music became known through the choir performances throughout Europe. His fame rests primarily on his lovely motets, canons, and masses.

1520   Andrea Gabrieli   11

born circa 1520, Venice, Italy
died 1586, Venice, Italy

Composer of antiphonal music for as many as eight voices or instruments, he also wrote secular and religious vocal works. His ricercari and canzoni for keyboard are among the finest examples of sixteenth-century keyboard style.

1525   Giovanni Pierluigi de Palestrina   12

born 1525, Palestrina, Italy
died 1594, Rome, Italy

Italian composer whose works have been said to represent the purest expression of church style. In 1544 Palestrina accepted the post of organist at the cathedral of Palestrina, where he played the organ and taught music to the choir boys. In 1555 he succeeded Lassus as music director of the Cathedral of St. John Lateran in Rome, where he composed his famous *Lamentations on the Prophet Jeremiah*.

Dissatisfied with conditions at St. John's, he resigned and in 1561 accepted a post at Santa Maria Maggiore, also in Rome. Here Palestrina had more freedom to organize the musical part of the church services, and he kept the post for seven years. After losing his wife and two of his sons in an epidemic, Palestrina petitioned in 1580 to the Pope to become a priest; however, he subsequently changed his mind and, in 1581, married the widow of a wealthy furrier. With a partner, he carried on the business. It was at this time that he was composing some of his finest music. His fame spread beyond Italy to Germany and England. Palestrina wrote almost one hundred masses, hundreds of motets, and many madrigals.

1532   Orlandus Lassus   13

born 1532, Mons, Belgium
died 1594, Munich, Germany

Flemish composer, one of the great masters in music. Lassus stands with his contemporary, Palestrina, as representing the peak of what had been begun a century earlier by Josquin—a polyphonic style that went beyond its contrapuntal origins to express a wide gamut of emotion in a great diversity of subject matter.

He was a choir boy at the church of St. Nicholas in Mons. He had an exceptional voice and his first journeys took him to Milan, Naples, and then to Rome where he became choirmaster. In 1555 he settled in Antwerp, Belgium. That year saw the publication in Venice of his first works—a set of madrigals to poems in Italian by Petrarch and in the same year the publication in Antwerp of a collection including madrigals and motets to Italian, French, and Latin words. The following year he was offered a post at the Bavarian court and settled in Munich. He married and Munich remained his home base for thirty-eight years, until his death. During his life he received international acclaim.

With over 2,000 works to his credit, Lassus was one of the most prolific composers of the Renaissance. He wrote extensively in both secular and sacred genres in all the chief forms of his day. In addition to chansons, he wrote motets, madrigals, and masses. His most important contribution was in the motet, his favorite form. The *Seven Penitential Psalms*, a compositional project covering seven years, are among the best known of the motets for their profound and deeply moving expression. A shorter work that illustrates the way in which Lassus weds the music to the words is the motet, *Tristus est anima mea* (*Sorrowful Is My Soul*). (This is available for study in *Masterpieces of Music Before 1750*, published by W. W. Norton & Company.)

Lassus—like Mozart later—enjoyed the felicities of language. Combining this with a broad sense of humor, he wrote in some of his more intimate letters various humorous mixtures of French, Italian, "bad" Latin, and German.

1543   William Byrd   14

born 1543, Lincolnshire, England
died 1623, Stondon Massey, Essex, England

Appointed organist of Lincoln Cathedral in 1563, Byrd retained this provincial post until 1572, at which time he was appointed to serve with Thomas Tallis as organist at the Chapel Royal. Three years later, Queen Elizabeth granted to Byrd and Tallis the monopoly rights for publishing copper engraved musical manuscripts; Byrd retained this royal patent after Tallis' death in 1585. In 1575 they jointly published *Cantiones Sacrae* (*Sacred Songs*), the first volume of motets ever printed in England.

As a keyboard composer, Byrd was responsible for bringing English music for virginals to the highest level of sophistication yet achieved. He contributed to the *Parthenia* collection several fine sets of variations, including "The Carman's Whistle," and numerous pavanes and galliards—dance forms that he brought to a new level of expressiveness and craftsmanship.

Although a Roman Catholic living in strongly Anglican surroundings, Byrd managed to compose successfully and to publish music for both churches, including masses and motets for three, four, and five voices. In addition, Byrd wrote madrigals, as well as chamber music for consorts of viols.

1549   Thomás Luis de Victoria   15

born circa 1549, Avila, Spain
died 27 August 1611, Madrid, Spain

Spanish composer who wrote only religious music, filled with intensity and passion. He is considered to be an equal of Palestrina as a composer of polyphonic music. One of his most famous compositions is the *Requiem Mass*, written in memory of the Empress Maria and dedicated to her daughter, Princess Margaret.

1551   Giovanni Gabrieli   16

born 1551, Venice, Italy
died 12 August 1612, Venice, Italy

Appointed second organist at St. Mark's in Venice in 1585, Gabrieli perfected the techniques in antiphonal music already developed by his uncle, Andrea Gabrieli. He contributed to the development of the *trio sonata* and also the *concertate* vocal style, in which instruments play a part entirely independent of the vocal soloist's line. His major works include two volumes called *Sacrae Symphoniae* (*Sacred Symphonies*, 1597) and *Canzoni e Sonate* (*Canzonas and Sonatas*, 1615).

1557   Thomas Morley   17

born circa 1557, London, England
died 1603, London, England

Considered by many the father of the English madrigal, Morley wrote *A Plain and Easy Introduction to Practical Music* (1597), and with his pieces for lute, virginal, and consort he did much to cultivate secular music in England.

1560   Carlo Gesualdo   18

born circa 1560, Naples, Italy
died 8 September 1613, Naples, Italy

Gesualdo was a nobleman who bore the title "Prince of Venosa." He is important for his six books of five-part madrigals. The last two volumes are particularly special for their chromatic, highly expressive harmonies and unusual phrasings.

1562   John Dowland   19

born 1562, London, England
died 1626, London, England

One of Europe's great lutanists, Dowland was the first great and prolific composer of madrigals for solo voice with lute accompaniment. In this music, the lute replaced other vocal parts as accompaniment for the soloist.

1567   Claudio Monteverdi   20

born May, 1567, Cremona, Italy
died 29 November 1643, Venice, Italy

Monteverdi demonstrated his talents at an early age, publishing his first work, a collection of motets, in 1582 while he was studying music at Cremona Cathedral. Around 1590 he assumed his first post as a musician in Mantua. Here Monteverdi witnessed the preparation for an opera by the noted vocal composer, Giaches de Wert; the work, *Il Pastor Fido* (*The Faithful Shepherd*), was never performed, however. Having witnessed the backstage operations for the preparation of this opera, Monteverdi went about composing his own opera, *La Favola d'Orfeo* (*The Tale of Orpheus*). This work was produced in 1607 and became an immediate success.

In the meantime, in 1602, Monteverdi had assumed the duties of *maestro di musica* at the Mantuan court. He had already issued five successful volumes of madrigals, including the landmark fifth volume containing intimations of the new *basso continuo*. The additional success in 1607 of *Orfeo* established Monteverdi's pre-eminence among Italian composers. In his operas Monteverdi discovered the dramatic possibilities of *recitativo* style—solo singing with simple chordal accompaniment—and combined it with popular dance and madrigal forms. Inspired by his success with *Orfeo*, Monteverdi went on composing operas, including his last and best work, *L'Incoronazione di Poppea* (*The Coronation of Poppea*), finished in 1642.

In 1613, Monteverdi was appointed *maestro di cappella* at St. Mark's in Venice, a position he held until his death. By then he had published a total of nine volumes of madrigals, three masses, vespers, and motets. Generally credited with the abandonment of Renaissance polyphony, Monteverdi stressed clear understanding of the words and their emotional impact.

1583   Girolamo Frescobaldi   21

born September 1583, Ferrara, Italy
died 1 March 1643, Rome, Italy

Organist in S. Peter's in Rome from 1608 until his death, Frescobaldi composed madrigals, motets, and hymns for the church. His major contribution was in the realm of keyboard music, both for organ and harpsichord. Through his student, Froberger, Frescobaldi exerted a great deal of influence upon the development of German baroque keyboard style.

1585   Heinrich Schütz   22

born 8 October 1585, Köstritz, Germany
died 6 November 1672, Dresden, Germany

Although trained as a choir boy, Schütz studied law at Marburg University until 1609, at which time he went to Venice to study music under Giovanni Gabrieli. He published a book of madrigals in 1611. Gaining an appointment in 1617 as music director of the chapel of the elector of Saxony in Dresden, Schütz remained in that city for the rest of his life, excepting travels to Italy (1628) and Copenhagen (1633).

The music of Schütz consists largely of church music, including the *Musikalische Exequien* (1636), the first German language setting of the requiem mass. His music ties together the Venetian antiphonal style with the German baroque polyphonic style in *Symphoniae Sacrae* (*Sacred Symphonies*, 1664) and other masterpieces of baroque church music.

1632   Jean-Baptiste Lully   23

born 28 November 1632, Florence, Italy
died 22 March 1687, Paris, France

Although born in Florence, Lully was brought to Paris in 1646 to serve Mlle. d'Orleans, cousin of Louis XIV. By 1652 he was a member of the King's orchestra and became its conductor shortly thereafter. Appointed court composer and royal music director in 1662, Lully encountered Molière, the great dramatist, and composed music for several of his plays between 1663 and 1671. Perhaps the best known of these plays is *Le Bourgeois Gentilhomme* (*The Bourgeois Gentleman*).

In 1672, Lully became director of the Paris Opera and discovered his natural idiom; he founded a new style of French opera, differing from the Italian style in that it emphasized drama rather than pure musical effects. For his operatic works, Lully developed the French overture. He also wrote over thirty ballets and included ballets in his operas. He retained his post as director of opera until 1687, having composed works including *Alceste* (1677) and *Armide* (1686) during his tenure there.

1653   Arcangelo Corelli   24

born 17 February 1653, Fusignano, Italy
died 9 January 1713, Rome, Italy

Little is known about Corelli's early life except that he studied counterpoint under Matteo Simonelli and violin with Giovanni Battista Bassani. He traveled in Germany and probably in France as well, finally settling in Rome in 1685. There he was employed by Cardinal Pietro Ottoboni, for whom he composed the concerti grossi and violin works for which he is remembered. His concerti grossi became models for Vivaldi and Bach. These works featured a variety of melodic and rhythmic inspiration. Corelli also contributed to the flowering violin technique that the baroque composer increasingly demanded from the performer.

1659   Henry Purcell   25

born circa 1659, probably London, England
died 21 November 1695, London, England

Purcell was a choir boy in the Chapel Royal until his voice changed. He later became keeper of the instruments. In 1677 he was appointed as composer for the King's violins, and he succeeded his teacher, John Blow, in the position of organist at Westminster Abbey two years later. By 1683 he had been appointed organ-maker and keeper of the King's wind instruments.

From 1680 he began composing music for the theater, including pieces for Dryden's *King Arthur* (1691), Shakespeare's *The Fairy Queen* (based on *A Midsummer Night's Dream*, 1692), and Dryden's *The Indian Queen* (1695). He wrote an outstanding opera, *Dido and Aeneas* (1689)—still frequently performed today—and a great deal of practical music for royal use, including marches and anthems. In 1683 he published a volume of twelve sonatas. He also composed church music, including the *Ode for St. Cecilia's Day* (1694).

1660   Alessandro Scarlatti   26

born 2 May 1660, Palermo, Italy
died 24 October 1725, Naples, Italy

Scarlatti worked as *maestro di cappella* to the viceroy of Naples. He composed more than one hundred operas in the Neapolitan style, including *La Principessa fedele* (*The Faithful Princess*, 1710), and *Tigrane* (1715). He also composed chamber music, solo vocal pieces, and keyboard works.

1668   François Couperin   27

born 10 November 1668, Paris, France
died 12 September 1733, Paris, France

Composer and keyboard player, Couperin was a member of a musical family of long standing. He studied under his father, Charles, and with Jacques Thomelin. In 1685 he succeeded his father as organist at St. Gervais; and in 1693 he followed Thomelin as organist of the royal chapel.

Gaining the favor of Louis XIV through his brilliance at the keyboard, Couperin was appointed court clavecinist and organist to the King in 1701. In this post he composed music for the enjoyment of the King, including the *Concerts royaux* (*Royal Concerts*, 1715); he also gave music lessons to members of the court. Outstanding among his works are the *Pièces de clavecin* (*Harpsichord Pieces*, 1713–1730), a collection in four volumes of dance suites of a programmatic nature.

Couperin also composed chamber music, including the *Apothéose de Lully* (*Apotheosis of Lully*), a tribute to his predecessor, combining the Italian trio sonata style with the French style. Nearly all his music is filled with wit and deep insight into the expressive capabilities of the harpsichord.

1678   Antonio Vivaldi   28

born 1678, Venice, Italy
died July 1741, Vienna, Austria

Italian violinist, who was ordained as a priest in 1703. He taught violin intermittently between 1704 and 1740 at the conservatory in Venice. This position required him to turn out two concerti grossi per month. Thus, his output is very large! Most notable are the *Concerti Grossi*, Op. 3, subtitled "L'Estro harmonico" ("The Inspiration of Harmony"). Vivaldi's concerti were modelled after Corelli's but represent a more bravura style. Another famous set of concerti grossi is subtitled "The Four Seasons." Vivaldi also composed vocal music, including a "Gloria" and thirty-nine operas. His lyrical and energetic style exerted great influence on J. S. Bach, who transcribed several of Vivaldi's concerti for different instruments.

1681   Georg Philipp Telemann   29

born 14 March 1681, Magdeburg, Germany
died 25 June 1767, Hamburg, Germany

Extremely prolific composer of chamber music, operas, church music, passions, French overtures, oratorios, and cantatas. Telemann worked both in churches and for noble patrons. Founder of the Leipzig Collegium Musicum, he also served as *Kapellmeister* at Eisenach, where he knew J. S. Bach.

1683   Jean Philippe Rameau   30

born 25 September 1683, Dijon, France
died 12 September 1764, Paris, France

Born the son of an organist, Rameau originally prepared to study law, but decided at the age of eighteen to follow his father's career. In 1701 he visited Italy. From 1705 to 1708 he worked in Paris, and he settled there permanently in 1722.

In that year he established his reputation as a theorist with the publication of *Traité de l'harmonie* (*Treatise on Harmony*), the first of seven treatises he wrote on harmonic theory and acoustics. These books are still read and debated today.

In 1733, Rameau acquired a wealthy patron and began to compose operas. Of his twenty-two operas, among the best known are *Hippolyte et Aricie* (1733) and *Castor et Pollux* (1737). Rameau also wrote chamber music and keyboard music. By 1745, Rameau had achieved national prominence through the lavish productions of his operas at Versailles. Toward the end of his life his reputation suffered as a result of the aesthetic dispute between Italian and French opera composers. Rousseau and the encyclopedists also attacked his music and harmonic theories.

1685   George Frederick Handel   31

born 23 February 1685, Halle, Germany
died 14 April 1759, London, England

The son of a barber-surgeon, Handel began organ lessons in 1693 and served as organist in Halle Cathedral from 1697 to 1703, while attending the university there.

1703–1706: Employed as musician at opera house in Hamburg; in 1705 his *St. John Passion* and his opera *Almira* were performed.

1706–1709: Visited Italy, composed vocal music. His reputation was carried back to Germany and led to his appointment as *Kapellmeister* to the elector of Hanover.

1710: Left Hanover for London, where his opera *Rinaldo* was performed the following year.

1712: Took up permanent residence in London, eventually being naturalized as an English citizen.

1719–1741: Chiefly engaged in producing operas and, later, oratorios. Major works include forty-six operas, among them *Julius Caesar* (1724) and *Xerxes* (1738); and thirty-two oratorios, including *Israel in Egypt* (1739), *Messiah* (1742), and *Judas Maccabeus* (1746). Also wrote two major sets of concerti grossi and eighteen organ concerti.

1751: While working on *Jeptha*, he was forced to stop because of failing vision, which eventually developed into incurable blindness.

1752–1759: Handel continued to perform public harpsichord recitals in spite of his blindness. He was tended to by a young musician, John Christopher Smith, who took dictation and conducted Handel's music. April 6, 1759, Handel fainted in the orchestra pit during the season's final performance of *Messiah*. He died eight days later.

1685   Johann Sebastian Bach   32

born 21 March 1685, Eisenach, Germany
died 28 July 1750, Leipzig, Germany

Early years:
Born into a family of professional musicians that had been outstanding for upwards of 200 years.

1695:   Orphaned, moved to Ohrdruf to live with his eldest brother, Johann Christoph.

1700–1702:   Attended St. Michael's Church School at Lüneburg. Greatly influenced by outstanding organist, Georg Böhm, at nearby Johannes-Kirche. Walked to Hamburg to hear organist Johann Reinken and to Celle to hear the court orchestra. In Celle heard music of Couperin, also chamber music that influenced his later compositions in Cöthen.

1703:   Became organist at St. Boniface Church, Arnstadt, and composed earliest familiar organ works, including *Prelude and Fugue in C Minor* and *Toccata and Fugue in C Major*.

1705:   Gained one month's leave, traveled to Lübeck to hear and study under Buxtehude, German master of organ music. Remained for five months before returning to Arnstadt. The visit fired his imagination and provided compositional models for study.

1706:   Reprimanded by his Arnstadt employers for his extended absence and for change in his organ style after his return. Is accused of confusing the congregation during the singing of the chorales with his spontaneous variations on the chorale melodies, and is ordered to return to simple accompaniments.

1707:   Married his cousin, Maria Barbara. Accepted position as organist at Mühlhausen.

The Weimar Period:

1708:   Became court organist and chamber musician to Duke Wilhelm Ernst and composed some of his greatest organ works: the *Orgelbüchlein* and the toccatas, preludes, and fugues.

1714:   Visited Cassel and astonished Frederick I of Sweden with his feet that worked the pedals "as if they had wings." Was appointed concertmaster of the Weimar orchestra and began composing a flood of cantatas, fulfilling the constant need for new music.

1716:   At the death of the *Kapellmeister*, Bach—not being offered the post—decided to go elsewhere.

The Cöthen Period:

1717:   On August 1 became *Kappelmeister* for Prince Leopold of Anhalt-Cöthen. During this period he wrote concerti, harpsichord suites, inventions, and the first book of *The Well-Tempered Clavier*.

1720:   Maria Barbara died, after having borne seven children. Bach considered leaving Cöthen to forget.

1721:   Remarried to Anna Magdalena Wilcken, daughter of a court musician. Composed six concerti grossi for various soloists and orchestra, and presented them to the Margrave of Brandenburg in an effort to secure a position. These works are now famous as the *Brandenburg Concerti*.

1722:   June 5, Johann Kuhnau, cantor at Leipzig's St. Thomasschule, died. Bach was chosen as replacement only as a last resort after Telemann and one Christoph Graupner both turned down the job.

The Leipzig Period:

1723:   May 3, signed the bond becoming director of music and cantor at St. Thomas Church. Also was music teacher of the boys in the church school who performed in the choir each Sunday.

1729:   Became *Kapellmeister* to Prince of Saxe-Weissenfels; composed one of the greatest religious masterpieces of all time, the *St. Matthew Passion;* and took over the Collegium Musicum, a group of amateur musicians from the university. Most of the keyboard concerti were composed for performance by this group.

1730–1738: Engaged in controversy with town council, arguing that influx of students not required to study music was damaging the choirs and orchestras used in the churches.

1738: Completed his monumental *Mass in B Minor,* one of his few works based on the Catholic liturgy—in Latin.

1740: Bach's son, Carl Philipp Emanuel, was appointed to court of Frederick the Great. Seven years later, while visiting his son at court, J. S. Bach was given a theme by Frederick and asked to improvise on it. The resulting work, completed after Bach returned home, was the *Musical Offering,* a collection of chamber works, including an intricate series of canons.

1742: Composed the *Goldberg Variations,* thirty variations on an aria, for use by his student, Goldberg, to help Count Hermann Keyserlingk, an insomniac, sleep at night.

1744: Completed the second book of *The Well-Tempered Clavier.*

1748–1750: Worked on his final composition, a thorough, but never completed, exploration of fugal techniques—*The Art of the Fugue.* Despite loss of his eyesight, Bach continued the work. Ten days before his death from a stroke, Bach's vision returned, giving him time to carry the last fugue—a giant work with four planned subjects—through the exposition of the theme that used the letters of his own name: B A C H. (The German letters sound B♭ A C B .)

1685   Domenico Scarlatti   33

born 26 October 1685, Naples, Italy
died 23 July 1757, Madrid, Spain

Scarlatti wrote over five hundred keyboard sonatas of surprising harmonic freedom and technical virtuosity. The son of Alessandro, Scarlatti also composed operas in the early part of his career when he served in Rome and the Vatican. His reputation is based mainly on his keyboard works, however; and these are a staple in every harpsichordist's repertoire.

1698   Giuseppe Sammartini   34

born circa 1698, Milan, Italy
died 15 January 1770, Milan, Italy

An Italian composer who moved to London, Sammartini became music director for the Prince of Wales as well as an esteemed oboist. In 1737 he published his *Dueti per Flauti* (*Duets for Flute*) and his *Sonate a tre* (*Trio Sonatas*), in which he partially abandoned use of the continuo. Sammartini was also among the first to detach the Italian sinfonia from its place at the opening of an opera and allow it to stand as a concert piece.

1710   Giovanni Battista Pergolesi   35

born 4 January 1710, Iesi, Italy
died 16 March 1736, Pozzuoli, Italy

Frail and tubercular, Pergolesi trained as a violinist and composed oratorios, sacred dramas, *opera serie*, and *opera buffe*. One of his most famous works is *La Serva Padrona* (*The Maid-Mistress*, 1733), an entr'acte that served as a model of that form for several decades. Stravinsky based his neoclassical ballet, *Pulcinella* (1920) on music of Pergolesi.

1714   Carl Philipp Emanuel Bach   36

born 8 March 1714, Weimar, Germany
died 15 December 1788, Hamburg, Germany

The second son of Johann Sebastian Bach, Emanuel studied at the St. Thomas School in Leipzig and at the University of Frankfurt. Appointed court keyboard musician for Frederick the Great in 1740, he continued in that position until 1767.

Having left Frederick's employ, Bach was appointed *Kapellmeister* to Princess Amalia's court at Hamburg. Here he gave concerts and directed music in the city's five principal churches until his death.

C. P. E. Bach stands as a transitional figure between the baroque and classical eras. Writing in the *Sturm und Drang* (Storm and Stress) style of the period, Bach was predominant in crystallizing sonata-form and the preclassical symphony. Haydn, Mozart, and Beethoven all spoke of their debt to him.

Among the finest keyboard players of his day, Bach is considered the father of modern keyboard playing. Besides his numerous fine compositions (about 210 of them) he also wrote the first standard work on keyboard technique: *Versuch über die wahre Art das Klavier zu spielen* (*Essay on the True Art of Playing the Keyboard*, 2 volumes, 1753 and 1762).

Being skilled in many forms, Bach wrote cantatas, keyboard pieces, symphonies, and chamber music. All his works continually develop the harmonic and formal structures that were to become standard in the classical era.

1714   Christoph Willibald Gluck   37

born 2 July 1714, Erasbach, Bavaria, Germany
died 15 November 1787, Vienna, Austria

Gluck received his early training in Prague, then became a member of the chamber orchestra in Vienna in 1736. Having traveled to Italy and fallen under the influence of Sammartini, Gluck produced his first opera in Milan—*Artaserse* (1741). He then went to London and met Handel in 1745 and continued traveling around Europe with an opera company for which he composed original works.

In 1754, Gluck was appointed court *Kapellmeister* by Empress Maria Theresa, and he settled in Vienna. *Don Juan* (1761), a landmark work of dramatic ballet, was followed the next year by the revolutionary opera, *Orfeo ed Eurydice*. Gluck was responsible for bringing opera away from the courtly dryness that pervaded much opera of the day. He favored a cogent dramatic plot with music that reflected the drama. Gluck's attempt to remove the heroic from opera and make it meaningful for common people was well timed to coordinate with similar changes that were taking place in society.

Gluck revised *Orfeo* (1774), and also *Alceste* (1776) for the Paris Opera, and composed *Iphigénie en Aulide* (1774) and *Iphigénie en Tauride* (1779). His last opera, *Echo et Narcisse* (1779) was a failure, and he retired to Venice. Gluck's operas had a great influence on Mozart and Cherubini.

1732   Franz Joseph Haydn   38

born 31 March 1732, Rohrau, Austria
died 31 May 1809, Vienna, Austria

1738–1739: Educated at a relative's school at Hainburg.

1740–1749: Continued studies at the choir school of St. Stephen's Cathedral in Vienna.

1755: Wrote first set of string quartets for his patron Karl Joseph Fürnberg. Patron obtained position for Haydn as music director to Count Morzin. For his new employer, Haydn wrote his first symphony (1759).

1761–1790: Served as *Kapellmeister* to Prince Esterhazy. Haydn, in his Esterhazy period, was extremely prolific. He supplied the court with all ceremonial, entertainment, and functional music. During this period he wrote masses, operas, concertos, overtures, symphonies, and chamber music. Included among the works written at Esterhazy's court are the *St. Cecilia's Mass* (1769–1772), about ninety symphonies, *The Seven Last Words* (1785), and about sixty string quartets. About 1781 he became acquainted with Mozart.

1791–1795: Made two visits to London and wrote and conducted twelve "London" symphonies. These represent the peak of the development of sonata-form in the classical symphony.

1795: Settled in Vienna and produced two oratorios: *The Creation* (1797–1798) and *The Seasons* (1799–1801).

1743   Luigi Boccherini   39

born 19 February 1743, Lucca, Italy
died 28 May 1805, Madrid, Spain

Italian composer and cellist whose 90 string quartets and 125 string quintets show a classical clarity of structure.

1746   William Billings   40

born 7 October 1746, Boston, Massachusetts
died 26 September 1800, Boston, Massachusetts

The first American composer to devote himself entirely to music, Billings is known for his "fuguing tunes." *When Jesus Wept* is an especially beautiful round.

He published six books containing hymns, psalm tunes, and original compositions. William Schumann composed *New England Triptych* (1956) based on Billings' melodies.

1752   Muzio Clementi   41

born 23 January 1752, Rome, Italy
died 10 March 1832, Evesham, England

Italian keyboard performer and composer who moved to London and became one of the first and finest mass producers of pianos. His keyboard sonatas are original in concept and influenced Beethoven.

1756   Wolfgang Amadeus Mozart   42

born 27 January 1756, Salzburg, Austria
died 5 December 1791, Vienna, Austria

Mozart was the son of Leopold Mozart, himself a distinguished musician in Salzburg. In the year of his son's birth, Leopold published a book on violin technique. He was assistant *Kapellmeister* to the Archbishop of Salzburg at the time.

In 1762, Wolfgang published his first set of violin sonatas; primitive in execution, they are nonetheless remarkable for a child of six. During the 1760's, Leopold took Wolfgang and his sister Nannerl—keyboard prodigies each—on tours of various European courts. They spent five months in Paris in 1763, then went to London where Wolfgang met one of Bach's sons. Three of Mozart's earliest piano concertos are transcriptions of sonatas by the "London Bach," to which Wolfgang added orchestra parts and keyboard cadenzas.

1768:   Composed his first operas: *Bastien und Bastienne* and *La Finta semplice* (*The Simple Schemer*).

1769–1771:   Traveled to Italy and met Padre Martini, a theory teacher, and the singer Farinelli, both important to his musical development. Returned to Salzburg where he became concertmaster and organist. At the end of 1771 the Archbishop died and was succeeded by Hieronymus Colloredo, who was to harass Mozart for the next ten years. Unceasing conflict arose, partly due to personalities, but also because of Mozart's frequent absences on tours. During this period, as throughout his life, Mozart wrote pieces on commission. One reason for Mozart's traveling was to cultivate potential patrons. In Salzburg, Mozart could not express himself in all forms, his church position calling mainly for masses and motets.

1772–1773:   Traveled to Milan, then returned to Salzburg where he feverishly completed five symphonies and some chamber music. In the summer of 1773, father and son went to Vienna. There Haydn's string quartets inspired Mozart. Mozart's six quartets, K. 387–465, were dedicated to Haydn.

1773–1775:   Went to Munich and was commissioned to write an opera. The result was *La Finta giardiniera* (*The Girl in Gardener's Guise*). Returning to Salzburg in March 1775, Mozart composed some vocal works and the five violin concertos.

1776–1777:   Remained in Salzburg composing masses and vocal pieces, three piano concertos—including one for three piano soloists—three serenades, and numerous divertimenti.

1777:   Because Wolfgang felt stifled in Salzburg, his father asked permission for them to go on a tour. The Archbishop refused. Wolfgang quit, and Colloredo fired them both. He rehired the father, however, so Leopold reluctantly sent Wolfgang off with his mother. After their visit to Mannheim the distinct style of the orchestra there influenced his later work.

1778:   Mozart's mother died in Paris.

1779–1780:   Returned to Salzburg and composed the *Coronation Mass,* a two-piano concerto, vespers, and chamber music.

1780:   Success of his opera *Idomeneo* in Vienna resulted in Mozart's moving to and settling in Vienna. He married Constanze Weber in 1782.

1781–1791:   Period of great opera production, including *The Abduction from the Seraglio* (1782), *The·Marriage of Figaro* (1786), *Don Giovanni* (1787), *Cosi fan tutte* (*Women Are Like That,* 1790), and *The Magic Flute* (1791). Public taste being fickle, Mozart—lacking regular patronage—was financially unsuccessful during his last years. Commissioned to write a requiem in 1791, he believed it was destined to be his own. He died just after beginning the sixth section of the *Requiem* and was buried in an unmarked pauper's grave. The *Requiem* was completed by an apprentice of Mozart's (Süssmayr) and stands as one of his greatest achievements.

1760   Luigi Cherubini   43

born 14 September 1760, Florence, Italy
died 15 March 1842, Paris, France

Italian composer who moved to Paris to make his mark, writing works of romantic emotional stress with classical refinement of form. His opera, *Medea,* is a striking dramatic work. Cherubini became the director of the Paris Conservatory and his pedagogical influence is still felt today.

1770   Ludwig van Beethoven   44

born 16 December 1770, Bonn, Germany
died 26 March 1827, Vienna, Austria

Beethoven's early musical education was with his father and Christian Neefe.

1778:   Made his first public appearance in Cologne in the Elector's Orchestra.

1783–1792:   Held various musical positions in Bonn. First piece, *Variations on a Theme by Dressler,* was published in 1783, followed in 1784 by three piano sonatas. Neefe also taught Beethoven German literature and philosophy.

1787:   Visited Vienna and met Mozart, for whom his admiration was vast.

1792:   Studied briefly in Vienna with Haydn, but their personalities clashed. He remained in Vienna when the court at Bonn collapsed and his position vanished.

1794: Began study of counterpoint with Albrechtberger. He was accepted into society because of recommendations of Count Waldstein, a noble friend in Bonn (and to whom he was later to dedicate one of his most remarkable piano sonatas).

1795: Made public debut as pianist.

1796: First lengthy trips to Prague and Berlin.

1797–1800: Period of great output: six piano sonatas, a dozen sets of variations, violin sontatas, two piano concertos, chamber music, and songs.

1800: *First Symphony* was performed. Op. 18 string quartets completed and performed by Schuppanzigh and his quartet. Schuppanzigh remained one of Beethoven's closest friends.

1802: Aware for several years of a hearing defect, Beethoven despaired in October and contemplated suicide. He ruled this out, however, feeling that it was his duty to produce all of which he was capable before dying.

1805: His only opera, *Fidelio,* met with a cold reception. He revised it several times and the 1814 performance was a success.

1806: Composed the *"Rasumowsky" String Quartets,* the *Piano Concerto No. 4,* and his *Violin Concerto.*

1808: *Fifth* and *Sixth* symphonies, as well as the *Choral Fantasy,* composed and performed. Nearly accepted an offer to go to Cassel as court composer, but his student and patron, Archduke Rudolph, along with Prince Lobkowitz and Prince Kinsky, agreed to pay Beethoven 4,000 gulden a year to stay in Vienna.

1810: Contemplated marrying Therese Malfatti, but she rejected him.

1812: Wrote a love letter to "the Immortal Beloved," a woman whose identity is uncertain. Also completed the *Symphonies No. 7* and *No. 8.*

1815: Made last appearance as pianist in a concert for the Empress of Russia's birthday. He could no longer hear the orchestra because his hearing had deteriorated so severely. Brother Karl died, and Beethoven was given guardianship of his nephew, Karl.

1818: Composed the *Hammerklavier Sonata,* one of the most spectacular works in the entire piano literature.

1819–1823: Composed the *Missa Solemnis (Solemn Mass)* and the last three piano sonatas. At the October 3rd opening of the Josephstadter Theatre, Beethoven's conducting of his *Overture for the Consecration of the House* was disastrous.

1824: Completed the *Ninth Symphony* with its choral "Ode to Joy," which he had envisioned several years earlier. He was totally deaf and as the audience applauded, he had to be turned around to *see* their response. After this, he withdrew to chamber music, completing the last string quartets in 1825. These works are regarded by many as the most sublime music ever composed.

1782   Niccolò Paganini   45

born 27 October 1782, Genoa, Italy
died 27 May 1840, Nice, France

Legendary Italian violin virtuoso, whose life was filled with love affairs and rumors of his league with the devil. He traveled around Europe astounding audiences with his technique, which was most effectively displayed in the several violin concerti that he composed for himself.

1786   Carl Maria von Weber   46

born 18 November 1786, Eutin, Germany
died 5 June 1826, London, England

Weber traveled widely as a boy, studied music with Michael Haydn, and wrote his first opera at thirteen, *Die Macht der Liebe und des Weins* (*The Power of Love and Wine*, 1799). He became conductor at Breslau in 1804 and, after several such conductorships, achieved the directorship of the German Opera at Dresden. His most outstandingly successful opera, *Der Freischütz* (*The Freeshooter*, 1820), was followed by the lesser successes *Euryanthe* (1823) and *Oberon* (1826). Weber also wrote instrumental music including *Invitation to the Dance* (1819) for piano, two piano concerti, cantatas, and two masses. As one of the first romantic composers, he reduced Italian influence in German opera; and he himself was highly influential on Richard Wagner.

1791   Giacomo Meyerbeer   47

born 5 September 1791, Berlin, Germany
died 2 May 1864, Paris, France

German composer and pianist. He was a piano student of Clementi and first played in public at the age of seven, but his fame rests on his operas. Best known are *L'Africaine* (*The Woman from Africa*), written over a period of many years and first performed in Paris in 1865; *Le Prophète* (*The Prophet*, 1849); and *Les Huguenots* (*The Huguenots*, 1836).

1792   Gioacchino Rossini   48

born 29 February 1792, Pesaro, Italy
died 13 November 1868, Passy, France

Rossini studied music in Bologna, and in 1808 a cantata of his was performed and won first prize. In 1810, Rossini produced his first opera in Venice, *La Cambiale di Matrimonio* (*The Marriage Contract*). By the age of twenty-one he had written eleven more operas that were performed in Venice, Milan, Bologna, and Ferrara. He quickly became the foremost operatic composer in Italy. Between 1815 and 1823, Rossini worked for the impressario, Domenico Barbaja, whose mistress he married in 1822. Products of this period include *The Barber of Seville* (1816), *Otello* (1816), and *La Gazza Ladra* (*The Thieving Magpie*, 1817).

After spending a successful season in London in 1823, Rossini was appointed music director of the Theatre Italien in Paris the following year. Composing his masterpiece, *William Tell*, in 1829, Rossini then stopped composing opera (at the age of thirty-seven); and during the remainder of his life he composed only the

Stabat Mater (1847), the *Petite Messe solennelle* (*Short Solemn Mass,* 1864), and a few instrumental and vocal pieces.

1797   Franz Schubert   49

born 31 January 1797, Vienna, Austria
died 19 November 1828, Vienna, Austria

Schubert was the son of a schoolmaster who taught him to play the violin.

1808:   Joined the court chapel choir and studied composition with Antonio Salieri.

1811:   First extant song—*Hagars Klage* (*Hagar's Lament*). First string quartets were composed for family performance during seminary school holidays.

1813:   Faced with the decision to become either a school teacher or composer. Began teaching.

1814–1815:   Continued composing while teaching. Finished two symphonies, piano pieces, choral music, and two masses. Became friends with Hans von Schober, who encouraged him to forsake teaching.

1816:   Boarded with Schober while continuing to compose over 100 songs, including *Der Wanderer* (*The Wanderer*), two more symphonies, a fourth mass, and chamber music.

1817:   Schober persuaded opera star, Johann Vogl, to visit Schubert and sing some of his lieder. They performed together in Vienna's drawing rooms. Songs include *An die Musik (To Music)* and *Die Forelle (The Trout)*.

1818:   Started teaching again. In July he received an appointment as music-master for Count Johann Esterhazy. Moved to Hungary and gave up teaching.

1820:   Completed the *"Trout" Quintet*, based on the earlier song. Began *Fifth Mass in A^b Major*, which was completed in 1822. Met Baron von Schönstein, a baritone, who became another great interpreter of Schubert's lieder.

1821:   *Der Erlkönig (The Erlking)* was published, along with other lieder.

1822:   Collaborated with Schober on the opera *Alfonso und Estrella*. Completed piano work, *The Wanderer Fantasy*. Wrote two movements of the *8th Symphony*.

1823:   Began *Die Schöne Müllerin* (*The Pretty Maid of the Mill*) song cycle. Broke with dishonest publishers after selling the rights to Opp. 1–14. Illness undermined him. Suffered several artistic failures on the stage, including *Rosamunde*.

1825:   Performances of his music in Vienna were increasingly popular. He had a productive summer holiday in Austria.

1827:   Composed the *Winterreise* (*Winter's Journey*) cycle. On March 19, Schubert met the dying Beethoven for the first time, although they had lived in the same city for years. A week later, Schubert was a torchbearer at Beethoven's funeral.

1828:   Feverish outpouring of songs, piano pieces, and the final symphony, despite failing health. His weakened condition made him easy prey for typhoid, from which he died.

1797   Gaetano Donizetti   50

born 29 November 1797, Bergamo, Italy
died 8 April, 1848 Bergamo, Italy

Opera composer who studied in Naples and Bologna before joining the army, at which time he composed his first work, *Enrico di Borgogna*. During the next twelve years he produced thirty-one operatic works, including *Zoraide di Granata*, his first success; his most popular works also stem from this period: *L'Elisir d'Amore (The Elixir of Love*, 1832) and *Lucia di Lammermoor* (1835). When his opera *Poliuto* (1839) was censored, he moved to Paris and composed *Don Pasquale* (1843), his most well-known opera buffa.

1801   Vincenzo Bellini   51

born 3 November 1801, Catania, Italy
died 24 September 1835, Puteax, France

Italian opera composer who wrote in the *bel canto* style. He studied at Naples Conservatory, then won commissions through the impressario, Domenico Barbaja. His operas include *Il Pirata* (*The Pirate*, 1827), *La Sonnambula* (*The Sleepwalker*, 1831), *Norma* (1831), and *I Puritani* (*The Puritans*, 1835).

1804   Mikhail Glinka   52

born 1 June 1804, Novospasskoi, Russia
died 15 February 1857, Berlin, Germany

A trip to Italy inspired Glinka to give up his civil service career to compose operas. His works were the foundation of the Russian national school. The two most outstanding of his operas are *A Life for the Czar* (1836) and *Russlan and Ludmilla* (1842).

1809   Felix Mendelssohn-Bartholdy   53

born 3 February 1809, Hamburg, Germany
died 4 November 1847, Leipzig, Germany

Mendelssohn was the son of a wealthy banker and grandson of the noted philosopher, Moses Mendelssohn.

1811: Family moved to Berlin. Felix received private tutoring and took piano lessons from Ludwig Berger, violin lessons from Wilhelm Henning, and composition lessons from C. F. Zelter.

1818: Made public debut as pianist.

1820–1828: Began serious composing. Early works: *Octet for strings* (1825) and overture to *A Midsummer Night's Dream* (1826).

1829: Began historic revival of music of Bach with performance of *St. Matthew Passion* at Berlin Singakademie—the first performance of the work since before Bach's death in 1750. Made first important conducting tour in England, meeting Latour, Clementi, Cramer, and Moscheles. Side trip to Scotland inspired the *Hebrides Overture* (1830) and the *"Scottish" Symphony* (1830).

1830: Paid last visit to Goethe in Weimar before the poet's death.

1830–1831: Traveled in Italy, saw the paintings of Titian, which inspired the *"Italian" Symphony* (1832).

1831: Traveled in Switzerland, studying the play *William Tell* by Schiller. Continued on to Paris, where he met Liszt, Herz, Meyerbeer, Chopin, and Kalkbrenner.

1832: Returned to London for successful performances conducting the London Philharmonic Society. Composed *Capriccio Brilliant* and the first volume of *Songs Without Words*, all for piano. Returned to Leipzig and conducted the *Walpurgisnacht*, the *"Reformation"* Symphony, *Midsummer Night's Dream Overture*, and other works.

1835–1847: Conducted the very important Gewandhaus concerts in Leipzig and founded the Leipzig Conservatory (1843).

1837: Married Cecile Jeanrenaud.

1839: Composed *"Ruy Blas" Overture.*

1844: Completed the *Violin Concerto in E Minor,* one of the most popular works in this form.

1846: Finished the oratoria *Elijah,* which was first performed at the Birmingham Festival.

1810   Frédéric Chopin   54

born 22 February 1810, Zelazowa Wola, Poland
died 17 October 1849, Paris, France

1816–1822: Took music lessons from Adalbert Zywny, a violinist, composer, and pianist. After 1818 began playing in Warsaw salons as a prodigy. For his own performances he began composing brief piano pieces, many based on Polish melodies, and most in some song or dance form.

1826–1829: Studied composition with Joseph Elsner at the Warsaw Conservatory.

1829: Toured Germany and Italy. Began composing the Op. 10 *Études,* dedicated to Liszt.

1830: Gave a concert of his music in Warsaw including his second piano concerto and gained reputation as leading national composer of Poland.

1831: Settled in Paris as fashionable piano teacher. Was engaged for a time to Maria Wodzinska.

1832: Began the Op. 25 *Études,* dedicated to the Countess d'Agoult.

1836: Met the brilliant writer George Sand (Aurore Dudevant), and lived with her for nine years. Composed the Op. 28 *Préludes.* In Paris he was one of a group of musicians, artists, and authors who were representative of French Romanticism.

1837: Visited England with Camille Pleyel.

1838: Visited the isle of Majorca with George Sand; upon returning to Paris, lived a retiring life, teaching and composing.

1846–1849: Composed last works—mazurkas and waltzes.

1810   Robert Schumann   55

born 8 June 1810, Zwickau, Germany
died 29 July 1856, Endenich, Germany

Schumann was the son of a bookseller.

1820–1828: Attended the *Gymnasium*, then was sent to Leipzig to study law, but instead he studied literature and music.

1822: Began composing while at school.

1829: Went to Heidelberg with friend Thibaut and learned choral music of Handel, Bach, and Palestrina.

1830: Persuaded mother to allow him to leave the study of law and begin piano study. His teacher was Friedrich Wieck. Moved into Wieck's house. Schumann's lessons halted when Wieck went on tour with his daughter, Clara, a piano prodigy.

1831–1832: Studied theory with Heinrich Dorn.

1833: Experimented with a mechanical device to strengthen his fingers and instead virtually crippled his right hand, ending his plans for a concert career.

1834–1844: Founded and edited a music journal, *Neue Zeitschrift für Musik*, in which he expounded on the latest trends in Romanticism, particularly as seen in the music of Schubert, Chopin, and Brahms.

1835–1840: Began spending time daily with Clara Wieck when she was home from touring. Her father grew alarmed that marriage might end her career, but Robert and Clara did indeed determine to marry. While her father took her on tour, Schumann composed *Davidsbünderltänze, Noveletten, Kinderszenen (Scenes from Childhood)*, and *Kreisleriana*—all important collections of character pieces for piano.

1840: Began composing lieder on poems of Heine, Goethe, Eichendorff et al. Married Clara after a court order prohibited her father from further interference. Much of Schumann's great outpouring of love songs date from this year, including *Frauenliebe und leben* and *Dichterliebe*.

1843: Toured Russia with Clara with great success for both.

1848: Composed the opera *Genoveva*.

1851: Served as municipal music director in Düsseldorf.

1854–56: Mental breakdown, feared since youth, struck him. He attempted suicide, then begged to be placed in a sanitorium. Clara finally submitted, and he spent his last two years in Endenich sanitorium.

1811   Franz Liszt   56

born 22 October 1811, Raiding, Hungary
died 31 July 1886, Bayreuth, Germany

1811–1825: Born into a noble family. Liszt's father gave him musical training and took him on a concert tour. He studied with Czerny, Salieri, and Reicha.

1833: He met Countess Marie d'Agoult, a brilliant and liberal aristocrat.

1835: Liszt eloped with the Countess to Switzerland and Italy.

1837: Cosima born, a daughter who will later marry Richard Wagner.

1837–1847: Traveled incessantly, concertizing in Europe. Slowly broke away from the Countess.

1848–1858: Served Grand Duke Carl Friederich as *Kapellmeister* in Weimar. In this post he encouraged younger musicians like Brahms, Berlioz, and Wagner. Composed a large number of works, making Weimar a musical center. Began new affair with Princess Carolyne von Sayn-Wittgenstein.

1861: Marriage plans with Carolyne aborted.

1865: Was ordained as abbé and continued to teach in Budapest, Weimar, and Rome.

1875: Agreed to become president of a newly founded National Academy of Music in Budapest, where he was a national hero.

1876–1886: Traveled to Rome, Paris, England, and Bayreuth, where he heard a memorable performance of Wagner's *Tristan und Isolde* just weeks before his death.

1813   Richard Wagner   57

born 22 May 1813, Leipzig, Germany
died 13 February 1883, Venice, Italy

Wagner was largely self-educated.

1834–1836: Was music director at theatres in Magdeburg and Königsberg. Married Minna Planer, 1836.

1837–1839: Enjoyed first period of success while conducting at Riga. Was forced to flee with Minna from his debtors; they went first to London, then to Paris.

1839–1842: Period of poverty and unemployment in Paris. He composed *The Flying Dutchman* as a German opera, forsaking the French grand opera style of Meyerbeer.

1842–1849: Returned to Germany and produced *Rienzi* (1842), which won him appointment as music director for the Royal Saxon court at Dresden. Became champion of German opera, producing works of Weber and Gluck with more success than his own, which included *Dutchman*, *Tannhäuser*, and *Lohengrin*. Began work on the *Ring of the Nibelungen*, which was not completed until twenty-five years later.

1849: Participated in the May uprising in Dresden with anarchist Bakunin and fled to escape arrest. Sought exile in Zurich.

1850–1853. Concertized theories of art synthesis, in which drama, music, and dance are all equal elements in an opera. Major volumes: *Opera and Drama*, *The Art Work of the Future*, and *Art and Revolution*.

1850–1858: Carried on an affair with Mathilde Wesendonck, which in some degree inspired *Tristan und Isolde*. The creation of this opera was affected by Wagner's study of Schopenhauer's *The World as Will and Idea*.

1864: Ludwig II became king and offered Wagner patronage which, among other things, allowed *Tristan* to be produced at last.

1865: Wagner left Munich for political reasons and settled again in Switzerland, at Triebschen, where he remained for six years.

1868: Presented *Die Meistersinger (The Mastersingers)*.

1870: Married Cosima von Bülow, the former wife of his good friend, conductor-pianist Hans von Bülow, and the daughter of Franz Liszt. To his new wife, Wagner dedicated his autobiography, *Mein Leben (My Life)*, which he had undertaken at the request of Ludwig II.

1872: April 21, Cosima and Wagner took up residence in Bayreuth and began plans for a festival theater technically equipped so that the entire four operas of the *Ring Cycle* could be performed as Wagner intended them. May 22, Richard's fifty-ninth birthday, was the day the foundation stone of the theater was laid.

1876:   August 7–9, dress rehearsals for *The Ring* took place, with King Ludwig present. August 13–17, the public premiere of the entire *Ring Cycle* was given. The festival immediately met with financial difficulties.

1873–1876:   Wagner made conducting appearances to help finance the festival.

1881:   Completed *Parsifal,* his final opera, then retired to Venice to write more essays and nurse his failing health.

1813   Giuseppe Verdi   58

born 10 October 1813, Le Roncole, Italy
died 27 January 1901, Milan, Italy

Verdi was the son of a tavern keeper. He became the protégé of Antonio Barezzi, a merchant from nearby Busseto.

1831:   Barezzi sent him to Milan where he studied three years under Vincenzo Lavigna.

1834:   Returned to Busseto and married Barezzi's daughter, Margherita, in 1836.

1839:   His first opera, *Oberto,* was produced.

1840:   His wife died.

1842:   Established a reputation in Italy with *Nabucco.*

1847–1849:   Lived in Paris with mistress, Guiseppina Strepponi.

1851:   *Rigoletto* was a success in Italy.

1853:   Produced *Il Trovatore* and *La Traviata* with success.

1855–1870: Presented a number of large and spectacular operas in Paris, including *Don Carlo* (1867).

1859:   Staged *Un Ballo in maschera* (*A Masked Ball*) in Rome.

1861–1865:   Went to St. Petersburg to present *La Forza del destino* (*The Force of Destiny*). Was elected to the Italian parliament but took no active role and later resigned.

1871–1901—The Later Years:

1871:   *Aida,* set in Egypt and composed for the opening of the Suez Canal.

1873:   *Manzoni Requiem,* decicated to the memory of the great Italian patriot.

1887:   Arrigo Boïto—himself the composer of the superb opera *Mephistophele*—enticed Verdi into composing two marvelous Shakespearian operas, his last works. (Boïto wrote the librettos.) The tragedy of *Otello* is contrasted by the comedy of *Falstaff* (1893).

1895–1897:   Composed *Te Deum* and *Stabat Mater.*

1818   Charles Gounod   59

born 17 June 1818, Paris, France
died 18 October 1893, St. Cloud, France

After studying in Rome and learning the music of Palestrina, Gounod worked in Paris, producing operas. His most successful work was *Faust* (1859). This opera was given at both the first and last performances of the old Metropolitan Opera House in New York. During and after the Franco-Prussian war, he lived in England, where his oratorios, *La Redemption* and *Mors et Vita* (*Death and Life*), were performed in 1882 and 1885. Gounod also composed an opera based on Shakespeare's *Romeo and Juliet*.

1822   César Franck   60

born 10 December 1822, Liège, Belgium
died 8 November 1890, Paris, France

Composer and organist whose fame rests chiefly on his instrumental works. Franck studied composition in Paris with Leborne, piano with Zimmerman, and organ with Benoist. In 1838 he won the Grand Prix d'Honneur for piano. His first important work, an oratorio, *Ruth*, was given at Paris in 1846. In 1851 Franck obtained a position as organist at the church of St. Jean-St. François. In 1853 he became chapel master. In 1858 he became organist at Ste. Clotilde, a position which he held until his death. In 1872 he became professor of organ at the Paris Conservatory, numbering among his students Vincent d'Indy and Ernest Chausson. Franck's innovative use of chromatic harmony (influenced by Wagner), which he combined with the strong contrapuntal lines of Bachian counterpoint, influenced a whole new generation of young French musicians. Among his works are: *Symphony in D Minor*, completed in 1888 when he was sixty six; *Piano Quintet in F Minor* (1879); *String Quartet in D Major* (1889); a tone poem, *Le Chasseur maudit* (*The Hunter Who Was Damned*, 1883); *Piano and Violin Sonata in A Major* (1886); *Les Béatitudes* (*The Beatitudes*, 1869–1879): and *Symphonic Variations for Piano and Orchestra* (1886). Among his many works for organ are *Prelude, Fugue and Variations*, Op. 18, and *Three Chorales*.

1824   Bedrich Smetana   61

born 2 March 1824, Leitomischl, Czechoslovakia
died 12 May 1884, Prague, Czechoslovakia

A child prodigy at the piano, Smetana conducted the Philharmonic Society in Sweden until 1861, when he returned to Prague to compose nationalistic operas. The most outstanding of these was the *Bartered Bride* (1866), which led to his appointment as director of the National Theater in Prague. He held this post until 1874, when he lost his hearing. In that same year he completed the nationalist symphonic cycle *Ma Vlast* (*My Life*), which includes the famous tone poem, *Moldau*. He finally suffered a mental breakdown and died in an asylum.

1824   Anton Bruckner   62

born 4 September 1824, Ansfelden, Austria
died 11 October 1896, Vienna, Austria

The son of a poor school teacher, Bruckner studied music and then attended a teacher's college at Linz, serving as a schoolmaster during the 1840's. Settling in Vienna in 1868, he served nearly the rest of his life as a teacher at the conservatory. A great follower of Wagner, Bruckner's nine symphonies are large and grand works that are loosely structured. His compositions were not really appreciated during his life, but his influence on Gustav Mahler was great. His symphonies are now regularly featured by the major symphony orchestras.

1829   Louis Moreau Gottschalk   63

born 8 May 1829, New Orleans, Louisiana
died 18 December 1869, Rio di Janeiro, Brazil

American pianist and composer. He was a child prodigy who later became a pupil of Berlioz. Much of his music reflects the folk melodies of the New World and is filled with the rhythms of the Caribbean. Well before Dvorak wrote his *New World Symphony*, Gottschalk was using American Negro folk songs in his music.

1833   Johannes Brahms   64

born 7 May 1833, Hamburg, Germany
died 3 April 1897, Vienna, Austria

Brahms was the son of a musician. Showing early talent, he studied piano with Otto Cossel and Edward Marxsen.

1846–1853: Marxsen taught him theory. Brahms made money by composing under a pseudonym and playing in bars and brothels. He sent a package of manuscripts to Schumann that was returned unopened. A period of depression was relieved by a tour with Hungarian violinist, Remenyi. He met Joseph Joachim, violin virtuoso, who introduced him to Liszt.

1853–1856: Through Joachim, he met Schumann, who wrote an encouraging article about him in *Neue Zeitschrift für Musik*. Brahms became friendly with the entire Schumann family.

1856–1859: Composed in Hamburg. *First Piano Concerto* was performed to a cool reception in 1859.

1860: Drew up manifesto with Joachim declaring opposition to Wagnerism. Brahms preferred strictly classical forms and composed *Variations on a Theme of Handel* for piano.

1862: Trip to Vienna, met Hanslick, an influential critic, who later championed Brahms over Wagner.

1865–1872: Toured with Joachim. His mother died, and he subsequently composed the *German Requiem* in her memory.

1868: He witnessed the first performance of the entire work, resulting in his greatest public success thus far.

1872–1875: Directed Society of Friends of Music, composed orchestral *Variations on a Theme of Haydn* (also arranged in a two-piano version).

1876:   Completed *Symphony No. 1*, fifteen years after beginning the work. This symphony has become a mainstay of the modern orchestral repertoire.

1879:   Was offered an honorary doctorate at University of Breslau and composed *Academic Festival Overture* for the occasion.

1881:   Composed the *Second Piano Concerto*, dedicated to Marxsen.

1883:   Composed the *Third* and *Fourth* symphonies.

1886:   Resided at Thun, Switzerland, and composed last orchestral work, *Double Concerto for Violin and Cello*.

1890–1895:   Led a semi-retired life composing mostly piano music, including Opp. 116–119, collections of intermezzi, capriccios, and other short forms.

1896:   Clara Schumann, his great friend, died; he was moved to compose *Eleven Chorale Preludes* for organ, his last compositions.

1833   Alexander Borodin   65

born 12 November 1833, St. Petersburg, Russia
died 27 February 1887, St. Petersburg, Russia

In addition to composing, Borodin was a professional chemist. In 1862 he met with Balakirev, who became the leader of "The Five." Although he composed three symphonies, two string quartets, and songs, Borodin's most monumental work was the opera *Prince Igor*, which was a life-long project and was completed posthumously by Glazunov.

1835   Charles Camille Saint-Saëns   66

born 9 October 1835, Paris, France
died 16 December 1921, Algiers, Algeria

Extremely brilliant and precocious, Saint-Saëns entered the Paris Conservatory at thirteen. He composed piano concerti for his own use and championed instrumental chamber music when it was unpopular in France. He was regarded as a traditionalist, noted for his humorous attacks on the music of Debussy and the modernists. A very prolific composer, his works include *Danse Macabre* (1874), *Introduction and Rondo Capriccioso* (1863), and the opera *Samson et Dalila* (1877).

1838   Georges Bizet   67

born 25 October 1838, Paris, France
died 3 June 1875, Bougival, France

The only son of a family of professional musicians, Bizet's precocious talents were carefully cultivated by his family. He entered the Paris Conservatoire at ten and was influenced by the music of Gounod. He won many prizes including the Prix de Rome in 1857. He spent three years in Rome, where he found the music of Palestrina "deadly boring," then he returned to Paris and composed the operas *Les Pecheurs de Perles* (*The Pearl Fishers*, 1863) and *La Joli Fille de Perth* (*The*

Pretty Girl from Perth, 1867). He also composed several vocal and piano works at this time. In 1870, when the Franco-Prussian war broke out, Bizet joined the National Guard. He continued composing all the same, completing *Jeux d'enfants* (*Children's Games*) in 1871 and *L'Arlesienne* the following year.

His final and greatest work, the opera *Carmen*, was completed in 1875, in spite of his own failing health and the nervous breakdown suffered by his wife. The premiere should have been an astounding success because—as Bizet himself said —*Carmen* is a work of "clarity, and vivacity, full of color and melody." When the audience response was far less than overwhelming, Bizet retreated to his room and was found later "with his head in his hands, crying bitter tears . . ." The opera managed to last for forty-eight performances in Paris, while Bizet retired to Bougival and died. Within the same year, the Vienna Opera gave triumphant performances of *Carmen*, and it has become and remained a world favorite ever since.

1839   Modest Mussorgsky   68

born 21 March 1839, Karevo, Russia
died 28 March 1881, St. Petersburg, Russia

The youngest son of a wealthy landowner, Mussorgsky learned piano from his mother. He attended cadet school in St. Petersburg, then joined a regiment of Imperial Guard. He was fascinated by folklore.

1849: Took piano lessons from Anton Herke, a pupil of Henselt.

1852: First piano piece, *Porte-Enseigne Polka*.

1857: Through Alexander Dargomizhky he met Cesar Cui and Mily Balakirev, and joined "The Five," a group of composers devoted to developing a Russian national compositional style.

1859: Visited Moscow and was filled with patriotic spirit.

1860: May-August, suffered mental/nervous crisis.

1861–1863: Returned to Karevo to manage the family estate after the freeing of the serfs.

1863: Was forced by financial straits to enter civil service and served as head clerk until 1867. During this period in St. Petersburg he lived in a commune, sharing aesthetic and political ideas with five other young men.

1867: Composed *Night on Bald Mountain*, a tone poem.

1868: Began his most daring effort to date, a setting of Gogol's prose comedy, *The Marriage*. Only completed one act.

1869: First version of opera, *Boris Godunov*, completed while again working as a clerk.

1870: September-December—set to his own words *The Nursery*, a song cycle of naturalistic studies of childhood.

1872: Second version of *Boris Godunov* was rejected, as the first had been, by the Opera Committee of the Maryinsky Theatre. In 1874 the opera finally appeared at the theatre. Began collecting historical material for two other operas, *Khovantchina* and *The Fair at Sorochinsk*—both of which were to remain unfinished.

1874: Piano version of *Pictures at an Exhibition* completed, to be later orchestrated by Ravel (and others).

1875–76: Began to suffer effects of heavy drinking. Suffered periods of dementia.

1879: Toured the Ukraine and Crimea, accompanying the contralto Daria Leonova.

1880: Obliged to leave government service on January 13.

1881: Made his final public appearance on February 15 at a performance of his *The Destruction of Sennacherib*. Eight days later he suffered a fit of alcoholic epilepsy and died soon thereafter.

1840   Peter Ilich Tchaikovsky   69

born 7 May 1840, Viatka, Russia
died 6 November 1893, St. Petersburg, Russia.

Tchaikovsky was the son of a mine inspector.

1850–1859: Family moved to St. Petersburg where Tchaikovsky studied music and jurisprudence.

1861: Began theory lessons with Nicholai Zaremba and was influenced by Anton Rubenstein.

1865: Graduated from St. Petersburg Conservatory.

1866–1878: Was professor of harmony at new Moscow Conservatory.

1869: Unsuccessful opera, *The Voyevoda*.

1870: *Romeo and Juliet*, a tone poem that is still popular today.

1877: Married, but remained so only nine disastrous weeks. Suffered nervous breakdown and began correspondence with Nadezdha von Meck, who became his benefactress and confidante.

1877–1878: Moved to Switzerland, then Italy. Enjoyed one of his few untroubled periods, composing the *Fourth Symphony* and the opera *Eugene Onegin*. Resigned from Moscow Conservatory and went to Florence.

1879: Returned to Moscow for moderately successful premiere of *Eugene Onegin* and then left again for Berlin, Paris, and Rome.

1882–1883: Composed the tone poem *Mazeppa*, which won him the order of St. Vladimir, bestowed upon him by the tzar.

1885: Recovering his health, he began conducting his own music and gaining new friends. Took a house near Maidanovo and was semi-retired while revising the opera *Vakula the Smith*.

1887: *Vakula* was performed, renamed *The Little Shoes*. Tchaikovsky conducted, and the work was a success. Started extended series of conducting appearances.

1888: Toured Europe, meeting special success in London. After tour, he settled in new home in Frolovskoye.

1889: Second concert tour of Europe as conductor. Spent summer working on *Sleeping Princess* ballet.

1890: Received letter in December from Nadezdha von Meck, stating her impending financial ruin would mean cancellation of allowance he had lived on for many years. Her situation improved, however, much to his relief.

1891: He undertook composition of the *Nutcracker* ballet. Was severely crushed by the death of his sister, Alexandra. Traveled to United States, keeping a journal.

1892: Another concert tour in Poland and Germany. Sought rest in Vichy, then went to newest and last home near Klin to work on the *Sixth Symphony*, the *"Pathétique."* *The Nutcracker* was premiered on December 17.

1893: Made final tour of Europe. The *"Pathétique"* was a failure at its premiere in St. Petersburg. He died of cholera on November 6.

1841 Antonin Dvorak   70

born 8 September 1841, Nelahozeves, Czechoslovakia
died 1 May 1904, Prague, Czechoslovakia

Dvorak studied at the Organ School in Prague for two years, then played viola with the Czech National Theatre from 1861 to 1871. He first gained attention with a performance of his *Hymnus* for chorus and orchestra (1873). He won the Austrian state prize in 1875 for a symphony he had written and performed the previous year.

Championed by Liszt, Brahms, and Hans von Bülow, Dvorak gained an international reputation as composer and teacher, receiving honorary degrees from Cambridge and Prague universities. While serving as Artistic Director of the National Conservatory of Music in New York (1892–1895), Dvorak composed his most famous symphony *From the New World* (1893). He returned to Prague in 1895, where he remained until his death. His output includes nine symphonies, tone poems, concerti, chamber music, and piano works. His music is noted for its rhythmic and melodic variety and its dependence upon Czech folk sources.

1843 Edvard Grieg   71

born 15 June 1843, Bergen, Norway
died 4 September 1907, Troldhaugen, Norway

Norwegian composer who was persuaded by his meeting with Norwegian nationalist composer, Rikard Nordraak (1864), to use Norwegian folk melodies in his compositions. He composed music for piano, the famous *Piano Concerto in A Minor*, the *Peer Gynt Suites* for orchestra, and more than 125 songs.

1844 Nicolai Rimski-Korsakov   72

born 18 March 1844, Tikhvin, Russia
died 21 June 1908, St. Petersburg, Russia

Born an aristocrat, Rimski-Korsakov went to the naval academy at St. Petersburg, from which he graduated in 1862. However, the year before, he had met Balakirev, who encouraged him to compose; and he wrote his first symphony while still in the navy (1862–1865). In 1871 Rimski was appointed professor of composition at St. Petersburg Conservatory, and he also spent time conducting in Europe that year.

At first he devoted his efforts to orchestral music: *Spanish Capriccio* (1887), *Scheherezade* (1888), and *Easter Overture* (1888). He then wrote sixteen operas, the best known being *Le Coq d'Or (The Golden Cockerel,* 1906–1907). He wrote more than eighty songs based on Russian folk tunes and became a member of "The Five." As a master orchestrator, Rimski numbered among his pupils Glazunov and Stravinsky.

1845   Gabriel Fauré   73

born 12 May 1845, Pamiers, France
died 4 November 1924, Paris, France

A student of Saint-Saëns, Fauré served several churches as organist and was a professor of composition at the Paris Conservatory. His students included Ravel, Nadia Boulanger, and Georges Enesco. Fauré's music for chamber ensembles and solo piano influenced contemporary French music with its delicacy and clarity. He was an outstanding composer of song settings of contemporary French poems. His larger works include the *Requiem* (1887) and the orchestral suite *Pelléas et Mélisande* (1898).

1857   Edward Elgar   74

born 2 June 1857, Broadheath, England
died 23 February 1934, Worcester, England

One of England's outstanding composers in the nineteenth century, Elgar served as organist at Worcester until 1889, when he moved to London. After two years of composing in London, he retired to Worcestershire, where he completed his major works, including two of the five *Pomp and Circumstance* marches, *The Black Knight* for chorus and orchestra (1893), the *Enigma Variations* for orchestra (1899), and the oratorio *The Dream of Gerontius* (1900).

1858   Giacomo Puccini   75

born 22 December 1858, Lucca, Italy
died 29 November 1924, Brussels, Belgium

Puccini represented the fifth generation of a family of local church musicians.
1880–1883:   Studied at Milan Conservatory, chiefly under Ponchielli. His first opera, *Le Villi* (1883), attracted attention.
1889:   *Edgar,* an opera based on Alfred de Musset's novel, was a total failure.
1891:   Settled in Torre del Lago, Tuscany, for thirty years.
1893:   Achieved international fame with the opera *Manon Lescaut.*
1896:   Composed the perennial favorite, *La Bohème,* and assumed leadership among the younger Italian composers. *La Bohème* gives a picture of Bohemian life in Paris about 1830. The librettists for this opera also provided Puccini with the texts for *Tosca* and *Madama Butterfly.*
1900:   *Tosca* demonstrated Puccini's increasing mastery at depicting powerful emotions.

1904:   *Madama Butterfly,* initially a failure in Milan, was later a great success.

1910:   *Girl of the Golden West,* set in the American West, was a success in New York, but not elsewhere. The plot is unusual in that it is one of the few standard operas set in the United States (but sung in Italian).

1917:   *La Rondine,* an attempt at comedy, was perhaps the least successful of Puccini's later works.

1918:   The *Trittico* (*Triptych*), comprising a set of three one-act operas—the tragedy *Suor Angelica* (*Sister Angelica*), the mystery *Il Tabarro* (*The Clock*), and the delightful comedy *Gianni Schicchi.*

1921:   Moved to Viareggio.

1924:   Died, leaving the nearly complete score of the oriental opera *Turandot,* completed by Franco Alfano.

1860   Hugo Wolf   76

born 13 March 1860, Windischgraz, Yugoslavia
died 22 February 1903, Vienna, Austria

Composer of over two hundred art songs, Wolf was heavily influenced harmonically and texturally by Wagner. Wolf was the chief supporter of Wagnerism in his capacity as critic of the *Wiener Salonblatt,* launching scathing attacks on Brahms during the years 1883–1887. His song cycles include the *Möricke Lieder* (1888), the *Goethe Lieder* (1889), and the *Italienisches Liederbuch* (1890–1896). He died in an insane asylum.

1860   Isaac Albéniz   77

born 29 May 1860, Camprodón, Spain
died 18 May 1909, Cambo-les-Bains, France

Composer and piano virtuoso who used Debussy's Impressionism to convey the flavor of Spain in his works. These are mostly for piano, including his popular twelve sketches entitled *Iberia.*

1860   Gustav Mahler   78

born 7 July 1860, Kalischt, Czechoslovakia
died 18 May 1911, Vienna, Austria

Mahler was the son of a Jewish shopkeeper.

1869–1875:   Attended grammar school in Jihlava.

1875–1878:   Studied at the Vienna Conservatory and was devoted to Wagner, and also Bruckner, whom he met in 1878.

1880:   Became *Kapellmeister* at Hall in Austria. First major composition, *Das klagende Lied,* failed to win a prize. Began successful career as opera conductor in Austria and Germany.

1883–1900:   Period of composition based on German folk poems: *Lieder eines fahrenden Gesellen* (*Songs of a Wayfarer*, 1883–1885); songs from *Des Knaben Wunderhorn* (*The Youth's Magic Horn*, 1888); and the first four symphonies, all of which include folk material. The *Second*, *Third*, and *Fourth* symphonies include chorus and vocal soloists.

1883: Journey to Bayreuth, where Mahler was deeply moved upon hearing Wagner's *Parsifal*. Became *Kapellmeister* at Cassel, conducting all types of opera.

1885: Moved to Prague and assumed duties of *Kapellmeister*.

1886: Expanded his knowledge of opera scores while working as second *Kapellmeister* in Leipzig.

1888: Won first appointment as music director, in Budapest, but left in 1891 because he was dissatisfied with conflict between conservatives and new audiences crying for national opera.

1891–1897: Served as *Kapellmeister* in municipal theater in Hamburg. Conducted opera in London in 1892. Completed *Second* and *Third* symphonies. Converted to Roman Catholicism in 1895, partially to offset anti-Semitic prejudices in Vienna.

1897–1907: With the backing of Brahms, Mahler gained appointment as director of the Imperial Opera in Vienna. Built the company, the audience, and his reputation. His personality and extreme concern over all details offended many, and he realized he should resign. Period of works based on poems of Friedrich Rückert—*Kindertotenlieder* (*Songs of the Death of Children*, 1904) and the fifth through seventh symphonies.

1902: Married Alma Schindler.

1907–1911: Directed New York Metropolitan Opera and, after 1909, the New York Philharmonic Society as well. Period of symphonic expansion both of form and instrumentation. Song cycle *Das Lied von der Erde* (*The Song of the Earth*, 1907–1910) and the last symphonies, including the *Eighth*, also known as "*Symphony of a Thousand*" because of the huge number of orchestral, choral, and solo vocal musicians called for, and the unfinished *Tenth*. Returned to Europe in 1910. Collapsed from nervous strain in Vienna.

1861   Edward MacDowell   79

born 18 December 1861, New York City
died 23 January 1908, New York City

American composer who trained in Paris and Germany, made his reputation in Europe as a pianist, then returned to America and chaired Columbia University's new music department (1896–1904). Far more representative of German Romanticism than of American indigenous music, MacDowell's works include *Indian Suite* (1897) for orchestra, two piano concertos, and *Woodland Sketches* (1896) for piano.

1862   Frederick Delius   80

born 29 January 1862, Bradford, England
died 10 June 1934, Grezsur-Loing, France

English composer who studied at Leipzig and was influenced by Grieg. He composed many orchestral suites, richly chromatic in harmony and late Romantic in flavor. Despite blindness that resulted from an illness in 1922, Delius continued to compose. His works include *A Village Romeo and Juliet*, an opera (1901); *In a Summer Garden, Eventyr,* and *A Song of Summer,* all large orchestral works; and several miniature orchestral works.

1862   Claude Debussy   81

born 22 August 1862, Saint Germain-en-Laye, France
died 25 March, 1918, Paris, France

Formative years:

1872:   Piano lessons with Mme. Maute de Fleurville, former student of Chopin and mother-in-law of the poet Verlaine, whose work was later to influence the young composer greatly.

1872–1884:   Studied at the Paris Conservatoire. Worked under Massenet and briefly under Franck. Won Grand Prix de Rome in 1884 with *L'Enfant prodigue* (*The Prodigal Son*). Traveled to Russia, Italy, and Switzerland with Mme. von Meck (Tchaikovsky's benefactress) as her "house painist."

1887–1891—Important formative influences:

a. Frequented literary circles: Baudelaire, Verlaine, Mallarmé. Symbolist poetry.

b. Traveled to Germany and heard Wagner's music dramas; also met Brahms.

c. In Paris, heard Javanese Gamelan at Exposition of 1889; met and was influenced by Satie.

d. Saw piano score of Mussorgsky's opera *Boris Godunov,* which influenced him tremendously.

Artistic Maturity:

1892:   *L'Après-midi d'un faune* (*Afternoon of a Faun*), ballet after an eclogue by Mallarmé. Crystallization of impressionistic style. Began work on his only finished opera, *Pelléas et Mélisande* (not completed and heard until 1902), based on Maeterlinck's symbolist play of the same title. The years 1887–1902 saw tremendous production of *chansons,* including the *Cinq Poèmes de Baudelaire* and the *Ariettes oubliées* (*Forgotten Songs*) (Verlaine).

1893:   *String Quartet,* and *Nocturnes* for orchestra.

1899:   Married Rosalie Texier. Marriage failed. Debussy later eloped with Emma Bardac (1904).

1903–1909:   Important instrumental works exemplary of the composer's impressionistic style: *La Mer* (*The Sea*) (orchestra), *Images, Estampes, Children's Corner* (piano solo).

1909–1914:   Various conducting engagements in Paris, London, Vienna, Budapest, Moscow, and elsewhere.

1910–1913:   *Preludes,* Books 1 and 2, for piano.

Late Works:

1912:   *Jeux* (*Games*), ballet.

1915–1917:   Works for small groups of non-impressionistic, abstract character—three sonatas for piano and various instruments; *12 Études* for piano; *En blanc et noir* (*In White and Black*) for two pianos.

1863   Pietro Mascagni   82

born 7 December 1863, Leghorn, Italy
died 2 August 1945, Rome, Italy

Composer of *Cavalleria rusticana* (*Rustic Chivalry,* 1890), a one-act opera in the *verismo* or realistic style, dealing with everyday events that occur among common people in a small town.

1864   Richard Strauss   83

born 11 June 1864, Munich, Germany
died 8 September 1949, Garmisch-Partenkirchen, Germany

Strauss was the son of an eminent horn player.
1868:   Began music lessons.
1883–1884:   Left the University of Munich and gained recognition for *Symphony in D Minor* (1881), *Violin Concerto* (1883), and *Serenade for Wind Instruments* (1884).
1885–1886:   Conducted Meinigen Orchestra.
1886–1889:   Became third conductor at Munich Opera.
1889–1894:   Served in Weimar as *Hofkapellmeister.* Produced first major works in his mature style—*Don Juan* (1889) and *Death and Transfiguration* (1889), both tone poems for orchestra.
1894–1895:   Appointed conductor of Berlin Philharmonic. Married singer Pauline de Ahna. Composed *Till Eulenspiegel's Merry Pranks* (1895), *Thus Spake Zarathustra* (1896), *Don Quixote* (1898), and *Ein Heldenleben* (*A Hero's Life,* 1899)—all tone poems that have achieved great popularity.
1898–1918:   Served as *Hofkapellmeister* in Berlin. Composed his greatest operas: *Salome* (1905), *Elektra* (1909), *Der Rosenkavalier* (*The Cavalier of the Rose,* 1911), and *Die Frau ohne Schatten* (*The Woman Without a Shadow,* 1919).
1919–1924:   Co-musical director at Vienna Opera.
1929:   Hugo von Hofmannsthal, his friend and librettist since *Elektra,* died. Collaborated next with Stefan Zweig, the famous Jewish novelist, on *Die schweigsame Frau* (*The Silent Woman*).
1933–1935:   Became president of a *Reichsmusikkammer* (a Nazi music organization) until political pressure caused his retirement.
1936–1945:   His political stand on Nazism unclear. He continued working under government surveillance.

1865   Carl Nielsen   84

born 9 June 1865, Nörre Lyndelse, Denmark
died 2 October 1931, Copenhagen, Denmark

The first major Danish symphonist, Nielsen's music is unmistakably Danish in character and spirit. Beginning with his first symphony, Nielsen developed his theory of "progressive tonality."

1865   Jean Sibelius   85

born 8 December 1865, Tavastehus, Finland
died 20 September 1957, Jarvenpää nr. Helsingfors, Finland

Finnish nationalist composer. In 1885, Sibelius attended Helsingfors University to study law, but his great love of music led him to enter the conservatory at Helsingfors before he had completed even a year of law study. At the conservatory he studied violin with Vasiliev and Csillag, and composition with Wegelius. In 1893 he returned to the conservatory as a professor of theory. A pension from the government, granted in 1897 in recognition of his work, enabled him to devote all his time to composition. The Finnish national epic *Kalevala* inspired much of his work. He is best known for his seven symphonies and his tone poems. Among the latter are *Finlandia* (1899), *Four Legends from the Kalevala* (1893–1895), and *Pohjola's Daughter* (1906).

1866   Erik Satie   86

born 17 May 1866, Honfleur, France
died 1 July 1925, Paris, France

A composer who enjoyed entertaining with whimsical deceptions, Satie was one of the "bohemians" who rebelled against excessive Romanticism at the turn of the century.

Much of Satie's music is without programmatic content. But it is often fancifully titled just for the sake of being odd. His ballet *Parade* (1917), on which he collaborated with Jean Cocteau and Picasso, includes orchestration for a siren and a wheel-of-fortune. In one of his piano pieces, Satie instructs the performer to play "like a nightingale with a toothache." These eccentricities were a result of his attempt to burst the romantic balloon and to challenge what he considered stagnant conventions of beauty.

Although his works are largely experimental, Satie's harmonic style and his economy of forces influenced Debussy and Ravel; and it was also critical for two post-World-War-I groups: *Les Six* and the School of Arcueil. Among his most popular pieces are the *Gymnopedies* (1888), *Three Pieces in the Shape of a Pear* for piano four-hands, and the "symphonic drama" *Socrate* (1919) for women's voices and orchestra.

1868   Scott Joplin   87

born 24 November 1868, Texarkana, Texas
died 11 April 1917, New York City

American ragtime pianist and composer, Joplin was one of the most important figures in classic ragtime. In his teens he traveled as an itinerant musician throughout Texas, Louisiana, and the Mississippi Valley, and the folk music he heard and the musicians he listened to influenced his later work greatly. In 1893 he met many ragtime pianists at the World's Columbian Exposition in Chicago. Among these pianists was Otis Saunders, one of the great ragtime pioneers. It was

Saunders who persuaded Joplin to write down some of the music he was playing. Joplin and Saunders became very close friends and later played ragtime together in Sedalia, Missouri. In 1899 at the Maple Leaf Club in Sedalia, John S. Stark, a music publisher, heard Joplin play. This was a turning point in Joplin's career for out of this meeting came the publication of the ragtime classic, *Maple Leaf Rag*. The association between Joplin and Stark was to continue throughout their lives. Joplin's interest in opera became important around 1903 and was to dominate the entire latter part of his life. His first opera, *Guest of Honor* (1903), was a failure, as was his second opera, *Treemonisha* (1911). Joplin published and copyrighted *Treemonisha* at his own expense, and his disappointment at its failure darkened the close of his career and contributed to his failing health. Among Scott Joplin's most famous rags are: *Maple Leaf Rag* (1899), *Sunflower Slow Drag* (1901), *Easy Winners* (1901), *The Entertainer* (1902), and *Heliotrope Bouquet* (1907). The complete works of Joplin were published in 1971 by the New York Public Library.

1872   Alexander Scriabin   88

born 6 January 1872, Moscow, Russia
died 27 April 1915, Moscow, Russia

Scriabin abandoned a career in the military to study music at the Moscow Conservatory in 1888. He won a medal there in 1892 and taught piano at the conservatory from 1898 to 1904. After that he concentrated on composing and concertizing, and he toured the United States in 1906.

His early works for piano show the influence of Chopin and Liszt, the former exerting his influence especially in Scriabin's *Preludes*, Opp. 33, 44, and 48. His later works reflect his fascination with mysticism, most notably in the *Dances*, Op. 73, and in the ten piano sonatas. Wagner's influence may be felt in his orchestral works, which include *Poem of Ecstasy* (1908) and *Poem of Fire* (1910). Much of Scriabin's music was based on a "mystic chord"—a chromatic thirteenth chord.

1872   Ralph Vaughan Williams   89

born 12 October 1872, Down Ampney, Gloucestshire, England
died 26 August 1958, London, England

A student of Max Bruch and Maurice Ravel, Vaughan Williams helped revive the English musical tradition that had been stagnant since the days of Purcell, Tallis, and other early English composers. Vaughan Williams was a professor of composition at the Royal College of Music and conductor of the London Bach Choir. His most important works are his nine symphonies. The later symphonies exhibit advanced harmonic techniques. *Fantasia on Greensleeves* and *Fantasia on a Theme of Thomas Tallis* are well known.

1873   Sergei Rachmaninoff   90

born 1 April 1873, Novgorod, Russia
died 28 March 1943, Beverly Hills, California

Composer and piano virtuoso, Rachmaninoff graduated from the St. Petersburg and Moscow conservatories. He toured Russia, performing his own music, including the *Prelude in C♯ Minor* that he wrote at the age of twenty. He left Russia in 1917, moving first to Switzerland, then to the United States, while continuing his concert career. He also composed an opera, *Francesca da Rimini* (1905), four piano concertos, and numerous songs. The *Second Piano Concerto* and the *Rhapsody on a Theme of Paganini*—also for piano and orchestra—remain among the most popular of modern concert pieces.

1874   Arnold Schoenberg   91

born 13 September 1874, Vienna, Austria
died 13 July 1951, Los Angeles, California

1882:   Began violin lessons and composed duets to play with his teacher.

1880's and 1890's: Death of his father forced him to work in a bank. Three friends turned him toward music: Oscar Adler, who taught him theory; David Bach; and Alexander von Zemlinsky, who taught him counterpoint.

1899:   First public performance of his music in Vienna, a string quartet. Was encouraged to compose *Verklärte Nacht* (*Transfigured Night*) for string sextet.

1900:   Began composing *Gurrelieder*, a cantata for solo voices, chorus, and huge orchestra, which was completed 1913.

1901:   Married Zemlinsky's sister, Mathilde. Moved to Berlin and became conductor of music-hall songs and operettas.

1902:   Composed tone poem *Pelléas und Mélisande*, unaware of Debussy's opera of the same name.

1903:   Returned to Vienna and began a long teaching career. Students included Berg and Webern. His music had many harsh critics, but supporters like the Rosé String Quartet performed his music despite violently hostile audiences.

1908:   *Piano Pieces*, Op. 11, and the song-cycle *Das Buch der hängenden Garten* (*The Book of the Hanging Garden*), Op. 15, are the first works in which the tonal system is entirely abandoned, an event in music history of overwhelming importance.

1910–1911:   Wrote *Treatise on Harmony*. Met actress Albertine Zehme, and at her suggestion wrote *Pierrot Lunaire*, three cycles of seven poems each, for voice and chamber ensemble. The solo voice part is a mixture of song and speech known as *Sprechstimme*.

1912–1915:   Made international tour conducting his own music. At concerts in March, 1913, the police were called to quell audience protest.

1915–1923:   Served in armed forces and wrote poems for a projected trilogy of oratorios. Returned to Vienna and founded *Verein für musikalische Privat-Aufführungen,* an organization that sponsored performances of contemporary works.

1923:   First serial pieces: *Five Piano Pieces*, Op. 23, and *Serenade*, Op. 24. Developed twelve-tone technique and used it nearly all his life. His wife died.

1925:   Married Gertrud Kolisch, sister of violinist Rudolf Kolisch.

1925–1930:   Composed *Third String Quartet* (1927) and *Variations for Orchestra* (1928). Both were greeted stormily.

1933:   Dismissed from his teaching post by the Nazi government. He moved to Paris, then to the United States, settling in Los Angeles.

1936: The *Violin Concerto* and the *Fourth String Quartet,* both important twelve-tone works. In following period, he produced tonal works that use elements of the twelve-tone system: *Kol Nidre* and *Variations on a Recitative* (1943).

1944: Retired from teaching. Completed *A Survivor of Warsaw* (1947).

1951: At his death, his great biblical opera *Moses und Aron* remained unfinished.

1874   Gustav Holst   92

born 21 September 1874, Cheltenham, England
died 25 May 1934, London, England

Of predominantly English ancestry, Holst was a friend of the English composer, Ralph Vaughan Williams. Neuritis prevented a career as a pianist, so Holst took up the trombone and performed in several opera orchestras. His own compositions include operas, choral works, and numerous orchestral pieces. *The Planets* (1916) is one of his better-known orchestral works.

1874   Charles Ives   93

born 20 October 1874, Danbury, Connecticut
died 19 May 1954, New York City

Ives was the son of a band leader. Played in his father's band while a boy, then studied organ with Dudley Buck.

1893–1902: Served as organist in churches in New Haven; Bloomfield, New Jersey; and New York, while working as an insurance clerk. (He eventually achieved a position of great eminence in the insurance field.)

1898: Graduated from Yale, where he studied with Horatio Parker.

1906–1916: Composed his major works, each progressively more experimental in character. His style is characterized by the *Piano Sonata No. 2,* "Concord, Mass., 1840–1860," that was written between 1909 and 1915, a work which demonstrates his harmonic complexity as well as his interest in native American themes.

1923: Stopped composing and retired from his insurance company due to ill health.

1947: His *Third Symphony,* composed in 1904, was performed and won a Pulitzer Prize.

1875   Maurice Ravel   94

born 7 March 1875, Ciboure, France
died 28 December 1937, Paris, France

1882: Began taking piano lessons with Henri Ghys.
1886: Took harmony lessons from Charles René.
1889: Entered Paris Conservatory, studied harmony with Pessard and com-

position with Fauré. Studied and was influenced by Chabrier, Satie, Liszt, and the Russians.

1893–1898:   Early compositions for piano demonstrated his already distinct individual style.

1898–1899:   First public performance of the songs, *Scheherazade*, was unfavorably reviewed; he was branded a revolutionary. As a consequence, he was refused the Prix de Rome in 1902 and 1903.

1899:   *Pavane pour une infante défunte (Pavane for a Dead Princess)*.

1901:   *Jeux d'eau (Play of the Water)* for piano.

1902:   *String quartet*.

1905:   In spite of the high level of already published works, the committee for the Prix de Rome declared him ineligible to compete. Some of his previous critics became outraged at this treatment.

1908:   *Miroirs (Mirrors)* and *Gaspard de la nuit* were further developments of his original harmonic style.

1912:   *Ma Mère l'oye (Mother Goose)* orchestrated from piano score; also *Valses nobles et sentimentales*. His most significant orchestral piece, a ballet for Diaghilev—with choral background—performed: *Daphnis et Chloe*.

1913:   *Trois Poèmes de Mallarmé*, representing the change of style toward the simple and abstract—concentrating on line more than on color.

1914–1922   *Le Tombeau de Couperin* and the *Sonata for Violin and Cello*, landmarks of the later style. Although depressed by World War I, he was anxious to serve and finally joined the air force.

1919:   Suffered neurasthenia attack.

1920:   *La Valse*, expressing his bitterness. He created a sensation by refusing the decoration of the Legion of Honor; he disliked official posts and distinctions and was still bitter over the Prix de Rome rejection. He left Paris and semi-retired in a villa at Montfort l'Amaury. He composed sporadically and collected mechanical toys.

1922:   Orchestrated Mussorgsky's *Pictures at an Exhibition*. Visited London, Venice, and Holland.

1928:   Composed *Bolero*, an orchestral experiment in crescendo technique, utilizing a Spanish dance rhythm and two simple themes (with no development). Toured the United States and went to England to receive an honorary degree from Oxford.

1930–1931:   Composed two piano concertos. One, for the left hand alone, for Paul Wittgenstein, the concert pianist who lost an arm in the war.

1932:   Toured Europe conducting the *G Major Piano Concerto*. October auto accident precipitated a nervous breakdown from which he never recovered.

1876   Manuel de Falla   95

born 23 November 1876, Cadiz, Spain
died 14 November 1946, Atta Gracia, Cordoba, Argentina

Early in his career de Falla won a prize for his opera *La Vida Breve (The Short Life*, 1905). His reputation was assured by *Nights in the Gardens of Spain* (1916) and Diaghilev's production of his ballet *The Three-Cornered Hat* (1919).

1877   Ernst von Dohnányi   96

born 27 July 1877, Poszony, Hungary
died 9 February 1960, New York City

Dohnányi wrote in a late romantic idiom. He produced three operas, three symphonies, and the *Variations on a Nursery Theme* for piano and orchestra. *Ruralia Hungarica* is a collection of piano pieces based on Hungarian folk sources and showing some of the composer's most adventurous harmonic writing.

1879   Ottorino Respighi   97

born 9 July 1879, Bologna, Italy
died 18 April 1936, Rome Italy

Italian composer. While in St. Petersburg, he studied with Rimski-Korsakov. Although he wrote operas, ballets, and chamber music, he is best known for his symphonic poems, among them *Le Fontane di Roma* (*The Fountains of Rome*, 1917) and *I Pini di Roma* (*The Pines of Rome*, 1924).

1880   Ernest Bloch   98

born 24 July 1880, Geneva, Switzerland
died 15 July 1959, Portland, Oregon

Although born in Switzerland, Bloch spent the greater part of his creative life in the United States, eventually becoming a citizen. He studied violin with Ysaÿe and composition with Rasse at the Brussels Conservatory in Belgium. In 1917 he settled in New York City and taught at the Mannes School of Music. During this period he frequently conducted his own compositions in many cities, among them New York where he directed the New York Philharmonic for a performance of his *C-Sharp Minor Symphony*. In 1919 he won the Coolidge Prize for his *Suite for Viola and Piano*. In 1927 he won first prize offered by the magazine, *Musical America* for his *America: An Epic Rhapsody*. In it Bloch attempted to portray in music the history of the United States. Returning to the United States in 1939 after a brief period in Switzerland, Bloch eventually moved to Oregon where he spent the remainder of his life. During this time he devoted himself chiefly to composition. Among his works are: *Trois Poèmes juifs* (1913) for orchestra; *Schelomo* (1916), a rhapsody for cello and orchestra; *Baal Shem* (1923) for violin and piano; the *Israel Symphony* (1912–1916), with voices; *Suite Modale* (1957) for flute solo and strings; and the *Concerto Grosso No. 1* (1924–1925). He wrote one opera, *Macbeth*, which was produced at the Opéra-Comique in Paris in 1910.

1881   Béla Bartók   99

born 25 March 1881, Nagyszentimiklos, Hungary
died 26 September 1945, New York City

1886: Mother taught him piano. Began writing music at age nine.

1891: Made debut as pianist.

1894: Began studying music with Laszlo Erkel, then at Budapest Academy of Music.

1904: First major orchestral work, *Kossuth Symphony*, performed in Budapest. Became interested in Hungarian folk music. Traveled through the country studying musical traditions and taking copious notes. Results first shown in *Twenty Hungarian Folksongs* (1908), on which he collaborated with Kodály. Throughout his career his music utilized authentic folk rhythms and melodies.

1907–1934: Served as professor of piano at Budapest Academy while continuing to compose and to study folk music.

1907–1917: Married one of his pupils.

1919: Composed *The Miraculous Mandarin*.

1920's: Made concert tours as pianist, performing his own works.

1923: Divorced his wife and married Ditta Pasztory, a pianist.

1926–1939: Composed *Mikrokosmos*, a teaching collection of 153 pieces for piano in six volumes.

1927: Opera *Bluebeard's Castle* performed in Budapest.

1927–1928: Completed *Third* and *Fourth* string quartets.

1936: *Music for Strings, Percussion, and Celesta*.

1940: Moved to the United States; composed *Concerto for Two Pianos, Percussion, and Orchestra*. Worked as a research associate in folk music at Columbia University.

1882   Igor Stravinsky   100

born 17 June 1882, Oranienbaum, Russia
died 6 April 1971, New York City

Stravinsky was the son of a leading bass at the St. Petersburg Opera.

1890–1906: Took piano lessons and studied harmony and counterpoint texts. Studied law at the university, as his father desired, while learning orchestration from Rimski-Korsakov.

1906: Married cousin, Catherine Gabrielle, who encouraged him to become a composer. Completed *Symphony* and a cycle of songs.

1908: First works performed. Encouraging response led him to compose *Scherzo fantastique* and *Fireworks*. The performance of these works the following year brought him to the attention of Serge Diaghilev, who invited him to compose for the Ballet Russe.

1910–1919—The ballet period:

Firebird created a world reputation for Stravinsky. *Petrouchka* (1911). *Le Sacre du printemps* (*The Rite of Spring*, 1913) caused a riot at Paris premiere, with its pagan rhythms, harsh dissonance, and exotic orchestration. *L'Histoire du soldat* (*The Soldier's Tale*, 1918) evidences humor, using dances like the tango and ragtime.

1919–1950—The neoclassic period:

1919: *Pulcinella* ballet marked the influence of baroque composer, Pergolesi, both in style and in actual use of Pergolesi's themes.

1922–1928: *Mavra*, a comic opera with a Russian subject; *Octet for Winds;*

Oedipus Rex, an opera-oratorio; *Apollon musagète,* a classical ballet; *The Fairy's Kiss,* a tribute to Tchaikovsky using some of his melodies.

1930:   *Symphony of Psalms,* a work for chorus and orchestra, featuring a double fugue as the middle movement.

1934:   Having lived in Paris since 1919, Stravinsky became a French citizen, knowing that he could not return to the Soviet Union under Stalin.

1938:   *Dumbarton Oaks Concerto,* inspired by Bach's *Brandenburg Concerti.*

1939:   Moved permanently to the United States, first lecturing at Harvard University, then settling in Hollywood. He continued to tour the world as guest conductor.

1950:   *The Rake's Progress,* opera written in the neoclassic style. Premiere in Venice was an international event.

1952–1971—Period of abstract works:

Utilized twelve-tone technique, also medieval modes. *Septet* (1953); *Agon* (1957), a ballet; *Threni* (1958), a work for chorus, soloists, and orchestra, based on words of the Prophet Jeremiah.

1962:   Made appearance as conductor in Russia.

1966–1971:   *Requiem Canticles,* one of the last large works, for chorus and orchestra.

1882   Zoltan Kodály   101

born 16 December 1882, Kecskemet, Hungary
died 6 March 1967, Budapest, Hungary

Kodály was a scholar of Hungarian folk music and, together with Bartók, collected great numbers of folk pieces. His music includes an opera, *Hary Janos* (1925), and orchestral works such as the *Galanta Dances* (1933). Much influenced by folk music research, his compositions are highly nationalistic. He is known for his reform of school music in Hungary, developing a teaching method that is still influential in several countries, including the United States. The method is based on his extensive research into the folk sources of Hungarian music and is predicated on the idea that singing is the base upon which to build all music learning.

1883   Anton von Webern   102

born 3 December 1883, Vienna, Austria
died 15 September 1945, Mittersill, Austria

Studied musicology at Vienna University, receiving his Ph.D., in 1906, after which he studied composition with Arnold Schoenberg.

1908–1914:   Held various conducting poses in Europe. *Passacaglia for Orchestra* (1908) is a fairly conventional work, but his *Five Pieces for Orchestra* (1913) shows full conversion to atonality.

1918:   Settled in Mödling, composing and teaching composition.

1924:   Adopted twelve-tone technique in *Three Sacred Songs* and became one of the most austere and pointillistic composers after Schoenberg. Works of the period before World War II include *Trio* for violin, viola, and cello (1927); and *Symphony* (1928).

1930's: The Nazis banned Webern's music as "cultural Bolshevism." His teaching and lecturing continued in secret. Works from this period are still relatively short and austere, including *Concerto for Nine Instruments* (1934), *Das Augenlicht* (1935), and a set of *Piano Variations* (1936).

1940–1945:   Three great works show the culmination of his genius: the first and second cantatas, and the *Variations for Orchestra.*

1945:   Moved his family to Mittersill, near Salzburg, for safety, but he was accidentally shot by an American soldier. (Webern was apparently taking an evening stroll, in violation of the strict curfew in effect during the early days of the post-war period.)

1883   Edgard Varèse   103

born 22 December 1883, Paris, France
died 6 November 1965, New York City

Having begun his career as an engineer, Varèse studied mathematics and science. Determined to become a musician, he studied at the Schola Cantorum under d'Indy and Roussel, and then went to the Paris Conservatory to study with Widor.

In Berlin he founded a chorus and conducted orchestras. Many of his early works from this period were destroyed by him later as being unworthy first attempts. During World War I he served in the French army; then in 1915 he came to the United States, where he settled permanently. His composition *Hyperprism* (1923) aroused adverse reaction but helped circulate his name in musical circles. After *Equatorial* (1934) he stopped composing for twenty years, resuming his study of mathematics and science. In the 1950's he turned to electronic composition, demonstrated by his work *Deserts* (1954).

Although his works were frowned upon in the 1920's and 1930's, the public caught up with his aesthetics during the 1960's. Varèse is now regarded as one of the boldest pioneers of the new music.

1885   Alban Berg   104

born 9 February 1885, Vienna, Austria
died 24 December 1935, Vienna, Austria

Berg was born into an upper-middle-class family.

1904–1911:   Worked with Schoenberg, who gave him great encouragement. Composed the impressionistic *Seven Early Songs* (1905–1908) and *Piano Sonata,* Op. 1 (1908). Married singer Helene Nahowski in 1911.

1914:   His works from this time were less and less tonal. *Four Pieces for Clarinet and Piano* (1913) and *Three Orchestral Pieces* (1914) demonstrated his attempts to synthesize Schoenberg with the architectural strength of Mahler and the harmonic subtleties of Debussy.

1917–1926:   Period of mastery of atonality and serial style. Products of this period included the opera *Wozzeck* (1917–1921), *Chamber Concerto* (1925), and *Lyric Suite* (1926).

1928–1935:   Although serial, *Lulu* (1928–1935) and the *Violin Concerto* (1935) show evidence of tonality. Berg died having completed just thirteen works.

1887   Heitor Villa-Lobos   105

born 5 March 1887, Rio de Janeiro, Brazil
died 17 November 1959, Rio de Janeiro, Brazil

At the age of 18, Villa-Lobos was an accomplished cellist, touring northern Brazil and studying his country's folk music. His compositons, numbering more than 2,000, include church music, chamber music, and symphonies. During the 1920's he toured Europe as a conductor; there he came under the influence of Ravel. During the 1930's he composed his famous series of suites *Bachianas Brasileiras*—Brazilian music in the style of Bach.

1890   Jacques Ibert   106

born 15 August 1890, Paris, France
died 5 February 1962, Paris, France

French composer. Won the Prix de Rome in 1919, while at the Paris Conservatory, for his cantata, *Le Poète et la Fée* (*The Poet and the Fairy*). A symphonic suite, *Escales* (*Ports of Call*, 1922), written in Rome, is a well-known work.

1890   Frank Martin   107

born 15 September 1890, Geneva, Switzerland
died 21 November 1974, Naarden, Holland

Swiss composer. His early works show the influence of Franck and the French Impressionists. The *Petite Symphonie Concertante*, written for harp, harpsichord, piano, and two string orchestras, is one of his best-known works. In *Le Vin herbe*, a dramatic oratorio, based on the subject of Tristram, he has combined twelve-tone techniques with chordal and homophonic writing.

1890   Bohuslav Martinů   108

born 8 December 1890, Policka, Czechoslovakia
died 28 August 1959, Liestal, Switzerland

Martinů wrote operas, chamber music, and six symphonies. His first symphony was commissioned by Serge Koussevitsky and was performed in 1942. Among his better-known works are *Fantasia Concertante* (1959) and a *Sonata for Flute and Piano* (1945).

1891   Sergei Prokofiev   109

born 23 April 1891, Sontsovka, Russia
died 5 March 1953, Moscow, Russia

Taught the piano by his mother, Prokofiev wrote a piano score at the age of nine for an opera, *The Giant*. Two years later he finished another opera score, *On Desert Islands*. That same year he began studying with Reinhold Glière in Moscow, under whose guidance he wrote two more operas. In 1904, Prokofiev entered the St. Petersburg Conservatory, where he studied under Rimsky-Korsakov, Liadov, Essipova, and Tcherepnin. By the time of his graduation in 1914, he had completed the *Scythian Suite* for orchestra, a piano concerto, (for which he had won the Anton Rubinstein prize), four piano sonatas, and another opera.

His early style is austere and pure. Prokofiev avoided sentimental program music and romantic devices; instead his music depends on rhythmic and dynamic power.

During the Russian Revolution, Prokofiev left Russia, traveling to Japan and the United States, before settling in Paris. There, he worked closely with Serge Diaghilev in producing ballets, including *Chout* (*The Buffoon*, 1920), *L'Enfant prodigue* (*The Prodigal Son*, 1928), and *Le Pas d'acier* (*The Steel Trot*, 1921). In 1933 he moved back to Moscow and produced a variety of works: *Peter and the Wolf* (1936); a ballet, *Romeo and Juliet* (1935–1936); an opera, *War and Peace* (1941–1952); and scores for the films *Lieutenant Kije* (1933) and *Alexander Nevsky* (1938). Although he sometimes hinted at polytonality, Prokofiev was basically a tonal composer. His rhythmic boldness and unusual harmonies had great influence on the next generation of Soviet composers.

1892   Arthur Honegger   110

born 10 March 1892, Le Havre, France
died 27 November 1955, Paris, France

Although Honegger prized his opera *Antigone* highly, it has been mainly his oratorios that have met with success. These include *Le Roi David* (*King David*), *Les Cris du monde* (*The Cries of Mankind*), and *La Danse des morts* (*Dance of the Dead*).

1892   Germaine Tailleferre   111

born 19 April 1892, Paris, France

The sole female member of *Les Six*, she later developed an interest in the eighteenth-century French masters and wrote solo piano pieces and chamber music.

1892   Darius Milhaud   112

born 4 September 1892, Aix-en-Provence, France
died 24 June 1974, Geneva, Switzerland

An extremely prolific composer, his dramatic compositions are important: *Orestes, Christoph Colombe*, and *Maximilian and Bolivar*. His ballet, *La Création du monde* (*Creation of the World*, 1923) is popular. A member of *Les Six*, Milhaud's compositions number in the several hundreds. He taught composition at Mills College for many years prior to his death.

1893   Douglas Moore   113

born 10 August 1893, Cutchogue, New York
died 25 July 1969, Greenport, New York

American composer of broad interests whose successes were chiefly in American-subject operas, such as *The Devil and Daniel Webster* (1939) and *The Ballad of Baby Doe* (1955).

1894   Walter Piston   114

born 20 January 1894, Rockland, Maine

Composer of finely-crafted music. His six symphonies show a master technician working in an absolute style coupled with occasional touches of Americanism. Author of several highly-used textbooks on various aspects of the musical craft.

1895   Carl Orff   115

born 10 July 1895, Munich, Germany

German composer, educator, and musicologist. His first stage work, and perhaps his most famous composition, is *Carmina Burana* (1935–1936), a scenic oratorio. *Antigonae*, first performed at the Salzburg Festival of 1949, is a musical play in which Orff has reverted to the principles of the ancient theater, emphasizing the unity of music with drama and dance.

1895   Paul Hindemith   116

born 16 November 1895, Hanau, Germany
died 28 December 1963, Frankfurt, Germany

Hindemith pursued his conservatory studies from 1909 until 1917, when he served in the German army. After the war, Hindemith became dissatisfied with his style of composition, which was heavily influenced by Brahms; for ten years he searched for a style that he could cultivate as his own. Coming into contact with the International Society for Contemporary Music, Hindemith was on his way to becoming a world figure like Stravinsky, and later, Bartók. The major products of this period of search are the *Third Quartet* and *Kleine Kammermusik*.

His opera *Mathis der Maler* (*Mathis the Painter*), which typifies his style, was scheduled for performance in 1934, but the premiere was banned by the Nazis.

In 1937, Hindemith finally left Germany and traveled for two years before settling in the United States, where he became a professor at Yale. During these years he wrote some orchestral works, but the period was dominated by the composing of sonatas for various solo instruments.

Shortly after his series of Norton Lectures at Harvard, delivered in 1949 and 1950, he returned to Europe, becoming a professor and conductor at Zurich University.

1896   Virgil Thomson   117

born 25 November 1896, Kansas City, Missouri

Thomson studied in Paris and was unmistakably influenced by Satie and *Les Six*. He first rose to prominence in 1928 with *Four Saints in Three Acts*, an opera with text by Gertrude Stein. Most of his music has wit, simplicity, and directness; and much of it is based on American hymn tunes and folk songs. His work includes *Symphony on a Hymn Tune* (1928), a ballet entitled *Filling Station* (1937), and *The Mother of Us All* (1947), a second opera with text by Gertrude Stein.

1896   Roger Sessions   118

born 28 December 1896, Brooklyn, New York

An American influenced by Ernest Bloch and Schoenberg, his works include concerti for piano and for violin, and five symphonies that are dense in texture and individualistic in character. Sessions has taught several generations of American composers at the University of California and Princeton University. His opera *Montezuma* has been produced in Berlin.

1897   Henry Cowell   119

born 11 March 1897, Menlo Park, California
died 11 December 1965, Shady, New York

A developer of tone cluster technique, whose music drew on American folk tunes and later on music of the Orient. His *Hymn and Fuguing Tunes*, Nos. 1–8 (1943–1947) were based on the "fuguing tunes" of William Billings, the eighteenth-century New England composer.

1898   Roy Harris   120

born 12 February 1898, Lincoln County, Oklahoma

Composer of chamber works and choral pieces that are filled with Americana and use tonal techniques in a conservative style. His work includes both a choral piece and an orchestral work based on *When Johnny Comes Marching Home* and pieces utilizing numerous other American folk and patriotic songs. His *Symphony No. 3* (1938) is among his better-known works.

1898   George Gershwin   121

born 26 September 1898, Brooklyn, New York
died 11 July 1937, Hollywood, California

With the publication of *Swanee* in 1919, twenty-one-year-old Gershwin's popularity began. He collaborated with his brother Ira on several Broadway musical hits, including *Lady Be Good* (1924) and *Strike Up the Band* (1929). In compositions like *Rhapsody in Blue* (1924) for piano and orchestra, Gershwin combined the mood of America with a European-derived formal structure. His most enduring work is the folk opera, *Porgy and Bess* (1935).

1899   Francis Poulenc   122

born 7 January 1899, Paris, France
died 30 January 1963, Paris, France

An excellent pianist from an early age, Poulenc cultivated an image as a social rebel; his style of composition tended toward witty flippancy. The works of the early 1940's show some abandonment of mannerism. In his final period he adopted a more serious approach in two operas: *Dialogue des Carmélites* and *La Voix humaine*.

1899   Carlos Chávez   123

born 13 June 1899, Mexico City, Mexico

One of the outstanding composers produced by Mexico. Chávez' travels to Europe influenced his style, and his ballet *H. P.* ("Horsepower") of 1927 resembles the work of the Italian futurists. Other works embody the spirit and rhythms of pre-Columbian Latin America; his *Sinfonia India* (1935) is characteristic of his nationalistic style.

1900   Kurt Weill   124

born 2 March 1900, Dessau, Germany
died 3 April 1950, New York City

Composer of music for the theater, he collaborated with Bertolt Brecht in 1928 on *The Threepenny Opera* and again on the even more socially critical *Rise and Fall of the City of Mahagonny*. Leaving Germany in 1933, Weill moved to America and composed several Broadway musicals, among them *Lady in the Dark, Knickerbocker Holiday,* and *Street Scene*. His folk opera, *Down in the Valley,* is frequently performed today.

1900   Otto Luening   125

born 15 June 1900, Milwaukee, Wisconsin

A composer who has experimented with electronic synthesizers and with recorded tape music, Leuning's output includes two symphonic poems, a symphony,
a suite for strings, and an opera *Evangeline.*

1900   George Antheil   126

born 8 July 1900, Trenton, New Jersey
died 12 February 1959, New York City

A pioneer in the use of non-musical sounds in serious musical forms, his major
work, *Ballet méchanique,* scored for anvils, bells, pianos, etc., was followed by
works in a more traditional vein.

1900   Ernst Krenek   127

born 23 August 1900, Vienna, Austria

Twelve-tone composer who settled in America in 1938. His output includes the
jazz-influenced opera, *Jonny Spielt auf!* (1927), as well as electronic music.

1900   Aaron Copland   128

born 14 November 1900, Brooklyn, New York

After several years of piano study, Copland took harmony lessons from Rubin
Goldmark, attended the Fontainbleau School of Music in France, and studied for
three years with Nadia Boulanger. His early works, including the *Dance Symphony* and the *Piano Variations*, strove to discover a place for jazz in the more
serious forms.

Copland simplified his style and began composing music for specific functions.
His movie scores include *Of Mice and Men, Our Town, The Heiress*—for which
he won an Academy Award—and *The Red Pony.* He began drawing his inspiration from American folk music and American history, in such works as *Rodeo,
Billy the Kid*, and *Appalachian Spring.*

Continuing to utilize a simple, clear style, Copland has recently composed
works capturing the moods of growth, strength, and beauty in the modern world
with pieces like *Fanfare for the Common Man* and *Music for a Great City.* Copland has concentrated on serialism in some of his most recent works.

1901   Harry Partch   129

born 24 June 1901, Oakland, California

Partch formulated a forty-three-tone scale and developed new instruments needed for the performance of his microtonal music. His theories are set forth in his book entitled *Genesis of a Music*. A few of his instruments are elongated violas, kitharas with seventy-two strings, harmonic canons with forty-four strings, boos (made of giant Philippine bamboo reeds), and cloud-chamber bowls.

Reverting to classical Greek concepts, he has attempted to combine music with dance and speech into a single entity. Among his works are the following: *8 Hitchhiker Inscriptions from a Calif. Highway Railing* and *U.S. Highball—a Musical Account of a Transcontinental Hobo Trip*, written for chorus and instruments; *King Oedipus* (produced 1952); and *Plectra and Percussion Dances: Castor and Pollux* (1952).

1902   William Walton   130

born 29 March 1902, Oldham, England

A composer with a broad spectrum, Walton's output includes symphonies, chamber music, concertos, and choral works. Included among his *oeuvre* is the *Te Deum*, which was performed at Queen Elizabeth II's coronation in 1953. His best-known work is the impish *Façade*, written in collaboration with the poetess Edith Sitwell.

1903   Aram Khachaturian   131

born 6 June 1903, Tiflis, Russia

Khachaturian, the son of a bookbinder, did not take up the study of music until he was a teen-ager. He studied composition at the Moscow Conservatory under Miaskovsky. In his music he often uses the scales and melodies of his native Caucasus. Among his most popular works is the brilliant *Piano Concerto* (1936). The *Violin Concerto* (1940) won the Stalin Prize. He has also written a ballet, *Gayne* (1942), and symphonies.

1904   Luigi Dallapiccola   132

born 3 February 1904, Pisino, Yugoslavia
died 19 February 1975, Florence, Italy

Italian composer. In the 1930's he turned to twelve-tone writing. This is evidenced in his opera *The Prisoner* (1949) and *Canti di liberazione* (*Songs of Liberation*, 1954) for chorus and orchestra.

1904   Goffredo Petrassi   133

born 16 July 1904, Zagarolo (nr. Rome), Italy

Petrassi was greatly influenced by Alfredo Casella in combining modern techniques with old forms. He also developed an interest in twelve-tone techniques. Among his works is *Nonsense* for chorus a cappella (1952) and *Concerto No. 5* for orchestra (1955).

1904   Dmitri Kabalevsky   134

born 30 December 1904, St. Petersburg, Russia

Russian composer and pianist. He has written in a wide variety of genres—operas, chamber music, orchestral works, and choral works. Among these are *Requiem* (1963), concertos for violin and for cello, and *Colas Breugnon: Overture* (1938).

1905   Michael Tippett   135

born 2 January 1905, London, England

English composer and teacher. An oratorio, *Child of our Time,* written in 1944, is the story of a boy trapped by an inhuman wartime machine. He has also written a *Concerto for Double String Orchestra* (1939) and an opera *The Midsummer Marriage,* from which the *Ritual Dances* are often performed.

1906   Dmitri Shostakovich   136

born 25 September 1906, St. Petersburg, Russia

Revealing his musical talents at an early age, Shostakovich entered Petrograd Conservatory at age thirteen as a piano student. He won first prize in the International Chopin Competition in 1927. His talents as a symphonist had already been revealed in his *Symphony No. 1.*

Although his love of Russia is basic, and he does not openly object to the principles of ideologically controlled art, Shostakovich has often been officially attacked for his dissonance and avant-garde techniques. Since he never totally abandoned tonality, his music has survived these repressive onslaughts.

Appointed in 1937 as professor at the Leningrad Conservatory, Shostakovich has occupied an important place in Russia's musical life. He has composed program music; and several of his fifteen symphonies portray events in Russian history. He has also written operas—including *Lady Macbeth from Minsk*—piano music, and concertos for violin and for piano.

1908   Olivier Messiaen   137

born 10 December 1908, Avignon, France

Messiaen's father was a professor of literature; his mother was the poetess, Cécile Sauvage. Messiaen spent much of his youth at Grenoble, where he taught himself the piano. In 1919, at age eleven, he entered the Paris Conservatory to study composition. Winning several prizes during the 1920's, Messiaen carried on private studies of Hindu rhythms, bird songs, and microtonal music.

Leaving the conservatory, Messiaen was appointed organist at the Trinité in Paris in 1931, the same year that his orchestral work *Les Offrandes oubliées (Forgotten Offerings)* won attention. In 1936, Messiaen was co-founder, along with Jolivet, Lesur, and Baudrier, of the Jeune-France group, representing the vanguard of Parisian composers.

Always a devout Christian, Messiaen demonstrated his religious devotion in a series of works written between 1932 and 1951. His work *Quatre études de rhythme (Four Rhythmic Studies,* 1949) has been extremely influential. Messiaen's theories are expounded in *Technique de mon language musical* (1944) and in a treatise on rhythm. His teachings have been important to many younger composers, especially Pierre Boulez.

1908   Elliott Carter   138

born 11 December 1908, New York City

One of the most significant American composers since World War II, Carter writes music that is thoroughly logical in its structure and style. A student of Gustav Holst and Nadia Boulanger, Carter has taught at Yale and Columbia. His music includes three string quartets—one of which won the Pulitzer Prize—and the *Concerto for Harpsichord, Piano, and Two Chamber Orchestras.*

1910   Samuel Barber   139

born 9 March 1910, West Chester, Pennsylvania

American composer in the late romantic European tradition. Barber is best known for his *Adagio for Strings,* two symphonies, and the opera, *Vanessa.*

1910   William Schuman   140

born 4 August 1910, New York City

Winner of the first Pulitzer Prize in music for his cantata, *A Free Song* (1942). Schuman's music is often based on American tunes. Filled with dynamic energy, Schuman's style features a skillful handling of counterpoint, texture, and orchestral color. He has composed symphonies, string quartets, and a violin concerto.

1910   Rolf Liebermann   141

born 14 September 1910, Zurich, Switzerland

One of the few Swiss composers to have adopted the twelve-tone system, Liebermann's works include *Furioso* for orchestra (1947) and *Symphony No. 1* (1949).

1911   Alan Hovhaness   142

born 8 March 1911, Somerville, Massachusetts

American composer. His style is distinctive because of his extensive use of Armenian modal music. He also has had a strong interest in Indian and Oriental music. Among his better known works are *A Fantasy on Japanese Woodprints* (1965), *Flute Player of the Armenian Mountains* (1946), and *Mysterious Mountain*. He has also written symphonies, songs, and chamber works.

1911   Gian-Carlo Menotti   143

born 7 July 1911, Cadegliano, Italy

Italian-born American composer of operas, sometimes for radio or television. His works include *The Medium* (1946), *The Telephone* (1947), and *Amahl and the Night Visitors* (1951), the popular Christmas favorite, which was originally performed on television.

1911   Vladimir Ussachevsky   144

born 3 November 1911, Hailar, Manchuria

Considered a conservative composer of electronic music, he collaborated with Otto Luening in obtaining an electronic music studio at Columbia University in the early 1950's.

1912   John Cage   145

born 5 September 1912, Los Angeles, California

One of the most influential American composers to emerge since the Second World War, John Cage was a student of Cowell and Schoenberg. His pioneering works for *prepared piano*—including *Amores* (1943) and the *Sonatas and Interludes* (1946–1948)—gained him public attention. Cage has also been a pioneer in *musique concrète* and electronic music. *Imaginary Landscape No. 5* (1952) is made up of taped fragments from forty-three jazz records. The disposition and order of these fragments is determined through chance procedures.

It is in the area of chance music and in musical "silence" that Cage has voyaged to the very edge of credibility. *Music for Piano* (1953) is notated in whole notes; rhythmic patterns are to be created by the player as he wishes. In *Music for Piano,* both the tempo and dynamic level are left to the discretion of the player. In his book *Silence* (1961), Cage states: "And what is the purpose of writing music? One is, of course, not dealing with purposes but dealing with sounds." In the composition *4' 33"*, a piano piece "performed" in silence, the only sounds are those that occur by chance within the hall as the pianist quietly sits at the keyboard. The composition *0' 00"*—"to be performed in any way by anyone"—is typical of Cage's more extreme work. In 1969 Cage and Lejaren Hiller composed/produced *HPSCHD*. The media used are harpsichords, amplified sound tapes, motion picture projectors, foreign language instructions, and psychedelic slides. During the performance the audience is to come and go as it pleases.

In sum, Cage is the true successor to Eric Satie, gloriously carrying on the tradition of *dada*.

1913   Witold Lutoslawski   146

born 25 January 1913, Warsaw, Poland

Studied composition under Maliszewski at the Warsaw Conservatory. Among his well-known works are several albums of children's songs, and his *Variations on a Theme of Paganini* (1941).

1913   Benjamin Britten   147

born 22 November 1913, Lowestoft, Suffolk, England

English composer who is well known for *A Young Person's Guide to the Orchestra*, based on a theme of Henry Purcell. Of major interest are his operas, such as *Peter Grimes, Billy Budd*, and *The Turn of the Screw*, which have revived the English opera tradition. Britten founded the English Opera Group in 1947.

He has also done a set of musical parables that includes *The Prodigal Son, Curlew River*, and *The Burning Fiery Furnace*. Through his collaboration with the Russian cellist Rostropovich, Britten has composed several pieces for cello, including a suite for unaccompanied cello. He has also toured extensively as pianist with the noted English tenor, Peter Pears.

1916   Milton Babbitt   148

born 10 May 1916, Philadelphia, Pennsylvania

Because he is a mathematician as well as a musician, Babbitt has been able to approach music along the lines of analysis and experiment. He has composed twelve-tone works for brass, piano, and chamber ensembles. In this area he was one of the first to explore serialization of non-pitch elements, such as durations and dynamics. *Three Compositions for Piano*, and *Composition for Four Instruments* are works written before 1950 that typify Babbitt's interest in total control through serialization. Among his better-known works are *Vision and Prayer* (1961) and *Relata I and II* (1968) for orchestra. Babbitt is Professor of Music at Princeton University and has traveled widely as a lecturer on contemporary music.

1916   Alberto Ginastera   149

born 11 April 1916, Buenos Aires, Argentina

Ginastera attended the National Conservatory in Argentina, where his gifts as a composer were recognized early. He is a nationalist and the rhythms of the folk and popular music of Argentina flow through much of his music. Among his works are a ballet, *Estancia,* a piano concerto (1961), and two operas, *Don Rodrigo* (1964) and *Bomarzo* (1967).

1918   George Rochberg   150

born 5 July 1918, Paterson, New Jersey

American composer. Published a book about twelve-tone music, entitled *The Hexachord and Its Relation to the Twelve-tone Row.* His symphonic poem, *Night Music,* won the George Gershwin Memorial Award in 1952. In recent works, he has integrated the music of Bach, Mozart, and Mahler into his own atonal fabric.

1918   Leonard Bernstein   151

born 25 August 1918, Lawrence, Massachusetts

A student of Walter Piston, Fritz Reiner, Randall Thompson, and Serge Koussevitsky, Bernstein has achieved renown as a pianist, conductor, and composer. His compositions cover a wide range: symphony, opera, Broadway musical, and liturgical music. Retiring in 1969 after ten years as Musical Director of the New York Philharmonic, Bernstein remains their lifetime laureate conductor. Among his best works are the *Second Symphony "Age of Anxiety,"* for piano and orchestra (1949); a one-act opera, *Trouble in Tahiti* (which he conducted at Brandeis University in 1952), *West Side Story* (1957), and *Mass, A Theatre Piece for Singers, Players, and Dancers* (1971), created for the opening of the John F. Kennedy Center for the Performing Arts.

1920   Bruno Maderna   152

born 21 April 1920, Venice, Italy
died 13 November 1973, Darmstadt, West Germany

Conductor and serial composer, Maderna's works include *Compositions in 3 Tempi, Music in Two Dimensions,* and *Concerto for Oboe and Chamber Orchestra.*

1922   Yannis Xenakis   153

born 29 May 1922, Athens, Greece

Former assistant to the noted architect Le Corbusier, Xenakis composes with "textural blocks" of sound. His dispersion of musicians within the audience to

create an impression of sonic immersion is part of his experimental use of time/
space.

1923   György Ligeti   154

born 28 May 1923, Dicsöszentmarton, Hungary

In 1957–1958 he worked in the Studio for Electronic Music in Cologne. After
teaching at the Stockholm Music Academy in 1961, he eventually settled in
Vienna. His later works are in the area of experimental music. The *Poème Sym-
phonique* (premiered in 1965) is written for one hundred metronomes. *Atmos-
phères* (1961) for orchestra is one of his better-known pieces. His music was
featured in the remarkable futuristic film, *2001, A Space Odyssey*.

1924   Luigi Nono   155

born 29 January 1924, Venice, Italy

Nono is a serialist composer often utilizing Webern's pointillism and displaying
social conscience in such works as *Sul Ponte di Hiroshima* and the opera
Intolleranza.

1925   Pierre Boulez   156

born 26 March 1925, Montbrison, France

One of the most significant composers to emerge from France since World War
II, Boulez is among the most advanced of the avant-garde composers. He has
experimented with *musique concrète,* as in his work *Polyphonie X* (1951). He
also has used aleatoric techniques, as in his *Third Piano Sonata,* in which the performer may arrange the five parts in an order of his choice.

Boulez first began his aesthetic development in Paris in the 1940's, when he was
a student of Messiaen. He studied twelve-tone composition with René Leibowitz,
then moved to total serialism. After World War II, Boulez conducted a theater
orchestra in Paris. In 1954 he organized the "Domaine musical," a yearly concert
series featuring avant-garde works. He soon achieved a reputation as a conductor,
making his American debut in 1964. He had already made his mark as a composer in 1955 with his masterpiece *Le Marteau sans maître* (*The Hammer Without a Master*). In 1966 he disavowed all connection with the French government
in protest of the appointment of conservative composer Marcel Lewandowski as
head of the bureau of the Cultural Ministry. In 1969 Boulez was named to succeed Leonard Bernstein as conductor of the New York Philharmonic.

1925   Luciano Berio   157

born 10 October 1925, Oneglia, Italy

One of the first Italian composers of electronic music. He has used electronic sound, traditional instruments, the spoken word, and music borrowed from earlier composers (mainly Mahler) to create a musical collage in *Sinfonia*, a work performed with the Swingle Singers.

1925   Gunther Schuller   158

born 22 November 1925, New York City

American composer and French horn player, Schuller studied music with his father, a professional violist. When he was barely twenty he played first horn with the Metropolitan Opera Orchestra. He coined the term *Third Stream*, which refers to a blending of the improvisatory elements of jazz with classical forms. One of his best-known works is *Seven Studies on Themes of Paul Klee* (1959). He has also written *Symphony for Brass and Percussion* (1959) and *Concertino for Jazz Quartet and Orchestra* (1959). His opera, *The Visitation* (1965), was premiered with great success in Hamburg.

1926   Morton Feldman   159

born 12 January 1926, New York City

American composer of the avant garde, with special interest in chance concepts. He was strongly influenced by abstract Impressionism and modern painting, and experimented with time-space concepts in music. *Out of "Last Pieces"* (1962) is written on graph paper. In this music he allows the performer to play a given number of notes in any manner he chooses.

1926   Hans Werner Henze   160

born 1 July 1926, Gütersloh, Westphalia, Germany

Possessing versatility in many compositional forms, Henze's style encompasses both tonal and atonal idioms. His output includes several ballets and operas and demonstrates his expertise in combining late romantic orchestration with serial compositional techniques.

1926   Earle Brown   161

born 26 December 1926, Lunenburg, Massachusetts

A student of John Cage, Brown has developed even further his teacher's unique systems of nontraditional notation, sometimes using pictures and symbols rather than notes on a staff.

1928   Jean Barraqué   162

born 17 January 1928, Paris, France

French composer who uses a highly developed serial system, producing a texture as dense and intense as that of late Beethoven. His life-long work, *La Mort de Virgile* (*The Death of Virgil*), was projected for a twenty-five-hour duration and is comprised of both orchestral and choral movements.

1928   Karlheinz Stockhausen   163

born 22 August 1928, Mödrath, Germany

After studies with Messiaen, Stockhausen decided that for his purposes all musical techniques, forms, and media of the past were obsolete. In every subsequent composition, he has striven to invent new expressions, and he has become one of the great experimenters in modern music.

Using Webern's serial technique in his *Kontrapunkte No. 1* (1953), for example, Stockhausen perfected a pointillist system in which notes are sprinkled on the score like paint upon a canvas. His affiliation with Pierre Schaeffer led him into *musique concrète* and electronic media. A new "open form" was developed, in which the performer is given several fragments that he may play in any order he desires. *Klavierstück XI* (1956) is this type of work; the performer may choose from nineteen fragments, six tempi, and various dynamic levels. "Controlled chance" is the key element in open form as developed by Stockhausen.

In 1953, Stockhausen became an associate at the Cologne Radio, where he established one of the first major studios for electronic music. His main electronic work began with *Gesang der Jünglinge* (*Song of the Youth*, 1956) for children's voices and electronically recorded sounds.

Another area in which Stockhausen has experimented is that of "spatial dimension," in which ideally the audience would sit in the center of a spherical auditorium with music converging on all sides. His work *Gruppen* (1957) was his first effort in this area.

1929   Toshiro Mayuzumi   164

born 20 February 1929, Yokohama, Japan

Japanese avant-garde composer. Among his better-known works are *Nirvana Symphony* (1957–1958), *Pieces for Prepared Piano and Strings*, and *Samsara*, a symphonic poem (1962).

1929   Henri Pousseur   165

born 23 July 1929, Malmédy, Belgium

Member of the avant-garde school, Pousseur studied with Pierre Boulez and was influenced by Webern. In addition to compositions for traditional instruments, he has written several electronic scores, among which *Trois visages de Liège* (1961) is one of his better known. It is cast in three movements: I, Air and Water; II, Voice of the City; and III, Forges.

1929   George Crumb   166

born 24 October 1929, Charleston, West Virginia

American avant-garde composer whose distinctive style employs unusual timbres and rhythmic patterns. Crumb is also noted for introducing aleatoric passages into otherwise fully composed pieces. *Night Music I* (1963), for soprano, celesta, piano, and percussion, is an instrumental work that also includes a vocal setting of two poems by Federico Garcia Lorca; it is a particularly interesting work because of the variety of sounds produced by direct manipulation of the piano strings, and the haunting, eerie glissando produced by a water gong. *Ancient Voices of Children* (1970) is a cycle of five songs, also on texts of Lorca, for mezzo-soprano, boy soprano, oboe, mandolin, harp, electric piano, and percussion. In this music Crumb displays a great talent for using the quality of the human voice to evoke specific moods. Crumb's *Echoes of Time and the River* won the Pulitzer Prize in 1968.

1930   Toru Takemitsu   167

born 8 October 1930, Tokyo, Japan

Organized a group called the "Experimental Laboratory" for the purpose of combining modern serial techniques with traditional Japanese music. He has written *Coral Island* (1963) for soprano and orchestra and a *Requiem* for strings (1961).

1931   Sylvano Bussotti   168

born 1 October 1931, Florence, Italy

Italian composer who studied both music and art. In his experimental music he has attempted to combine these disciplines, employing a special optical notation in his writing. Among his works are *Fragmentations* (1962) for harp; and *Memoria* (1962), written for baritone, chorus, and orchestra.

1933   Krzystof Penderecki   169

born 23 November 1933, Debica, Poland

Graduated from Cracow Conservatory in 1958. His interest lies in discovering new sounds and performance techniques. *Strophes*, one of his early compositions, was performed at the 1959 Warsaw Festival and was well received. *Threnody for the Victims of Hiroshima* (1960), written for fifty-two strings, shows his highly original methods of composition. In this work he uses tone clusters; glissandos; "noise" resulting from tapping an instrument with the fingers; and shrill high unstable pitch sounds, achieved by placing the finger on the string directly next to the bowing point. Among his choral works are *Stabat Mater* (1962) for three choirs and *Dies Irae* (*Auschwitz Oratorio*, 1967).

APPENDIXES

Appendix I

A SHORT GUIDE
TO THE FUNDAMENTALS
OF MUSIC

Pitch

Pitch is the term used to designate the "highness" or "lowness" of a particular sound. Technically, pitch refers to the *number of vibrations per second* of a particular musical tone. The more vibrations per second, the higher the pitch of a tone; the fewer vibrations, the lower the pitch. The number of vibrations per second is spoken of as the *frequency*. For example, the frequency of "orchestra *A*" (the pitch to which an orchestra tunes) is 440—that is, 440 vibrations per second. This pitch is commonly referred to as *A 440*.

EXAMPLE 1   Octave Reference Chart

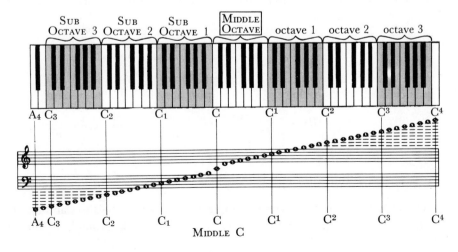

The term *octave*, abbreviated *8ve*, refers in the above chart to a span of eight notes. C^2 is spoken of as being an octave higher than C^1.

The Staff

The musical graph in use today consists of five lines and the adjacent spaces. This is known as the *staff*. A staff may be used for high, middle, or low register voices or instruments.

In the evolution of notation, an eleven-line staff evolved for keyboard instruments, because of their great range. Visual orientation to eleven lines and their spaces was difficult, however, and the necessity for something simpler resulted in the system that is in use today. It is a modification of the eleven-line system. The middle line of the eleven is left out except when the note on that line is needed, and then only a short segment of the line is used—enough on which to write the note. This short line is called a *leger line*. Leger lines and their adjacent spaces are used above or below the staff.

EXAMPLE 2

G clef locates G above MIDDLE C → TREBLE STAFF

MIDDLE C

F clef locates F below MIDDLE C → BASS STAFF

The *G clef* and the *F clef* shown in their proper positions on the Great Staff are stylized versions of the actual letters G and F. These are the two clefs most commonly in use today, but there is a third clef that is used in orchestral scores in writing for instruments in the middle register. This is the *C clef* and locates *middle C*. It is used with two different five-line staves, the alto staff and the tenor staff.

EXAMPLE 3

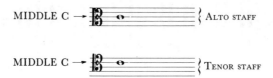

MIDDLE C → ALTO STAFF

MIDDLE C → TENOR STAFF

Sharps and Flats

The Octave Reference Chart (Example 1) shows that the lines and spaces of the staff coincide with the white notes of the keyboard. Example 4 illustrates the black and white keys of the keyboard; the distance between any two adjacent keys is a *half-step* (also called a *semitone*). (Each key is indicated by an arrow.) The distance between two adjacent white keys is a *whole step* (or *whole tone*), with the exception of E-F and B-C.

EXAMPLE 4

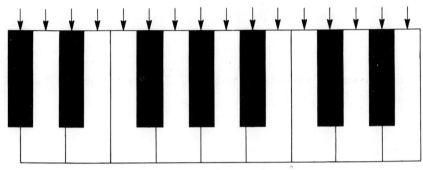

In order to raise the pitch of a tone by a semitone, a *sharp* (♯) is placed in front of the note.

EXAMPLE 5

C   C-sharp

In order to lower the pitch of a tone by a semitone, a *flat* (♭) is placed in front of the note.

EXAMPLE 6

D   D-flat

Enharmonics

When one pitch has two designations, such as *C-sharp* and *D-flat*, either of these designations is the *enharmonic equivalent* of the other. Composers use enharmonics to facilitate notation during modulation or to simplify certain key signatures.

At certain times in the course of a composition, it is necessary to raise by a semitone the pitch of a tone that is already sharped. For this, the *double-sharp* (×) is used.

EXAMPLE 7

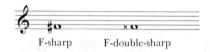

F double-sharp is the enharmonic of G. To lower a note that is already flatted, the *double-flat* (♭♭) is used.

EXAMPLE 8

Naturals

The *natural* (♮) cancels the effect of any sharp or flat, including double-sharps and double-flats, returning the note to its pitch unsharped or unflatted. Sharps, flats, and naturals are known as *accidentals*.

The overtone series

When a musical tone is produced, it is ordinarily accompanied by a series of *overtones*. These overtones are for the most part not distinguishable separately by the human ear; however, they serve all together to invest the tone with body and timbre (tone color). Listed below are the fundamental and first fifteen overtones for C^2. (In this example, the fundamental is shown as No. 1.) It is not possible to represent on the musical staff the exact pitch of the notes of the overtone series; this may be done only with a graph. The most notable deviations in pitch from what can be shown on the staff are represented by black notes, which are lower in pitch than indicated.

EXAMPLE 9

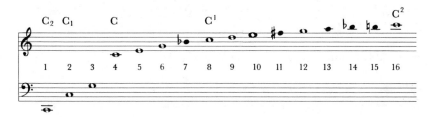

Intervals

An *interval* is the distance between two tones. The distance between two tones sounded together may be referred to as a *harmonic interval*. When the two tones are sounded in succession, the distance may be referred to as a *melodic interval*.

EXAMPLE 10

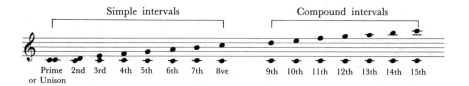

Diatonic and chromatic intervals

The Greek word *diatonic* means "across the tones," and refers in practical usage to the tones associated with a given key. Thus, the white-note pattern C D E F G A B is a diatonic pattern. A diatonic semitone consists of an interval that uses two letters that stand in succession. E-F and B-C are diatonic semitones, as well as minor seconds. Furthermore, C-Db and F♯-G are diatonic semitones. C-C♯ and Gb-G♮, however, are *chromatic* semitones. *Chroma*, also from the Greek, means "color"; and one meaning of the term *chromatic* is the "colored" alteration of a tone produced by raising or lowering it with the application of an accidental.

EXAMPLE 11

TABLE OF INTERVALS

Selected Diatonic Intervals (in the Key of C Major):

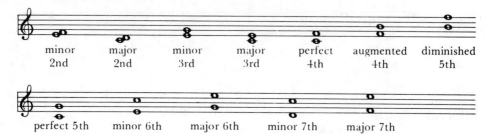

Selected Chromatic Intervals (Associated with the Key of C):

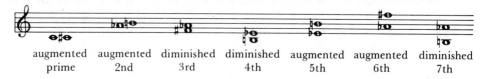

Interval Inversion

The *inversion* of an interval takes place when the positions of the two notes on the staff are reversed so that the lower note becomes the upper. This can also be accomplished by raising the lower note, or lowering the upper note, the distance of an octave. Thus, the interval F̲ becomes C̲ .

EXAMPLE 12

Consonance and dissonance

Consonance and dissonance help create the effect of tension and release in a composition.

> *consonance:* A combination of tones regarded as stable
> and not requiring resolution.

> *dissonance:* A combination of tones creating tension
> and requiring resolution.

Scales

A *scale* is a theoretical abstraction of the tones used in a piece of music. Named from the Italian word *scala,* meaning "ladder," it is an arranged series of notes. The normal scale consists of the diatonic tones used in a particular *mode.*

Modes

Music during the Middle Ages and the Renaissance, until about 1600, was written in what are called the *modes.* Each of these modes may be represented by a *diatonic scale* that uses only the white notes of the piano keyboard and is represented by the lines and spaces of the staff.

There were originally four authentic modes—the Dorian, Phrygian, Lydian, and Mixolydian—to which were added the Aeolian, Locrian, and Ionian. It can be seen in the next example that the distinguishing feature of each mode depends upon the particular arrangement of the whole-steps and half-steps.

EXAMPLE 13

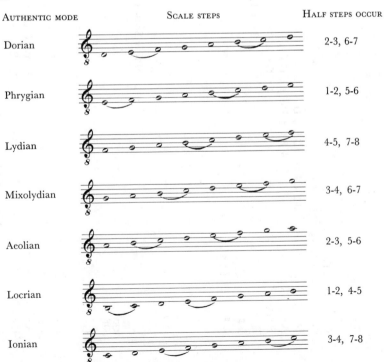

AUTHENTIC MODE	SCALE STEPS	HALF STEPS OCCUR
Dorian		2-3, 6-7
Phrygian		1-2, 5-6
Lydian		4-5, 7-8
Mixolydian		3-4, 6-7
Aeolian		2-3, 5-6
Locrian		1-2, 4-5
Ionian		3-4, 7-8

Major Scales, Keys with Sharps

KEY OF	Scale	KEY SIGNATURE SPECIFIED AS
C	C D E F G A B C	—
G	G A B C D E F♯ G	1 sharp
D	D E F♯ G A B C♯ D	2 sharps
A	A B C♯ D E F♯ G♯ A	3 sharps
E	E F♯ G♯ A B C♯ D♯ E	4 sharps
B	B C♯ D♯ E F♯ G♯ A♯ B	5 sharps
F♯	F♯ G♯ A♯ B C♯ D♯ E♯ F♯	6 sharps
C♯	C♯ D♯ E♯ F♯ G♯ A♯ B♯ C♯	7 sharps

Major Scales, Keys with Flats

KEY OF	Scale	KEY SIGNATURE SPECIFIED AS
C	C D E F G A B C	—
F	F G A B♭ C D E F	1 flat
B♭	B♭ C D E♭ F G A B♭	2 flats
E♭	E♭ F G A♭ B♭ C D E♭	3 flats
A♭	A♭ B♭ C D♭ E♭ F G A♭	4 flats
D♭	D♭ E♭ F G♭ A♭ B♭ C D♭	5 flats
G♭	G♭ A♭ B♭ C♭ D♭ E♭ F G♭	6 flats
C♭	C♭ D♭ E♭ F♭ G♭ A♭ B♭ C♭	7 flats

Major and minor modes

With the constant changing of pitches by the application of accidentals and the "growing art" of harmony, the Ionian and Aeolian modes emerged to become the two modes that since have been the basis of harmony of Western music (until the twentieth century, when their hegemony began to diminish).

With only two modes in common usage, the old mode-distinguishing names gradually went out of general use, and the two modes were referred to by the specific difference in pitch of the third scale-step as related to the tonic. Thus, the Ionian mode became the *major mode,* and the Aeolian mode became the *minor*

The *key signatures* of all the major keys and their relative minor keys may be illustrated in the Circle of Fifths (Ex. 14).

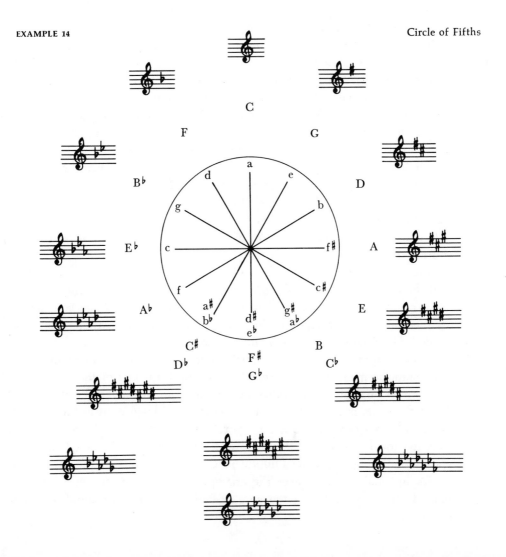

EXAMPLE 14   Circle of Fifths

The major keys and their relative minors are paired around the circle, the major keys outside and the minor keys inside. The important enharmonic keys are shown. Clockwise motion represents key relations in ascending perfect fifths; counterclockwise, in descending perfect fifths. Proceeding around the circle of fifths clockwise from C shows the sharp keys in succession, with each succeeding key note a perfect fifth higher than the preceding one. Proceeding from C counterclockwise shows the flat keys in succession, with each key note a perfect fifth lower than the preceding one.

Tonality

Tonality embraces the concept of key or mode, but it is not synonymous with either; it is a larger concept. One may think of tonality as a process in which one note—the tonic—predominates over all the other notes as they gravitate around it. The tonic is constantly departed from as the other notes and their relationship to the tonic are explored.

The essence of tonality in the classical period is that the key center may shift while the basic tonal center remains unchanged. In other words, there may be modulation to closely related or distantly related keys, *but the exploration of these keys is always in relation to the basic tonal center*, which ultimately returns. This is true not only throughout a symphonic movement, but throughout an entire symphony. There is always the connecting thread between even the most distant key center and the basic tonal center. The new key center amounts to an exploration or a side excursion. The concept of tonality embraces the idea that there will be a return to the basic tonal center.

A diagram of the first movement of Mozart's *Symphony No. 41* illustrates this process (Ex. 18, pp. 498–499).

Note that the basic key center is adhered to for the first 36 measures and then that the dominant becomes the principal key center throughout the remainder of the exposition. The strong relationship of the dominant to the tonic is illustrated by the fact that upon repetition of the exposition no modulation of any kind is needed. The dominant just "falls into" the tonic.

In the recapitulation, there is a brief excursion into the subdominant, and then back onto the main road, the basic tonality, until the end of the movement. Inspection or analysis of the other movements should only make it clearer that Mozart's *Symphony No. 41* is not in the key of C major, but in the "tonality of C major." That is to say, C as the central note and major as the main mode provide the tonal center for the entire work. Note that Sir Donald Francis Tovey speaks of Schubert's *String Quintet in C Major* as "one of the greatest of all essays in tonality." Whatever the analogy—an essay, a journey, a quest—the point is that tonality is at the core of much of our most significant musical experience.

Duration

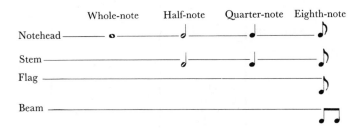

NOTES			RESTS
𝅝		whole	▬
𝅗𝅥 or 𝅗𝅥		half	▬
𝅘𝅥 or 𝅘𝅥		quarter	𝄽
𝅘𝅥𝅮 or 𝅘𝅥𝅮		eighth	𝄾
𝅘𝅥𝅯 or 𝅘𝅥𝅯		sixteenth	𝄿
𝅘𝅥𝅰 or 𝅘𝅥𝅰		thirty-second	𝅀
𝅘𝅥𝅱 or 𝅘𝅥𝅱		sixty-fourth	𝅁

	Whole-note	Half-note	Quarter-note	Eighth-note
Notehead	𝅝	𝅗𝅥	𝅘𝅥	𝅘𝅥𝅮
Stem		𝅗𝅥	𝅘𝅥	𝅘𝅥𝅮
Flag				𝅘𝅥𝅮
Beam				𝅘𝅥𝅮𝅘𝅥𝅮

The tie and the dot

The binary system of the division of note values does not contain within itself any way to denote a duration three-quarters of the given value of a particular note. If three-quarters of the length of a whole-note is desired, this problem in notation is solved by joining a half-note and a quarter-note by means of a *tie*.

In the evolving "shorthand" of notation, the tied quarter ultimately became a *dot*.

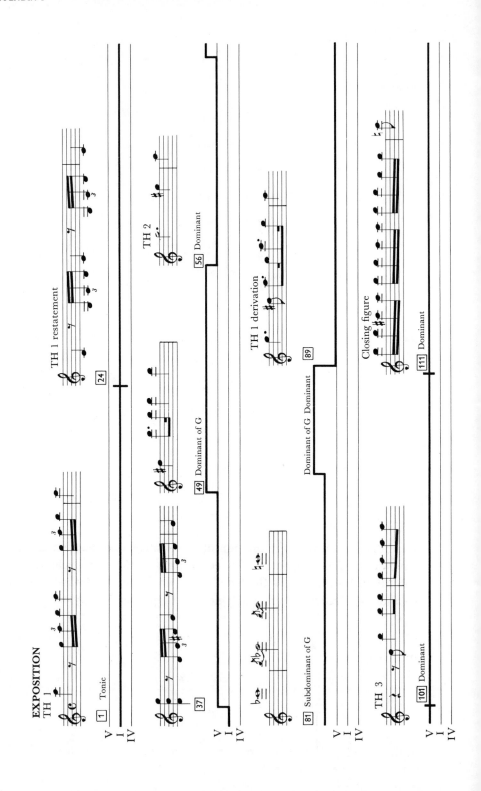

Symphony No. 41 ("Jupiter"), K. 551, Mvt. I, Mozart

EXAMPLE 18

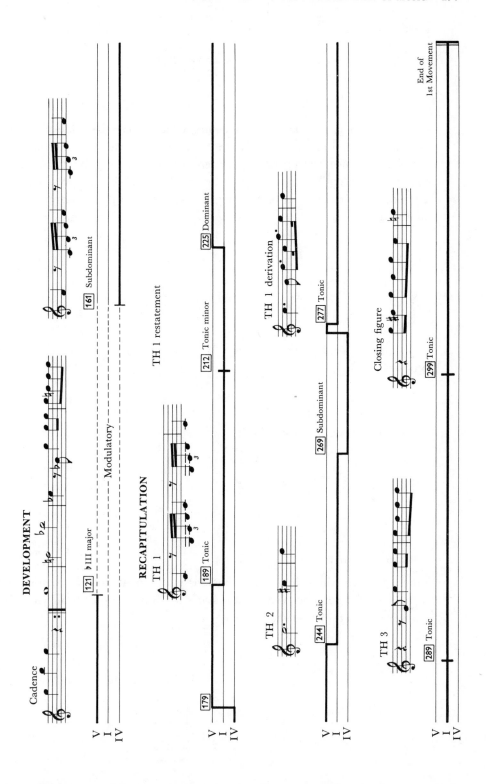

EXAMPLE 19

The dot in this case equals a quarter-note, which is half the value of the half-note preceding. In certain English and other editions of music, this shorthand dot representing the tied quarter is still written with the spacing shown in Example 19, but modern usage has moved the dot closer to the note it follows, as in Example 20. Thus, a dot placed after any note or rest adds to it half its value, as in Example 21.

EXAMPLE 20

EXAMPLE 21

	NOTES		RESTS

Triplets and duplets

Where there are duple and triple divisions within main accents, this is taken care of by a special notation. When three notes are wanted in place of two, a *triplet* is written and bracketed as shown below.

EXAMPLE 22

Time signature

At the beginning of each piece of music, a *time signature* is placed on the staff (directly after the key signature) to show the method of measuring time in that particular piece of music.

Vertical *bars* (or *bar-lines*) placed on the staff throughout the piece divide the music into *measures*. The lower number of the time signature designates what note value is to be the measuring unit; the upper number designates how many of these will occur in each measure. Thus, the time signature $\frac{2}{4}$ ("two-four") specifies that a quarter (note or rest) is the measuring unit, and that there are two beats in each measure. No bar-line is necessary at the beginning.

EXAMPLE 23

Any combination of note values or rests that are equivalent to two quarter-notes may appear in each measure.

EXAMPLE 24

The following table presents the signs and symbols most commonly used in music.

SIGNS AND SYMBOLS

	TERM	MEANING	USAGE OR PLACEMENT
	staccato mark	note so indicated played shorter than its value	dot placed above or below note
stacc.	staccato	same as above, but applying to several notes	above notes at point of usage
	"wedge" mark	not as short as staccato, and accented	above or below note
	accent	note so indicated to be accented	above or below note
marc.	marcato	"marked," a slightly lighter accent than preceding entry	above notes at point of usage
	legato	notes to be connected without separation; to be played smoothly	above or below notes
	tie	two notes of same pitch to sound as one continuous tone	connects notes separated by bar-line, or of unequal values
	tenuto mark	hold note full value, or even slightly longer; sometimes also means "slightly pressing"	above or below note
	comma	short breathing space: it may or it' may not interrupt the rhythmic pace	between two notes, especially between phrases
	pause	short pause of silence	at end of phrase
	pause, fermata, hold	longer pause of silence or sound	over bar-line or rest (silence); over note (sound)
G.P.	grand pause, general pause	silence for all instruments	over a measure of rest in all parts

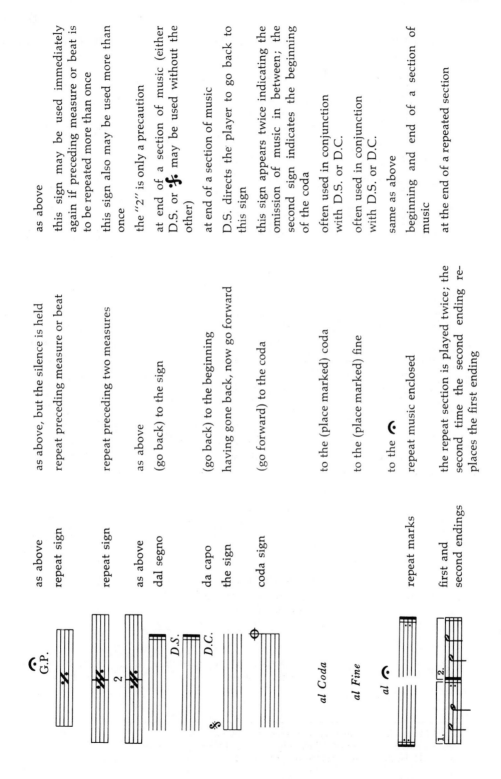

as above (G.P.)	as above, but the silence is held	as above
repeat sign	repeat preceding measure or beat	this sign may be used immediately again if preceding measure or beat is to be repeated more than once
repeat sign	repeat preceding two measures	this sign also may be used more than once
as above	as above	the "2" is only a precaution
dal segno	(go back) to the sign	at end of a section of music (either D.S. or 𝄋 may be used without the other)
da capo	(go back) to the beginning	at end of a section of music
the sign	having gone back, now go forward	D.S. directs the player to go back to this sign
coda sign	(go forward) to the coda	this sign appears twice indicating the omission of music in between; the second sign indicates the beginning of the coda
al Coda	to the (place marked) coda	often used in conjunction with D.S. or D.C.
al Fine	to the (place marked) fine	often used in conjunction with D.S. or D.C.
al ⊙	to the ⊙	same as above
repeat marks	repeat music enclosed	beginning and end of a section of music
first and second endings	the repeat section is played twice; the second time the second ending replaces the first ending	at the end of a repeated section

TYPE OF METER		BEATS PER MEASURE	TIME SIGNATURES
Simple	duple	2	$\frac{2}{1}$ $\frac{2}{2}$ $\frac{2}{4}$ $\frac{2}{8}$ $\frac{2}{16}$ $\frac{2}{32}$
	triple	3	$\frac{3}{1}$ $\frac{3}{2}$ $\frac{3}{4}$ $\frac{3}{8}$ $\frac{3}{16}$ $\frac{3}{32}$
Common*		4	$\frac{4}{4}$ also: C
Compound†		6 or 2	$\frac{6}{1}$ $\frac{6}{2}$ $\frac{6}{4}$ $\frac{6}{8}$ $\frac{6}{16}$ $\frac{6}{32}$
		9 or 3	$\frac{9}{1}$ $\frac{9}{2}$ $\frac{9}{4}$ $\frac{9}{8}$ $\frac{9}{16}$ $\frac{9}{32}$
		12 or 4	$\frac{12}{1}$ $\frac{12}{2}$ $\frac{12}{4}$ $\frac{12}{8}$ $\frac{12}{16}$ $\frac{12}{32}$
Asymmetrical**		5 or combinations of 2's and 3's	$\frac{5}{1}$ $\frac{5}{2}$ $\frac{5}{4}$ $\frac{5}{8}$ $\frac{5}{16}$ $\frac{5}{32}$
		7 or combinations of 3's and 4's	$\frac{7}{1}$ $\frac{7}{2}$ $\frac{7}{4}$ $\frac{7}{8}$ $\frac{7}{16}$ $\frac{7}{32}$
Mixed		Alternating combinations usually of 2's, 3's or 4's	$\frac{3}{4} + \frac{2}{4}$ (typical)
Polymeter		Any number of beats, but heard simultaneously with different beat groups	$\frac{6}{8}$ $\frac{3}{4}$ (typical)
Changing		According to the measure of the moment	Any combination at any time

* Meters in 8 are usually multiples of common meter.
† Compound meters can have higher beat numbers: 15, 18, etc.
** 1) Higher beat numbers are possible: 10, 11, 13, etc.

METERS

EXAMPLE	ILLUSTRATIONS FROM THE REPERTOIRE
	Beethoven *Symphony No. 1*, Mvt. 4
	Tchaikowsky *Symphony No. 5*, Mvt. 3
	Beethoven *Symphony No. 5*, Mvt. 4
	Brahms *Symphony No. 1*, Mvt. 1
	Tchaikowsky *Symphony No. 4*, Mvt. 1
	Tchaikowsky *Symphony No. 5*, Mvt. 2
	Ravel General Dance, *Daphnis and Chloe*, Suite No. 2
	Prokofiev *Piano Sonata No. 7*, Mvt. 3
	Bartók *Mikrokosmos*, Vol. 6, Bulgarian Dance No. 1 meter: $\frac{4}{4} + \frac{2}{8} + \frac{3}{8}$
	Mozart *Don Giovanni*, Act I, Ball Scene meters: $\frac{3}{8}$ $\frac{2}{4}$ $\frac{3}{4}$
	Bartók *Music For Stringed Instruments, Percussion and Celesta*, Mvt. 4 meter: varied

2) Inner combinations—other than 3's or 4's—are possible:

Ex.:

Appendix II

SYNOPTIC LISTING OF MUSICAL FORMS WITH SUGGESTED LISTENING

The instrumental and vocal forms that follow should not be considered mutually exclusive. Vocal music, more often than not, will include instrumental forces. And instrumental music, such as the symphony, occasionally will include vocal forces.

Forms based on the sonata pattern

A *sonata* is an aggregate form ordinarily consisting of three or four loosely linked movements, contrasted in tempo and style.

The solo sonata The *solo sonata* is written either for a single instrument with complete range such as the piano, organ, or harpsichord or for instruments such as oboe, violin, or cello with a keyboard instrument. Properly these last should be termed *duo sonatas*.

> *Suggested Listening:* Beethoven, *Sonata*, Op. 81a, "*Les Adieux*," for piano; Hindemith, *Sonata for Bassoon and Piano* (1939).

The symphony A *symphony* is a sonata for full orchestra. Symphonies are often more extensive than sonatas for solo or chamber ensemble. The term *symphony (sinfonia)* is also used in baroque music to define instrumental forms prefacing choral or instrumental works.

> *Suggested Listening:* Bizet, *Symphony in C.*

Trio, quartet, quintet   Chamber music media such as the *trio*, the *quartet*, and the *quintet* ordinarily follow standard sonata patterns. Their charm comes from an intimate character, not unlike that of the solo sonata, combined with the subtlety of musical dialogue found in all ensemble.

> *Suggested Listening:* Schubert, *"Trout" Quintet* for violin, viola, cello, contrabass, piano; Debussy, *Quartet in G Minor*, Op. 10, for two violins, viola, cello.

The concerto   A *concerto* is a sonata for one or more soloists with orchestra. It is almost always in three movements. There is no Scherzo or Minuet. *Cadenzas*, brilliant sections for soloist alone, are featured. The *concerto grosso*, originating in baroque music, features a small body of soloists, the *concertino*, set in opposition to a larger instrumental group, the *tutti*. A concerto for orchestra does not call for any set type or number of soloists. Rather, any or all instruments in the orchestra may lead momentarily without being considered *the* exclusive soloist or soloists.

> *Suggested Listening:*   Mozart, *Concerto for Clarinet*, K. 622; Brahms, *Concerto for Violin and Cello,* Op. 102; Beethoven, *Concerto for Violin, Cello, and Piano*, Op. 56; Bloch, *Concerto Grosso No. 2* (1952); Bartók, *Concerto for Orchestra* (1943).

The sonatine   A *sonatine* (sometimes *sonatina*) is a sonata of reduced dimensions. *Sonatina form* means sonata-allegro with absent or truncated development section.

> *Suggested Listening:* Ravel, *Sonatine for Piano* (1905).

Variation forms

Variation technique occurs in all forms. Whenever any musical element is repeated, with however slight change, it produces variation. Variation forms may be complete in one movement or part of aggregate structures.

Theme and variations   The *theme and variation* form is an additive structure consisting of a theme repeated an indeterminate number of times, each time varied. In some variations the theme remains crystal clear, while in others the transformations may actually suggest a new theme. The last variation is often climactic and dazzling, following one of slow, meditative character.

> *Suggested Listening:* Rachmaninoff, *Rhapsody on a Theme of Paganini*, Op. 43, for piano with orchestra.

Passacaglia and chaconne   The *passacaglia* and *chaconne* have an additive structure with a theme considerably shorter than that of theme and variations; indeed, these forms often extend for just a few bars. The passacaglia features an opening theme in the bass. Both forms tend to be more contrapuntal than theme and variations. *Ground* and *ostinato* are structures nearly identical with passacaglia, both suggesting a short figure in the bass overlaid with variations for each repetition. The notes of the ostinato usually do not change, and it may be heard in registers other than the bass.

> *Suggested Listening:* Brahms, *Symphony No. 4*, Op. 98, Mvt. IV (chaconne); Copland, *Passacaglia* (1922) for piano.

Chorale prelude   The *chorale prelude* is an instrumental form, usually for organ and based on the *chorale*, a vocal form (see below). In one common version, individual phrases from the chorale are separated by transitions. These transitions continue as polyphonic commentary to the chorale phrases themselves. It is primarily a contrapuntal form.

> *Suggested Listening:* J. S. Bach, *Wachet auf, ruft uns die Stimme* for organ (see analysis, Chapter 5).

Free forms

Many forms, both single and aggregate, are diverse in their use of structural pattern. For example, a rhapsody may be in the style of a rambling free improvisation, or it may follow strong classical structural patterns. The *Rhapsody in G Minor*, Op. 79, for piano, by Brahms, for example, is cast in a powerful sonata-allegro form; and the *Rhapsody on a Theme of Paganini* by Rachmaninoff is set as a theme with twenty-four variations.

Prelude   The *prelude* can be either functional, as a preface to another piece, or independent. Many structural patterns are possible.

> *Suggested Listening:* Shostakovich, *24 Preludes and Fugues*, Op. 84, for piano (functional); Puccini, *Prelude to Act II* of *Tosca* (functional); Chopin, *24 Preludes*, Op. 28, for piano (independent); Debussy, *Prélude à l'Après-midi d'un faune* for orchestra (independent) (see analysis, Chapter 8).

Overture   The *overture* is similar to the prelude, but usually for full orchestra and substantial in dimensions. It is often cast in sonata-allegro form.

> *Suggested Listening:* functional overture: Beethoven, *"Leonore" Overture No. 3*, Op. 72b, for orchestra; concert overture: Brahms, *Academic Festival Overture*, Op. 80, for orchestra.

Fantasie   A *fantasie* is a work in free form, resembling an improvisation. In baroque and pre-baroque music it is sometimes prefatory to a fugue.

> *Suggested Listening:* Vaughan Williams, *Fantasie on a Theme by Tallis* (1910) for orchestra; J. S. Bach, *Fantasia and Fugue in G Minor* for organ.

Rhapsody   A *rhapsody* is a work cast in any of various forms, usually imposing and substantial. The term is not used consistently by composers. It refers more often to style rather than to form.

> *Suggested Listening:* Liszt, *Hungarian Rhapsodies* for piano.

Character piece   A *character piece* is a work displaying one mood, emotion, or idea. Such pieces are often programmatic. Typical titles are *Impromptu*, *Intermezzo*, *Song Without Words*, *Album Leaves*, and *Ballad*. The form is often ternary.

> *Suggested Listening:* Bernstein, *Four Anniversaries* (1948) for piano.

Tone poem   A *tone poem* is a substantial single-movement composition, usually orchestral, of programmatic content. The sonata-allegro form is much used, but other forms are also common.

> *Suggested Listening:* Richard Strauss, *Death and Transfiguration*, Op. 24, for orchestra.

Suite   A *suite* is any collection of pieces loosely bound together and contrasted to one another in style. Typical is the *dance suite*. This last, in the Baroque, consists primarily of dances, such as the *minuet, gavotte, gigue,* and is variously called *French suite, English suite, partita,* or simply suite.

> *Suggested Listening:* J. S. Bach, *Suite No. 2* for flute with strings; Bartók, *Dance Suite* (1923) for orchestra; Vaughan Williams, *Folk Song Suite* for military band.

Opera and ballet suite   The *opera* or *ballet suite* is a selection of excerpts from an opera or ballet.

> *Suggested Listening:* Kodály, *Háry János Suite* (1926) from the opera *Háry János;* Stravinsky, *Firebird Suite* (1910), for orchestra, from the ballet *The Firebird.*

Incidental music   *Incidental music* is music written to accompany a play.

> *Suggested Listening:* Schubert, *Rosamunde*, Op. 26, for orchestra.

Divertimento   A *divertimento* is a suite of light, entertaining character. Other titles are *Serenade* and *Cassation.*

> *Suggested Listening:* Ibert, *Divertissement* (1930) for orchestra.

Ballet   A *ballet* is an extended theater-piece for dance, often divided into acts or scenes. Ballet is similar to opera but with the "text" danced rather than sung. A ballet may be a full-length work or may be short enough to be included with two or three other ballets in a single program.

> *Suggested Listening:* Milhaud, *La Création du monde.*

Contrapuntal structures

Contrapuntal structures do not segmentize easily and therefore are to be described according to contrapuntal technique rather than according to parts or sections.

Fugue   Fugue is the combination of two or more melodic parts, using techniques of imitation and motivic transformation.

> *Suggested Listening:* J. S. Bach, *The Well-Tempered Clavier*, Books I, II, for keyboard.

Invention   An *invention* is a brief contrapuntal composition in two or three melodic parts (voices). A prominent feature is inversion of the parts. Inversions are often canonic.

> *Suggested Listening:*   J. S. Bach, *2- and 3-part Inventions* for keyboard.

Canon   The *canon* is a contrapuntal form based on continuous imitation.

> *Suggested Listening:* Franck, *Sonata for Violin and Piano*, Mvt. IV.

Toccata   A *toccata* is a primarily contrapuntal work originally for keyboard, but also for orchestra, featuring brilliant display work. In baroque music a toccata is sometimes appended to a fugue and occasionally divided into several movements.

> *Suggested Listening:* J. S. Bach, *Toccata and Fugue in F* for organ.

Vocal music

While all intelligible music must possess form, form is less apparent and freer in vocal music than in instrumental music. The sonata-allegro pattern is diffuse and ineffective without motivic transformation and a sturdy overall superstructure including exposition, development, and recapitulation. But a song or an aria may very well ramble on, its inner segments only loosely connected, and still be intelligible. What makes this possible, of course, is the text, which largely dictates what the structure will be. Unmetered prose set to music tends to produce loose structures, while rhymed poetry suggests closer-knit forms.

Each stanza of a poem is frequently set to the same music, as in a church hymn. This form is called a *strophic* song. When each stanza is set to different music, the song is termed *through composed*.

Single member forms

Recitative is a rhythmically free and melodically somewhat static setting of a narration or dialogue. The shape of the melodic line closely follows the natural speech inflection of the voice. If the accompaniment (often played by harpsichord or organ) is minimal, it is called *secco;* if dramatic and elaborate (usually orchestral), it becomes *accompagnato*. It is seen mostly in opera, oratorio, and cantata. Instrumental recitative, as in the first section of Mvt. IV in Beethoven's *Ninth Symphony,* is a simulation of vocal recitative.

> *Suggested Listening:* Mozart, recitatives from *Don Giovanni;* Schoenberg, *Variations on a Recitative,* Op. 40 (1943), for organ.

Plain song, sometimes called *plain chant,* is a form used for settings of the liturgy. *Gregorian chant* is the setting of early Roman Catholic Church texts. Only gentle accents occur, with an undulating, gentle pulse. The melodic intervals are small, with conjunct motion primary.

> *Suggested Listening:* "Dies Irae" from the Requiem Mass of the Roman Catholic Church. (Also listen to utilization of this chant in: Saint-Saëns, *Dance Macabre,* Op. 40, for orchestra; Berlioz, *Symphonie Fantastique,* Op. 14, for orchestra; Rachmaninoff, *Rhapsody on a Theme of Paganini;* Liszt, *Totentanz* for piano and orchestra.)

A *song* is a setting of a poetic text for solo voice. A *part song* is for several voices. Songs are often ternary in structure.

The true *folk song* is anonymously composed and undergoes considerable modification as it is transmitted from singer to singer. Also, songs and airs, such as *Au Clair de la lune,* written by Lully in the seventeenth century, and the simple songs of Stephen Foster have become folk songs with the passing of the years and through their immense popularity.

> *Suggested Listening:* Copland, *Old American Songs* (1950–1954) for voice with orchestra or piano.

The *art song*, termed *Lied* in German and *chanson* in French, is a setting by a master composer of a fine poem. Because both text and music are often of the highest caliber, the form is one of the richest in the vocal literature. Art songs are usually performed by a single voice accompanied by piano, but an orchestra is sometimes used.

Suggested Listening: Schubert, *Winterreise*. (The final song in this cycle, "Der Leiermann," is analysed in Chapter 7).

An *aria* is a song occurring usually in a large aggregate work such as an opera, oratorio, cantata, or passion. The accompaniment is orchestral and the aria amplifies and comments on emotions suggested in preceding recitatives. An *aria da capo*, found often in baroque works, is ternary, with the final part exactly duplicating the first part (and therefore not written out the second time). A loose ternary pattern is common for many other arias. A *concert aria* is not written as part of an aggregate work but otherwise follows the dimensions and structure of the above. An *arioso* is a hybrid between a recitative and an aria, showing considerable lyricism but tending to the rhetorical.

Suggested Listening: Verdi, "Addio del Passato" from *La Traviata*. (See Chapter 7.)

A *hymn* is a simple setting of a religious or patriotic poem, suitable to be sung by untrained voices. Hymns are usually strophic in structure.

Suggested Listening: Billings, *Chester*.

A *chorale* is an early hymn originating in the German Lutheran Church, and often seen in SATB arrangement as part of larger works such as the cantata and *passion*. The chorale consists of short musical phrases punctuated by cadences, each with a fermata. The chorale as used by J. S. Bach is a compendium of harmonic devices of his time and formed the cornerstone of traditional harmony until its dissolution in the twentieth century.

Suggested Listening: J. S. Bach, chorales in the *St. Matthew Passion*.

An *anthem* is a choral setting in English, usually of a religious text, accompanied often by church organ, but sometimes done *a cappella* or with other instruments.

> *Suggested Listening:* S. S. Wesley, *Blessed Be the God and Father.*

A *motet* is a contrapuntal, choral setting of a sacred text, often in Latin, and frequently unaccompanied.

> *Suggested Listening:* Byrd, *Ego sum Panis vivum,* unaccompanied.

A *madrigal* is a setting of a secular text for mixed vocal ensemble. It contains a mixture of chordal and contrapuntal textures.

> *Suggested Listening:* Bennet, *Thyrsis, Sleepest Thou,* unaccompanied.

Aggregate vocal forms

A *song cycle* is a group of art songs loosely related musically, frequently on poems by a single author.

> *Suggested Listening:* Mussorgsky, *Songs and Dances of Death* for voice with piano.

An *opera* is a play set to music, with most, if not all, of the words of the text (called *libretto*) sung. It includes many sections, any of which may follow diverse structural patterns: overtures (or preludes), recitatives, arias, duets, ensembles, choruses, ballets, incidental music, etc. *Number opera* features the above-mentioned individual forms. In *continuous opera,* the demarcation between and identification of these is not salient. There is a continuous flow of music closely following the dramatic development of the play.

Some opera, especially that in a lighter vein, contains considerable spoken dialogue, e.g., English *ballad opera, singspiel, opera comique,* and *operetta.*

> *Suggested Listening:* number opera: Mozart, *The Marriage of Figaro;* operetta with spoken dialogue: J. Strauss, Jr., *Die Fledermaus;* continuous opera: Richard Strauss, *Elektra.*

An *oratorio* is a setting of a religious text with a similar structure and with forms as in opera. There are no costumes, scenery, or ballet. The soloists are often in fours, SATB. A narrator singing recitatives is commonly featured.

> *Suggested Listening:* Mendelssohn, *St. Paul* with soloists, chorus, orchestra.

A *cantata* is similar to an oratorio. However, cantatas are not always on a sacred text and are often shorter. Two kinds are the solo cantata and the choral cantata. A *passion* is an extensive cantata (or oratorio) on one of the Gospel accounts of the Passion of Christ.

> *Suggested Listening:* J. S. Bach, *Cantata No. 211 ("Coffee Cantata")* for STB, flute, strings.

A *mass* is a setting in Latin of certain portions of the liturgy of the Roman Catholic Church. Five of these portions are, the Kyrie, the Gloria, the Credo, the Sanctus, and the Agnus Dei. A mass for the dead is called a *requiem* and includes a slightly different arrangement, including the dramatic portion, the Dies Irae. A mass that is more suitable for performance in the concert hall than in church is called a *concert mass.*

> *Suggested Listening:* Schubert, *Mass No. 2 in G Major* for soprano, chorus, and orchestra.

Appendix III

GLOSSARY OF TECHNICAL TERMS

Technical terms not defined in this glossary are explained elsewhere in the text.

Absolute music music existing solely for itself, without extra-musical content or inferences.

Accent an emphasis on single or simultaneous tones achieved in various ways —through dynamics, duration, pitch location, etc. Also, as in *metrical accent*, associated with the relationship of a strong beat to a weak beat.

Accidental a notated sharp, flat, or natural that raises or lowers the pitch of a tone by a half-step.

Alberti bass an accompaniment figure in keyboard music that consists of broken chords in close position.

Arco an instruction to a string player to use the bow after a *pizzicato* passage.

Arpeggio a chord the individual tones of which are played successively rather than simultaneously.

Articulation the manner in which tones are played relative to clarity or to *legato* /*staccato*. Also the way a tone is produced on a specific instrument.

Asymmetrical meter a meter of unequal groups of beats, indicated by a time signature such as $\frac{5}{4}$, $\frac{7}{8}$, etc.

Atonal music without key or tonal center.

Bar see *Measure*.

Bar lines vertical lines on the staff that indicate the beginning and end of a measure.

Basso continuo   the bass line in a baroque ensemble piece, played by a combination of bass instrument (cello, bassoon) and keyboard (harpsichord, organ). The keyboard part was usually left for the performer to "realize," often with the aid of numerical figures written below the bass line. See *Figured bass.*

Bel canto   a singing style that emphasizes beauty of sound and line rather than dramatization of the text.

Blue note   in blues, the lowering in pitch of either the third or seventh scale steps of the major scale.

C clef   a clef now used for middle-register instruments, such as the viola, cello, and bassoon.

Cadence   a short progression of chords that holds back or terminates the flow of music.

Cadenza   the improvisatory portion of a work, often of a brilliant character and usually rhythmically free, mainly performed by a concerto soloist with the orchestra silent.

Canon   a contrapuntal texture in which one voice precisely imitates another.

Cantilena   refers to instrumental playing in a flowing, lyric style.

Cantus firmus   the established tune against which another voice is set.

Chalumeau   the lowest register of the clarinet.

Changing meter   meter in which different time signatures appear in succession.

Chord   a group of three or more tones commonly sounding together, but often arpeggiated (see *Arpeggio*).

Chord progression   a succession of two or more chords normally providing a sense of harmonic cohesion.

Chromatic   characterized by the interval of the minor second, as in the *chromatic scale;* also referring to notes lying outside a given diatonic mode.

Chromatic scale   a stepwise ordering of the twelve different notes within an octave.

Chromaticism   in tonal music, the use of tones not in the particular diatonic scale being used; the term is often used in connection with music that modulates frequently.

Clef   a symbol placed on the staff to specify the pitch name for each line and space.

Composite organum   the two voices of organum doubled at the octave above.

Conjunct motion   linear motion characterized by the interval of a second.

Consonance   a quality associated with an interval or chord regarded as stable and not requiring resolution.

Counterpoint   the setting of one melodic line against another.

Crescendo   gradually getting louder.

Descant   florid melody set against a *cantus firmus.*

Diatonic   referring to the natural tones of the modes; opposed to *chromatic.*

Diminuendo   gradually getting softer.

Dissonance   a quality associated with an interval or chord regarded as unstable and usually requiring resolution.

Dominant   the note a fifth above the tonic; also a triad built on that note.

Double-flat   lowers a note that is already flatted.

Double-sharp   raises a note that is already sharped.

Double-stop   two notes played simultaneously on two different strings of a member of the violin family.

Double-tonguing   a technique that wind players, mostly brass, use to execute rapid passages with alternating articulation of "T" and "K."

Downbeat   the first beat of a measure.

Dynamics   pertaining to volume of tone; loudness and softness.

Enharmonic   refers to a pitch with two letter-name designations. Examples: C♯ and D♭.

F clef   the clef used for low-register voices or instruments and for the lower register of keyboard music.

Figured bass   numbers signifying intervals to be played above a given bass line; see *Basso continuo.*

Flat   a sign placed in front of a tone to lower its pitch by a half-step.

Flutter tongue   rapid fluttering of the tongue while producing a tone on a wind instrument, similar to the German and French way of pronouncing the letter "R."

Free organum   organum in which the voices do not proceed in consistent parallel motion.

Frequency   the number of vibrations per second of a tone.

Fugato   an imitative section in the style of a fugue exposition.

Fugue   a polyphonic texture in two or more voices in which imitation of a given subject is the principal compositional element. Also, a single work based upon this kind of texture.

Fugue exposition   the opening of a fugue in which the subject is presented successively in each voice.

G clef   the clef used for high-register voices or instruments and for the higher register of keyboard music.

Glissando   continuous sliding up or down a scale with one tone merging into another.

Half-cadence   a progression of chords ending on the dominant triad.

Half-step   the smallest distance between any two adjacent tones of the chromatic scale; a *semitone*.

Harmonic minor   the scale resulting from the raising of the seventh scale-degree of the natural minor scale by a half-step.

Homophony   a texture in which one predominant melodic part is supported closely by subsidiary harmonic elements.

Idée fixe   a recurring idea; the cyclic theme representing the beloved in Berlioz's *Symphonie fantastique*.

Imitation   one melodic part imitating another in close succession.

Improvisation   the performance of music as it is being composed.

Instrumentation   the specific number and kinds of instruments that form an orchestra or other instrumental group. Also, the instruments called for in a specific piece.

Interval   the distance between two tones measured by diatonic or chromatic scale-steps.

Inversion   the process of reversing two notes of an interval so that the lower becomes the upper; or the exchange of bass note in a chord. Also, the restructuring of a melody wherein ascending and descending motions are replaced, respectively, by descending and ascending motions of the same intervallic sizes.

Isorhythm   in early polyphonic music, the repetition of the same rhythmic pattern throughout a substantial portion of a piece.

Key   the letter designation of a tonal center, which can either be major or minor. Examples: E♭ major, B minor.

Key signature   the grouping of sharps or flats associated with the key of a piece at the beginning of a staff. The sharps or flats remain in effect throughout the piece unless cancelled by naturals or replaced by another key signature.

Legato   a style of playing (articulation) in which each note is connected to the following note.

Leger line   a short line used above or below a staff in order to extend it. Thus, middle C is notated in the treble staff on the first leger line below the staff, the lowest line of which is E above middle C.

Leitmotif   (leading motive): a characteristic motive associated with a specific concept, person, or object, as in Wagner's music dramas.

Major mode   the diatonic scale containing half-steps between the third and fourth, and seventh and eighth scale-steps—the remaining intervals of the scale being whole steps. Originally the Ionian mode.

Measure   the span from one downbeat to the next, as indicated by bar lines.

Mediant   the note midway between the tonic and the dominant; the third scale-step.

Melismatic   a style in which an extended series of tones are sung to one syllable, effecting a *melisma*.

Melodic minor   the scale resulting from the raising of the sixth and seventh scale-degrees of the natural minor scale each by a half-step.

Metrical modulation   a process in which tempo is adjusted through changing metronomic designations for successive note values.

Minor mode   the diatonic scale containing half-steps between the second and third, and fifth and sixth scale-steps—the remaining intervals of the scale being whole steps. Originally the Aeolian mode.

Mixed meter   refers to different meters appearing in alternate measures.

Mode   any one of various diatonic scales that may begin on any line or space of the staff.

Modulation   the process of gradual or abrupt transition from one key to another.

Monody   recitative-like melodic line sustained by block chords.

Motive   a short melodic and/or rhythmic idea.

Musica ficta   the use of chromatic alterations in early music, not written in the score but introduced by the performer.

Musique concrète   a type of composition that uses sounds, pitched or unpitched, transformed by various kinds of electronic manipulation.

Natural   a sign that restores the basic pitch of a tone that has been flatted or sharped.

Natural minor   the unaltered scale of the minor mode. See *Harmonic minor* and *Melodic minor.*

Note value   the symbol that represents the duration of a tone.

Obbligato   a subsidiary melodic line set against a primary melodic line. See *Descant.*

Octave   an interval between two pitches in which the higher of the two pitches vibrates at twice the frequency of the lower. The choice of the term *octave* is based on the eight members of the diatonic scale as represented by *do* (1), *re* (2), *mi* (3), *fa* (4), *sol* (5), *la* (6), *ti* (7), *do* (8).

Orchestration   the manner in which instrumental timbres are combined, as specified in a composer's orchestral score.

Organum   in early music, the coupling of a lower voice with an upper voice in parallel motion.

Ornament   the addition of one or more tones above or below a specific tone, indicated by various symbols, such as grace notes, trills, mordants, etc.

Ostinato   a short melodic figure repeated over and over again, usually in the bass; a ground.

Pandiatonic   the seemingly indiscriminate use of several tones of a scale or mode melodically and/or harmonically.

Parallel chords   successive chords with the same intervallic structure.

Parallel motion   the movement of two melodic lines in the same direction and separated throughout by the same vertical interval; for example, parallel thirds.

Pedal point   the continuous or repeated sounding of a note, usually in the bass, often while contrasting melodic and harmonic elements are sounding.

Pentatonic mode   a mode of five notes that have the relationship found among the notes C D E G A; associated with Oriental music.

Phrasing   the manner in which a performer shapes the inner components of a melodic line or lines in terms of dynamics, tone connection, articulation, duration, and tempo.

Pizzicato   refers to plucking a string instrument instead of bowing it.

Polyphony   the combining and blending of two or more melodic lines.

Polytonality   two or more keys sounding together.

Quodlibet   the process of combining two or more unrelated melodies into a single comprehensible texture.

Range   the notes that can be played from low to high by an instrument; similarly the span of notes that can be sung by a voice. Also, the low-high span of a passage of music.

Recitative   a vocal passage, usually with no clear melody, that adheres to normal speech rhythms. Found normally as a prelude to or transition between arias in an opera or oratorio.

Register   a specific area within the total spectrum of sound, generally denoted as soprano, alto, tenor, or bass.

Retrograde   the presentation of a melodic passage backwards.

Rhythm   everything pertaining to the element of time in music, including the duration of sounds and rests.

Rhythmic pattern   a group of note values used as a unifying structural element in a composition. See *Motive*.

Root   the fundamental note of a chord.

Rubato   deviation from strict tempo, slowing down normally followed by compensatory speeding up. Especially associated with the performance of Chopin's piano music but employed for music of all periods.

Scale   a theoretical abstraction of the basic set of notes used in a piece of music. Also a running passage in a piece or an exercise practiced by musicians.

Scale-step   a particular member of a scale, ordered numerically; for example, the tonic is the first scale-step, the dominant the fifth, etc. Also called *scale-degree*.

Scat   jazz singing that employs nonsense syllables.

Score   the musical graphing of the notes of a composition, in which each instrument or voice is represented by the appropriate staff or staves. A score may consist of just one staff at a time—as in solo violin music—or of a large number of staves—as in orchestral music.

Semitone   see *Half-step*.

Sequence   repetition of a melodic pattern beginning on different notes.

Serial technique   an approach to composition in which the notes to be used (normally all twelve) are placed in a specific order or *row* and are used in this order (or transformations of it, such as *inversion* and *retrograde*), melodically and harmonically, throughout the work.

Sharp   a sign placed in front of a tone to raise its pitch by a half-step.

Sprechstimme   a cross between speaking and singing in which the pitch is not maintained but is rather barely suggested and then immediately moved away from.

Staccato   a style of playing (articulation) in which each note is detached and generally lasts about half its notated value.

Staff   the five lines and their adjacent spaces which, with the appropriate clef, specify pitch location.

Stretto   refers to the overlapping of melodic entries in a contrapuntal texture.

Subdominant   the note a fifth below the tonic; also a triad built on that note.

Subject   the principal melodic idea of a fugue or similar contrapuntal piece.

Syllabic   a melodic style in which one syllable is sung per each tone; opposed to *melismatic*.

Syncopation   the accentual deviation from the metrically regular flow of beats; the stressing of weak beats.

Tempo   the speed at which a piece is played.

Tessitura   the vocal range of a musical passage.

Theme   a melodically striking component of a composition.

Tie   a curved line connecting two notes of the same pitch, indicating that the sound should continue without interruption.

Timbre   see *Tone color*.

Time signature   the double number placed after the clef at the beginning of a piece of music and elsewhere in a piece. The lower number signifies the size of the beat, such as a quarter-note, half-note, etc.; the upper number signifies the number of beats per measure. The symbols "C" and "₵" are also time signatures, denoting 4/4 and 2/2, respectively.

Tonality   the gravitation of several notes around a primary note; see *Key*.

Tone   a sound of specific pitch produced by an instrument, voice, or electronic device.

Tone cluster   any vertical chord consisting of two or more adjacent major or minor seconds.

Tone color   the distinguishing quality of sound of an instrument or voice; timbre.

Tonic   the key tone. The first and principal note of a diatonic scale; that is, *do*.

Transcription   the rendering of a piece for a different set of voices and/or instruments.

Transposition   the exact reproduction (in notation or in performance) of a pattern of tones starting at a different pitch.

Tremolo   the quick repetition of the same tone on bowed instruments; the quick alternation of different tones on a keyboard or other instrument.

Triad   a three-note chord built in thirds.

Triple tonguing   a technique used mainly by brass players to execute rapid passages in triplets, with the articulations "T," "T," "K."

Triplets   the division of any durational note value into thirds.

Tritone   an interval spanning three whole tones; an augmented fourth.

Trope   musical and textual insertions in a liturgical service.

Tune   a simple melody easily played, sung, and remembered.

Twelve-tone technique   serial compositional technique utilizing all twelve notes of the chromatic scale. See *Serial technique.*

Unison   a sounding of the same tone by two or more voices or instruments.

Up-beat   the beat preparatory to the first beat of a measure.

Variation   any alteration or transformation of a musical idea in a composition. Also one section of a set of variations.

Whole-tone   a distance of two adjacent semitones or half-steps.

Whole-tone scale   a scale found mainly in impressionistic music, with six successive whole-tones comprising an octave.

INDEX*

* The index does not include items listed in the Glossary, or the names of musical works included in the Chronological Biographies and Appendices. Page numbers in italics indicate Chronological Biographies.

535